Daily treasure

Daily treasure

366 daily readings from
The Treasury of David
by C. H. Spurgeon

Compiled by James M. Renihan

 **EVANGELICAL PRESS**

EVANGELICAL PRESS
Faverdale North Industrial Estate, Darlington, DL3 0PH, England

Evangelical Press USA
P. O. Box 84, Auburn, MA 01501, USA

e-mail: sales@evangelical-press.org

web: www.evangelical-press.org

First published 2000

British Library Cataloguing in Publication Data available

ISBN 0 85234 464 3

Printed and bound in Great Britain by Creative Print & Design, Ebbw Vale, Wales.

Preface

Charles Haddon Spurgeon's *The Treasury of David* is quite accurately described by its title: it is a true treasure. Not only does it bring the reader through the whole Psalter — the riches of the Word of God, but it also provides him or her with bountiful material for profound spiritual reflection. The whole range of sanctified emotions may be found in the Psalms, and in this work Spurgeon has helped to make them accessible to every believer. Drawing from the vault of his unique wisdom and experience, as well as his superb gifts as an expositor, and supplementing this with an amazing collection of quotations from other commentators, he has constructed an almost unending source of benefit for devotional meditation.

In editing *Daily Treasure*, I have been frequently faced with difficult choices. It is all gold, silver and precious gems — when they are freely provided in such abundance, how does one decide which to take and which to leave? This has been a constant dilemma. I am sure that if someone else had pursued this project, the end result would be different, and perhaps better. I hope that those who know the work best will not be disappointed in the way that I have condensed the material.

My method of editing has been simple. Generally, I have followed the divisions in the Psalms used by Spurgeon himself. In addition, in most cases, I have followed the order of his comments on the verses of each psalm. In several instances, however, I have reordered material: phrases, sentences, or even paragraphs so as to present a more cohesive devotional. Charles Spurgeon had an enormously varied vocabulary, often using archaic and colloquial words and expressions. I have altered many of these words in an attempt to make the material more accessible to the modern reader. The supplementary readings have been very difficult to select. Some have been obvious, especially when a psalm arises from a particular historical setting recorded in Scripture. But at other times, my choices have been very subjective. I have tried not to repeat readings except in a very few cases.

It is my prayer that many will be blessed and helped by this material. It has been a tremendously profitable experience personally. Often it has made me pray, or give thanks, or confess my sins, or worship the living God. May the spiritual legacy of the 'Prince of Preachers' live on through this distillation of his wonderful work.

This book is dedicated to my mother, Lillian Renihan. She is lovingly known as Grammie, not only to her many grandchildren, but also to the members of her church family, Heritage Baptist Church, Worcester, Massachusetts. With two sons in the ministry, and her grandchildren professing their faith in Christ, she is a wonderful demonstration of how the Lord answers the simple prayers of a mother. *Soli Deo Gloria!*

James M. Renihan
Escondido, California

The life and legacy of
Charles Haddon Spurgeon (1834-1892)[1]

Charles Haddon Spurgeon was born into a godly home in the heart of rural Essex on 19 June 1834, only ten days after the death of the pioneer Baptist missionary, William Carey (1761-1834). Spurgeon's forebears originally came from the Netherlands, which they had left in the sixteenth century due to religious persecution. Both Spurgeon's father, John Spurgeon (1811-1902), and his grandfather, James Spurgeon (1776-1864), were Congregationalist preachers, and it was during an extended stay over a number of years in the home of his grandfather that Spurgeon was first exposed to the writings of the Puritans. James Spurgeon was the pastor of the Congregational church in the village of Stambourne in the heart of rural Essex. Here in the parsonage the young Spurgeon discovered a library of Puritan folios. They had been collected by Henry Havers (1620-c.1712), who had pastored the Stambourne church after his ejection from the Church of England in 1662 when he refused to comply with the Act of Uniformity.

Despite Spurgeon's tender years and the fact that as a young child he found it very difficult to lift these large and weighty Puritan volumes, he would later write that as a boy he was never happier than when in the company of these Puritan authors.[2] In time Spurgeon would be rightly convinced that commitment to the Calvinism and the spirituality of the Puritans was vital for the well-being of Baptist churches and associations.

It was at the home of his grandparents that a remarkable incident took place during the summer of 1844. A visiting preacher by the name of Richard Knill (d.1857) had preached for Spurgeon's grandfather, and afterwards spent some time with the young Spurgeon, endeavouring, in Spurgeon's later words, 'to lead me to the Saviour'. As Knill was leaving the home of Spurgeon's grandparents he took the young boy upon his knee and said in the hearing of a number of people, 'I think this little man will one day be a preacher of the gospel, and I hope a successful one. I think you will preach in Rowland Hill's Chapel; and when you do, tell the people this verse, "God moves in a mysterious way, etc." ' According to a letter that Spurgeon later wrote to Knill in 1853, these words were regarded by Spurgeon's friends with 'half the reverence of prophecy'.[3] Knill's predictions about the young Spurgeon were indeed fulfilled and Spurgeon never forgot the incident.[4]

Conversion and baptism

However, despite such godly surroundings it was not until January 1850 that Spurgeon was soundly converted. By this time he was quite conscious of his lost estate, and secretly wished that he was a frog or a toad — anything but a human being with a conscience and an awareness of the existence of a holy God. 'I reckoned that the most defiled creature ... was a better thing than myself, for I had sinned against Almighty God.'[5]

Now, Charles worshipped at his father's church in Tollesbury, nine miles to the south of Colchester, where his parents lived. One Sunday in January 1850, John Spurgeon recommended that his son stay and worship at a Nonconformist church in Colchester — very possibly Colchester

Baptist Church — due to a fierce snowstorm that was raging outside.[6] However, the snow was falling so heavily that Spurgeon was unable to reach the Nonconformist church recommended by his father and he was compelled to turn aside into what was then a small Primitive Methodist chapel called Artillery Street Chapel (now Spurgeon Memorial Evangelical Church). Here there were gathered a dozen or so people.[7]

'I had heard of the Primitive Methodists,' Spurgeon wrote a number of years later in his own inimitable account of his conversion, 'how they sang so loudly that they made people's heads ache; but that did not matter to me. I wanted to know how I might be saved, and if they could tell me that, I did not care how much they made my head ache.' When it was evident that the minister of the congregation was snowed in by the storm, 'a very thin-looking man, a shoemaker, or tailor' — a man who spoke in the broad dialect common to rural Essex — went into the pulpit to preach. His text was Isaiah 45:22: 'Look unto me, and be ye saved, all the ends of the earth'. He began thus:

> My dear friends, this is a very simple text indeed. It says, 'Look'. Now lookin' don't take a deal of pain. It ain't liftin' your foot or your finger; it is just, 'Look'. Well, a man needn't go to College to learn to look. You may be the biggest fool, and yet you can look. A man needn't be worth a thousand a year to be able to look. Anyone can look; even a child can look. But then the text says, 'Look unto *Me*'. Ay! Many on ye are lookin' to yourselves, but it's no use lookin' there. You'll never find any comfort in yourselves. Some look to God the Father. No, look to Him by-and-by. Jesus Christ says, 'Look unto *Me*'. Some on ye say, 'We must wait for the Spirit's workin'.' You have no business with that just now. Look to *Christ*. The text says, 'Look unto *Me*.'

After the preacher had elaborated what looking to Christ meant for about ten minutes or so, Spurgeon said the poor man 'was at the end of his tether'. It was at this point in the service that the preacher noticed Spurgeon under the gallery, and with so few present, knew him to be a stranger. Fixing his eyes on Spurgeon, he said to him, 'Young man, you look very miserable.' It was as if the man had read Spurgeon's heart, for this was his very state indeed when it came to spiritual matters. The preacher continued: 'And you always will be miserable — miserable in life, and miserable in death — if you don't obey my text; but if you obey my text, this moment, you will be saved.' Then, lifting up his hands, he shouted, as, Spurgeon said, only a Primitive Methodist could do, 'Young man, look to Jesus Christ. Look! Look! Look! You have nothin' to do but look and live.'

As soon as the preacher had uttered these words, Spurgeon said that he saw at once the way of salvation. 'When I heard that word, "Look!" what a charming word it seemed to me! Oh! I looked until I could almost have looked my eyes away. There and then the cloud was gone, the darkness had rolled away, and that moment I saw the sun; and I could have risen that instant and sung with the most enthusiastic of them, of the precious blood of Christ, and the simple faith which looks alone to Him.'

Four months later, on 3 May, Spurgeon, with the agreement of his Congregationalist parents, was baptized in the River Lark not far from Isleham in Cambridgeshire. His later description of his baptism is particularly noteworthy as it reflects to a great degree the biblical meaning of this ordinance. Spurgeon said that after he had taken a few steps into the river and 'noted the people on the ferry-boat, and in boats, and on either shore, I felt as if Heaven, and earth, and hell, might all gaze upon me, for I was not ashamed, there and then, to own myself a follower of the Lamb'.[8] Later his mother remarked to him that she had often prayed to God for his conversion, but she had never asked him to make her son a Baptist. Charles could not resist the temptation to reply that God had not only answered her prayers, but, with his usual generosity, had given her more than she had asked for!

Serving Christ

After his baptism Spurgeon found an unquenchable desire to serve Christ. 'I could scarcely content myself even for five minutes without trying to do something for Christ,' he later wrote with regard to this period of his life.[9] Every Saturday he would regularly visit some seventy people, spend time with each of them, and 'endeavour to draw their attention to spiritual realities'.[10]

He also began to speak in more public settings, and his 'compelling and captivating preaching'[11] soon led to an invitation to pastor the Baptist church in Waterbeach, a small hamlet a few miles north-east of Cambridge. Spurgeon laboured here from the autumn of 1851 to April 1854. In those two and a half years the membership of the small Baptist chapel more than doubled, going from 40 to 100. Moreover, it was here that Spurgeon came to the conviction that God had placed his seal upon his ministry, for it was in this hamlet that the first individual — the wife of a poor labourer — was converted under his preaching.

As a community Waterbeach was well known for drunkenness and profanity, riot and iniquity. Spurgeon's preaching ministry, though, altered the entire complexion of the town. In his words: 'it pleased the Lord to work signs and wonders in our midst. He showed the power of Jesus's name, and made us witnesses of that Gospel which can win souls, draw reluctant hearts, and mould the life and conduct of men afresh'.[12]

The call to London

In November 1853 Spurgeon was one of three speakers at an anniversary meeting of the Cambridge Sunday School Union. A certain George Gould, a deacon at Loughton Baptist Church, Essex, was present at this meeting in Cambridge and was quite impressed with Spurgeon's evident gift for public speaking. A short while later Gould met a friend by the name of Thomas Olney, one of the deacons of Park Street Chapel, an historic London Baptist congregation. When the latter mentioned the fact that their church was pastorless and in quite a depressed state, Gould urged his friend to invite Spurgeon to preach for a Sunday. Spurgeon was duly invited and preached on 11 December 1853.

The congregation who heard Spurgeon that Sunday was thrilled with his preaching and the deacons quickly arranged for Spurgeon to return for three more Sundays in January 1854. He was subsequently invited to supply the pulpit for several months, and in April of that year, at the tender age of nineteen, he accepted a call to be the pastor of the church.

In his letter of acceptance, written on 28 April, he emphasized that he had not sought the pastorate of the London congregation; in fact, he said, he 'trembled at the idea of preaching in London'. Yet, he wrote, he was convinced that God was directing him to the London church, a high honour indeed when he thought of the 'glorious names' of his predecessors. He did not explicitly mention the names of any of his predecessors, but undoubtedly he had in mind the three outstanding men which the church had had as pastors during the previous couple of centuries: Benjamin Keach (1640-1704), a prolific author, who had pastored the congregation from 1668 to 1704; John Gill (1697-1771), the doyen of eighteenth-century Baptist theologians, who had been the minister of the church from 1720 till his death; and

John Rippon (1750-1836), an influential preacher, hymnwriter and historian, who was pastor for no less than 63 years, from 1773 to 1836. 'Blessed be the name of the Most High', he continued, 'if he has called me to this office, He will support me in it — otherwise, how should a child, a youth, have the presumption thus to attempt the work which filled the heart and hands of Jesus?'[13]

God's blessing

Within a few months it was quite evident that God had indeed called the 'Cambridgeshire lad' to the pulpit of this historic congregation. The church was built to seat 1,200, but it soon proved far too small for the crowds that thronged to sit under Spurgeon's preaching. In 1855 the chapel was consequently expanded to seat 1,500. A year later, however, this renovated chapel had also been outgrown, and the decision was made to build what would become known as the Metropolitan Tabernacle. Completed in 1861, the Tabernacle could seat 5,000 and accommodate another 1,000 standing. For the rest of Spurgeon's pastorate the Tabernacle saw an average of 5,000 at each Sunday morning and evening service. And while Spurgeon and his fellow elders were careful not to make a huge membership their goal — indeed Spurgeon had a healthy distrust of all such statistics — 14,691 were added to the church during Spurgeon's time there, of which roughly 10,800 were by conversion and baptism.

Spurgeon's success as a preacher certainly owed little to his physical appearance, for he was of average height, fairly stout as he grew older, and had two unduly prominent front teeth. In the words of a certain Monckton Milnes: 'When he went into the pulpit, he might be taken for a hairdresser's assistant; when he left it he was an inspired apostle.'[14]

Augustine Birrell records that when he went to hear Spurgeon preach the only seat he could find was in the topmost gallery, between a woman eating an orange and a man sucking peppermints. Finding this combination of odours unendurable, he was about to leave, when, he said, 'I heard a voice and forgot all else.'[15] In his recent biography of Spurgeon, Mike Nicholls emphasizes the importance of Spurgeon's voice to his success as a preacher. He possessed, Nicholls writes, 'one of the great speaking voices of his age, musical and combining compass, flexibility and power'.[16]

Spurgeon, though, looked to quite a different source for the blessings that attended his ministry. In a speech which he gave at a celebration held in honour of his fiftieth birthday in 1884, the Baptist preacher forthrightly declared that the blessing which he had enjoyed in his pastorate 'must be entirely attributed to the grace of God, and to the working of God's Holy Spirit...Let that stand as a matter, not only taken for granted, but as a fact distinctly recognized'.[17]

'Energetic activist'

Not only was Spurgeon the pastor of what was then the largest Protestant congregation in the world, but he also had a variety of other irons in the fire. During the week he was frequently called upon to speak at English Nonconformist church functions apart from those of the Tabernacle. In 1856 he founded a pastors' college, which twenty years later had 110 men training for vocational ministry as well as a considerable number of men studying in its evening classes.[18]

Spurgeon also took seriously the church's responsibility to care for the poor and needy. For instance, in 1869 he established an orphanage, which eventually housed 500 children, and which he regularly visited. His manifest fatherly concern for the physical and spiritual well-being of the children endeared him to many of them. Writing in December 1887 from Menton, France, for example, he wished them a merry Christmas and expressed his sorrow at having to be away from them at such a time. 'I hope', he continued, 'you will all enjoy yourselves none the less, and be as happy as kittens.'[19] Further evidence of Spurgeon's deep commitment to these children is the fact that he wanted to be buried on the grounds of the orphanage — a wish that was not to be fulfilled.

Spurgeon also gave his support to a number of other philanthropic ventures and social activities. He spoke against the blatant immorality of prostitution, rampant in Victorian London, and urged that 'the men who frequent brothels should be punished as well as the women who traffic their bodies'.[20]

Nor was he slow to condemn the institution of slavery in the pre-Civil War United States. In no uncertain terms he publicly declared that he considered 'slavery to be a crime of crimes, a soul-destroying sin, and an iniquity which cries aloud for vengeance'. When pressed to write a letter on the subject, he wrote a 'red-hot letter' to the *Watchman and Reflector* in which he stated: 'I do from my inmost soul detest slavery anywhere and everywhere, and although I commune at the Lord's table with men of all creeds, yet with a slaveholder I have no fellowship of any kind or sort.'[21] It is not surprising that such sentiments were bitterly attacked in the Southern United States, where there was an outpouring of anger, even hatred, against Spurgeon, and where his books were boycotted and burnt in Southern bonfires.

Other Spurgeonic enterprises included a Book Fund — a charitable agency for Christian workers which was run by his wife Susannah — a colportage society, and the publication of a monthly magazine, *The Sword and the Trowel*, which was begun in 1865 and which enjoyed a wide circulation. Like many other evangelicals of his day and true to his earliest longings after conversion to serve the Lord Christ, Spurgeon was an 'energetic activist'. But, first and foremost, Spurgeon was a preacher, and a preacher without peer in the Victorian era.

Christ-centred

Four characteristics predominate in all of Spurgeon's sermons and writings. First, they are Christ-centred and Christ-exalting. Spurgeon was thus faithful to the intentions that he declared when the Tabernacle first opened in 1861.

> I would propose that the subject of the ministry in this house, as long as this platform shall stand, & as long as this house shall be frequented by worshippers, shall be the person of Jesus Christ. I am never ashamed to avow myself a Calvinist; I do not hesitate to take the name of Baptist; but if I am asked what is my creed, I reply, 'It is Jesus Christ'. My venerated predecessor, Dr. Gill, has left a body of divinity, admirable & excellent in its way; but the body of divinity to which I would pin & bind myself for ever, God helping me, is not his system, or any other human treatise; but Jesus Christ, who is the sum & substance of the gospel, who is in himself all theology, the incarnation of every precious truth, the all-glorious personal embodiment of the way, the truth, & the life.[22]

We find the same emphases in a sermon that he preached on 24 April 1891 to graduates of his college who had gathered for the annual conference that took place under the auspices of the Tabernacle. 'Ah, brothers! The Holy Ghost never comes to glorify *us*, or to glorify a denomination, or, I think, even to glorify a systematic arrangement of doctrines. He comes to glorify Christ. If we want to be in accord with him, we must preach in order to glorify Christ.'[23]

Spurgeon was conscious that devotion to the doctrines of grace and dedication to Baptist principles can well exist without the all-essential heart of Christianity, namely, devotion to the Lord Jesus. He was determined that when he preached it would be the Lord Jesus who was pre-eminently exalted in his sermons. As Nigel Lacey, an English Baptist pastor, has observed, a preaching ministry that did not centre upon his Saviour, Spurgeon detested.[24]

At the same time it should be understood that he never sought to conceal his doctrinal convictions as a Calvinistic Baptist. In a remarkable address which he gave at the Tabernacle on 19 August 1861 in honour of the centenary of the birth of William Carey, he declared to a packed auditorium of 6,000 that Carey's theology was profoundly influenced by what he called 'the noblest type of divinity that ever blessed the world', that is, the theological convictions of Jonathan Edwards (1703-1758), the great eighteenth-century American theologian.

He then went on to emphasize that 'Carey was the living model of Edwards' theology, or rather of pure Christianity. His was not a theology which left out the backbone and strength of religion — not a theology, on the other hand, all bones and skeleton, a lifeless thing without a soul: his theology was full-orbed Calvinism, high as you please, but practical godliness so low that many called it legal.' Moreover, Spurgeon stated that he admired 'Carey all the more for being a Baptist: he had none of that false charity which might prompt some to conceal their belief for fear of offending others; but at the same time he was a man who loved all who loved the Lord Jesus Christ'.[25]

A passion for the salvation of the lost

Spurgeon's sermons and books drew men and women to worship and adore the living God. They had a distinctly evangelistic thrust. In a sermon entitled 'Soul Winning', preached in 1869 on Proverbs 11:30 — 'He that wins souls is wise' — Spurgeon bared his heart in this regard.

> Even if I were utterly selfish, and had no care for anything but my own happiness, I would choose, if I might, under God, to be a soul-winner, for never did I know perfect, overflowing, unutterable happiness of the purest and most ennobling order, till I first heard of one who had sought and found a Saviour through my means. I recollect the thrill of joy which went through me! ... Oh! the joy of knowing that a sinner once at enmity has been reconciled to God, by the Holy Spirit, through the words spoken by our feeble lips. Since then, by grace given to me, the thought of which prostrates me in self-abasement, I have seen and heard of, not hundreds only, but even thousands of sinners turned from the error of their ways by the testimony of God in me. Let afflictions come, let trials be multiplied as God willeth, still this joy preponderates above all others, the joy that we are unto God a sweet savour of Christ in every place, and that as often as we preach the Word, hearts are unlocked, bosoms heave with a new life, eyes weep for sin, and their tears are wiped away as they see the great Substitute for sin, and live.[26]

Spurgeon's sermons so resonated with a passion for the salvation of the lost that Hyper-Calvinistic Baptists in London frequently criticized him for being an Arminian, despite the fact that Spurgeon was unrelenting in his opposition to

Arminianism. William Williams, a close friend of Spurgeon, recalled one occasion when Spurgeon met his leading Hyper-Calvinistic critic, the Strict Baptist preacher James Wells (1803-1872). Spurgeon remarked that he would like to have a tour of Wells' church some day. Wells responded by saying that he would be happy to show Spurgeon over his church, on the provision that the latter visited on a Monday. Wells would then have time before the following Sunday to have the building fumigated and so purge away any trace of Arminianism![27] Although, from one perspective, this snatch of conversation is but kindly banter, from another perspective, it well reveals how Spurgeon's Hyper-Calvinistic critics regarded him and that chiefly because he insisted on urging all of his hearers to repent and believe the gospel.[28]

Devoted to the Scriptures

Also prominent in Spurgeon's verbal and written utterance was the fact that he treated the Scriptures with reverence, and this produced a like effect in his hearers. 'Bible hearers,' Spurgeon noted in 1891, 'when they hear indeed, come to be Bible lovers.'[29] Now, it comes as a surprise to many admirers of Spurgeon to be told that he never preached a consecutive series of sermons on a book of the Bible. Fearful that such a style of preaching might quench the Spirit, Spurgeon chose the text for his Sunday morning sermon on the previous evening. The Sunday evening sermon was generally outlined on Sunday afternoon. Yet, it must be noted that his week before would be replete with reading in materials relating to Scripture and to the various branches of theology. His work-day would often extend past midnight, sometimes consuming eighteen hours a day. By the weekend there would be quite a number of texts vying for attention. Spurgeon, though, had to be certain that the text that he selected to preach on was also Spirit-chosen. Once the text was decided on, he would spend time meditating on it, and then jot down a brief outline, from which he would preach extemporaneously.[30]

Moreover, as Nigel Lacey has noted, there is little doubt that Spurgeon's sermons are expository. His sermons reveal that he paid close attention to the text he was expounding.[31] What Spurgeon once said of the seventeenth-century Baptist evangelist John Bunyan (1628-1688) is equally true of himself: 'Read anything of his, and you will see that it is almost like reading the Bible itself... Prick him anywhere; and you will find that his blood is Bibline, the very essence of the Bible flows from him. He cannot speak without quoting a text, for his soul is full of the Word of God.'[32]

Owned by the Spirit of God

The final characteristic of Spurgeon's preaching and writing that needs to be noted is that it was Spirit-anointed. When he preached, as one of his hearers once put it, 'the pentecostal fire fell from heaven upon the people'.[33]

Now, surely one of the major reasons for this anointing on Spurgeon's preaching was the fact that central to the content of his preaching was the Lord Jesus — the glory of his person and the marvel of his work. As Spurgeon warned graduates of the pastors' college who had gathered for the annual conference in 1891: 'If we do not make the Lord Jesus glorious; if we do not lift him high in the esteem of men, if we do not labour to make him King of kings, and Lord of lords; we shall not have the Holy Spirit with us. Vain will be rhetoric, music, architecture, energy, and social status: if our one design be not to magnify the Lord Jesus, we shall work alone and work in vain'.[34]

Spurgeon made the same point somewhat more quaintly when he stated in his sermon 'Receiving the Holy Ghost', preached in July of 1884: 'the Holy Spirit always keeps sweet company with Jesus Christ'.[35]

The Downgrade Controversy

In his final years Spurgeon suffered from a disease of the kidneys. This physical problem appears to have been exacerbated by his involvement as one of the leading protagonists in what is known as the Downgrade Controversy. During the 1880s Spurgeon was concerned by what he saw rightly as the inroads of liberal theology into British Baptist ranks. Sensing that something definite needed to be said to the issue, he published a series of articles in *The Sword and the Trowel* over the course of 1887, in which he urged his fellow Baptists to deal with the problem head on and proclaim their wholehearted commitment to evangelical orthodoxy. As Spurgeon had examined the preaching of some of his Baptist contemporaries, he had noticed in their sermons that the 'Atonement is scouted, the inspiration of Scripture is derided, the Holy Spirit is degraded into an influence, the punishment of sin is turned into fiction, and the resurrection into a myth'.[36] Spurgeon's protest, however, fell largely on deaf ears, and in October of that year the Baptist preacher felt he had no recourse but to lead the Tabernacle out of the Baptist Union.

Over the winter of 1887-1888 a naive, though well-intentioned, group of eirenical individuals within the Union made common cause with some of Spurgeon's opponents to attempt a reconciliation between the pastor of the Tabernacle and the Union. Spurgeon, though, rightly chose commitment to the truths of the Scriptures and the God who gave them over the preservation of denominational unity, and these attempts at reconciliation failed. The climax came at the annual meeting of the Baptist Union in April 1888. Spurgeon was not present, though his brother, James Archer Spurgeon (1837-1899), the co-pastor of the Tabernacle, was. Spurgeon's supporters and the eirenicists within the Union had both drawn up doctrinal statements. Prior to the debate about the issue on 23 April, however, a mediating statement was drafted and overwhelmingly accepted by the delegates at the meeting. Those of Spurgeon's supporters who voted in favour of this statement — including Spurgeon's own brother, James, who seconded the approval of the statement — actually believed that they had won a great victory. Spurgeon was convinced otherwise and the succeeding decades showed that he was right. As Willis B. Glover has written: 'Spurgeon's insight into the religious life of his own times was proved by subsequent events. He did stand on the eve of a great evangelical depression, and unquestionably the theological confusion of his day and the disturbance to religious traditions wrought by higher criticism had a great deal to do with the decline of evangelicalism.'[37]

Spurgeon recognized that without clear and distinct doctrinal parameters evangelicalism was helpless against the onslaught of liberal theology. Many of the eirenicists within the Union felt that acceptance of the new theological perspectives spawned by the rise of higher criticism would not intrinsically affect or harm Christian spirituality. Spurgeon saw the folly of such a position: 'the coals of orthodoxy are necessary to the fire of piety'.[38]

The stress of this controversy took a great toll on Spurgeon and almost certainly contributed to the rapid decline of his health in 1891. He died at Menton, a resort on the French Riviera not far from the Italian border, where he had annually taken vacations since the mid-1870s. Spurgeon had gone there with his wife in October of that year in the hope that a change of scenery and weather would facilitate a recovery of health. It was not to be. The Prince of Preachers died in the last hour on the final day of January 1892.

Not long before his death he had whispered to his secretary, Joseph W. Harrald, 'Remember, a plain stone, C. H. S. and no more; no fuss.' [39]His wishes went unheeded. After the return of his body to England, it 'lay in state' at the Tabernacle, with as many as 50,000 mourners coming to pay their last respects. On the day of the funeral, thousands lined the streets along which the funeral procession passed, with shops, and even pubs, closing their doors for the day. His body was laid to rest in an ornate tomb. On top of his coffin was placed a Bible, open at the very text instrumental in his conversion so many years before: 'Look unto me, and be ye saved, all the ends of the earth: for I am God, and there is none else' (Isaiah 45:22).[40]

His true memorial

His lasting memorial, though, was in the lives of countless men and women who had been touched by the Spirit of God at work in his life and ministry. To take but one example: in October 1889 a young man by the name of D. C. Davidson left his home in Michigan to go abroad to do postgraduate work in theology. His mother had wanted him to study at Yale, but he was determined to come into vital contact with what he called 'the leading minds of Europe'. After a stay of four months in Edinburgh, he crossed over from Great Britain to Germany in 1890 and eventually made his way to Berlin. Yet, instead of being a place where his faith was deepened and established, the German capital proved to be a veritable furnace in which his faith in God was tried to the very depths. Of his time in Berlin he said that a 'horror of great darkness' came over his soul there as he was exposed to liberal German theology. 'I have encountered many a fiery temptation', he later wrote, 'but I have never had a temptation cross my pathway so subtle and dangerous as that of German destructive criticism.'[41]

With his faith well nigh shattered he returned to England, where for three months he regularly went to hear Charles Haddon Spurgeon preach what must have been some of his final sermons. Sitting under Spurgeon's preaching brought spiritual revitalization and healing to his soul.

When Spurgeon preached the simple old doctrines of the Cross, the pentecostal fire fell from heaven upon the people. I have seen the multitudes in that tabernacle moved by the breath of God, when that man spoke, as the trees of the forest are moved by the wind. It seemed to me that I was in the third heaven, compared to the cess-pool of German criticism in which I had been wallowing. What could I do but bow down before my Maker and worship, crying, 'The Lord, He is God! The Lord, He is God!'...The glory of God seemed to fill Mr Spurgeon's tabernacle...The poisonous effects of the destructive criticism which had permeated my heart, were consumed like stubble, by the holy fire of God. I saw the Scriptures with new eyes. They became inexpressibly precious to me and the Christ whom they reveal.[42]

When Davidson returned to the United States he did so with the resolve 'that while life lasts, I would "preach the Word", and blow the gospel trumpet with no uncertain sound'.[43]

Although Spurgeon's voice was stilled in 1892, through the ongoing publication of his sermons and books the Holy Spirit continues to honour Spurgeon's ministry and to draw sinners to know and to worship the Triune God.

Michael Haykin
Professor of Church History
Heritage Baptist College and Theological Seminary
Cambridge, Ontario, Canada

Notes

1 Much of this biographical sketch appeared in an earlier form in *The Evangelical Baptist*, 40, No.1 (November 1992), 6-7, 9-10; 40, No.2 (December 1992), 10-12, and appears here by permission.

2 *C.H. Spurgeon: The Early Years 1834-1859* (London: The Banner of Trust, 1962), 11.

3 *Letters of Charles Haddon Spurgeon*, selected Iain H. Murray (Edinburgh: The Banner of Truth Trust, 1992), 39.

4 Mike Nicholls, *C. H. Spurgeon: The Pastor Evangelist* (Didcot, Oxfordshire: Baptist Historical Society, 1992), 2-3. On Knill, see W.Y. Fullerton, *Spurgeon* (Chicago: Moody Press, 1966), 37-38.

5 Cited Arnold Dallimore, *Spurgeon* (1984 ed.; repr. Edinburgh: The Banner of Truth Trust, 1985), 17.

6 For evidence that the church to which Spurgeon was headed on the morning of his conversion was Colchester Baptist Church, see Henry Spyvee, *Colchester Baptist Church—The First 300 Years, 1689-1989* (Colchester: Colchester Baptist Church, 1989), 59.

7 For the following account of Spurgeon's conversion, see [Susannah Spurgeon and J. W. Harrald], *C.H. Spurgeon: The Early Years, 1834-1859* (1897-1899 ed.; revised and abridged London: The Banner of Truth Trust, 1962), 87-88.

8 *Spurgeon: The Early Years*, 149.

9 Nicholls, *Spurgeon*, 5.

10 *Letters*, 27.

11 Nicholls, *Spurgeon*, 5.

12 Cited Ernest W. Bacon, *Spurgeon: Heir of the Puritans* (London: George Allen & Unwin Ltd, 1967), 32.

13 *Letters*, 50-51.

14 Cited E. J. Poole-Connor, *Evangelicalism in England* (London: The Fellowship of Independent Evangelical Churches, 1951), 226.

15 Cited *ibid.*, 226-227.

16 *Spurgeon*, 37.

17 *C. H. Spurgeon's Autobiography*, compiled Susannah Spurgeon and J. W. Harrald (London: Passmore and Alabaster, 1900), IV, 243.

18 Nicholls, *Spurgeon*, 82. Nicholls devotes an entire chapter in his biography to Spurgeon as an 'innovative educator'. See *ibid.*, 69-96.

19 *Letters*, 109.

20 Cited Nicholls, *Spurgeon*, 61. Nicholls details Spurgeon's social activities in the chapter of his biography entitled 'Energetic Activist'. See *ibid.*, 55-68. On his activism, see also James M. Gordon, *Evangelical Spirituality* (London: SPCK, 1991), 167-168.

21 Cited Nicholls, *Spurgeon*, 120. For his attitude to slavery, see also *ibid.*, 61, 118-121.

22 *C. H. Spurgeon's Autobiography*, compiled Susannah Spurgeon and J. W. Harrald (London: Passmore and Alabaster, 1899), III, 1.

23 'Honey in the Mouth!', *The Metropolitan Tabernacle Pulpit*, 37:381.

24 'Spurgeon—The Preacher', *Grace Magazine* (January 1992), 6. On the Christocentric nature of Spurgeon's entire life, see Richard Ellsworth Day, *The Shadow of the Broad Brim. The Life Story of Charles Haddon Spurgeon: Heir of the Puritans* (Philadelphia: The Judson Press, 1934), 217-227.

25 'C. H. Spurgeon's tribute to William Carey', Supplement to the *Baptist Times*, (16 April 1992), [1].

26 *The Metropolitan Tabernacle Pulpit*, 15:27.

27 *Personal Reminiscences of Charles Haddon Spurgeon* (London: The Religious Tract Society, 1895), 60. It says much for Spurgeon's character that when he learned that Wells was dying in 1871, he wrote him a comforting letter, in which he called Wells 'a father in the Gospel' and mentioned that he was asking the Lord, 'the tender lover of our souls, to lay under you His supporting

arms'. 'May your sick chamber,' he continued, 'be the very gate of heaven to your soul, the presence of the Lord filling the house with glory' (*Letters*, 73-74).

28 Lacey, 'Spurgeon', 6-7. For a good study of Spurgeon as an evangelist, see W. E. Payne, 'C. H. Spurgeon and Soul Winning', *The Fellowship for Reformation and Pastoral Studies*, 19, No.4 (January 1991). On Spurgeon's relationship to Hyper-Calvinism, see especially Iain H. Murray, *Spurgeon v. Hyper-Calvinism. The Battle for Gospel Preaching* (Edinburgh: The Banner of Truth Trust, 1995).

29 *The Greatest Fight in the World* (London: Passmore and Alabaster, 1891), 24.

30 William R. Estep, 'The Making of A Prophet: An Introduction to Charles Haddon Spurgeon', *Baptist History and Heritage*, 19, No.4 (October 1984), 10.

31 'Spurgeon', 6.

32 Cited Iain H. Murray, *The Forgotten Spurgeon* (London: The Banner of Truth Trust, 1966), 42.

33 D. C. Davidson, 'In the Furnace of Unbelieving Theology', *The Banner of Truth*, 293 (February 1988), 18.

34 *Greatest Fight in the World*, 64.

35 *The Metropolitan Tabernacle Pulpit*, 30:395.

36 'Another Word concerning the Downgrade', *The Sword and the Trowel* (August 1887), 397.

37 *Evangelical Nonconformists and Higher Criticism in the Nineteenth Century* (London: Independent Press Ltd, 1954), 166-167.

38 Cited David P. Kingdon, 'C. H. Spurgeon and the Downgrade Controversy' in *The Good Fight of Faith* (London: The Westminster Conference/Evangelical Press, 1971), 48.

39 Cited *Letters*, 211.

40 Eric Hayden, 'The day my father saw Spurgeon buried', *Baptist Times* (January 30, 1992), 7.

41 'In the Furnace of Unbelieving Theology', 16-18.

42 *Ibid.*, 18-19.

43 *Ibid.*, 19.

Psalm 1:1-3

Suggested further reading: Matthew 5:1-12

See how this book of Psalms opens with a benediction, just as the famous sermon of our Lord upon the Mount did! The word translated 'blessed' is a very expressive one. Since it is plural, we might read it, 'Oh, the blessednesses!' and we may well regard it as a joyful acclamation of the gracious man's felicity. May the same benediction rest on us!

Here the gracious man is described both negatively (v. 1) and positively (v. 2). Mark the gradation in the first verse: he walks not in the counsel of the ungodly, nor stands in the way of sinners, nor sits in the seat of the scornful. When men are living in sin they go from bad to worse. They have taken their degree in vice, are installed as true Doctors of damnation, and are looked up to by others as Masters in evil. But the blessed man, the man to whom all the blessings of God belong, can hold no communion with such characters as these. He keeps himself pure from these lepers; he puts evil things away from him as garments spotted by the flesh; he comes out from among the wicked, and goes outside the camp, bearing the reproach of Christ. Oh, for grace to be separate from sinners in this way.

Now note his positive character: 'His delight is in the law of the Lord.' It is the daily bread of the true believer. And yet, in David's day, how small was the volume of inspiration, for they had scarcely anything save the first five books of Moses! How much more, then, should we prize the whole written Word which it is our privilege to have in all our houses! But, alas, how this angel from heaven is ill treated! We are not all Berean searchers of the Scriptures. How few among us can lay claim to the benediction of the text! Perhaps some of you can claim a sort of negative purity, because you do not walk in the way of the ungodly; but let me ask you: Is your delight in the law of God? Do you study God's Word? Do you make it your right-hand man, your best companion and hourly guide? If not, this blessing does not belong to you.

He is 'like a tree planted by the rivers of water, that brings forth its fruit in its season'; the man who delights in God's Word, being taught by it, brings forth patience in the time of suffering, faith in the day of trial, and holy joy in the hour of prosperity. Fruitfulness is an essential quality of a gracious man, and that fruitfulness should be seasonable.

Meditation: *I have no rest, but in a nook, with* the Book (Thomas à Kempis).

Psalm 1:4-6

Suggested further reading: 2 Peter 2:4-11

We now come to the second section of the psalm. In verse 4 the contrast of the ill estate of the wicked is employed to heighten the colouring of that fair and pleasant picture which precedes it. The more forcible translation of the Vulgate and of the Septuagint version is 'Not so the ungodly, not so.' And by this we are to understand that whatever good thing is said of the righteous is not true in the case of the ungodly. Oh, how terrible it is to have a double negative put upon the promises, and yet this is just the condition of the ungodly! Note the use of the term 'ungodly', for, as we have seen in the opening of the psalm, these are the beginners in evil, and are the least offensive of sinners. Oh! if this is the sad state of those who quietly continue in their morality, and neglect their God, what must be the condition of open sinners and shameless infidels? The first sentence is a negative description of the ungodly, and the second is the positive picture. Here is their character, they are 'like chaff', intrinsically worthless, dead, unserviceable, without substance, and easily carried away. Here, also, mark their doom, 'the wind drives away'; death shall hurry them with its terrible blast into the fire in which they shall be utterly consumed. The ungodly shall stand to be judged, but not to be acquitted. Fear shall lay hold upon them there; they shall not stand their ground; they shall flee away; they shall not stand in their own defence, for they shall blush and be covered with eternal contempt.

Well may the saints long for heaven, for no evil men shall dwell there. All our congregations upon earth are mixed. Sinners mix with saints, as dross mingles with gold. Righteous Lots are this side of heaven continually vexed by the men of Sodom. Let us rejoice then, that in 'the general assembly and church of the firstborn' above, there shall by no means be admitted a single unrenewed soul. Sinners cannot live in heaven. They would be out of their element. A fish could sooner live upon a tree than the wicked in paradise. Heaven would be an intolerable hell to an impenitent man, even if he could be allowed to enter. May God grant that we have a name and a place in his courts above! The Lord is constantly looking on the way of the wicked, and though it may be often in mist and darkness, yet the Lord knows it. Not only shall they perish themselves, but their way shall perish too. The righteous carves his name upon the rock, but the wicked writes his remembrance in the sand. The very 'way' of the ungodly shall perish.

May the Lord cleanse our hearts and our ways, so that we may escape the doom of the ungodly, and enjoy the blessedness of the righteous!

Meditation: *The righteous go a way that God knows, and the wicked go a way that God destroys; and seeing that these ways can never meet, how should the men that go these ways meet?* (Sir Richard Baker).

Psalm 2:1-6

Suggested further reading: Revelation 4

This psalm begins abruptly, and well it may: it is surely no little wonder that the sight of creatures in arms against their God should amaze the psalmist's mind. We see the 'nations raging', roaring like the sea, tossed to and fro with restless waves, as the ocean in a storm; and then we note the people in their hearts 'imagining a vain thing against God'. Where there is much rage there is generally some folly, and in this case there is an excess of it. It was not temporary rage, but deep-seated hate, for they 'set themselves' resolutely to withstand the Prince of Peace. Gathering impudence by the traitorous proposition of rebellion, they add 'let us cast away' as if it were an easy matter. However mad the resolution to revolt from God, it is one in which man has persevered ever since his creation, and he continues in it to this very day. To a graceless neck the yoke of Christ is intolerable, but to the saved sinner it is easy and light. We may judge ourselves by this: do we love that yoke, or do we wish to cast it from us?

Let us now turn our eyes from the wicked council-chamber and raging tumult of man, to the secret place of the majesty of the Most High. What does God say? What will the King do to the men who reject his only-begotten Son, the Heir of all things? Mark the quiet dignity of the Omnipotent One, and the contempt he pours on the princes and their raging people. He has not taken the trouble to rise up and do battle with them: he despises them, he knows how absurd, how irrational, how futile are their attempts against him, he therefore laughs at them. After he has laughed he will speak. At the moment when their power is its strongest, and their fury most violent, then shall his Word go forth against them. And what is it that he says? It is a very galling sentence, 'Despite your malice, despite your tumultuous gatherings, despite the wisdom of your counsels, despite the craft of your lawgivers, "Yet have I set my king upon my holy hill of Zion."' Is not that a grand exclamation! He has already done that which the enemy seeks to prevent. Jehovah's will is done, and man's will frets and raves in vain. God's Anointed is appointed, and shall not be disappointed. Look back through all the ages of infidelity, hearken to the high and hard things which men have spoken against the Majesty of heaven, and then remember that God is saying all the while, 'Yet have I set my king upon my holy hill of Zion.' Even now he reigns in Zion, and our glad lips sound forth the praises of the Prince of Peace. In him is Zion's best safeguard; let her citizens be glad in him.

Meditation: *Whatever the plots of hell and earth may be to the contrary, Christ reigns by his Father's ordination* (Stephen Charnock).

Psalm 2:7-12

Suggested further reading: Revelation 5

This psalm wears something of a dramatic form, for now another person is introduced as speaking. We have looked into the counsel-chamber of the wicked, and to the throne of God, and now we behold the Anointed declaring his rights of sovereignty, and warning the traitors of their doom.

Christ the Anointed himself comes forward, as the risen Redeemer, 'declared to be the Son of God with power, according to the spirit of holiness, by the resurrection from the dead' (Rom. 1:4). Looking into the angry faces of the rebellious kings, the Anointed One seems to say, 'If this is not enough to make you silent, "I will declare the decree".' Now this decree is directly in conflict with the device of man, for its tenor is the establishment of the very dominion against which the nations are raging. The words 'You are my Son' are a noble proof of the glorious divinity of our Immanuel. What a mercy to have a divine Redeemer in the Godhead of our Lord! Let us not attempt to fathom it, for it is a great truth, a truth reverently to be received, but not irreverently to be scanned.

It was a custom among great kings to give to favoured ones whatever they might ask. So Jesus has but to ask and have. Here he declares that his very enemies are his inheritance. He declares this decree to their face, and 'Lo, here!' cries the Anointed One, as he holds aloft in that once pierced hand the sceptre of his power: 'He has given me this, not only the right to be a king, but the power to conquer.'

The scene again changes, and counsel is given to those who have taken counsel to rebel. They are exhorted to obey, and give the kiss of homage and affection to him whom they have hated. 'Be wise,' delay no longer, your warfare cannot succeed, therefore desist and yield cheerfully to the one who will make you bow if you refuse his yoke. Let reverence and humility be mingled with your service. He is a great God, and you are but puny creatures; bend, therefore, in lowly worship. Fear, without joy, is torment; and joy, without holy fear, would be presumption. Note the benediction with which the psalm closes. Have we a share in this blessedness? Do we trust in him? Our faith may be slender as a spider's thread; but if it is real, we are in our measure blessed. The more we trust, the more fully we shall know this blessedness. We may therefore close the psalm with the prayer of the apostles: 'Lord, increase our faith.'

Meditation: *The fear of God promotes spiritual joy; it is the morning star which ushers in the sunlight of comfort* (Thomas Watson).

Psalm 3:1-4

Suggested further reading: 2 Samuel 15:13-17

The poor broken-hearted father complains of the multitude of his enemies. Here is a note of exclamation to express the wonder of woe that amazed and perplexed the fugitive father: 'Their hosts are far superior to mine! Their numbers are too great for my reckoning!' David complains before his loving God of the worst weapon of his enemies' attacks, and the bitterest drop of his distresses. If all the trials which come from heaven, all the temptations which ascend from hell, and all the crosses which arise from earth, could be mixed and pressed together, they would not make a trial so terrible as that which is contained in verse 2. It is the bitterest of all afflictions to be led to fear that there is no help for us in God. And yet remember our most blessed Saviour had to endure this in the deepest degree when he cried, 'My God, my God, why have you forsaken me?' He knew full well what it was to walk in darkness and to see no light. This was the curse of the curse. To be deserted by his Father was worse than to be the despised of men. Surely we should love him who suffered this bitterest of temptations and trials for our sake. It will be a delightful and instructive exercise for the loving heart to mark the Lord in his agonies as portrayed here, for there is here, and in very many other psalms, far more of David's Lord than of David himself.

In reply, David avows his confidence in God: 'You are a shield for me.' The word signifies more than a shield; it means a protection which shall surround a man entirely: above, beneath, around, without and within. Oh, what a shield is God for his people! He wards off the fiery darts of Satan from beneath, and the storms of trials from above, while, at the same instant, he speaks peace to the tempest within the breast. David knew that though he was driven from his capital in contempt and scorn, he should yet return in triumph, and by faith he looks upon God as honouring and glorifying him. Oh, for grace to see our future glory amid present shame! Indeed, there is a present glory in our afflictions, if we could but discern it; for it is no mean thing to have fellowship with Christ in his sufferings.

Good men often find that, even in secret, they pray better aloud than they do when they utter no vocal sound. There is one in the sanctuary who hearkens from the seventh heaven, and he has 'heard me out of his holy hill'. Answers to prayers are sweet cordials for the soul. We need not fear a frowning world while we rejoice in a prayer-hearing God.

Meditation: *Persuade yourselves, with David, that the Lord is your defender, who has compassed you round about, and is, as it were, a 'shield' that covers you on every side* (Thomas Tymme).

Psalm 3:5-8

Suggested further reading: 2 Samuel 16:5-14

David's faith enabled him to 'lie down'; anxiety would certainly have kept him on his toes, watching for an enemy. He was able to sleep, in the midst of trouble, surrounded by foes. There is a sleep of presumption; may God deliver us from it! There is a sleep of holy confidence; may God help us so to close our eyes! But David says he 'awoke' also. Some sleep the sleep of death; but he, though exposed to many enemies, reclined his head on the bosom of his God, slept happily beneath the wing of providence in sweet security, and then awoke in safety, conscious that the Lord had preserved him.

Buckling on his harness for the day's battle, our hero sings, 'I will not be afraid of ten thousands of people.' Observe that he does not attempt to underestimate the number or wisdom of his enemies. He reckons them at tens of thousands, and he views them as cunning huntsmen chasing him with cruel skill. Yet he trembles not, but looking his enemy in the face he is ready for the battle. But David is too wise to venture to the battle without prayer; he therefore falls to his knees, and cries aloud to Jehovah. His only hope is in his God, but that is so strong a confidence that he feels the Lord has but to 'arise' and he is saved. It is enough for the Lord to stand up, and all is well. He compares his enemies to wild beasts, and he declares that God has broken their jaws, so that they could not injure him: Rejoice, O believer, you have to do with a dragon whose head is broken, and with enemies whose teeth are dashed from their jaws!

The final verse contains the sum and substance of Calvinistic doctrine. Search Scripture through, and you must, if you read it with a candid mind, be persuaded that the doctrine of salvation by grace alone is the great doctrine of the Word of God: 'Salvation belongs to the Lord.' This is a point concerning which we are daily fighting. Our opponents say, 'Salvation belongs to the free will of man; if not to man's merit, yet at least to man's will'; but we hold and teach that salvation from first to last, in every iota of it, belongs to the Most High God. It is God who chooses his people. He calls them by his grace; he quickens them by his Spirit, and keeps them by his power. It is not of man, neither by man; 'not of him that wills, nor of him that runs, but of God that shows mercy'. May we all learn this truth experimentally, for our proud flesh and blood will never permit us to learn it in any other way.

Meditation:
  Rise, my soul! adore and wonder!
  Ask, 'O why such love to me?'
  Grace hath put me in the number
  Of the Saviour's family:
  Hallelujah!
  Thanks, eternal thanks to thee.

Psalm 4:1-5

Suggested further reading: Genesis 50:15-21

This is an instance of David's common habit of pleading past mercies as a ground for present favour. It is not to be imagined that he who has helped us in six troubles will leave us in the seventh. God does nothing by halves, and he will never cease to help us until we cease to need. Observe that David speaks first to God and then to men. Surely we should all speak more boldly to men if we had more constant communion with God. He who dares to face his Maker will not tremble before the sons of men.

The name by which the Lord is addressed here deserves notice, since it is not used in any other part of Scripture. It means, 'You are the author, the witness, the maintainer, the judge, and the rewarder of my righteousness; to you I appeal from the calumnies and harsh judgements of men.' Herein is wisdom, let us imitate it and always take ours, not to the petty courts of human opinion, but to the superior court, the King's Bench of heaven. Then we shall say with David, 'God has enlarged my heart with joy and comfort when I was like a man imprisoned by grief and sorrow.' The best of men need mercy as surely as the worst of men. All the times of deliverance of saints, as well as the pardons of sinners, are the free gifts of heavenly grace. God is a never-failing comforter.

We are next led from the closet of prayer into the field of conflict. Note again the undaunted courage of the man of God. He allows that his enemies are great men, but still he believes them to be foolish men, and therefore chides them, as though they were but children. He tells them that they 'love worthlessness and seek falsehood'. Fools will not learn, and therefore they must be told the same thing again and again, especially when it is such a bitter truth that is to be taught them, namely the fact that the godly are the chosen of God, and are, by distinguishing grace, set apart and separated from among men. Election is a doctrine that unrenewed men cannot endure, but, nevertheless, it is a glorious and well-attested truth, and one that should comfort the tempted believer. Election is the guarantee of complete salvation, and an argument for success at the throne of grace. He who chose us for himself will surely hear our prayers. O beloved, when you are on your knees, the fact of your being 'set apart' as God's own peculiar treasure should give you courage and inspire you with fervency and faith. Since he chose to love us he cannot but choose to hear us.

Meditation: *Let us remember that the experience of one of the saints concerning the verity of God's promises, and the certainty of the written privileges of the Lord's people is a sufficient proof of the right that all his children have to the same mercies, and a ground of hope that they also shall partake of them in their times of need* (David Dickson).

Psalm 4:6-8

Suggested further reading: Isaiah 9:1-7

There were many, even among David's own followers, who wanted to see rather than to believe. Alas! this is the tendency of us all! Sometimes even the regenerate groan after the sense and sight of prosperity, and are sad when darkness covers all good from view. As for worldlings, this is their unceasing cry: 'Who will show us any good?' Never satisfied, their gaping mouths are turned in every direction, their empty hearts are ready to drink in any fine delusion that impostors may invent; and when these fail, they soon yield to despair, and declare that there is no good thing in either heaven or earth. The true believer is a man of a very different mould. His face is not downward like the beasts', but upward like the angels'. He does not drink from the muddy pools of Mammon, but from the fountain of life above. The light of God's countenance is enough for him. This is his riches, his honour, his health, his ambition, his ease. Give him this, and he will ask no more. This is joy unspeakable, and full of glory. Oh, for more of the indwelling of the Holy Spirit, that our fellowship with the Father and with his Son Jesus Christ may be constant and abiding!

'It is better', it has been said, 'to feel God's favour one hour in our repenting souls, than to sit whole ages under the warmest sunshine that this world affords.' Christ in the heart is better than corn in the barn, or wine in the vat. Corn and wine are but fruits of the world, but the light of God's countenance is the ripe fruit of heaven. 'You are with me' is a far more blessed cry than 'Harvest home.' Let my granary be empty, I am yet full of blessings if Jesus Christ smiles upon me; but if I have the whole world, I am poor without him.

A sweet evening hymn is found in verse 8! He who has the wings of God above him needs no other curtain. The protection of the Lord is better than bolts or bars. Armed men kept the bed of Solomon, but we do not believe that he slept more soundly than his father, whose bed was the hard ground, and who was haunted by bloodthirsty foes. How many of our sleepless hours might be traced to our untrusting and disordered minds. They slumber sweetly whom faith rocks to sleep. There is no pillow so soft as a promise, no coverlet so warm as an assured interest in Christ. O Lord, give us this calm repose, that like David we may lie down in peace, and sleep each night while we live; and may we lie down joyfully in the appointed season, to sleep in death, to rest in God!

Meditation: *While men of the world, from the world, are seeking their chief good, let us desire Christ's favour which infinitely transcends corn and wine, and all the good things which perish with use* (Robert Hawker).

Psalm 5:1-7

Suggested further reading: Matthew 6:5-15

There are two sorts of prayers — those expressed in words, and the unuttered longings that abide as silent meditations. Words are not the essence but the garments of prayer. Moses at the Red Sea cried to God, though he said nothing. Yet the use of language may prevent distraction of mind, may assist the powers of the soul, and may excite devotion. David, we observe, uses both modes of prayer, and craves for the one a hearing, and for the other a consideration. What an expressive word! 'Consider my meditation.' If I have asked that which is right, give it to me; if I have omitted to ask that which I most needed, fill up the vacancy in my prayer. Let your holy soul consider it as presented through my all-glorious Mediator; then regard it in your wisdom, weigh it in the scales, judge my sincerity, and the true state of my necessities, and answer me in due time for your mercy's sake! Let us cultivate the spirit of prayer, which is even better than the habit of prayer. We should begin to pray before we kneel down, and we should not cease when we rise up.

The morning is the most fitting time for communion with God. An hour in the morning is worth two in the evening. While the dew is upon the grass, let grace drop upon the soul. The Hebrew used by David has a full meaning. It is the word used for the laying in order of the wood and the pieces of the victim upon the altar, and it is used for the putting of the shewbread on the table. I will arrange my prayer, or, as old Master Trapp has it, 'I will marshal up my prayers.'

Now that the psalmist has expressed his resolution to pray, we hear him offering up his prayer. He is pleading against his cruel and wicked enemies. He begs God to put them away from him, because they were displeasing to God himself. Let us learn here the solemn truth of the hatred that a righteous God must bear toward sin. He will not grant it the least shelter. Oh, how foolish we are if we attempt to entertain two guests so hostile to one another as Christ Jesus and the devil! Rest assured, Christ will not live in the parlour of our hearts if we entertain the devil in the cellar of our thoughts. Earthly kings were accustomed to having fools in their trains, but the only wise God will have no fools in his palace above.

After describing the character and fate of the wicked, David turns to the condition of the righteous. He will enter into God's house — not in his own merits, but because of the multitude of God's mercies. He approaches with confidence because of immeasurable grace.

Meditation: *God's judgements are all numbered, but his mercies are innumerable* (C. H. Spurgeon).

Psalm 5:8-12

Suggested further reading: Romans 3:9-20

Now we come to the second part, in which the psalmist
repeats his arguments and then reinforces the same points
again. As a little child is led by his father, as a blind man is
guided by his friend, so it is safe and pleasant walking when
God leads the way. When we have learned to give up our
own way, and long to walk in God's way, it is a happy sign
of grace; and it is no small mercy to see the way of God
with clear vision straight before our face.

The description of depraved man has been copied by
the apostle Paul as being an accurate description of the
whole human race, not only of David's enemies, but of all
men by nature. The picture is remarkable, 'Their throat is
an open tomb', full of loathsomeness, pestilence and death.
But, worse than that, it is an open tomb, with all its evil
gasses issuing forth, to spread death and destruction all
around. In addition, their tongues are full of flattery. A
smooth tongue is a great evil; many have been bewitched
by it. There are many human anteaters that with their long
tongues covered with oily words entice and entrap the un-
wary and so make their gain. When the wolf licks the lamb,
he is preparing to wet his teeth in its blood. In the tenth
verse, the psalmist speaks as a judge, ex officio; he speaks
as God's mouth, and in condemning the wicked he gives us
no excuse whatever for uttering anything by way of mal-
ediction upon those who have caused us personal offence.
O impenitent man, may it be known that all your godly

friends will give their solemn assent to the awful sentence of the Lord, which he shall pronounce on you in the day of doom.

Joy is the privilege of the believer. When sinners are destroyed our rejoicing shall be full. They laugh first and weep ever after; we weep now, but shall rejoice eternally. This holy bliss of ours has a firm foundation, for O Lord, we are 'joyful in you'. The eternal God is the well-spring of our bliss. We love God, and therefore we delight in him. Jehovah has ordained his people the heirs of blessedness, and nothing shall rob them of their inheritance. With all the fulness of his power he will bless them, and all his attributes shall unite to satiate them with divine contentment. Nor is this merely for the present, but the blessing reaches into the long and unknown future. 'You, O Lord, will bless the righteous.' This is a promise of infinite length, of unbounded breadth, and of unutterable preciousness.

Meditation: *Where can we go for shelter but unto God our Maker! When the lion of the forest begins to roar, how he will terrify and vex us, till he that permits him to trouble us for a while, is pleased to chain him up again* (Timothy Rogers).

Psalm 6:1-7

Suggested further reading: Isaiah 54:1-10

This psalm is commonly known as the first of the Penitential Psalms, and certainly its language well suits the lip of a
penitent, for it expresses at once the sorrow (vv. 3, 6, 7), the
humiliation (vv. 2 and 4), and the hatred of sin (v. 8). These
are the unfailing marks of the contrite spirit when it turns
to God. The psalmist is very conscious that he deserves to
be rebuked, and he feels, moreover, that the rebuke must
come upon him in some form or other, if not for condemnation, then for conviction and sanctification.

This is the right way to plead with God if we would
prevail. Do not urge your goodness or your greatness, but
plead your sin and your smallness. Cry, 'I am weak, therefore, O Lord, give me strength and do not crush me.' When
the soul has a sense of sin, it is enough to make the bones
shake; it is enough to make a man's hair stand up on end to
see the flames of hell beneath him, an angry God above
him, and danger and doubt surrounding him. The psalmist
still had, however, some hope; but that hope was only in
his God. He therefore cries, 'O Lord, how long?' The coming of Christ into the soul in his priestly robes of grace is
the grand hope of the penitent soul; and, indeed, in some
form or other, Christ's appearance is, and ever has been,
the hope of the saints.

As God's absence was the main cause of his misery, so
his return would be enough to deliver him from his trouble.
He knows where to look, and what arm to lay hold upon.

He does not lay hold on God's left hand of justice, but on his right hand of mercy. He knew his iniquity too well to think of merit, or appeal to anything but the grace of God. If we turn to justice, what plea can we urge? But if we turn to mercy we may still cry, notwithstanding the greatness of our guilt, 'Save me for your mercies' sake.'

Poor trembling sinners, may the Lord help you to use this forcible argument. It is for God's glory that a sinner should be saved. When we seek pardon, we are not asking God to do that which will stain his banner, or put a blot on his shield. He delights in mercy. It is his peculiar, darling attribute. Mercy honours God. Do not we ourselves say, 'Mercy blesses him that gives, and him that takes'? And surely, in some diviner sense, this is true of God, who, when he gives mercy, glorifies himself.

Meditation: *It is no light matter to feel oneself a sinner, condemned at the bar of God* (C. H. Spurgeon).

Psalm 6:8-10

Suggested further reading: Matthew 25:31-46

David has found peace, and rising from his knees he begins to sweep his house of the wicked. The best remedy for
us against an evil man is a long space between us both.
Repentance is a practical thing. It is not enough to bemoan
the desecration of the temple of the heart, we must scourge
out the buyers and sellers, and overturn the tables of the
money-changers. A pardoned sinner will hate the sins that
cost the Saviour his blood. Grace and sin are quarrelsome
neighbours, and one or the other must go to the wall.

Does weeping speak? In what language does it utter its
meaning? Why, in that universal tongue which is known
and understood in all the earth, and even in heaven above.
Weeping is the eloquence of sorrow. It is an unstammering
orator, needing no interpreter, but understood of all. Is it
not sweet to believe that our tears are understood even when
words fail! Let us learn to think of tears as liquid prayers,
and of weeping as a constant dropping of importunate
intercession which will wear its way surely right into the
very heart of mercy, despite the stony difficulties which
obstruct the way. My God, I will 'weep' when I cannot plead,
for you hear the voice of my weeping.

The Holy Spirit had wrought into the psalmist's mind
the confidence that his prayer was heard. This is frequently
the privilege of the saints. Praying the prayer of faith, they
are often infallibly assured that they have prevailed with
God. We read of Luther that, having on one occasion

wrestled hard with God in prayer, he came leaping out of his closet crying, '*Vicimus, vicimus*'; that is, 'We have conquered, we have prevailed with God.' Assured confidence is no idle dream, for when the Holy Ghost bestows it upon us, we know its reality, and could not doubt it, even though all men deride our boldness.

David knows that the doom of his enemies shall come upon them suddenly. Death's day is doom's day, and both are sure and may be sudden. The Romans were known to say, 'The feet of the avenging Deity are shod with wool.' With noiseless footsteps vengeance nears its victim, and its destroying stroke shall be sudden and overwhelming.

Thus the psalm, like those that precede it, shows the different states of the godly and the wicked. O Lord, let us be numbered with your people, both now and for ever!

Meditation: *David's tears were music to God's ears. It is a sight fit for angels to behold, tears dropping from a penitent eye as pearls* (Thomas Watson).

Psalm 7:1-7

Suggested further reading: 2 Corinthians 1:8-14

David appears before God to plead with him against the Accuser, who had charged him with treason and treachery. The case is opened here with an avowal of confidence in God. Whatever may be the emergency of our condition we shall never find it amiss to retain our reliance upon our God.

Among David's foes there was one mightier than the rest, who had dignity, strength and ferocity, and was, therefore, 'like a lion'. From this foe he urgently seeks deliverance. Perhaps this was Saul, his royal enemy; but in our own case there is one who goes about like a lion, seeking whom he may devour, concerning whom we should ever cry, 'Deliver us from the evil one.' We must be ready for this trial, for it will surely come upon us. If God was slandered in Eden, we shall surely be maligned in this land of sinners.

The second part of this wandering hymn contains a prot-estation of innocence, and an invocation of wrath upon his own head, if he were not clear from the evil imputed to him. So far from hiding treasonable intentions in his hands, or ungratefully requiting the peaceful deeds of a friend, he had even allowed his enemy to escape when he had him completely in his power. From these verses we may learn that no innocence can shield a man from the slanders of the wicked. David had been scrupulously careful to avoid any appearance of rebellion against Saul, whom he con-stantly styled 'the Lord's anointed'; but all this could not protect him from lying tongues. As the shadow follows the substance, so envy pursues goodness. It is only at the tree heavy with fruit that men throw stones. If we would live without being slandered we must wait till we get to heaven. Let us be very heedful not to believe the flying rumours that are always harassing gracious men. If there are no believers in lies there will be but a dull market in falsehood, and good men's characters will be safe. Ill will never spoke well. Sinners have an ill will to saints, and therefore, be sure they will not speak well of them.

David's sorrow makes him view the Lord as a judge who had left the judgement-seat and retired into his rest. Faith would move the Lord to avenge the quarrel of his saints. He never slumbers, yet he often seems to do so; for the wicked prevail, and the saints are trodden in the dust. God's silence is the patience of long-suffering, and if wearisome to the saints, they should bear it cheerfully in the hope that sinners may be led by that means to repentance.

Meditation: *The applause of the wicked usually denotes some evil, and their censure imports some good* (Thomas Watson).

Psalm 7:8-17

Suggested further reading: John 3:31-36

David has now seen in the eye of his mind the Lord ascending to his judgement-seat, and beholding him seated there in royal state, he draws near to him to urge his suit anew. Our petitioner rises at once, and cries with earnestness and humility, 'Judge me, O Lord, according to my righteousness, and according to my integrity within me.' His hand is on an honest heart, and his cry is to a righteous judge. He sees a smile of complacency upon the face of the King, and in the name of all the assembled congregation he cries aloud, 'Oh, let the wickedness of the wicked come to an end; but establish the just.' Is not this the universal longing of the whole company of the elect?

The judge has heard the cause, has cleared the guiltless, and uttered his voice against the persecutors. Let us draw near, and learn the results of the great tribunal. There is the slandered one with his harp in hand, hymning the justice of his Lord, and rejoicing aloud in his own deliverance. Crooked sinners, with all their craftiness, are foiled by the upright in heart. God defends the right. Filth will not abide for long on the pure white garments of the saints, but shall be brushed off by divine providence, to the vexation of the men by whose base hands it was thrown upon the godly. When God shall try our cause, our sun has risen, and the sun of the wicked is set for ever. O believer, do not fear all that your foes can do or say against you, for the tree that God plants, no winds can hurt. He has not given you

up to be condemned by the lips of persecutors. Your enemies cannot sit on God's throne, nor blot your name out
of his book. Let them alone, then, for God will find time for
his revenge.

He not only detests sin, but is also angry with those who
continue to indulge in it. We do not have an insensible and
stolid God to deal with; he can be angry, no, he is angry
today and every day with you, ungodly and impenitent sinners. The best day that ever dawns on a sinner brings a
curse with it. Sinners may have many feast days, but no
safe days. From the beginning of the year even to its ending, there is not an hour in which God's oven is not hot,
and burning in readiness for the wicked, who shall be as
stubble.

We conclude with the joyful contrast. In this all these
psalms are agreed; they all exhibit the blessedness of the
righteous, and make its colours more glowing by contrast
with the miseries of the wicked. Praise is the occupation of
the godly, their eternal work, and their present pleasure.

Meditation: *To bless God for mercies is the way to increase
them; to bless him for miseries is the way to remove them*
(William Dyer).

Psalm 8:1-4

Suggested further reading: 1 Corinthians 1:26-31

Unable to express the glory of God, the psalmist utters a note of exclamation. 'O LORD, our Lord!' We need not wonder at this, for no heart can measure, no tongue can utter, the half of the greatness of Jehovah. The whole creation is full of his glory and radiant with the excellence of his power; his goodness and his wisdom are manifested on every hand. The countless myriad of terrestrial beings, from man the head, to the creeping worm at the foot, are all supported and nourished by the divine bounty. The solid fabric of the universe leans upon his eternal arm. He is universally present, and everywhere is his name excellent. His glory exceeds the glory of the starry heavens; above the region of the stars he has set fast his everlasting throne, and there he dwells in light ineffable. Returning to the text we are led to observe that this psalm is addressed to God, because none but the Lord himself can fully know his own glory. The believing heart is ravished with what it sees, but God alone knows the glory of God. No words can express the excellence of the divine name; and therefore it is left as a note of exclamation. The very name of Jehovah is excellent; what must his person be!

Not only in the heavens above is the Lord seen, but the earth beneath is also telling forth his majesty. In the sky, the massive orbs, rolling in their stupendous grandeur, are witnesses of his power in great things, while here below, the lisping utterances of babes are the manifestations of his strength in little ones. How often will children tell us of a God whom we have forgotten! How their simple prattle refutes those learned fools who deny the being of God! Many men have been made to hold their tongues, while young children have borne witness to the glory of the God of heaven.

When other arguments and motives produce little effect on certain minds, no considerations seem likely to have a more powerful tendency to counteract this deplorable propensity in human beings than those that are borrowed from objects connected with astronomy. They show us what an insignificant being — what a mere atom, indeed, man appears amidst the immensity of creation! Though he is an object of the paternal care and mercy of the Most High, yet he is but as a grain of sand to the whole earth, when compared to the countless myriads of beings that people the amplitudes of creation.

Meditation: *My readers must be careful to note the design of the psalmist, which is to enhance, by this comparison, the infinite goodness of God; for it is, indeed, a wonderful thing that the Creator of heaven, whose glory is so surpassingly great as to ravish us with the highest admiration, condescends so far as to graciously take upon him the care of the human race* (John Calvin).

Psalm 8:5-9

Suggested further reading: Hebrews 2:5-9

These verses may set out man's position among the creatures before he fell; but as they are, by the apostle Paul,
appropriated to man as represented by the Lord Jesus, it is
best to give most weight to that meaning. In order of dignity, man stood next to the angels, although a little lower;
this was accomplished in the Lord Jesus, for he was made a
little lower than the angels by the suffering of death. Man
in Eden had the full command of all creatures and they
came before him to receive their names as an act of homage to him as the vicegerent of God to them. Jesus in his
glory is now Lord, not only of all living, but also of all
created things. With the exception of he who put all things
under him, Jesus is Lord of all, and his elect, in him, are
raised to a dominion wider than that of the first Adam, as
shall be seen more clearly at his coming. Well might the
psalmist wonder at the singular exaltation of man in the
scale of being, when he marked his utter nothingness in
comparison with the starry universe.

'You have made him a little lower than the angels' — a
little lower in nature, since they are immortal, and just a
little, because time is short; and when that is over, saints
are no longer lower than the angels. The margin reads, 'a
little while inferior to'. 'You crown him.' The dominion that
God has bestowed on man is a great glory and honour to
him; for all dominion is honour, and the highest is that
which wears the crown. A full list is given of the subjugated

creatures, to show that all the dominion lost by sin is restored in Christ Jesus. Let none of us permit the possession of any earthly creature to be a snare to us, but let us remember that we are to reign over them, and not to allow them to reign over us. We must keep the world under our feet, and we must shun that base spirit which is content to let worldly cares and pleasures sway the empire of the immortal soul.

In the final verse, like a good composer, the poet returns to his keynote, falling back, as it were, into his first state of wondering adoration. What he started with as a proposition in the first verse, he closes with as a well-proven conclusion. Oh, for grace to walk worthy of that excellent name which has been named upon us, and which we are pledged to magnify!

Meditation: *Truly, this is how it is with the Christian: all the creatures are his servants, and so long as he keeps his heart at a holy distance from them, and maintains his lordship over them, not laying in his bosom those that God has put 'under his feet', all is well; he marches to the duties of God's worship in a goodly order. He can be private with God, and they will not be bold enough to crowd in to disturb him* (William Gurnall).

Psalm 9:1-6

Suggested further reading: Isaiah 11:1-5

The songster begins his hymn with a holy resolution. It sometimes needs all our determination to face the foe and bless the Lord in the teeth of his enemies; vowing that whoever else may be silent we will bless his name. Here, however, the overthrow of the foe is viewed as complete, and the song flows with sacred fulness of delight. Gladness and joy are the appropriate spirit in which to praise the goodness of the Lord. Birds extol the Creator in notes of overflowing joy, the cattle low his praise with tumultuous happiness, and the fish leap up in his worship with excess delight. Moloch may be worshipped with shrieks of pain, and Juggernaut may be honoured by dying groans and in-human yells, but he whose name is Love is best pleased with the holy mirth and sanctified gladness of his people. Daily rejoicing is an ornament to the Christian character, and a suitable robe for God's choristers to wear.

God's presence is evermore sufficient to work the defeat of our most furious foes, and their ruin is so complete when the Lord takes them in hand, that even flight cannot save them; they fall to rise no more when he pursues them. We must be careful, like David, to give all the glory to the one whose presence gives the victory. If we have here the ex-ulting of our conquering Captain, let us make the triumphs of the Redeemer the triumphs of the redeemed, and rejoice with him at the total discomfiture of all his foes.

While God lives my right shall never be taken from me. If we seek to maintain the cause and honour of our Lord we may suffer reproach and misrepresentation, but it is a rich comfort to remember that he who sits in the throne knows our hearts, and will not leave us to the ignorant and ungenerous judgement of erring man.

God rebukes before he destroys, but once he comes to blows with the wicked he does not cease until he has dashed them in pieces so small that their very name is forgotten. The psalmist exults over the fallen foe. He bends, as it were, over his prostrate form, and insults his once vaunted strength. He plucks the boaster's song out of his mouth, and sings it for him in derision. This is how our glorious Redeemer asks of death, 'Where is your sting?' and of the grave, 'Where is your victory?' The spoiler is spoiled, and he who made captive is led into captivity himself. Let the daughters of Jerusalem go out to meet their King, and praise him with timbrel and harp.

Meditation: *As a vessel reveals what liquor it holds by its scent, so should our mouths smell continually of that mercy which has refreshed our hearts: for we are called vessels of mercy* (William Cowper, 1612).

Psalm 9:7-14

Suggested further reading: Acts 17:22-31

In the light of the past the future is not doubtful. Since the same almighty God fills the throne of power, we can, with unhesitating confidence, exult in our security for all time to come. The enduring existence and unchanging dominion of our Jehovah are the firm foundations of our joy. The enemy and his destructive ways shall come to a perpetual end, but God and his throne shall 'endure for ever'. The eternity of divine sovereignty yields unfailing consolation.

Whatever earthly courts may do, heaven's throne ministers judgement in uprightness. Partiality and respect of persons are things unknown in the dealings of the Holy One of Israel. How the prospect of appearing before the impartial tribunal of the Great King should act as a check to us when tempted to sin, and as a comfort when we are slandered or oppressed! He who gives no quarter to the wicked in the day of judgement is the defence and refuge of his saints in the day of trouble. There are many forms of oppression; it comes to us both from man and from Satan; and for all its forms, a refuge is provided in the Lord Jehovah. Ignorance is worst when it amounts to ignorance of God, and knowledge is best when it exercises itself upon the name of God. This most excellent knowledge leads to the most excellent grace of faith. Oh, to learn more of the attributes and character of God! Unbelief, that hooting nightbird, cannot live in the light of divine knowledge; it flies before the sun of God's great and gracious name.

Memories of the past and confidences concerning the future conducted the man of God to the mercy seat to plead for the needs of the present. He divided all his time between praising and praying. How could he have spent it more profitably? His first prayer is one suitable for all persons and occasions; it breathes a humble spirit, indicates self-knowledge, appeals to the proper attributes, and to the fitting person. In sickness, in sin, in despair, in temptation, we have been brought very low, and the gloomy portal has seemed as if it would open to imprison us; but underneath us were the everlasting arms, and, therefore, we have been uplifted even to the gates of heaven. We must not overlook David's object in desiring mercy; it is God's glory. Saints are not so selfish as to look only to self; they desire mercy's diamond that they may let others see it flash and sparkle, and may admire he who gives such priceless gems to his beloved. When David speaks of his declaring all God's praise, he means that, in his deliverance, grace in all its heights and depths would be magnified.

Meditation: *To show forth all God's praise is to enter largely into the work. An occasional 'God, I thank you' is no fit return for a perpetual stream of rich benefit* (William S. Plumer).

Psalm 9:15-20

Suggested further reading: Deuteronomy 8:11-20

In considering this terrible picture of the Lord's overwhelming judgements of his enemies, we are called upon to ponder and meditate upon it with deep seriousness by the two words, meditate and pause (selah). Consider, and tune your instrument. Contemplate and solemnly adjust your hearts to the solemnity that is so well becoming the subject. Let us approach these verses in a humble spirit, and notice that the character of God requires the punishment of sin. 'The Lord is known by the judgement he executes', his holiness and abhorrence of sin are thus displayed. A ruler who winked at evil would soon be known by all his subjects to be evil himself, and, on the other hand, he who is severely just in judgement in the same way reveals his own nature. So long as our God is God, he will not, he cannot, spare the guilty, except through that one glorious way in which he is just, and yet the justifier of the one who believes in Jesus.

The justice which has punished the wicked, and preserved the righteous, remains the same, and therefore, in days to come, retribution will surely be meted out. How solemn is the seventeenth verse, especially in its warning to those who forget God. The moral who are not devout, the honest who are not prayerful, the benevolent who are not believing, the amiable who are not converted, these must all have their portion with the openly wicked in the hell which is prepared for the devil and his angels. There are whole nations of such people; those who forget God are far more numerous than the profane or profligate, and according to the very forceful expression of the Hebrew, the nethermost hell will be the place into which all of them shall be hurled headlong. Forgetfulness seems a small sin, but it brings eternal wrath upon the man who lives and dies in it.

Prayers are the believer's weapons of war. When the battle is too hard for us, we call in our great ally, who, as it were, lies in ambush until faith gives the signal by crying out, 'Arise, O Lord.' Although our cause may be all but lost, it shall soon be won again if the Almighty does but stir himself. He will not suffer man to prevail over God, but with swift judgements will confound their glorying. In the very sight of God the wicked will be punished, and he who is now all tenderness will have no heart of compassion for them, since they had no tears of repentance while their day of grace endured.

Meditation: Before leaving this psalm, it will be very profitable if the student will peruse it again as the triumphal hymn of the Redeemer, as he devoutly brings the glory of his victories and lays it down at his Father's feet. Let us joy in his joy, and our joy shall be full (C. H. Spurgeon).

Psalm 10:1-11

Suggested further reading: 2 Peter 2:12-22

To the tearful eye of the sufferer the Lord seemed to 'stand' still, as if he calmly looked on, and did not sympathize with his afflicted one. No, even more, the Lord appeared to be 'afar off', no longer 'a very present help in trouble', but an inaccessible mountain, into which no man would be able to climb. The presence of God is the joy of his people, but any suspicion of his absence is distracting beyond measure. Let us, then, ever remember that the Lord is near us. The refiner is never far from the mouth of the furnace when his gold is in the fire, and the Son of God is always walking in the midst of the flames when his holy children are cast into them. Yet he that knows the frailty of man will little wonder that when we are sharply exercised, we find it hard to bear the apparent neglect of the Lord when he forbears to work our deliverance. It is not the trouble, but the hiding of our Father's face which cuts us to the quick. When our sun is eclipsed, it is dark indeed. If we need an answer to the question, 'Why do you hide yourself?' it is to be found in the fact that there is a 'needs-be', not only for trial, but also for heaviness of heart under trial. But how could this be the case, if the Lord should shine upon us while he is afflicting us? A smiling face and a rod are not fit companions. God bares the back that the blow may be felt; for it is only felt affliction which can become blest affliction. If we are carried in the arms of God over every stream, where would be the trial, and where the experience, which trouble is meant to teach us?

The fact that the man is proud and arrogant may go a long way to prove that he is vindictive and cruel. Haman's pride was the father of a cruel design to murder all the Jews. Nebuchadnezzar builds an idol; in pride he commands all men to bow before it; and then cruelly stands ready to heat the furnace seven times hotter for those who will not yield to his imperious will. Every proud thought is twin brother to a cruel thought. He who exalts himself will despise others, and one step further will make him a tyrant.

This cruel man comforts himself with the idea that God is blind, or, at least, forgetful: a fond and foolish fancy, indeed. Men doubt Omniscience when they persecute the saints. If we had a sense of God's presence with us, it would be impossible for us to ill-treat his children. In fact, there can scarcely be a greater preservation from sin than the constant thought of 'You, God, see me.'

Meditation: *There is not, in my judgement, a psalm which describes the mind, the manners, the works, the words, the feelings, and the fate of the ungodly with so much propriety, fulness, and light, as this psalm* (Martin Luther).

Psalm 10:12-18

Suggested further reading: 2 Peter 3:1-9

Thus has the trial proceeded. The case has been fully stated; and now it is but little wonder that the oppressed petitioner lifts up the cry for judgement, which we find in verse 12. With what bold language will faith address its God! Yet what unbelief is mingled with our strongest confidence. Fearlessly the Lord is stirred up to arise and lift up his hand, yet timidly he is begged not to forget the humble, as if Jehovah could ever be forgetful of his saints. This verse is the incessant cry of the church, and she will never refrain from it until her Lord shall come in his glory to avenge her of all her adversaries.

In these verses the description of the wicked is condensed, and the evil of his character traced to its source, namely, atheistic ideas with regard to the government of the world. We may at once perceive that this is intended to be another urgent plea with the Lord to show his power, and reveal his justice. When the wicked call God's righteousness into question, we may well beg him to teach them terrible things in righteousness. In verse 13, the hope of the infidel and his heart-wishes are laid bare. He despises the Lord, because he will not believe that sin will meet with punishment. If there was no hell for other men, there ought to be one for those who question the justice of it. This vile suggestion receives its answer in verse 14. God is all eye to see, and all hand to punish his enemies. From divine oversight there is no hiding, and from divine justice there is no fleeing. In the fifteenth verse we hear again the burden of the psalmist's prayer. Let the sinner lose his power to sin; stop the tyrant, arrest the oppressor, weaken the loins of the mighty, and dash in pieces the terrible. They deny your justice: let them feel it to the full. Indeed, they shall feel it; for God shall hunt the sinner for ever: so long as there is a grain of sin in him it shall be sought out and punished.

The psalm ends with a song of thanksgiving to the great and everlasting King, because he has granted the desire of his humble and oppressed people, has defended the fatherless, and punished the heathen who trampled upon his poor and afflicted children. Let us learn that we are sure to speed well, if we carry our complaint to the King of kings. Rights will be vindicated, and wrongs redressed, at his throne. His government does not neglect the interests of the needy, nor does it tolerate oppression in the mighty. Great God, we leave ourselves in your hand; to you we commit your church afresh. Arise, O God, and let the man of the earth — the creature of a day — be broken before the majesty of your power. Come, Lord Jesus, and glorify your people. Amen and Amen.

Meditation: *He that sits nearest the dust, sits nearest heaven* (Andrew Gray).

Psalm 11:1-3

Suggested further reading: Nehemiah 6:10-14

These verses contain an account of a temptation to distrust
God, with which David was, upon some unmentioned occasion, greatly exercised. It may be, that in the days when
he was in Saul's court, he was advised to flee at a time
when this flight would have been charged against him as a
breach of duty to the king, or a proof of personal cowardice. His case was like that of Nehemiah, when his enemies,
under the garb of friendship, hoped to entrap him by ad-
vising him to escape for his life. Had he done so, they could
then have found a ground for accusation. Nehemiah bravely
replied, 'Shall such a man as I flee?' and David, in a like
spirit, refuses to retreat, exclaiming, 'In the Lord I put my
trust: how can you say to my soul, "Flee as a bird to your
mountain"?' When Satan cannot overthrow us by presumption, how craftily will he seek to ruin us by distrust! He
will employ our dearest friends to argue us out of our confidence, and he will use such plausible logic, that unless
we once and for all assert our immovable trust in Jehovah,
he will make us like the timid bird which flies to the mountain whenever danger presents itself. How forcibly the case
is put! The bow is bent, the arrow is fitted to the string:
'Flee, flee, you defenceless bird, your safety lies in flight;
be gone, for your enemies will send their shafts into your
heart; haste, haste, for soon you will be destroyed!' David
seems to have felt the force of the advice, for it came home
to his soul; but yet he would not yield, but would rather

dare the danger than exhibit distrust in the Lord his God.
Doubtless, the perils that encompassed David were great
and imminent; it was quite true that his enemies were ready
to 'shoot secretly' at him. It was equally correct that the
very 'foundations' of law and justice were 'destroyed' under
Saul's unrighteous government: but what were all these
things to the man whose trust was in God alone? He could
brave the dangers, escape the enemies, and defy the injustice that surrounded him. His answer to the question, 'What
can the righteous do?' would be the counter-question, 'What
cannot they do?' When prayer engages God on our side,
and when faith secures the fulfilment of the promise, what
cause can there be for flight, however cruel and mighty our
enemies? With a sling and a stone, David had smitten a
giant before whom the whole hosts of Israel were trembling, and the Lord, who delivered him from the uncircumcised Philistine, could surely deliver him from King
Saul and his ruffians. There is no such word as 'impossibility' in the language of faith; that martial grace knows
how to fight and conquer, but she knows not how to flee.

Meditation: *Sinning times have ever been the saints' praying times* (William Gurnall).

Psalm 11:4-7

Suggested further reading: Isaiah 66:1-4

David here declares the great source of his unflinching courage. He borrows his light from heaven — from the great central orb of deity. The God of the believer is never far from him; he is not merely the God of the mountain fastnesses, but of the dangerous valleys and battle plains. Why, then, should we fear? What plots can men devise which Jesus will not discover? Satan has doubtless desired to have us, that he may sift us as wheat, but Jesus is in the temple praying for us, so how can our faith fail? What attempts can the wicked make that Jehovah shall not behold? And since he is in his holy temple, delighting in the sacrifice of his Son, will he not defeat every device, and send us a sure deliverance?

Nothing can be done in heaven, or earth, or hell, which he does not ordain and overrule. He is the world's great Emperor. God sees each man as much and as perfectly as if there were no other creature in the universe. He sees us always; he never removes his eye from us; he sees us entirely, reading the recesses of the soul as readily as the glancing of the eye. Is this not a sufficient ground of confidence, and an abundant answer to the solicitations of despondency? My danger is not hid from him; he knows my limits, and I may rest assured that he will not allow me to perish while I rely on him alone.

The delightful contrast of the last verse is well worth our observation, and it affords another overwhelming reason why we should be steadfast, immovable, not carried away with fear, or led to adopt worldly means to avoid trials. It is not only his office to defend righteousness, but his nature to love it. He would deny himself if he did not defend the just. It is essential to the very being of God that he should be just; fear not, then, the end of all your trials, but 'Be just, and fear not.' God approves, and, if men oppose, what does it matter? We need never be out of countenance, for God countenances us. He observes, he approves, he delights in the upright. He sees his own image in them, an image of his own fashioning, and therefore he looks on them with satisfaction. Shall we dare to put out our hand into iniquity in order to escape affliction? Let us have done with byways and short turnings, and let us keep to that fair path of right, along which Jehovah's smile shall light us. There is no room or reason for retreat. Advance! Let the vanguard push on! To the front! all powers and passions of our soul. On! on! In God's name, on! For 'The Lord of hosts is with us; the God of Jacob is our refuge.'

Meditation: *Take God into your counsel. Heaven overlooks hell. God at any time can tell you what plots are hatching there against you* (William Gurnall).

Psalm 12:1-5

Suggested further reading: 1 Kings 19:9-18

'Help, Lord.' A short, but sweet, suggestive, seasonable and serviceable prayer; a kind of angel's sword, to be turned every way, and to be used on all occasions. The psalmist sees the extreme danger of his position, for a man would be safer among lions than among liars. He feels his own inability to deal with such sons of the devil, and therefore turns to his all-sufficient Helper, the Lord, whose help is never denied to his servants, and whose aid is enough for all their needs. 'Help, Lord,' is a very useful exclamatory plea that we may dart up to heaven on occasions of emergency, whether in labour, learning, suffering, fighting, living or dying.

The death, departure, or decline of godly men should be a trumpet-call for more prayer. We must not, however, be rash in our judgement on this point, for Elijah erred in counting himself the only servant of God alive, when there were thousands whom the Lord held in reserve. The present times always appear to be peculiarly dangerous, because they are nearest to our anxious gaze, and whatever evils are rife are sure to be observed, while the faults of past ages are further off, and are more easily overlooked. Yet we expect that in the latter days, 'because iniquity shall abound, the love of many shall wax cold', and then we must even more thoroughly turn from man, and address ourselves to the churches' Lord, by whose help the gates of hell shall be kept from prevailing against us.

In due season the Lord will hear his elect, who cry to him day and night, and though he tolerates their oppressors for a long time, yet he will suddenly avenge them. Observe that the mere oppression of saints, however silently they bear it, is in itself a cry to God. Nothing moves a father like the cries of his children; he stirs himself up, wakes up his manhood, overthrows the enemy, and sets his beloved in safety. The needy dared not speak, and could only sigh in secret; but the Lord heard, and could rest no longer, but girded on his sword for the battle. It is a fair day when our soul brings God into her quarrel, for when his bare arm is seen, Philistia shall rue the day. The darkest hours of the church's night are those which precede the break of day. Man's extremity is God's opportunity. Jesus will come to deliver just when his needy ones will sigh, as if all hope had gone for ever. He who promises to set us in safety means by that, preservation on earth, and eternal salvation in heaven.

Meditation: *When men cease to be faithful to their God, he who expects to find them so to each other will be much disappointed* (George Horne).

Psalm 12:6-8

Suggested further reading: Psalm 119:105-112

What a contrast between the vain words of man, and the pure words of Jehovah! Man's words are yes and no, but the Lord's promises are yea and amen. For truth, certainty, holiness, faithfulness, the words of the Lord are pure as well-refined silver. In the original there is an allusion to the severest purifying process known to the ancients, through which silver was passed when the greatest possible purity was desired. The dross was all consumed, and only the bright and precious metal remained; so clear and free from all alloy of error or unfaithfulness is the book of the words of the Lord. The Bible has passed through the furnace of persecution, literary criticism, philosophic doubt and scientific discovery, and has lost nothing but those human interpretations that clung to it as alloy to precious ore. The experience of saints has tried it in every conceivable manner, but not a single doctrine or promise has been consumed in the most excessive heat. What God's words are, the words of his children should be. If we would be Godlike in conversation, we must watch our language, and maintain the strictest purity of integrity and holiness in all our communications.

To fall into the hands of an evil generation, so as to be baited by their cruelty, or polluted by their influence, is an evil to be dreaded beyond measure; but it is an evil foreseen and provided for in the text. It should be our daily prayer that we may rise above our age as the mountaintops above the clouds, and may stand out as a heaven-pointing pinnacle high above the mists of ignorance and sin which roll around us. O Eternal Spirit, fulfil in us the faithful saying of this verse!

When those in power are vile, their underlings will be no better. As a warm sun brings out noxious flies, so a sinner in honour fosters vice everywhere. Our turf would not so swarm with abominables if those who are styled honourables did not sanction the craft. Would to God that the glory and triumph of our Lord Jesus would encourage us to walk and work on every side; as like acts upon like, since an exalted sinner encourages sinners, our exalted Redeemer must surely excite, cheer and stimulate his saints. Nerved by a sight of his reigning power we shall meet the evils of the times in the spirit of holy resolution, and shall more hopefully pray, 'Help, Lord.'

Meditation: *It is true, indeed, despisers will esteem both God and his word as trifling; but oh, what an unknown treasure does the word, the promises, the covenant relation of the divine things of Jesus contain!* (Robert Hawker).

Psalm 13:1-2

Suggested further reading: Job 13:20-27

'How long?' This question is repeated no less than four times. It indicates very intense desire for deliverance, and great anguish of heart. And what if there is some impatience mingled within it? Is not this a more accurate portrait of our own experience? It is not easy to prevent desire from degenerating into impatience. Oh, for grace that, while we wait on God, we may be kept from indulging a murmuring spirit!

'How long, O Lord? Will you forget me for ever?' Ah, David! How like a fool you talk! Can God forget? Can Omniscience fail in memory? Above all, can Jehovah's heart forget his own beloved child? Ah! brethren, let us drive away the thought. 'For ever?' Oh, dark thought! It was surely bad enough to suspect a temporary forgetfulness, but shall we ask the ungracious question, and imagine that the Lord will cast away his people for ever? No, his anger may endure for a night, but his love shall abide eternally. 'How long will you hide your face from me?' This is a far more rational question, for God may hide his face, and yet he may still remember. A hidden face is no sign of a forgetful heart. It is in love that his face is turned away; yet to a real child of God, this hiding of his Father's face is terrible, and he will never be at ease until once more he has his Father's smile. 'How long shall I take counsel in my soul?' There is in the original the idea of 'laying up' counsels in his heart, as if his devices had become innumerable but unavailing.

In thinking like this, we have often been like David, for we have considered and reconsidered day after day, but have not discovered the happy means by which to escape from our trouble. 'How long shall my enemy be exalted over me?' The laughter of a foe grates horribly upon the ears of grief. For the devil to make fun of our misery is the last ounce of our complaint, and quite breaks down our patience; therefore let us make it a chief argument in our plea with mercy.

The careful reader will remark that the question 'How long?' is put in four shapes. The writer's grief is viewed, as it seems to be, as it is, as it affects himself within, and his foes without. We are all prone to play most on the worst string. We set up monumental stones over the graves of our joys. But who thinks of erecting monuments of praise for mercies received? We write four books of lamentations and only one of canticles, and are far more at home in wailing out a *Miserere* than in chanting a *Te Deum.*

Meditation: *Though it is proper to know our own hearts, for the purposes of conviction, yet, if we expect consolation from this quarter, we shall find ourselves sadly disappointed. Such, for a time, appears to have been the case of David. He seems to have been in great distress; and as is common in such cases, his thoughts turned inward. While thus exercised, he had sorrow in his heart daily: but, turning to God for relief, he succeeded, trusting in his mercy, his heart rejoiced in his salvation. There are many persons, who, when in trouble, imitate David in the former part of this experience: I wish we may imitate him in the latter* (Andrew Fuller).

Psalm 13:3-6

Suggested further reading: Hebrews 4:14-16

The mercy seat is the life of hope and the death of despair. The gloomy thought of God's having forsaken him is still upon the psalmist's soul, and he therefore cries, 'Consider and hear me.' He remembers at once the root of his woe, and cries aloud that it may be removed. Note the cry of faith, 'O Lord my God!' Is it not a very glorious fact that our interest in our God is not destroyed by all our trials and sorrows? Let the eye of my faith be clear, that I may see my God in the dark; let my eye of watchfulness be wide open, lest I become entrapped, and let the eye of my understanding be illuminated to see the right way. David feared that his trials would end his life, and he rightly uses his fear as an argument with God in prayer; for deep distress has within it a kind of claim upon compassion; not a claim of right, but a plea which has power with grace.

Another plea is urged in the fourth verse, and it is one that the tried believer may handle well when on his knees. It is not the Lord's will that the great enemy of our souls should overcome his children. This would dishonour God, and cause the evil one to boast. It is well for us that our salvation and God's honour are so intimately connected that they stand or fall together. Our covenant God will complete the confusion of all our enemies, and if for a while we become a laughing stock, the day is coming when the shame will change sides, and the contempt shall be poured on those to whom it is due.

What a change is found in the fifth verse! The rain is over and gone, and the time of the singing of birds has come. The mercy seat has so refreshed the poor weeper that he clears his throat for a song. Here is his confidence: 'I have trusted in your mercy.' For many a year it had been his rule to make the Lord his castle and tower of defence, and he smiles from behind the same bulwark still. Had he doubted the reality of his trust in God, he would have blocked up one of the windows through which the sun of heaven delights to shine.

The psalm closes with a sentence that is a refutation of the charge of forgetfulness that David had uttered in the first verse. So shall it be with us if we wait a while. The complaint that we utter in our haste shall be joyfully retracted, and we shall witness that the Lord has dealt bountifully with us.

Meditation: *None live so easily, so pleasantly, as those that live by faith* (Matthew Henry).

Psalm 14:1-3

Suggested further reading: 2 Chronicles 33:1-9

As no distinguishing title is given to this psalm, we would suggest as assistance to the memory, the heading, 'Concerning practical atheism'. The atheist is *the* fool pre-eminently, and *a* fool universally. He would not deny God if he were not a fool by nature, and having denied God it is no wonder that he becomes a fool in practice. Sin is always folly, and as it is the height of sin to attack the very existence of the Most High, so is it also the greatest imaginable folly. To say there is no God is to belie the plainest evidence, which is obstinacy; to oppose the common consent of mankind, which is stupidity; to stifle consciousness, which is madness.

Is this where man first becomes an unbeliever — in his heart, not in his head? And when he talks atheistically, is it a foolish heart speaking and endeavouring to clamour down the voice of conscience? We think so. If the affections were set upon truth and righteousness, the understanding would have no difficulty in settling the question of a present personal Deity. But as the heart dislikes the good and the right, it is no wonder that it desires to be rid of that Elohim, who is the great moral Governor, the Patron of rectitude and the Punisher of iniquity. It is a solemn reflection that some who worship God with their lips may in their hearts be saying, 'No God.' It is worthy of observation that he does not say there is no Jehovah, but there is no Elohim; deity in the abstract is not so much the object of attack as the covenant, personal, ruling and governing presence of God in the world. God as ruler, lawgiver, worker, Saviour, is the target at which the arrows of human wrath are shot. How impotent the malice! How horrible the insanity which leads a man who owes his all to God to cry out, 'No God'! How terrible the depravity which makes the whole race adopt this as their hearts' desire, 'No God'!

Without exception, all men have apostatized from the Lord their Maker, from his laws, and from the eternal principles of right. Like stubborn heifers they have sturdily refused to receive the yoke, like errant sheep they have found a gap and left the right field. The final phrase of verse 3 is an utter denial concerning any mere man that he of himself does good. What can be more sweeping? This is the verdict of the all-seeing Jehovah, who cannot exaggerate or mistake. What do the opponents to the doctrine of natural depravity say to this? Rather, what do we feel about it? Do we not confess that we by nature are corrupt, and do we not bless the sovereign grace which has renewed us in the spirit of our minds, that sin may no more have dominion over us, but that grace may rule and reign?

Meditation: *Who in the world is a greater fool, a more ignorant, wretched person, than he that is an atheist?* (Jeremy Taylor).

Psalm 14:4-7

Suggested further reading: Psalm 126

Hatred of God and corruptness of life are the motive forces that produce persecution. Men who, having no saving knowledge of divine things, enslave themselves to become workers of iniquity have no heart to cry to the Lord for deliverance, but seek to amuse themselves with devouring the poor and despised people of God. It is hard bondage to be a 'worker of iniquity'. As pikes in a pond eat up little fish, as eagles prey on smaller birds, as wolves rend the sheep of the pasture, so sinners naturally and as a matter of course persecute, malign and mock the followers of the Lord Jesus. While thus preying, they renounce all praying, and in this behave consistently, for how could they hope to be heard while their hands are full of blood?

Oppressors do not have it all their own way, they have their fits of trembling and their appointed seasons of over-throw. The most hardened of men have periods when their conscience casts them into a cold sweat of alarm. As cow-ards are cruel, so all cruel men are at heart cowards. The ghost of past sin is a terrible spectre to haunt any man, and though unbelievers may boast as loudly as they will, there is a sound in their ears which makes them ill at ease. God's presence with his people makes the company of godly men so irksome to the wicked because they perceive that God is with them. Shut their eyes as they may, they cannot but perceive the image of God in the character of his truly gra-cious people, nor can they fail to see that he works for their deliverance.

Notwithstanding their real cowardice, the wicked put on the lion's skin and lord it over the Lord's poor ones. Though fools themselves, they mock at the truly wise as if the folly were on their side. What can your God do for you now? Who is that God who can deliver out of our hand? Where is the reward for all your praying and beseeching? They thrust taunting questions of this sort into the faces of weak but gracious souls, and tempt them to feel ashamed of their refuge. Let us not be laughed out of our confidence by them, let us scorn their scorning and defy their jeers. We shall need to wait but a little, and then the Lord our refuge will avenge his own elect and ease himself of his adversaries, who once made so light of him and of his people.

The closing prayer is natural enough, for what would so effectually convince atheists, overthrow persecutors, stay sin, and secure the godly, as the manifest appearance of Israel's great salvation? Oh, that he had come! What happy, holy, halcyon, heavenly days should we then see! But let us not count him slack, for behold, he comes, he comes quickly! Blessed are all those who wait for him.

Meditation: *The wicked have cause enough to fear those in whom God delights* (Joseph Caryl).

Psalm 15

Suggested further reading: Isaiah 42:1-4

The first verse asks the question; the rest of the verses answer it. O high and holy one, who shall be permitted to have fellowship with you? The heavens are not pure in your sight, and you charge your angels with folly. Who, then, of mortal mould shall dwell with you, O dread consuming fire? A sense of the glory of the Lord and of the holiness that becomes his house, his service and his attendants, excites the humble mind to ask the solemn question before us. Where angels bow with veiled faces, how shall man be able to worship at all? The unthinking many imagine it to be a very easy matter to approach the Most High, and when professedly engaged in his worship they do not question in their heart whether or not they are fit for it. But truly humbled souls often shrink under a sense of utter unworthiness, and would not dare to approach the throne of the God of holiness if it were not for him, our Lord, our Advocate, who can abide in the heavenly temple, because his righteousness endures for ever. The question is raised, because it is a question. The questions in the text are asked of the Lord, as if none but the Infinite Mind could answer them sufficiently to satisfy the unquiet conscience. We must know from the Lord of the tabernacle what are the qualifications for his service, and when we have been taught by him, we shall clearly see that only our spotless Lord Jesus, and those who are conformed to his image, can ever stand with acceptance before the Majesty on high.

In answer to the question the Lord informs us by his Holy Spirit of the character of the man who alone can dwell in his holy hill. In perfection this holiness is found only in the Man of Sorrows, but in a measure it is wrought in all his people by the Holy Ghost. Faith and the graces of the Spirit are not mentioned, because this is a description of outward character, and where fruits are found the root may not be seen, although it is surely there. Those that rejoice that another, even the Lord Jesus, does everything for them, and they therefore hate legality, are the best doers in the world upon gospel principles.

Like the Lord Jesus, whose dominion is everlasting, the true Christian shall never lose his crown. He shall not only be on Zion, but like Zion, fixed and firm. He shall dwell in the tabernacle of the Most High, and neither death nor judgement shall remove him from his place of privilege and blessedness.

Meditation: *Let us take ourselves to prayer and self-examination, for this psalm is as fire for the gold, and as a furnace for silver. Can we endure its testing power?* (C. H. Spurgeon).

Psalm 16:1-5

Suggested further reading: John 17:1-11

We are not left to human interpreters for the key to this golden mystery, for, speaking by the Holy Spirit, Peter tells us, 'David speaks concerning HIM' (Acts 2:25). It has been the usual plan of commentators to apply the psalm both to David, to the saints, and to the Lord Jesus, but we will venture to believe that in it 'Christ is all', since in the ninth and tenth verses, like the apostles on the mount, we can see 'no man but Jesus only'.

Tempted in all points as we are, the manhood of Jesus needed to be preserved from the power of evil. Though in itself pure, the Lord Jesus did not confide in that purity of nature, but as an example to his followers, looked to the Lord, his God, for preservation. In his inmost heart the Lord Jesus bowed himself to do service to his heavenly Father, and before the throne of Jehovah his soul vowed allegiance to the Lord for our sakes. We are like him when our soul, truly and constantly in the presence of the heart-searching God, declares her full consent to the rule and government of the infinite Jehovah, saying, 'You are my Lord.' What wonders the eyes of Divine Love can see where the hands of Infinite Power have been graciously at work. It was this quicksighted affection which led Jesus to see in us a recompense for all his agony, and sustained him under all his sufferings by the joy of redeeming us from going down into the pit.

With what confidence and bounding joy does Jesus turn to Jehovah, whom his soul possessed and delighted in! Content beyond measure with his portion in the Lord his God, he had not a single desire with which to hunt after other gods. His cup was full, and his heart was full too; even in his sorest sorrows he still laid hold upon his Father with both hands, crying, 'My God, my God'. He had not so much as a thought of falling down to worship the prince of this world, although tempted with an 'all these will I give you'. We, too, can make our boast in the Lord; he is the meat and the drink of our souls. He is our portion, supplying all our necessities, and our cup yielding royal luxuries; our cup in this life, and our inheritance in the life to come. As children of the Father who is in heaven, we inherit, by virtue of our joint heirship with Jesus, all the riches of the covenant of grace; and the portion which falls to us sets upon our table the bread of heaven and the new wine of the kingdom. Who would not be satisfied with such dainty diet? Our shallow cup of sorrow we may well drain with resignation, since the deep cup of love stands side by side with it, and will never be empty.

Meditation: *Here, in effect, is shown that whosoever puts his trust in God shall be preserved* (Richard Greenham).

Psalm 16:6-11

Suggested further reading: Acts 2:25-32

Jesus found the way of obedience to lead into 'pleasant places'. Notwithstanding all the sorrows which marred his countenance, he exclaimed, 'Behold, I come; in the scroll of the book it is written of me, I delight to do your will, O my God, and your law is within my heart.' It may seem strange, but while no other man was ever so thoroughly acquainted with grief, it is our belief that no other man ever experienced so much joy and delight in service, for no other served so faithfully and with such great results in view as his recompense of reward. The joy which was set before him must have sent some of its beams of splendour down into the rugged places where he endured the cross, despising the shame, and must have made them in some respects pleasant places to the generous heart of the Redeemer.

The fear of death at one time cast its dark shadow over the soul of the Redeemer, and we read that 'he was heard in that he feared'. An angel appeared to him, strengthening him; perhaps the heavenly messenger reassured him of his glorious resurrection as his people's surety, and of the eternal joy into which he would admit the flock redeemed by blood. Then hope shone full upon our Lord's soul, and, as recorded in verses 8-11, he surveyed the future with holy confidence because he had his eye continually on Jehovah, and enjoyed his perpetual presence. He felt that thus sustained, he could never be driven from his life's grand design.

What an infinite mercy was this for us! In this immove-ableness, caused by simple faith in divine help, Jesus is to be viewed as our exemplar; to recognize the presence of the Lord is the duty of every believer: 'I have set the Lord always before me'; and to trust the Lord as our champion and guard is the privilege of every saint: 'because he is at my right hand, I shall not be moved'.

This way was first shown to Jesus, for he is the first-begotten from the dead, the first-born of every creature. He himself opened up the way through his own flesh, and then trod it as the forerunner of his own redeemed. The thought of being made the path of life to his people gladdened the soul of Jesus. 'In your presence is fulness of joy.' Christ, being raised from the dead, ascended into glory, to dwell in constant nearness to God, where joy is at its full for ever: the foresight of this urged him onward in his glorious but grievous toil. To bring his chosen ones to eternal happi-ness was the high ambition which inspired him, and made him wade through a sea of blood. O God, when the worldling's mirth has all expired, for ever with Jesus may we dwell 'at your right hand', where 'there are pleasures for evermore'.

Meditation: The glorified soul shall be for ever bathing itself in the rivers of pleasure. This is that which makes heaven to be heaven, 'We shall be ever with the Lord' (Thomas Watson).

Psalm 17:1-6

Suggested further reading: 1 Samuel 24:1-7

The troubled heart craves for the ear of the great Judge, persuaded that with him to hear is to redress. If our God could not or would not hear us, our state would be deplorable indeed; and yet some professors set such small store by the mercy seat that God does not hear them for the simple reason that they neglect to plead. Who can resist a cry? A real hearty, bitter, piteous cry might almost melt a rock; there can be no fear of its prevalence with our heavenly Father. A cry is our earliest utterance, and in many ways the most natural of human sounds; if our prayer, like the infant's cry, should be more natural than intelligent, and more earnest than elegant, it will be none the less eloquent with God.

The psalmist had been libelled, basely and maliciously libelled; and having brought his action before the highest court, he, like an innocent man, has no desire to escape the enquiry, but even invites and sues for judgement. He does not ask for secrecy, but would have the result made known to the world. Believers do not desire any other judge than God, or to be excused from judgement, or even to be judged on principles of partiality. No; our hope does not lie in the prospect of favouritism from God, and the consequent suspension of his law; we expect to be judged on the same principles as other men, and through the blood and righteousness of our Redeemer we shall pass the ordeal unscathed. It is a most assuring thing to be able to appeal at

once to the Lord, and call upon our Judge to be a witness
for our defence.

Under trial it is not easy to conduct ourselves aright; a
candle is not easily kept alight when many envious mouths
are puffing at it. In evil times prayer is peculiarly needful,
and wise men resort to it at once. 'You have always heard
me, O my Lord, and therefore I have the utmost confidence
in again approaching your altar.' Experience is a blessed
teacher. He who has tried the faithfulness of God in hours
of need has great boldness in laying his case before the
throne. 'Stoop out of heaven and put your ear to my mouth;
give me your ear all to myself, as men do when they lean
over to catch every word from their friend.' The psalmist
here comes back to his first prayer, and thus sets us an
example of pressing our suit again and again, until we have
a full assurance that we have succeeded.

Meditation: *Prayer is the best remedy in a calamity* (William
Gouge).

Psalm 17:7-15

Suggested further reading: 1 Samuel 24:8-15

God is the God of salvation; it is his present and perpetual habit to save believers; he puts forth his best and most glorious strength, using his right hand of wisdom and might, to save all those, of whatsoever rank or class, who trust themselves with him. Happy faith thus to secure the omnipotent protection of heaven! Blessed God, to be so gracious to unworthy mortals, when they have but grace to rely upon you! The right hand of God is interposed between the saints and all harm; God is never at a loss for means; his own bare hand is enough. He works without tools, as well as with them.

No part of the body is more precious, more tender, and more carefully guarded than the eye; and of the eye, no portion more peculiarly to be protected than the central apple, the pupil. The all-wise Creator has placed the eye in a well-protected position; it stands surrounded by projecting bones like Jerusalem encircled by mountains. Moreover, its great Author has surrounded it with many tunics of inward covering, besides the hedge of the eyebrows, the curtain of the eyelids, and the fence of the eyelashes; and, in addition to this, he has given to every man so high a value for his eyes, and so quick an apprehension of danger, that no member of the body is more faithfully cared for than the organ of sight. Thus, Lord, keep me, for I trust I am one with Jesus, and so a member of his mystical body.

The more furious the attack, the more fervent the psalm-ist's prayer. His eye rests singly upon the Almighty, and he feels that God has but to rise from the seat of his patience and the work will be performed at once. Let the lion spring upon us; if Jehovah steps between we need no better de-fence. When God meets our foe face to face in battle, the conflict will soon be over. David contrasts the sword of the Lord with human aids and relief, and rests assured that he is safe enough under the patronage of heaven.

To behold God's face and to be changed by that vision into his image, so as to partake in his righteousness, this is my noble ambition; and in the prospect of this I cheerfully waive all my present enjoyments. My satisfaction is to come; I do not look for it as yet. I shall sleep awhile, but I shall wake at the sound of the trumpet; wake to everlasting joy, because I arise in your likeness, O my God and King! Here below, good men have glimpses of glory to restrain their sacred hunger, but the full feast awaits them in the upper skies. Compared with this deep, ineffable, eternal fulness of delight, the joys of the worldling are as a glow-worm to the sun, or the drop of a bucket to the ocean.

Meditation: *If there is so much delight in God, when we see him only by faith, what will the joy of vision be, when we shall see him face to face!* (Thomas Watson).

Psalm 18:1-3

Suggested further reading: 2 Samuel 22:1-4

Here is a fixed resolution to abide in the nearest and most intimate union with the Most High. Our triune God deserves the warmest love of all our hearts. Father, Son and Spirit each have a claim upon our love. The solemn purpose never to cease loving naturally springs from present fervour of affection. It is wrong to make rash resolutions, but when made in the strength of God this is most wise and fitting.

Dwelling among the crags and mountain fastnesses of Judea, David had escaped the malice of Saul, and he compares his God to such a place of concealment and security. Believers are often hidden in their God from the strife of tongues and the fury of the storm of trouble. The clefts of the Rock of Ages are safe abodes. When almost captured, the Lord's people are rescued from the hand of the mighty by he who is mightier still. Our God is the strength of our life, our graces, our works, our hopes, our conflicts, our victories.

Faith must be exercised, or the preciousness of God is not truly known; and God must be the object of faith, or faith is mere presumption. The Lord furnishes his warriors with both offensive and defensive weapons. Our armoury is completely stored so that none need go to battle unarmed. Here are many words, but not too many; we might profitably examine each one of them if we had time, but summing up the whole, we may conclude with Calvin, that David here equips the faithful from head to foot.

In the third verse the happy poet resolves to invoke the Lord in joyful song, believing that his God would deal as well with him in all future conflicts as in the past. It is well to pray to God as the one who deserves to be praised, for then we plead in a happy and confident manner. If I feel that I can and do bless the Lord for all his past goodness, I am bold to ask great things of him. That word 'so' has much in it. To be saved singing is to be saved indeed. Many are saved mourning and doubting; but David had such faith that he could fight singing, and win the battle with a song still upon his lips. How happy a thing to receive fresh mercy with a heart already aware of mercy enjoyed, and to anticipate new trials with a confidence based upon past experiences of divine love!

Meditation: *Whoever comes to God as he should will not call in vain. The right kind of prayer is the most potent instrumentality known on earth* (William S. Plumer).

Psalm 18:4-19

Suggested further reading: 2 Samuel 22:5-20

Death like a cruel conqueror seemed to twist round about him the cords of pain. From all sides the hell-hounds barked furiously. A cordon of devils hemmed in the hunted man of God; every way of escape was closed up. The nets were drawn closer and closer until the contracted circle completely prevented the escape of the captive. Thus this good man's situation was hopeless, as hopeless as could be, so utterly desperate that none but an almighty arm could be of any service.

Prayer is that way upward from the pit of despair to which the spiritual miner flies at once when the floods from beneath break forth upon him. Note that he first invokes his God under the name of Jehovah, and then advances to a more familiar name, 'my God'. Thus faith increases by exercise, and he whom we at first viewed as Lord is soon seen to be our God in covenant. There is never a wrong time to pray; no distress should prevent us from using the divine remedy of supplication. Above the noise of the raging billows of death, or the barking dogs of hell, the feeblest cry of a true believer will be heard in heaven.

There was no great space between the cry and its answer. The Lord is not slack concerning his promise, but is swift to rescue his afflicted. David has in his mind's eye the glorious manifestations of God in Egypt, at Sinai, and on different occasions to Joshua and the judges; and he considers that his own situation exhibits the same glory of power and goodness, and that, therefore, he may accommodate the descriptions of former displays of the divine majesty into this hymn of praise.

After pining awhile in the prison-house Joseph reached the palace, and from the cave of Adullam David mounted to the throne. After pain, pleasure is sweet. Besieged souls delight in the broad fields of the promise when God drives off the enemy and sets open the gates of the city. The Lord does not leave his work half done, for having routed the foe, he leads out the captive into liberty. Free grace lies at the foundation. Rest assured, if we go deep enough, sovereign grace is the truth that lies at the bottom of every well of mercy. Deep sea fisheries in the ocean of divine bounty always bring the pearls of electing, discriminating love to light. Why Jehovah should delight in us is an answerless question, and a mystery that angels cannot solve; but that he does delight in his beloved is certain, and is the fruitful root of favours as numerous as they are precious. Believer, sit down, and inwardly digest the instructive truth now before us, and learn to view the uncaused love of God as the cause of all the loving-kindness in which we share.

Meditation: *God's grasp cannot be broken. None can pluck his chosen out of his hand* (William S. Plumer).

Psalm 18:20-24

Suggested further reading: 2 Samuel 22:21-25

Viewing this psalm as prophetic of the Messiah, these strongly-expressed claims to righteousness are readily understood, for his garments were white as snow; but considered as the language of David they have perplexed many. Yet the case is clear, and if the words are not strained beyond their original intention, no difficulty need occur. Although the dispensations of divine grace are wholly and completely sovereign and irrespective of human merit, yet in the dealings of providence there is often discernible a rule of justice by which the injured are eventually avenged, and the righteous ultimately delivered. David's early troubles arose from the wicked malice of envious Saul, who no doubt prosecuted his persecutions under cover of charges brought against the character of 'the man after God's own heart'. These charges David declares to have been utterly false, and asserts that he possessed a grace-given righteousness that the Lord had graciously rewarded in defiance of all his detractors. Before God, the man after God's own heart was a humble sinner, but before his slanderers he could with unblushing face speak of the 'cleanness of his hands' and the righteousness of his life. He who is not able to plead innocence at the bar of human equity knows little of the sanctifying power of divine grace. There is no self-righteousness in an honest man knowing that he is honest, nor even in his believing that God rewards him in providence because of his honesty, for this is often a most evident matter of fact; but it would be self-righteousness indeed if we transferred such thoughts from the region of providential government into the spiritual kingdom, for there grace reigns not only supreme but also alone in the distribution of divine favours. When a gracious man who has been slandered stoutly maintains his integrity, and vigorously defends his character, it is by no means in opposition to the doctrine of salvation by grace, nor is it any kind of evidence of a Pharisaic spirit. A godly man has a clear conscience, and knows he is upright. Is he to deny his own consciousness and despise the work of the Holy Ghost, by hypocritically making himself out to be worse than he is? A godly man prizes his integrity very highly, or else he would not be a godly man at all. Is he to be called proud because he will not readily lose the jewel of a reputable character? A godly man can see that, in divine providence, uprightness and truth are sure to bring their own reward in the long run. May he not, when he sees that reward bestowed upon him, praise the Lord for it? Indeed, must he not show forth the faithfulness and goodness of his God? Read the cluster of expressions in this and the following verses as the song of a good conscience, sung after safely riding out a storm of defamation, persecution and abuse, and there will be no fear of us rebuking the writer as one who set too high a price upon his own moral character.

Meditation: *To protect and preserve our good name is a great and necessary duty* (Joseph Caryl).

Psalm 18:25-28

Suggested further reading: 2 Samuel 22:26-29

The dealings of the Lord in his own case cause the grateful singer to remember the usual rule of God's moral government; he is just in his dealings with the sons of men, and metes out to each man according to his measure. Every man shall have his meat weighed in his own scales, his corn meted in his own bushel, and his land measured with his own rod. No rule can be more fair, to ungodly men more terrible, or to the generous more honourable. Note that even the merciful need mercy; no amount of generosity to the poor, or forgiveness to enemies, can set us beyond the need of mercy. Lord, have mercy upon me, a sinner.

The sinner's deviousness is sinful and rebellious; the only sense in which the same term can be applied to the Most Holy God is that of judicial opposition and sternness, in which the Judge of all the earth will act at cross-purposes with the offender, and let him see that all things are not to be made subservient to wicked whims and wilful fancies. We see then what the stubborn gain in the end by their obduracy; it is this, that God steels himself even more to break them in pieces, and if they are of stone, he causes them to feel that he has the hardness of iron. The Jewish tradition was that the manna tasted according to each man's mouth; certainly God shows himself to each individual according to his character.

There is a comforting assurance for the poor in spirit, whose spiritual grief admits of no sufficient solace from any other than a divine hand. They cannot save themselves nor can others do it, but God will save them. Those who look down on others with scorn shall be looked down upon with contempt before long. The Lord abhors a proud look. What a reason for repentance and humiliation! How much better to be humble than to provoke God to humble us in his wrath!

The metaphor of the twenty-eighth verse is founded upon the mournful nature of darkness and the delightfulness of light: 'Truly the light is sweet, and a pleasant thing it is for the eyes to behold the sun'; and even so, the presence of the Lord removes all the gloom of sorrow, and enables the believer to rejoice with exceeding great joy. The lighting of the lamp is a cheerful moment in the winter's evening, but the lifting up of the light of God's countenance is happier by far. It is said that the poor in Egypt will deprive themselves of bread to buy oil for the lamp, so that they may not sit in darkness; we could well afford to part with all earthly comforts if the light of God's love could but constantly gladden our souls.

Meditation: *God is not the author of sin, but he punishes the sinner justly* (Augustine).

Psalm 18:29-45

Suggested further reading: 2 Samuel 22:30-46

Some repetitions are not vain repetitions. Second thoughts upon God's mercy should be and often are the best. Our gratitude grows stronger and sweeter as we meditate upon divine goodness. The verses that we have now to consider are the ripe fruit of a thankful spirit; they are apples of gold as to matter, and they are placed in baskets of silver as to their language. They describe the believer's victorious career and his enemies' confusion.

God's dealings with his people are far past all fault and error; all his actions are resplendent with justice, truth, tenderness, mercy and holiness. Every way of God is complete in itself, and all his ways put together are matchless in harmony and goodness. Is it not a great consolation to believe that he who has begun to bless us will perfect his work, for all his ways are perfect? Nor must the divine word be without its song of praise. 'The word of the Lord is proven', like silver refined in the furnace. The doctrines are glorious, the precepts are pure, the promises are faithful, and the whole revelation is superlatively full of grace and truth. David had tried it, thousands have tried it, we have tried it, and it has never failed. It was fitting that when way and word had been extolled, the Lord himself should be magnified; hence it is added, 'He is a shield to all who trust in him.' No armour of proof or shield of brass secures the warrior as well as the covenant God of Israel protects his warring people. He himself is the shield of those who trust in him; what a thought is this! What peace may every trusting soul enjoy!

Having mentioned his God, the psalmist's heart burns, and his words sparkle; he challenges heaven and earth to find another being worthy of adoration or trust in comparison with Jehovah. The idols of the heathen he scorns to mention, snuffing them all out as mere nothings when Deity is spoken of. Who else creates, sustains, foresees and over-rules? Who but he is perfect in every attribute, and glorious in every act? To whom but Jehovah should creatures bow? Who else can claim their service and their love? Where can lasting hopes be fixed? Where can the soul find rest? Where is stability to be found? Where is strength to be discovered? Surely in the Lord Jehovah alone can we find rest and refuge.

Like scorched leaves or blasted trees our foes and Christ's foes shall find no sap and stamina remaining in them. Those who are strangers to Jesus are strangers to all lasting happiness; those who refuse to be watered from the river of life must soon fade. Thus, remembering conquests in the past, and with glad anticipation of victories yet to come, the sweet singer closes the description, and returns to more direct adoration of his gracious God.

Meditation: *David ascribes his victories to God. Thus we see that, although he was a valiant warrior, and skilled in arms, he arrogates nothing to himself* (John Calvin).

Psalm 18:46-50

Suggested further reading: 2 Samuel 22:47-51

The Lord possesses underived, essential, independent and eternal life. We serve no inanimate, imaginary, or dying God. He only has immortality. Like loyal subjects let us cry, 'Live on, O God. Long live the King of kings. By your immortality we dedicate ourselves afresh to you.' As the Lord our God lives so would we live to him. He is the ground of our hope, and let him be the subject of our praise. Our hearts bless the Lord, extolling him with holy love.

As our Saviour, the Lord should more than ever be glorified. We should publish abroad the story of the covenant and the cross, the Father's election, the Son's redemption, and the Spirit's regeneration. He who rescues us from deserved ruin should be very dear to us. In heaven they sing, 'Unto him that loved us and washed us in his blood'; the same music should be common in the assemblies of the saints below.

To rejoice in personal revenge is unhallowed and evil, but David viewed himself as the instrument of vengeance upon the enemies of God and his people, and had he not rejoiced in the success accorded to him he would have been worthy of censure. That sinners perish is in itself a painful consideration, but that the Lord's law is avenged upon those who break it is to the devout mind a theme for thankfulness. We must, however, always remember that vengeance is never ours, vengeance belongs to the Lord, and he is so just and at the same time so long-suffering in carrying it out, that we may safely leave its administration in his hands.

The writer winds up the psalm in verse 50 with a fulness of expression, indicating the most rapturous delight of gratitude. The word 'deliverance' is plural, to show the variety and completeness of the salvation; the adjective 'great' is well placed if we consider from what, to what, and how we are saved. All this mercy is given to us in our King, the Lord's Anointed, and those are blessed indeed who as his seed may expect mercy to be built up for evermore. The Lord was faithful to the literal David, and he will not break his covenant with the spiritual David, for that would involve the honour of his crown and character far more.

The psalm concludes in the same loving spirit that shone upon its commencement; happy are they who can sing on from love to love, even as the pilgrims marched from strength to strength.

Meditation: *Sometimes the Lord cheers and comforts the hearts of his people with smiling and reviving providences, both public and personal* (John Flavel).

Psalm 19:1-6

Suggested further reading: Romans 10:16-21

The book of nature has three leaves, heaven, earth and sea, of which heaven is the first and the most glorious. With its help we are able to see the beauties of the other two. Any book without its first page would be sadly imperfect, and especially the great Natural Bible, since its first pages, the sun, moon and stars, supply light to the rest of the volume, and are thus the keys, without which the writing which follows would be dark and undiscerned. Man walking erect was evidently made to scan the skies, and he who begins to read creation by studying the stars begins the book at the right place.

Any part of creation has more instruction in it than the human mind will ever exhaust, but the celestial realm is peculiarly rich in spiritual lore. The heavens declare, or are declaring, for the continuance of their testimony is intended by the participles employed. Every moment God's existence, power, wisdom and goodness are being sounded abroad by the heavenly heralds which shine upon us from above. He who would guess at divine sublimity should gaze upward into the starry vault; he who would imagine infinity must peer into the boundless expanse; he who desires to see divine wisdom should consider the balancing of the orbs; he who would know divine fidelity must mark the regularity of the planetary motions; and he who would attain some conceptions of divine power, greatness and majesty must estimate the forces of attraction, the magnitude of the fixed stars, and the brightness of the whole celestial train. It is not merely glory that the heavens declare, but the glory of God, for they deliver to us such unanswerable arguments for a conscious, intelligent, planning, controlling and presiding Creator, that no unprejudiced person can remain unconvinced by them. The testimony given by the heavens is no mere hint, but a plain, unmistakable declaration; and it is a declaration of the most constant and abiding kind. Yet for all this, to what avail is the loudest declaration to a deaf man, or the clearest showing to one spiritually blind? God the Holy Ghost must illuminate us, or all the suns in the Milky Way never will.

In the expanse above us God flies, as it were, his starry flag to show that the King is at home, and hangs out his escutcheon that atheists may see how he despises their denunciations of him. He who looks up to the firmament and then writes himself down as an atheist brands himself, at the same moment, as an idiot or a liar. It is strange that some who love God are still afraid to study the God-declaring book of nature. The wisest men are those who with pious eagerness trace the goings forth of Jehovah as much in creation as in grace; only the foolish have any fears that the honest study of the one should injure our faith in the other.

Meditation: *The heavens and the firmament are the theatres, as it were, of God's wisdom, and power and glory* (Obadiah Sedgewick).

Psalm 19:7-14

Suggested further reading: 1 Peter 2:1-3

He declares the doctrine revealed by God to be perfect, and yet David had but a very small part of the Scriptures. If a fragment, and the darkest and most historical portion at that, is perfect, what must the entire volume be? How more than perfect is the book which contains the clearest possible display of divine love, and gives us an open vision of redeeming grace! The gospel is a complete scheme or law of gracious salvation, presenting to the needy sinner everything that his terrible needs can possibly demand. There are no redundancies and no omissions in the Word of God, and in the plan of grace. Why then do men try to paint this lily and gild this refined gold? The gospel is perfect in all its parts, and perfect as a whole: it is a crime to add to it, treason to alter it, and felony to take from it. The practical effect of the Word of God is to turn the man to himself, to his God, and to holiness; and the turn or conversion is not outward alone, the soul is moved and renewed. The great means of the conversion of sinners is the Word of God, and the more closely we keep to it in our ministry the more likely are we to be successful. It is God's Word rather than man's comment on God's Word that is made mighty with souls.

His precepts and decrees are founded in righteousness, and are just what are right or fitted to the right reason of man. As a physician gives the right medicine, and a counsellor the right advice, so does the Book of God. Filth brings decay, but cleanness is the great foe of corruption. The grace of God in the heart is a pure principle, an abiding and incorruptible principle, which may be crushed for a time, but cannot be utterly destroyed.

Bible truth enriches the soul to the highest degree. The metaphor is one which gathers force as it is brought out; gold — fine gold — much fine gold; it is good, better, best, and therefore it is not just to be desired with a miser's avidity, but with more than that. As spiritual treasure is more noble than mere material wealth, so it should be desired and sought after with greater eagerness. Men speak of solid gold, but what is so solid as solid truth? For love of gold pleasure is forsworn, ease renounced, and life endangered; should we not be ready to do as much for love of truth?

Our near Kinsman's name, our Goel or Redeemer, makes a blessed ending to the psalm; it began with the heavens, but it ends with him whose glory fills heaven and earth. Blessed Kinsman, grant that we may now meditate acceptably upon your most sweet love and tenderness.

Meditation: *Old people are all for profit, the young for pleasure; here's gold for the one, indeed, the finest gold in great quantity; here's honey for the other, indeed, live honey dropping from the comb* (John Trapp).

Psalm 20:1-4

Suggested further reading: Hebrews 5:1-10

We have before us a national anthem fit to be sung at the outbreak of war, when the monarch was fastening on his sword for the fight. If David had not been vexed with wars, we might never have been favoured with such psalms as this. The first four verses are a prayer for the success of the king. It needs but a moment's reflection to perceive that this hymn of prayer is prophetic of our Lord Jesus, and is the cry of the ancient church on behalf of her Lord, as she sees a vision of him enduring a great fight of afflictions on her behalf. The militant people of God, with the great Captain of salvation at their head, may still plead in earnest that the pleasure of the Lord may prosper in his hand.

There may be much in a royal name, or a learned name, or a venerable name, but it will be a theme for heavenly scholarship to discover all that is contained in the divine name. The glorious power of God defended and preserved the Lord Jesus through the battle of his life and death, and exalted him above all his enemies. His warfare is now accomplished in his own proper person, but in his mystical body, the church, he is still beset with dangers, and only the eternal arm of our God in covenant can defend the soldiers of the cross, and set them on high out of the reach of their foes. The day of trouble is not over, the pleading Saviour is not silent, and the name of the God of Israel is still the defence of the faithful.

Out of heaven's sanctuary the angel came to strengthen our Lord, and from the precious remembrance of God's work in his sanctuary our Lord refreshed himself when on the tree. There is no help like that which comes from God, and no deliverance like that which comes out of his sanctuary. The sanctuary to us is the person of our blessed Lord, who was typified by the temple, and is the true sanctuary that God has pitched, and not man. Let us fly to the cross for shelter in all times of need, and help will be sent to us. Men of the world despise sanctuary help, but our hearts have learned to prize it above all material aid.

Christ's desire and counsel were both set upon the salvation of his people; the church of old desired for him good speed in his design, and the church in these latter days desires with all her heart the complete fulfilment of his purpose. In Christ Jesus sanctified souls may take hold of this verse as a promise; they shall have their desire, and their plans to glorify their Master shall succeed. We may have our own will when our will is God's will. This was always the case with our Lord, and yet he said, 'Not as I will, but as you will.'

Meditation: *What need for submission in our case; if it was necessary to him, how much more for us!* (C. H. Spurgeon).

Psalm 20:5-9

Suggested further reading: Isaiah 2:1-4

We should determinedly resolve that, come what may, we will rejoice in the saving arm of the Lord Jesus. The people in this psalm, before their king went to battle, felt sure of victory, and therefore began to rejoice beforehand. How much more ought we to do this who have seen the victory completely won! Unbelief begins weeping for the funeral before the man is dead; why should not faith commence piping before the dance of victory begins?

It is here asserted confidently that God's holiness and power would both come to the rescue of the Saviour in his conflict, and surely these two glorious attributes found congenial work in answering the sufferer's cries. Since Jesus was heard, we shall be. God is in heaven, but our prayers can scale those glorious heights; those heavens are holy, but Jesus purifies our prayers, and so they gain admittance. Our need is great, but the divine arm is strong, and all its strength is 'saving strength'; that strength, moreover, is in the hand which is most used and which is used most readily — the right hand. What encouragements are these for pleading saints!

The most dreaded war-engine of David's day was the war-chariot, armed with scythes which mowed down men like grass: this was the boast and glory of the neighbouring nations; but the saints considered the name of Jehovah to be a far better defence. As the Israelites might not keep horses, it was natural for them to regard the enemy's cavalry with more than usual dread. It is, therefore, all the greater evidence of faith that the bold songster can here disdain even the horse of Egypt in comparison with the Lord of hosts. Alas, how many in our day who profess to be the Lord's are as abjectly dependent upon their fellow-men or upon an arm of flesh in some shape or other, as if they had never known the name of Jehovah at all. Jesus, you alone be our rock and refuge, and never may we mar the simplicity of our faith. The name of our God is JEHOVAH, and this should never be forgotten; the self-existent, independent, immutable, ever-present, all-filling I AM. Let us adore that matchless name, and never dishonour it by distrust or creature-confidence. Reader, you must know it before you can remember it. May the blessed Spirit reveal it graciously to your soul! For those who rest on Jehovah, they are often cast down at the first onset, but an almighty arm uplifts them, and they joyfully stand upright. The victory of Jesus is the inheritance of his people. The world, death, Satan and sin shall all be trampled beneath the feet of the champions of faith, while those who rely upon an arm of flesh shall be ashamed and confounded for ever.

Meditation: *The armies in heaven which follow you have themselves no arms, and no strength but in following you* (Isaac Williams).

Psalm 21:1-6

Suggested further reading: Revelation 19:11-16

The king is most prominent throughout, and we shall gain most profit from reading it if our meditation of him at this time is sweet. We must crown him with the glory of our salvation, singing of his love and praising his power. The next psalm will take us to the foot of the cross; this introduces us to the steps of the throne.

Jesus is a royal person. The question, 'Are you a king then?' received a full answer from the Saviour's lips: 'You say rightly that I am a king. For this cause I was born, and for this cause I have come into the world, that I might bear witness to the truth.' He is not merely a king, but the King; King over minds and hearts, reigning with a dominion of love, before which all other rule is but mere brute force. He was proclaimed King even on the cross, for there, indeed, to the eye of faith, he reigned as on a throne, blessing with more than imperial generosity the needy sons of earth. Jesus has wrought out the salvation of his people, but as a man he found his strength in Jehovah his God, to whom he addressed himself in prayer upon the lonely mountain's side, and in the garden's solitary gloom. That strength so abundantly given is here gratefully acknowledged, and made the subject of joy. The Man of Sorrows is now anointed with the oil of gladness above his fellows. In this, let every subject of King Jesus imitate the King; let us lean upon Jehovah's strength, let us joy in it by unstaggering faith, let us exult in it in our thankful songs. Jesus not only has thus rejoiced, but he shall do so as he sees the power of divine grace bringing out from their sinful hiding-places those his soul's travail has purchased. We also shall rejoice more and more as we learn by experience and to a greater degree the strength of the arm of our covenant God. Our weakness unstrings our harps, but his strength tunes them anew. If we cannot sing a note in honour of our own strength, we can at any rate rejoice in our omnipotent God.

Jesus is most blessed in himself, for he is God over all, blessed for ever; but this relates to him as our Mediator, in which capacity blessedness is given to him as a reward. Just as the Lord swore to Abraham, the promised seed is an everlasting source of blessings to all the nations of the earth. He is set for this, ordained appointed, made incarnate with this very design, that he may bless the sons of men. Oh, that sinners had sense enough to use the Saviour for that end to which he is ordained, namely, to be a Saviour to lost and guilty souls.

Meditation: *Were there ten thousand millions of heavens created above these highest heavens, and again as many above them, and as many above them, till angels were wearied with counting, it were but too low a seat to fix the princely throne of that Lord Jesus (whose you are) above them all* (Samuel Rutherford).

Psalm 21:7-13

Suggested further reading: Revelation 19:17-21

Eternal mercy secures the mediatorial throne of Jesus. He who is Most High in every sense engages all his infinite perfections to maintain the throne of grace upon which our King in Zion reigns. He was not moved from his purpose, nor in his sufferings, nor by his enemies, nor shall he be moved from the completion of his designs. He is the same yesterday, today, and for ever. Other empires are dissolved by the lapse of years, but eternal mercy maintains his growing dominion evermore; other kings fail because they rest upon an arm of flesh, but our monarch reigns on in splendour because he trusts in Jehovah. It is a great display of divine mercy to men that the throne of King Jesus is still among them: nothing but divine mercy could sustain it, for human malice would overturn it tomorrow if it could. We ought to trust in God for the promotion of the Redeemer's kingdom, for in Jehovah, the King himself trusts: all unbelieving methods of action, and especially all reliance upon mere human ability, should be for ever discarded from a kingdom where the monarch sets the example of walking by faith in God.

The destruction of the wicked is a fitting subject for joy to the friends of righteousness; hence here, and in most scriptural songs, it is noted with calm thanksgiving. We pity the lost for they are men, but we cannot pity them as enemies of Christ. None can escape from the wrath of the victorious King, nor is it desirable that they should. Jehovah will himself visit the enemies of his Son with his anger. The Lord Jesus will, as it were, judge by commission from God, whose solemn assent and co-operation shall be with him in his sentences upon impenitent sinners. An utter destruction of soul and body, so that both shall be swallowed up with misery, and be devoured with anguish, is intended here. Oh, the wrath to come! The wrath to come! Who can endure it? Lord, save us from it, for Jesus' sake.

It is always right to praise the Lord when we remember his goodness to his Son, and the overthrow of his foes. The exaltation of the name of God should be the business of every Christian; but since such poor things as we fail to honour him as he deserves, we may invoke his own power to aid us. For a time the saints may mourn, but the glorious appearance of their divine Helper awakens their joy. Joy should always flow in the channel of praise. All the attributes of God are fitting subjects to be celebrated by the music of our hearts and voices, and when we observe a display of his power, we must extol it. He wrought our deliverance alone, and he alone shall have the praise.

Meditation: *Those that might have had Christ to rule and save them, but rejected him, and fought against him, even the remembrance of that will be enough to make them to eternity a fiery oven to themselves* (Matthew Henry).

Psalm 22:1-10

Suggested further reading: Mark 15:33-39

This is, more than all others, the Psalm of the Cross. For plaintive expressions rising up from unutterable depths of woe we may say of this psalm, 'There is none like it.' It is the photograph of our Lord's saddest hours, the record of his dying words, the memorial of his expiring joys. David and his afflictions may be here in a very modified sense, but, as the star is concealed by the light of the sun, he who sees Jesus will probably neither see nor care to see David. Before us we have a description both of the darkness and of the glory of the cross, the sufferings of Christ and the glory which shall follow. Oh, for grace to draw near and see this great sight! We should read reverently, pulling off our shoes from our feet, as Moses did at the burning bush, for if there is holy ground anywhere in Scripture it is in this psalm.

The Jews mocked, but the angels adored when Jesus cried this exceeding bitter cry. Nailed to the tree we behold our great Redeemer in extremities, and what do we see? Let us gaze with holy wonder, and mark the flashes of light amid the awful darkness of that midday-midnight. Our Lord's faith beams forth and deserves our reverent imitation; he keeps his hold upon his God with both hands and cries twice, 'My God, my God!' The spirit of adoption was strong within the suffering Son of Man, and he felt no doubt about his interest in his God. Oh, that we could imitate this cleaving to an afflicting God!

The Man of Sorrows had prayed until his speech failed him, and he could only utter moanings and groanings as men do in severe sicknesses, like the roarings of a wounded animal. To what extremity of grief was our Master driven! What strong crying and tears were those which made him too hoarse for speech! What must have been his anguish to find his own beloved and trusted Father standing afar off, and neither granting help nor apparently hearing prayer. This was good cause to make him 'roar'. Yet there was a reason for all this which those who rest in Jesus as their Substitute well know.

We may remind the Lord of his former loving-kindnesses to his people, and beseech him to be still the same. This is true wrestling; let us learn the art. Observe that ancient saints cried and trusted, and that in trouble we must do the same. The invariable result was that they were not ashamed of their hope, for deliverance came in due time; this same happy portion shall be ours. The prayer of faith can do the deed when nothing else can. Let us wonder when we see Jesus using the same pleas as ourselves, and immersed in griefs far deeper than our own.

Meditation: *Oh! how will our very hearts melt with love, when we remember that as we have been distressed for our sins against him, so he was in greater agonies for us?* (Timothy Rogers).

Psalm 22:11-21

Suggested further reading: Mark 15:21-25

The crucified Son of David continues to pour out his complaint and prayer. We need much grace that while reading we may have fellowship with his sufferings. May the blessed Spirit conduct us into a most clear and affecting sight of our Redeemer's woes.

Our Substitute had trouble in his inmost heart, for he said, 'The waters have come in, even unto my soul'; well might he cry, 'Be not far from me.' The absence of all other helpers is a telling plea. In our Lord's case none either could or would help him, it was necessary that he should tread the winepress alone; yet it was a sore aggravation to find that all his disciples had forsaken him, and loved ones and friends were put far from him. There is an awfulness about absolute friendlessness which is crushing to the human mind, for man was not made to be alone, and is like a dismembered limb when he has to endure heart-loneliness. Think of the Lord Jesus as a helpless, unarmed, naked man, cast into the midst of a herd of infuriated wild bulls. They were brutal as bulls, many, and strong, and the Rejected One was all alone, and bound naked to the tree. His position throws great force into the earnest entreaty, 'Be not far from me.' Our Lord's faith must have passed through a most severe conflict while he found himself abandoned to the tender mercies of the wicked, but he came off victorious by prayer, the very dangers to which he was exposed being used to add prevalence to his entreaties.

Turning from his enemies, our Lord describes his own personal condition in language that should bring the tears into every loving eye. He was utterly spent, like water poured upon the earth; his heart failed him, and had no more firmness in it than running water. His whole being was made a sacrifice, like a libation poured out before the Lord. He had long been a fountain of tears; in Gethsemane his heart welled over in sweat, and on the cross he gushed forth with blood. He poured out his strength and spirit, so that he was reduced to the most feeble and exhausted state.

Having experienced deliverance in the past from great enemies, who were strong as the wild oxen, the Redeemer utters his last cry for rescue from death, which is fierce and mighty as the lion. This prayer was heard, and the gloom of the cross departed. Thus faith, though sorely beaten, and even cast beneath the feet of her enemy, ultimately wins the victory. It was so in our Head, it shall be so in all the members. We have overcome the wild ox, we shall conquer the lion, and from both lion and ox we shall take the crown.

Meditation: *Oh, how different is that look which the awakened sinner directs to Calvary, when faith lifts up her eye to him who agonized, and bled, and died, for the guilty!* (John Morison).

Psalm 22:22-31

Suggested further reading: Hebrews 2:10-15

The transition is very marked: from a horrible tempest all is changed into calm. The darkness of Calvary at length passed away from the face of nature, and from the soul of the Redeemer, and beholding the light of his triumph and its future results the Saviour smiled. We have followed him through the gloom, let us attend him in the returning light.

The delights of Jesus are always with his church, and hence his thoughts, after much distraction, return at the first moment of relief to their usual channel; he forms fresh designs for the benefit of his beloved ones. He is not ashamed to call them brethren. Among his first resurrection words were: 'Go to my brethren.' Jesus anticipates happiness in having communication with his people; he purposes to be their teacher and minister, and fixes his mind upon the subject of his discourse. Not merely in a little household gathering does our Lord resolve to proclaim his Father's love, but in the great assemblies of his saints, and in the general assembly and church of the first-born. This the Lord Jesus is always doing by his representatives, who are the heralds of salvation, and labour to praise God. In the great universal church Jesus is the one authoritative teacher, and all others, so far as they are worthy to be called teachers, are nothing but echoes of his voice. Jesus reveals his object in declaring the divine name: that God may be praised. The church continually magnifies Jehovah for manifesting himself in the person of Jesus, and Jesus himself leads the song, and is both precentor and preacher in his church. Delightful are the seasons when Jesus communes with our hearts concerning divine truth; joyful praise is the sure result.

The reader must imagine the Saviour as addressing the congregation of the saints. He exhorts the faithful to unite with him in thanksgiving. The genius of the gospel is praise. Jew and Gentile saved by sovereign grace should be eager in the blessed work of magnifying the God of our salvation. All saints should unite in the song; no tongue may be silent, no heart may be cold. Christ calls us to glorify God, so can we refuse? Out from the inner circle of the present church the blessing is to spread in growing power until the remotest parts of the earth shall be ashamed of their idols, mindful of the true God, penitent for their offences, and unanimously earnest for reconciliation with Jehovah. Then shall false worship cease.

Sovereign grace shall bring out the blood-bought ones from among men. Nothing shall thwart the divine purpose. The chosen shall come to life, to faith, to pardon, to heaven. In this the dying Saviour finds a sacred satisfaction. Salvation's glorious work is done, there is peace on earth, and glory in the highest. 'It is finished': these were the expiring words of the Lord Jesus, as they are the last words of this psalm. May we by living faith be enabled to see our salvation finished by the death of Jesus!

Meditation: *True conversion to Christ will be accompanied with the worship of him* (Andrew Fuller).

Psalm 23

Suggested further reading: John 10:11-16

What condescension is this, that the infinite Lord assumes towards his people the office and character of a shepherd! It should be the subject of grateful admiration that the great God allows himself to be compared to anything which will set forth his great love and care for his own people. David had himself been a keeper of sheep, and understood both the needs of the sheep and the many cares of a shepherd. He compares himself to a creature weak, defenceless and foolish, and he takes God to be his provider, preserver, director, and, indeed, his everything. We must cultivate the spirit of assured dependence upon our heavenly Father. The sweetest word of all is that monosyllable, 'my'. He does not say, 'The Lord is the shepherd of the world at large, and leads forth the multitude as his flock,' but 'The Lord is my shepherd'; if he is a shepherd to no one else, he is a shepherd to me; he cares for me, watches over me, and preserves me. The words are in the present tense. Whatever the believer's position is, he is even now under the pastoral care of Jehovah.

The Christian life has two elements in it, the contemplative and the active, and both of these are richly provided for. First, the contemplative, 'He makes me to lie down in green pastures.' What are these 'green pastures' but the Scriptures of truth — always fresh, always rich, and never exhausted? Sweet and full are the doctrines of the gospel; fit food for souls, as tender grass is natural nutriment for sheep. The second part of a vigorous Christian's life consists in gracious activity. We not only think, but we act. We are not always lying down to feed, but are journeying onward towards perfection; hence we read, 'He leads me beside the still waters.' What are these 'still waters' but the influences and graces of his blessed Spirit? His Spirit attends us in various operations, like waters — in the plural to cleanse, to refresh, to fertilize, to cherish. When the soul grows sorrowful he revives it; when it is sinful he sanctifies it; when it is weak he strengthens it.

This is the joy of the Christian! You are with me. While I am here I will be a child at home with my God; the whole world shall be his house to me; and when I ascend into the upper chamber I shall not change my company, nor even change the house. I shall only go to dwell in the upper storey of the house of the Lord for ever. May God grant us grace to dwell in the serene atmosphere of this most blessed psalm!

Meditation: *By means of all the mercies of God bestowed on him, David came to be persuaded of the continuance of the favour of God towards him* (William Perkins).

Psalm 24:1-6

Suggested further reading: Isaiah 25:6-12

How very different this is from the ignorant Jewish notion of God which prevailed in our Saviour's day. The Jews said, 'The holy land is God's, and the seed of Abraham are his only people'; but their great Monarch had long before instructed them, 'The earth is the Lord's, and all its fulness.' The whole round world is claimed for Jehovah.

In the second verse we have the reason why the world belongs to God: namely, because he has created it, which is a title beyond all dispute. The world is Jehovah's, because from generation to generation he preserves and upholds it, having settled its foundations. Providence and creation are the two legal seals upon the title-deeds of the great Owner of all things. He who built the house and bears up its foundation has surely a first claim upon it.

In verses three to six we have the true Israel described. The men who shall stand as courtiers in the palace of the living God are not distinguished by race, but by character; they are not Jews only, nor Gentiles only, nor any one branch of mankind peculiarly, but a people purified and made fit to dwell in the holy hill of the Lord. It is uphill work for the creature to reach the Creator. Where is the mighty climber who can scale the towering heights? Nor is it height alone; it is glory too. Whose eye shall see the King in his beauty and dwell in his palace? In heaven he reigns most gloriously. Who shall be permitted to enter into his royal presence? God has made all, but he will not save all; there is a chosen company who shall have the singular honour of dwelling with him in his high abode. These choice spirits desire to commune with God, and their wish shall be granted them. Who is he that can gaze upon the Holy One, and can abide in the blaze of his glory? Certainly none may venture to commune with God upon the footing of the law, but grace can make us fit to behold the vision of the divine presence. There must be a work of grace in the core of the heart, or our religion is a delusion. May God grant that our inward powers may be cleansed by the sanctifying Spirit, so that we may love holiness and abhor all sin. The pure in heart shall see God, all others are but blind bats; stone-blindness in the eyes arises from stone in the heart. Dirt in the heart throws dust in the eyes.

We must not suppose that the persons who are described in this way by their inward and outward holiness are saved by the merit of their works; but their works are the evidences by which they are known. The fifth verse shows that in the saints grace reigns and grace alone. Such men wear the holy livery of the Great King because he has of his own free love clothed them with it.

Meditation: *The true saint wears the wedding garment, but he owns that the Lord of the feast provided it for him, without money and without price* (C. H. Spurgeon).

Psalm 24:7-10

Suggested further reading: Isaiah 12:1-6

These verses reveal to us the great representative man, who answered to the full character laid down, and therefore by his own right ascended the holy hill of Zion. Our Lord Jesus Christ could ascend into the hill of the Lord because his hands were clean and his heart was pure; and if we by faith in him are conformed to his image we shall enter too. We have here a picture of our Lord's glorious ascent. We see him rising from amidst the little group upon Olivet, and as the cloud receives him, angels reverently escort him to the gates of heaven. Let all things do their utmost to honour so great a prince; let the highest heaven put on unusual loftiness in honour of 'the King of glory'. He who, fresh from the cross and the tomb, now rides through the gates of the New Jerusalem is higher than the heavens; great and everlasting as they are, those gates of pearl are all unworthy of him before whom the heavens are not pure, and who charges his angels with folly.

'Who is this King of glory?' is a question full of meaning and worthy of the meditations of eternity. Who is he in person, nature, character, office and work? What is his pedigree? What is his rank and what his race? The answer given in a mighty wave of music is, 'The Lord strong and mighty, the Lord mighty in battle.' We know the might of Jesus by the battles which he has fought, the victories which he has won over sin, and death, and hell, and we clap our hands as we see him leading captivity captive in the majesty of his strength. Mighty hero, be crowned for ever King of kings and Lord of lords.

Dear reader, it is possible that you are saying, 'I shall never enter into the heaven of God, for I have neither clean hands nor a pure heart.' Look then to Christ, who has already climbed the holy hill. Follow in his footsteps, and rest upon his merit. He rides triumphantly into heaven, and you shall ride there too if you trust him. 'But how can I get the character described?' you say. The Spirit of God will give you that. He will create in you a new heart and a right spirit. Faith in Jesus is the work of the Holy Spirit, and has all virtues wrapped up in it. Faith stands by the fountain filled with blood, and, as she washes there, clean hands and a pure heart, a holy soul and a truthful tongue are given to her.

The closing note is inexpressibly grand. The Lord of hosts, Lord of men and angels, Lord of the universe, Lord of the worlds, is the King of glory. All true glory is concentrated upon the true God, for all other glory is but a passing pageant, the painted pomp of an hour. The ascended Saviour is here declared to be the Head and Crown of the universe, the King of glory.

Meditation: *Jesus of Nazareth is Lord of Hosts* (C. H. Spurgeon).

Psalm 25:1-7

Suggested further reading: Exodus 33:12-23

When the storm-winds are out, the Lord's vessels put about and make for their well-remembered harbour of refuge. What a mercy that the Lord will condescend to hear our cries in time of trouble, although we may have almost forgotten him in our hours of fancied prosperity.

It is but mockery to uplift the hands and the eyes unless we also bring our souls into our devotions. True prayer may be described as the soul rising from earth to have fellowship with heaven; it is taking a journey upon Jacob's ladder, leaving our cares and fears at the foot, and meeting with a covenant God at the top. Very often the soul cannot rise, she has lost her wings, and is heavy and earth-bound; she is more like a burrowing mole than a soaring eagle. In such dull seasons we must not give up prayer, but must, by God's assistance, exert all our power to lift up our hearts. Let faith be the lever and grace be the arm, and the dead lump will yet be stirred. But what a lift it has sometimes proved!

Suffering enlarges the heart by creating the power to sympathize. If we pray eagerly for ourselves, we shall not be able to forget our fellow-sufferers for long. None pity the poor like those who have been or are still poor, none have such tenderness for the sick as those who have been long in ill health themselves. We ought to be grateful for occasional griefs if they preserve us from chronic hardheartedness; for of all afflictions, an unkind heart is the worst. It is a plague to its possessor, and a torment to those around him. Prayer, when it is of the Holy Ghost's teaching, is never selfish; the believer does not sue for monopolies for himself, but would have all in similar circumstances partake of divine mercy with him.

In seasons of affliction we are usually tempted to fear that our God has forgotten us, or forgotten his usual kindness towards us; so the soul, as it were, reminds the Lord, and beseeches him to recollect those deeds of love which once he bestowed upon it. There is a holy boldness that ventures to deal with the Most High in this way; let us cultivate it. But there is also an unholy unbelief that suggests our fears; let us strive against it with all our might. With an unchangeable God it is a most effective argument to remind him of his ancient mercies and his eternal love. By tracing all that we enjoy to the fountain-head of everlasting love we shall greatly cheer our hearts.

Meditation: *Divine love is an eternal fountain that never ceases running while a vessel is empty or capable of holding more* (Elisha Coles).

Psalm 25:8-15

Suggested further reading: Exodus 34:1-9

It is no less true than wonderful that through the atonement the justice of God pleads as strongly as his grace for the salvation of the sinners whom Jesus died to save. Moreover, as a good man naturally endeavours to make others like himself, so will the Lord our God in his compassion bring sinners into the way of holiness and conform them to his own image; thus the goodness of our God leads us to expect the reclaiming of sinful men. We may not conclude from God's goodness that he will save those sinners who continue to wander in their own ways, but we may be assured that he will renew transgressors' hearts and guide them into the way of holiness. Let those who desire to be delivered from sin take comfort from this. God himself will condescend to be the teacher of sinners. What a ragged school is this for God to teach in!

'Who is the man that fears the Lord?' Let the question provoke self-examination. Gospel privileges are not for every pretender. Those whose hearts are right shall not err for want of heavenly direction. Where God sanctifies the heart he enlightens the head. We all wish to choose our way, but what a mercy it is when the Lord directs that choice, and makes free will to be good will! If we make our will God's will, God will let us have our will. God does not violate our will, but leaves much to our choice; nevertheless, he instructs our wills, and so we choose that which is well pleasing in his sight. The will should be subject to law; there is a way that we should choose, but so ignorant are we that we need to be taught, and so wilful that none but God himself can teach us effectually.

He who fears God has nothing else to fear. He shall lodge in the chamber of content. It is not abundance but content that gives true ease. Even here, having learned by grace both to abound and to be empty, the believer dwells at ease; but how profound will be the ease of his soul for ever! Saints have the key of heaven's hieroglyphics; they can unravel celestial enigmas. They are initiated into the fellowship of the skies; they have heard words that it is not possible for them to repeat to their fellows. The antiquity, security, righteousness, fulness, graciousness and excellence of God's covenant shall be revealed to their hearts and understandings, and above all, their own part in it shall be sealed to their souls by the witness of the Holy Spirit. The designs of love which the Lord has to his people in the covenant of grace, he has been pleased to show to believers in the Book of Inspiration, and by his Spirit he leads us into the mystery, even the hidden mystery of redemption.

Meditation: *Fear God, who is above all, and no need to fear man at all* (Augustine).

Psalm 25:16-22

Suggested further reading: 1 Peter 1:3-9

David's own eyes were fixed upon God, but he feared that the Lord had averted his face from him in anger. Unbelief often suggests that God has turned his back upon us. When we turn to God we need not fear that he will turn from us, but may boldly cry, 'Turn yourself to me.' The ground of quarrel is always in ourselves, and when that is removed there is nothing to prevent our full enjoyment of communion with God. When trouble penetrates the heart, it is trouble indeed. In the case before us, the heart was swollen with grief like a lake surcharged with water by enormous floods; this is used as an argument for deliverance, and it is a potent one. When the darkest hour of the night arrives we may expect the dawn; when the sea is at its lowest ebb the tide must surely turn; and when our troubles are enlarged to the greatest degree, then may we hopefully pray, 'Oh, bring me out of my distresses!'

Note the many trials of the saints; here we have no less than six words all descriptive of woe. 'Desolate, and afflicted, troubles enlarged, distresses, affliction and pain.' But note even more the submissive and believing spirit of a true saint; all he asks for is, 'Lord, look upon my evil plight.' He does not dictate or even express a complaint; a look from God will content him, and when that is granted he asks no more. Even more noteworthy is the way in which the believer under affliction discovers the true source of all the mischief, and lays the axe at the root of it. 'Forgive all my sins' is the cry of a soul that is more sick of sin than of pain, and would sooner be forgiven than healed. Blessed is the man to whom sin is more unbearable than disease, it shall not be long before the Lord shall both forgive his iniquity and heal his diseases. Men are slow to see the intimate connection between sin and sorrow, a grace-taught heart alone feels it.

Sorrow had taught the psalmist sympathy, and given him communion with the tried people of God; he therefore remembers them in his prayers: 'Israel', the tried, the wrestling, the conquering hero, fit representative of all the saints; Israel in Egypt, in the wilderness, in wars with Canaanites, in captivity, fit type of the church militant on earth. Jesus is the Redeemer from trouble as well as sin, he is a complete Redeemer, and from every evil he will rescue every saint. Redemption by blood is finished: O God, send us redemption by power. Amen and Amen.

Meditation: *We may not complain* of *God, but we may complain* to *God* (William Plumer).

Psalm 26:1-5

Suggested further reading: 2 Kings 20:1-7

Worried and worn out by the injustice of men, the innocent spirit flies from its false accusers to the throne of Eternal Right. He who dares to carry his suit into the King's
bench of heaven needed to have a clear case. Such an appeal as this is not to be made rashly on any occasion; and
as for the whole of our walk and conversation, it should
never be made at all, except as we are justified in Christ
Jesus. A far more fitting prayer for a sinful mortal is the
petition: 'Enter not into judgement with your servant.' David
held integrity as his principle, and walked in it as his practice. He had not used any traitorous or unrighteous means
to gain the crown, or to keep it; he was conscious of having
been guided by the noblest principles of honour in all his
actions with regard to Saul and his family. What a comfort
it is to have the approbation of one's own conscience! If
there is peace within the soul, the blustering storms of slander that howl around us are of little consideration.

The psalmist was so clear from the charge laid against
him, that he submitted himself unconditionally to any form
of examination that the Lord might see fit to employ. All
this is a very bold appeal, and made by a man like David,
who greatly feared the Lord, it manifests a most solemn
and complete conviction of innocence. The expressions
used here should teach us the thoroughness of the divine
judgement, and the necessity of being profoundly sincere
in all things, lest we be found wanting at the last. Our

enemies are harsh with us with the severity of spite, and a brave man endures this without a fear; but God's severity is that of unswerving right. Who shall stand against such a trial?

A sense of mercy received sets a fair prospect before the faithful mind in its gloomiest condition, for it yields visions of mercies yet to come, visions not visionary but real. Dwell, dear reader, upon that celestial word 'loving-kindness'. It has a heavenly savour. Is it not an unmatchable word, unexcelled, unrivalled? The goodness of the Lord to us should be before our eyes as a motive directing our conduct; we are not under the bondage of the law, but we are under the sweet constraints of grace, which are far more mighty, although far more gentle.

A man who does not hate evil terribly does not love good heartily. Men, as men, we must always love, for they are our neighbours, and therefore to be loved as ourselves; but evildoers, as such, are traitors to the Great King, and no loyal subject can love traitors. What God hates we must hate. Better to sit with the blind, and the halt, and the lame, at the table of mercy, than with the wicked in their feasts of ungodliness; indeed, it is better to sit on Job's dunghill than on Pharaoh's throne.

Meditation: *Let each reader see well to his company, for such as we keep in this world, we are likely to keep in the next* (C. H. Spurgeon).

Psalm 26:6-12

Suggested further reading: 2 Corinthians 6:11 – 7:1

The washing of hands is a significant action to show that we have no connection with a deed. David does not claim perfect innocence here, but he avows his innocence of the crimes he was slanderously accused of. There is, however, a sense in which we may be washed in absolute innocence, for the atoning blood makes every part of us clean. We ought never to rest satisfied short of a full persuasion of our complete cleansing by Jesus' precious blood.

The company of sinners is so distasteful to us here, that we cannot endure the thought of being bound up in the same bundle with them for all eternity. Our comfort is, that the Great Husbandman discerns the tares from the wheat, and will find a separate place for distinct characters. In the former verses we see that the psalmist kept himself clear of profane persons, and this is to be understood as a reason why he should not be thrust into their company at the end. Let us think of the doom of the wicked, and the prayer of the text will rise forcibly to our lips.

Trusting in God the psalmist resolves that the plain way of righteousness shall be his choice, and those who will, may prefer the tortuous paths of violence and deceit. Yet he is by no means a boaster, or a self-righteous vaunter of his own strength, for he cries for redemption and pleads for mercy. Our integrity is not absolute nor inherent, it is a work of grace in us and is marred by human infirmity. We must, therefore, resort to the redeeming blood and the throne of mercy, confessing that though we are saints among men, we must still bow as sinners before God.

The song began in the minor, but it has now reached the major key. Saints often sing themselves into happiness. The 'even place' upon which our foot stands is the sure, covenant faithfulness, eternal promise and immutable oath of the Lord of Hosts; there is no fear of falling from this solid basis, or of its being removed from under us. Established in Christ Jesus by being vitally united to him, we have nothing left to occupy our thoughts but the praises of our God. Let us not forsake the assembling of ourselves together, and when assembled, let us not be slow to contribute our portion of thanksgiving. Each saint is a witness to divine faithfulness, and should be ready with his testimony. As for the slanderers, let them howl outside the door while the children sing within.

Meditation: *As a man whose feet are firmly fixed upon even ground is apprehensive of no fall, so the pious worshippers of Jehovah feel no dread lest their adversaries should finally triumph over them* (William Walford).

Psalm 27:1-6

Suggested further reading: Exodus 14:19-31

Salvation finds us in the dark, but it does not leave us there; it gives light to those who sit in the valley of the shadow of death. After conversion our God is our joy, comfort, guide, teacher, and in every sense our light; he is light within, light around, light reflected from us, and light to be revealed to us. Note, it is not said merely that the Lord gives light, but that he is light; nor that he gives salvation, but that he is salvation. He, then, who by faith has laid hold upon God has all covenant blessings in his possession.

Divided aims tend to distraction, weakness, disappointment. The man of one book is eminent; the man of one pursuit is successful. Let all our affection be bound up in one affection, and that affection set upon heavenly things. God judges us very much by the desire of our hearts. He is the right target for aspirations. Our desires of the Lord should be sanctified, humble, constant, submissive, fervent, and it is well if, as with the psalmist, they are all molten into one mass. Under David's painful circumstances we might have expected him to desire repose, safety, and a thousand other good things; but no, he has set his heart on the pearl, and leaves the rest. 'To behold the beauty of the Lord' is an exercise both for earthly and heavenly worshippers. We must not enter the assemblies of the saints in order to see and be seen, or merely to hear the minister; we must repair to the gatherings of the righteous, intent upon the gracious object of learning more of the loving Father, more of the glorified Jesus, more of the mysterious Spirit, in order that we may more lovingly admire, and more reverently adore our glorious God. What a word is that, 'the beauty of the Lord'! Think of it, dear reader! Better still — behold it by faith! What a sight that will be when every faithful follower of Jesus shall behold 'the King in his beauty'! Oh, for that infinitely blessed vision!

Godly men of old prayed in faith, nothing wavering, and spoke of the answer to their prayers as a certainty. David was by faith so sure of a glorious victory over all those who beset him, that he arranged in his own heart what he would do when his foes all lay prostrate before him; that arrangement was just as gratitude suggested. Let who will, be silent; the believer, when his prayer is heard, must and will make his praise to be heard also. And let who will, sing unto the vanities of the world; the believer reserves his music for the Lord alone.

Meditation: *A heavenly mind gathers itself up into one wish and no more* (Jeremy Taylor).

Psalm 27:7-14

Suggested further reading: Isaiah 49:14-21

The pendulum of spirituality swings from prayer to praise. The voice that in the sixth verse was tuned to music is here turned to crying. As a good soldier, David knew how to handle his weapons, and found himself much at home with the weapon of 'all prayer'. Note the anxiety in his voice. Pharisees do not care a fig for the Lord's hearing them, so long as they are heard of men, or charm their own pride with their sounding devotions; but with a genuine man, the Lord's ear is everything.

In the eighth verse we are taught that if we would have the Lord hear our voice, we must be careful to respond to his voice. The true heart should echo the will of God as the rocks among the Alps repeat in sweetest music the notes of the peasant's horn. Observe that the command was in the plural, to all the saints, but the man of God turned it into the singular by a personal application, 'Your face, Lord, I will seek.' The voice of the Lord is very effectual where all other voices fail. The command to seek the Lord's face would be a painful one if the Lord, by withdrawing himself, rendered it impossible for the seeker to meet with him. A smile from the Lord is the greatest of comforts, his frown the worst of ills.

David does not pray to be indulged with his own way, but to be informed as to the path in which the righteous Jehovah would have him walk. This prayer evinces a humble sense of personal ignorance, great teachableness of spirit, and cheerful obedience of heart. Here help is sought, as well as direction; we not only need a map of the way, but also a guide to assist us in the journey. Here a path is desired which shall be open, honest, straightforward, in opposition to the way of cunning, which is intricate, tortuous, dangerous. Good men seldom succeed in fine speculations and doubtful courses; plain simplicity is the best spirit for an heir of heaven. Let us leave shifty tricks and political expediencies to the citizens of the world — the New Jerusalem owns plain men for its citizens.

Wait at the Lord's door with prayer; wait at his foot with humility; wait at his table with service; wait at his window with expectancy. Suitors often win nothing but the cold shoulder from earthly patrons after long and obsequious waiting; he speeds best whose patron is in the skies. David sets his own private seal to the word which, as an inspired man, he had been moved to write. It is his testimony as well as the command of God. Wait on the Lord.

Meditation: *Think not the government is out of Christ's hand, when men are doing many sad things, and giving many heavy blows to the work of God* (Ralph Erskine).

Psalm 28:1-5

Suggested further reading: Psalm 143:1-4

A cry is the natural expression of sorrow, and is a suitable utterance when all other modes of appeal fail us; but the cry must be directed to the Lord alone, for to cry to man is to waste our entreaties in the air. When we consider the readiness of the Lord to hear, and his ability to aid, we shall see good reason for directing all our appeals at once to the God of our salvation, and shall use language of firm resolve like that in the text. Mere formalists may be content without answers to their prayers, but genuine suppliants cannot. They are not satisfied with the results of prayer itself in calming the mind and subduing the will — they must go further and obtain actual replies from heaven, or they cannot rest; and those replies they long to receive at once, if possible; they dread even a little of God's silence. We stretch out empty hands, for we are beggars; we lift them up, for we seek heavenly supplies; we lift them towards the mercy seat of Jesus, for there our expectation dwells.

The best of the wicked are dangerous company in time, and would make terrible companions for eternity; we must avoid them in their pleasures, if we would not be confounded with them in their miseries. They have learned the manners of the place to which they are going: the doom of liars is their portion for ever, and lying is their conversation on the road. It is a sure sign of baseness when the tongue and the heart do not ring to the same note. Deceitful men are more to be dreaded than wild beasts: it would be better to be shut up in a pit with serpents than to be compelled to live with liars.

God works in creation — nature teems with proofs of his wisdom and goodness, yet blind atheists refuse to see him. He works in providence, ruling and overruling, and his hand is very manifest in human history, yet the infidel will not discern him. He works in grace — remarkable conversions are still met with at every hand, yet the ungodly refuse to see the operations of the Lord. Where angels wonder, carnal men despise. God condescends to teach, and man refuses to learn. If they would not see the hand of judgement upon others, they shall feel it upon themselves. They have become like old, rotten, decayed houses of timber, useless to the owner, and harbouring all manner of evil, and, therefore, the Great Builder will demolish them utterly. Incorrigible offenders may expect speedy destruction: they who will not mend shall be thrown away as worthless. Let us be very attentive to all the lessons of God's word and work, lest being found disobedient to divine will, we are made to suffer divine wrath.

Meditation: *He prays against his enemies, not out of any private revenge, but being led by the infallible spirit of prophecy, looking through these men to the enemies of Christ, and of his people in all ages* (David Dickson).

Psalm 28:6-9

Suggested further reading: Colossians 1:9-12

Saints are full of benedictions; they are a blessed people, and a blessing people; but they give their best blessings, the fat of their sacrifices, to their glorious Lord. Our psalm was prayer up to this point, and now it turns to praise. They who pray well will soon praise well: prayer and praise are the two lips of the soul. Real praise is established upon sufficient and constraining reasons; it is not irrational emotion, but rises, like a pure spring, from the deeps of experience. Answered prayers should be acknowledged. Do we not often fail in this duty? Would it not greatly encourage others, and strengthen ourselves, if we faithfully recorded divine goodness, and made a point of extolling it with our tongue? God's mercy is not such an inconsiderable thing that we may safely venture to receive it without so much as thanks. We should shun ingratitude, and live daily in the heavenly atmosphere of thankful love.

The Lord employs his power on our behalf, and, moreover, infuses strength into us in our hour of weakness. The psalmist, by an act of appropriating faith, takes the omnipotence of Jehovah to be his own. Dependence upon the invisible God gives great independence of spirit, inspiring us with confidence more than human. The heavenly experience of one believer is a pattern of the life of all. To all the militant church, without exception, the Lord is the same as he was to his servant David, 'the least of them shall be as David'. They need the same aid and they shall have it, for they are loved with the same love, written in the same book of life, and one with the same anointed Head.

The final verse is a prayer for the church militant, written in short words, but full of weighty meaning. We must pray for the whole church, and not for ourselves alone. Deliver your people from their enemies, preserve them from their sins, help them in their troubles, rescue them from their temptations, and ward off from them every ill. There is a plea hidden in the expression 'your people', for it may be safely concluded that God's interest in the church, as his own portion, will lead him to guard it from destruction. Grant positive blessings, peace, plenty, prosperity, happiness; make all your dearly purchased and precious heritage to be comforted by your Spirit. Revive, refresh, enlarge and sanctify your church. Be a shepherd to your flock, may their bodily and spiritual wants be plentifully supplied. By your word and ordinances, direct, rule, sustain and satisfy those who are the sheep of your hand. Carry them in your arms on earth, and then lift them into your bosom in heaven. Elevate their minds and thoughts, spiritualize their affections, make them heavenly, Christlike, and full of God. O Lord, answer this, our petition, for Jesus' sake.

Meditation: *Prayer is the best remedy in a calamity. This is indeed a general remedy for every malady* (William Gouge).

Psalm 29:1-4

Suggested further reading: Job 37:1-13

Neither men nor angels can confer anything upon Jehovah, but they should recognize his glory and might, and ascribe it to him in their songs and in their hearts. You great ones of earth and of heaven, kings and angels, join in offering worship to the blessed and only Potentate. You lords among men need to be reminded in this way, for you often fail where humbler men are ardent; but fail no longer, bow your heads at once, and loyally do homage to the King of kings. When will the day arrive when kings and princes consider it their delight to glorify their God?

Three times the admonition is given, for men are backward in glorifying God, and especially great men, who are often too puffed up with their own glory to spare time to give God his rightful praise, although nothing more is asked of them than is most just and right. Surely men should not need so much pressing to give what is due, especially when the payment is so pleasant. 'Worship the Lord', bow before him with devout homage and sacred awe, and let your worship be such as he appoints. In times past, worship was cumbered with ceremony, and men gathered around one dedicated building, whose solemn pomp was emblematic of 'the beauty of holiness'. But now our worship is spiritual, and the architecture of the house and the garments of the worshippers are matters of no importance, the spiritual beauty of inward purity and outward holiness being far more precious in the eyes of our thrice holy God. Oh, for grace ever to worship with holy motives and in a holy manner as becomes saints! In these two verses the call to worship chimes in with a loud pealing thunder, which is the church bell of the universe ringing kings and angels, and all the sons of earth to their devotions.

The thunder is not only poetically but instructively called 'the voice of the Lord', since it peals from on high. It surpasses all other sounds, it inspires awe, it is entirely independent of man, and has been used on some occasions as the grand accompaniment of God's speech to Adam's sons. An irresistible power attends the lightning reported by thunder. In an instant, when the Lord wishes, the force of electricity produces amazing results. Thompson speaks rightly of 'the unconquerable lightning', for it is the most powerful force used by God to demonstrate his ways, and none can measure its power.

As the voice of God in nature is so powerful, so it is in grace; the reader will do well to draw a parallel, and he will find much in the gospel that may be illustrated by the thunder of the Lord in the tempest. His voice, whether in nature or revelation, shakes both earth and heaven; see that you do not refuse the one who speaks. If his voice is as mighty as this, what must his hand be! Beware lest you provoke a blow.

Meditation: *Where the word of a king is, there is power, but what imperial voice shall be likened unto the majestic thunder of the Lord?* (C. H. Spurgeon).

Psalm 29:5-11

Suggested further reading: Job 37:14-24

Noble trees fall prostrate beneath the mysterious bolt, or stand in desolation as momentoes of its power. The greatest and most venerable of trees or men may not reckon upon immunity when the Lord vents his fury. The gospel of Jesus has a similar dominion over the most inaccessible of mortals; and when the Lord sends the word, it breaks hearts far more stout than the cedars. Not only the trees, but also the mountains themselves move as though they frisked and leaped like young bulls or antelopes. The glorious gospel of the blessed God has more than equal power over the rocky obduracy and mountainous pride of man. The voice of our dying Lord rent the rocks and opened the graves; his living voice still works the same wonders. Glory to his name, when the voice of his intercession is heard, the hills of our sins leap into his grave and are buried in the red sea of his blood!

Flames of fire attend the voice of God in the gospel, illuminating and melting the hearts of men; by these he consumes our lusts and kindles in us a holy flame of ever-inspiring love and holiness. God does not court the applause of men — his grandest deeds are wrought where man's inquisitive glance is completely unknown. Where no sound of man was heard, the voice of God was terribly distinct. The vast and silent plains trembled with fright. Silence paid homage to the almighty voice. Low-lying plains must hear the voice of God as well as lofty mountains; the poor as well as the mighty must acknowledge the glory of the Lord. Flood follows tempest, but Jehovah is ready for the emergency. No deluge can undermine the foundation of his throne. He is calm and unmoved, however much the deep may roar and be troubled: his government rules the most unstable and boisterous of created things. Jesus has the government upon his shoulders eternally; in the stormiest times our interests are safe in his hands. Satan is not king, but Jehovah Jesus is; therefore let us worship him, and rejoice evermore.

Why are we weak when we have divine strength to flee to? Why are we troubled when the Lord's own peace is ours? Jesus the mighty God is our peace — what a blessing is this today! What a blessing will be ours in that day of the Lord that will be in darkness, and will shed no light to the ungodly!

Dear reader, is not this a noble psalm to be sung in stormy weather? Can you sing amid the thunder? Will you be able to sing when the last thunders are let loose, and Jesus judges the living and the dead? If you are a believer, the last verse is your heritage, and surely that will set you singing.

Meditation: *There is far more royal power in the thunder of the Word, than in the word of thunder* (Joseph Caryl).

Psalm 30:1-5

Suggested further reading: 2 Samuel 7:1-11

I will extol your name, your character, your attributes, your mercy to me, your great patience with my people; but, I will especially speak well of you. O Jehovah, this will be my cheerful and constant employment! The psalmist's praise was reasonable. He had been drawn up like a prisoner from a dungeon, like Joseph out of the pit, and therefore he loved his deliverer. Grace has uplifted us from the pit of hell, from the ditch of sin, from the Slough of Despond, from the bed of sickness, from the bondage of doubts and fears: have we no song to offer for all this? How high has our Lord lifted us? Lifted us up into the children's place, to be adopted into the family; lifted us up into union with Christ, 'to sit together with him in heavenly places'. Lift high the name of our God, for he has lifted us above the stars.

David sent up prayers for himself and for his people when visited with the pestilence. He went at once to headquarters, and not round about to fallible means. God is the best physician, even for our bodily infirmities. We act very wickedly and foolishly when we forget God. Thrice happy is he who can claim the Lord himself to be his portion. Note how David's faith ascends the scale; he sang 'O Lord' in the first verse, but it is 'O Lord my God', in the second. Heavenly heart-music is something that ascends like the pillars of smoke that rose from the altar of incense. I could hardly pray, but I cried; I poured out my soul as a little child pours out its desires. I cried to my God: I knew to whom to cry; I did not cry to my friends, or to any arm of flesh. Hence the sure and satisfactory result, you have healed me. I know it. I am sure of it. I have the evidence of spiritual health within me now: glory to your name! Every humble suppliant with God who seeks release from the disease of sin shall act as quickly as the psalmist did, but those who will not so much as seek a cure need not wonder if their wounds putrefy and their soul dies.

He felt that he could not praise God enough himself, and therefore he would enlist the hearts of others. David would not fill his choir with reprobates, but with sanctified persons, who could sing from their hearts. He calls to you, people of God, because you are saints: and if sinners are wickedly silent, let your holiness constrain you to sing. You are his saints, chosen, blood-bought, called, and set apart for God; sanctified on purpose that you should offer the daily sacrifice of praise. Abound in this heavenly duty. Mourning only lasts till morning: when the night is gone the gloom shall vanish. This is adduced as a reason for saintly singing, and a forcible reason it is; short nights and merry days call for the psaltery and harp.

Meditation: *None but saints are fit to sing of holiness, and specially of God's holiness; but most specially with songs of holiness* (Sir Richard Baker).

Psalm 30:6-12

Suggested further reading: 2 Samuel 7:12-17

Because I happen to be prosperous today, I must not fancy that I shall be in my high estate tomorrow. As in a wheel, the uppermost spokes descend to the bottom in due course; so it is with mortal conditions. There is a constant revolution; many who are in the dust today shall be highly elevated tomorrow, while those who are now aloft shall soon grind the earth. Prosperity had evidently turned the psalmist's head, or he would not have been so self-confident. He stood by grace, and yet forgot himself, and so met with a fall. Reader, is there not much of the same proud stuff in all our hearts? Let us beware lest the fumes of intoxicating success get into our brains and make fools of us also.

He ascribed his prosperity to the Lord's favour — so good, it is right to acknowledge the hand of the Lord in all our stability and wealth. But observe that the good in a good man is not unmingled good, for this was alloyed with carnal security. He compares his state to a mountain: a molehill would have been nearer — we never think too little of ourselves. Ah, vain conceit, too common to us all! How soon the bubble bursts when God's people get conceit into their heads, and fancy that they are to enjoy immutability beneath the stars, and constancy upon this whirling orb.

Prayer is the unfailing resource of God's people. If they are driven to their wits' end, they may still go to the mercy seat. When an earthquake makes our mountain tremble, the throne of grace still stands firm, and we may come to it.

Let us never forget to pray, and let us never doubt the success of prayer. The hand that wounds can heal; let us turn to him who smites us, and he will hear our entreaties. Mirth and carnal amusements are a sorry prescription for a distracted and despairing mind: prayer will succeed where all else fails. David's prayer was an argument with God, an urging of reasons, a pleading of his cause. It was not a statement of doctrinal opinions, nor a narration of experience, much less a sly hit at other people under pretence of praying to God, although all these things and worse have been substituted for holy supplication at certain prayer meetings. He wrestled with the angel of the covenant with vehement pleadings, and therefore he prevailed. Head and heart, judgement and affections, memory and intellect were all at work to spread the case aright before the Lord of love.

If God hears prayer, it is a great act of mercy; our petitions do not merit a reply. It would be a shameful crime, if, after receiving God's mercies, we should forget to praise him. God would not have our tongues lie idle while so many themes for gratitude are spread on every hand. He would have no dumb children in the house. They are all to sing in heaven, and therefore they should all sing on earth.

Meditation: *What is praise? The rent we owe to God; and the larger the farm the greater the rent should be* (G. S. Bowes).

Psalm 31:1-13

Suggested further reading: 1 Samuel 23:1-5

The psalmist has one refuge, and the best one at that. He casts out the great sheet anchor of his faith in the time of storm. Though other things may be doubtful, David lays down most positively the fact that he relies upon the Lord; and he begins with it, lest under stress of trial he should afterwards forget it. This avowal of faith is the fulcrum by which he labours to uplift and remove his trouble. He dwells upon it as a comfort to himself and a plea with God. How can the Lord permit the man who depends alone upon him to be ultimately put to shame? This would not be dealing like a God of truth and grace. It would bring dishonour upon God himself if faith were not in the end rewarded. It will be an ill day indeed for religion when trust in God brings no consolation and no assistance.

The tried soul avows its full confidence in God. Faith's repetitions are not vain. The avowal of our reliance upon God in times of adversity is a principal method of glorifying him. The enemies of David were cunning as well as mighty; if they could not conquer him by power, they would capture him by craft. Our own spiritual foes are of the same order — they are of the serpent's brood, and seek to ensnare us by their guile. The prayer before us supposes the possibility of the believer being caught like a bird; and, indeed, we are so foolish that this often happens. The fowler does his work so deftly that any who are unsuspecting are soon surrounded by it. The text asks for the deliverance of the captive one, even out of the meshes of the net. This is a proper petition and one that can be granted; eternal love can rescue the saint from between the jaws of the lion and out of the belly of hell.

The ungodly act in concert in their onslaughts upon the excellent of the earth: it is a wonder how sinners are often better agreed than saints, and generally set about their wicked work with much more care and foresight than the righteous exhibit in holy enterprises. Observe the cruelty of a good man's foes! They will be content with nothing less than his blood — this is what they plot and scheme for. It is better to fall under the power of a lion than under the will of malicious persecutors, for the beast may spare its prey if it is fed to the full; but malice is unrelenting and cruel as a wolf. Of all fiends the most cruel is envy. What a terrible situation the psalmist found himself in, when the poisoned arrows of a thousand bows were all aimed at his life! Yet in all this his faith did not fail him, nor did his God forsake him. Here is encouragement for us.

Meditation: *If David prays against being ashamed, let us strive against it. Lovers of Jesus should be ashamed of being ashamed* (C. H. Spurgeon).

Psalm 31:14-24

Suggested further reading: 1 Samuel 23:6-13

Notwithstanding all afflicting circumstances, David's faith maintained its hold, and was not turned aside from its object. What a blessed saving clause is this! So long as our faith, which is our shield, is safe, the battle may be hard, but there is no question of its ultimate result. If that could be torn from us, we should be slain as surely as Saul and Jonathan were, upon the high places of the field. He proclaimed aloud his determined allegiance to Jehovah. He was no fair-weather believer, he could hold to his faith in a sharp frost, and wrap it about him as a garment fitted to keep out all the ills of time.

The sovereign arbiter of destiny holds in his own power all the issues of our life; we are not waifs and strays upon the ocean of fate, but are steered by infinite wisdom towards our desired haven. Providence is a soft pillow for anxious heads, an anodyne for care, a grave for despair. It is lawful to desire escape from persecution if it is the Lord's will; and when this may not be granted us in the form which we desire, sustaining grace will give us deliverance in another form, by enabling us to laugh to scorn all the fury of the foe.

Truly the life of faith is a miracle. When faith led David to his God, she set him singing at once. He does not tell us how great was God's goodness, for he could not; there are no measures that can set forth the immeasurable goodness of Jehovah, who is goodness itself. Holy amazement uses interjections where adjectives utterly fail. If we cannot measure we can marvel; and though we may not calculate with accuracy, we can adore with fervency. Heavenly mercy is not all hidden in the storehouse; it has already revealed itself in a thousand ways on behalf of those who are bold to avow their confidence in God. The goodness of the Lord has been displayed before their fellow men, that a faithless generation might stand rebuked. The proofs of the Lord's favour to believers are overwhelming; history teems with amazing instances, and our own lives are full of prodigies of grace. We serve a good Master. Faith receives a large reward even now, but looks for her full inheritance in the future. Who would not desire to take his lot with the servants of a Master whose boundless love fills all holy minds with astonishment? If saints do not love the Lord, who will? Love is the universal debt of all the saved family: who would wish to be exonerated from its payment? Reasons for love are given, for believing love is not blind. Every one of you, lift up your heads and sing for joy of heart. God is faithful, and does not fail even his little children who do but hope. Why then should we be afraid?

Meditation: *When the cloud of trouble hides the Lord's favour, faith knows it may shine again, and therefore prays through the cloud for its dissolving* (David Dickson).

Psalm 32:1-5

Suggested further reading: Romans 4:1-8

Like the Sermon on the Mount, this psalm begins with beatitudes. This is the second psalm of benediction. The first
psalm describes the result of holy blessedness, the thirty-
second details its cause. The first pictures the tree in full
growth, this depicts it in its first planting and watering. He
who in the first psalm is a reader of God's book is here a
suppliant at God's throne, accepted and heard. Note the
three words so often used to denote our disobedience: transgression, sin and iniquity are the three-headed dog at the
gates of hell, but our glorious Lord has silenced its barking
for ever against his own believing ones. The trinity of sin is
overcome by the Trinity of heaven. He is blessed indeed
who has a substitute to stand for him, to whose account all
his debts may be set down.

What a killer sin is! It is a pestilent disease! A fire in the
bones! While we smother our sin it rages within, and like a
gathering wound swells horribly and torments terribly. He
was silent as to confession, but not as to sorrow. Horror at
his great guilt drove David to incessant laments, until his
voice was no longer like the articulate speech of man, but
so full of sighing and groaning that it resembled the hoarse
roaring of a wounded beast. None know the pangs of conviction but those who have endured them. The Spanish
Inquisition, with all its tortures, was nothing to the inquest
which conscience holds within the heart. God's finger can
crush us — what must his hand be, and pressing so heavily

and continuously! Under terrors of conscience, men have little rest by night, for the grim thoughts of the day dog them to their chambers and haunt their dreams, or else they lie awake in a cold sweat of dread. God's hand is very helpful when it uplifts, but it is awful when it presses down. Better a world on the shoulder, like Atlas, than God's hand on the heart, like David.

After long lingering, the broken heart reminded itself of what it ought to have done at the first, and laid bare its bosom before the Lord. The lancet must be let into the gathering ulcer before relief can be afforded. The least thing we can do, if we would be pardoned, is to acknowledge our fault; if we are too proud for this we doubly deserve punishment. We must confess the guilt as well as the fact of sin. It is useless to conceal it, for it is well known to God; it is beneficial to us to acknowledge it, for a full confession softens and humbles the heart. We must as far as possible unveil the secrets of the soul, dig up the hidden treasure of Achan, and by weight and measure bring out our sins. Not only was the sin itself pardoned, but also its iniquity; the virus of its guilt was put away immediately, as soon as it was acknowledged.

Meditation: *God's pardons are deep and thorough: the knife of mercy cuts at the roots of the ill weed of sin* (C. H. Spurgeon).

Psalm 32:6-11

Suggested further reading: Isaiah 55:1-7

Remarkable answers to prayer very much quicken the prayerfulness of other godly persons. Where one finds a golden nugget, others feel inclined to dig. The benefit of our experience to others should reconcile us to it. No doubt the case of David has led thousands to seek the Lord with hopeful courage who, without such an instance to cheer them, might have died in despair. The mercy seat is the way to heaven for all who shall ever come there.

In the eighth verse, the Lord is the speaker, and gives the psalmist an answer to his prayer. Our Saviour is our instructor. The Lord himself deigns to teach his children to walk in the way of integrity; his holy word and the admonitions of the Holy Spirit are the directors of the believer's daily conversation. We are not pardoned that we may live after our own lusts from then on, but that we may be educated in holiness and trained for perfection. A heavenly training is one of the covenant blessings which adoption seals to us: 'All your children shall be taught by the Lord.' Understanding separates man from a brute; let us not act as if we were devoid of it. Men should take counsel and advice, and be ready to run where wisdom points the way. Alas! We need to be cautioned against stupidity of heart, for we are very apt to fall into it. He who sows sin will reap sorrow in heavy sheaves. Sorrows of conscience, of disappointment, of terror, are the sinner's sure heritage in time, and then sorrows of remorse and despair for ever. Let those who boast of present sinful joys remember the 'shall be' of the future, and take warning.

Faith is placed as the opposite of wickedness, since it is the source of virtue. Faith in God is the great charmer of life's cares, and he who possesses it dwells in an atmosphere of grace, surrounded with a bodyguard of mercies. May the Lord grant us at all times to believe in the mercy of God, even when we cannot see traces of its working, for to the believer, mercy is as all-surrounding as omniscience, and every thought and act of God is perfumed with it. The wicked have a hive of wasps around them; but we have a swarm of bees storing honey for us.

We are not to be glad in sin, or to find comfort in corn, and wine, and oil, but the garden of our soul's delight is to be in our God. That there is a God and such a God, and that he is ours, ours for ever, our Father and our reconciled Lord, is matter enough for a never-ending psalm of rapturous joy. Since God has clothed his choristers in the white garments of holiness, let them not restrain their joyful voices, but sing aloud and shout as those who find great spoil.

Meditation: *Reader, this is a delightful psalm! Have you, in perusing it, been able to claim a lot in the goodly land? If so, publish to others the way of salvation* (C. H. Spurgeon).

Psalm 33:1-11

Suggested further reading: Job 26:1-14

Joy is the soul of praise. To delight in God is most truly to extol him, even if we let no notes of song proceed from our lips. That God is, and that he is such a God, and our God, ours for ever and ever, should wake within us an unceasing and overflowing joy. To rejoice in temporal comforts is dangerous, to rejoice in self is foolish, to rejoice in sin is fatal, but to rejoice in God is heavenly. Even the righteous are not always glad, and need to be stirred up to enjoy their privileges.

God's ordinances, natural, moral and spiritual, are right, and especially his incarnate Word, who is the Lord our righteousness. Whatever God has ordained must be good, and just, and excellent. There are no anomalies in God's universe, except what sin has made; his word of command made all things good. When we look at his word of promise, and remember its faithfulness, what reasons we have for joy and thankfulness! His work is the outflow of his word, and it is true to it. He neither does nor says anything ill; in deed and speech he agrees with himself and the purest truth. There is no lie in God's word, and no sham in his works; in creation, providence and revelation, unalloyed truth abounds. To act truth as well as to utter it is divine, let not children of God ever yield their principles in practice any more than in heart. What a God we serve! The more we know of him, the more our better natures approve his surpassing excellence; even his afflicting works are according to his truthful word.

Creation was the fruit of a word. Jehovah said, 'Let there be light', and there was light. The Lord's acts are sublime in their ease. Creation came forth out of nothing, and was confirmed in existence. The same power which first up-lifted, now sustains the universe; although we may not observe it, there is as great a display of sublime power in confirming as in creating. Happy is the man who has learned to lean his all upon the sure word of the one who built the skies!

The cause of God is never in danger: infernal craft is outwitted by infinite wisdom, and satanic malice held in check by boundless power. He does not change his pur-pose, his decree is not frustrated, his designs are accom-plished. Men's purposes are blown to and fro like the thread of the gossamer or the down of the thistle, but the eternal purposes are firmer than the earth. Men come and go, sons follow their fathers to the grave, but the undisturbed mind of God moves on in unbroken serenity, producing ordained results with unerring certainty.

Meditation: *It is not an easy matter to praise God aright; it must be done with the very best of the very best* (John Trapp).

Psalm 33:12-22

Suggested further reading: Job 28:20-28

Israel was happy in the worship of the only true God. The chosen nation was indeed blessed to have received a revelation from Jehovah. While others grovelled before their idols, the chosen people were elevated by a spiritual religion that introduced them to the invisible God, and led them to trust in him. All who confide in the Lord are blessed in the largest and deepest sense, and none can reverse the blessing. Election is at the bottom of it all. The divine choice rules the day; none take Jehovah to be their God till he takes them to be his people. What an ennobling choice this is! We are selected to no mean estate, and for no ignoble purpose: we are made the peculiar domain and delight of the Lord our God. Being so blessed, let us rejoice in our portion, and show the world by our lives that we serve a glorious Master.

The Lord is represented as dwelling above and looking down below; seeing all things, but peculiarly observing and caring for those who trust in him. It is one of our choicest privileges to be always under our Father's eye, to be never out of sight of our best Friend. All Adam's sons are as well watched as was Adam himself, their lone progenitor in the garden. Ranging from the frozen pole to the scorching equator, dwelling in hills and valleys, in huts and palaces, the divine eye regards all the members of the family of man alike.

All men equally owe the possession of life to the Creator, and have therefore no reason to boast themselves. What reason has the vessel to glorify itself in the presence of the potter? God does not see men's acts in vain: he ponders and judges them. He reads the secret design in the outward behaviour, and resolves the apparent good into its real elements. This consideration is a token of a judgement to come, when the results of the divine thoughts will be meted out in measures of happiness or woe. Consider your ways, O man, for God considers them!

The eye of peculiar care is the glory and defence of God's people. None can take them unawares, for the celestial watcher foresees the designs of their enemies, and provides against them. They who fear God need not fear anything else: let them fix their eye of faith on him, and his eye of love will always rest upon them. Our soul, our life, must hang upon God; we are not to trust him with a few baubles, but with all we have and are. We, who trust, cannot but be of a glad heart, our inmost nature must triumph in our faithful God. The root of faith in due time bears the flower of rejoicing. Doubts breed sorrow, confidence creates joy.

Meditation: *Lest it should be thought that men obtain so great a good by their own efforts and industry, David teaches us expressly that it proceeds from the fountain of God's gracious, electing love that we are accounted the people of God* (John Calvin).

Psalm 34:1-10

Suggested further reading: 1 Samuel 21:10-15

David knows to whom praise is due, and what is due, and for what and when. To Jehovah, and not to second causes, our gratitude is to be rendered. The Lord has a monopoly in his creatures' praise by right. Even when a mercy reminds us of our sin, as in this case David's deliverance from the Philistine monarch was sure to do, we are not to rob God of his recompense of honour because our conscience justly censures our part in the transaction.

The confident expressions of tried believers are a rich solace to their less experienced brethren. We ought to talk of the Lord's goodness particularly so that others may be confirmed in their trust in a faithful God. It is well when the soul feels its own inability to glorify the Lord adequately, and therefore stirs up others to the gracious work; this is good both for the man himself and for his companions. Social, congregated worship is the outgrowth of one of the natural instincts of the new life. In heaven it is enjoyed to the full, and earth is most like heaven where it abounds.

David must have prayed in a very confused manner, and there must have been much self-sufficiency in his prayer, or he would not have resorted to methods of such dubious morality as pretending to be mad and behaving as a lunatic. Yet his poor limping prayer was accepted and brought him succour: the more reason for them celebrating the abounding mercy of the Lord. We may seek God even when we have sinned. If sin could blockade the mercy seat it would be all over for us, but the mercy is that there are gifts even for the rebellious, and an advocate for men who sin. The psalmist avows that his case was not at all peculiar, it was matched in the lives of all the faithful; each one of them, on looking to their Lord, were brightened up, their faces began to shine, their spirits were uplifted. What a means of blessing one look at the Lord may be! There is life, light, liberty, love, everything in fact, in a look at the crucified one.

Faith is the soul's taste; they who test the Lord by their confidence always find him good, and they themselves become blessed. Jehovah will not allow his faithful servants to starve. He may not give luxuries, but the promise binds him to supply necessities, and he will not run back from his word. Many whims and wishes may remain ungratified, but real wants the Lord will supply. No really good thing shall be denied to those whose first and main end in life is to seek the Lord. Men may call them fools, but the Lord will prove them wise.

Meditation: *Take a survey of heaven and earth and all things therein, and whatever upon sure ground appears good, ask it confidently of Christ* (David Clarkson).

Psalm 34:11-22

Suggested further reading: Proverbs 1:7-19

Though a warrior and a king, the psalmist was not ashamed
to teach children. Children are the most hopeful persons to
teach; wise men who wish to propagate their principles
take care to win the ear of the young. So far as they can be
taught by word of mouth, or learned by the hearing of the
ear, we are to communicate the faith and fear of God, in-
culcating upon the rising generation the principles and
practices of piety. We must get them away, apart from toys
and sports, and try to occupy their minds with better pursuits; for we cannot teach them well while their minds are
full of other things. We must drive at the main point always,
and keep the fear of the Lord ever uppermost in our teachings, and in so doing we may discreetly cast our own personality into the scale by narrating our own experiences
and convictions.

Life spent in happiness is the desire of all, and he who
can give the young a recipe for leading a happy life deserves to be popular among them. Mere existence is not
life; the art of living, truly, really, and joyfully living, is not
given to all men to know. To teach men how to live and
how to die is the aim of all useful religious instruction.
The rewards of virtue are the baits with which the young
are to be drawn to morality. While we teach piety towards
God we should also dwell much upon morality towards
man.

The Lord observes the righteous with approval and tender consideration; they are so dear to him that he cannot take his eyes off them; he watches each one of them as carefully and intently as if they were the only one creature in the universe. His eyes and ears are both turned towards his saints; his whole mind is occupied with them: if slighted by all others they are not neglected by him. He hears their cry at once, even as a mother is sure to hear her sick baby; the cry may be broken, plaintive, unhappy, feeble, unbelieving, yet the Father's quick ear catches each note of lament or appeal, and he is not slow to answer his children's voice. The same Lord who sends the afflictions will also recall them when his design is accomplished, but he will never allow the fiercest of them to rend and devour his beloved.

Divine love watches over every believer as it did over Jesus. No fatal injury shall happen to us, we shall neither be crippled nor maimed in the kingdom, but shall be presented after life's trials are over without spot or wrinkle or any such thing, being preserved in Christ Jesus, and kept by the power of God through faith unto salvation. Believer, you will never be deserted, forsaken, given up to ruin. God, even your God, is your guardian and friend, and bliss is yours.

Meditation: *Though our troubles are many in number, strange in nature, heavy in measure, yet God's mercies are more numerous, his wisdom more wondrous, his power more miraculous; he will deliver us out of all* (Thomas Adams).

Psalm 35:1-10

Suggested further reading: 2 Timothy 4:14-18

Lord, plead against those who plead against me; strive with those who strive against me; contend with my contenders. If they urge their suit in the lawcourt, Lord, meet them there, and beat them with their own weapons. Every saint of God shall have this privilege: the accuser of the brethren shall be met by the Advocate of the saints. If my adversaries try force as well as fraud, be a match for them: oppose their strength with your strength. Jesus does this for all his beloved; he is both intercessor and champion for them; whatever aid they need they shall receive from him, and in whatever manner they are assaulted they shall be effectually defended. Let us not fail to leave our situation in the Lord's hand. The help of man is vain, but the intervention of heaven is ever effectual. What is here asked for as a boon may be regarded as a promise, to all the saints; in judgement they shall have a divine advocate, in warfare a divine protection.

In vivid metaphor the Lord is pictured as coming forth armed for battle, and placing himself between his servant and his enemies. This poetic imagery shows how the psalmist realized the existence and power of God; and thought of him as a real and actual person, truly working for his afflicted. There is a law of retribution with God, which often works most wonderfully. Men set traps and catch their own fingers. They throw up stones, and they fall upon their own heads. How often Satan outwits himself, and burns his fingers with his own coals! This will doubtless be one of the aggravations of hell, that men will torment themselves with what were once the fond devices of their rebellious minds. They curse and are cursed; they kick the goads and tear themselves; they pour forth floods of fire, and it burns them within and without.

When rescued, David ascribes all the honour to the Judge of the right; to his own courageous arm he offers no sacrifice of boasting. He turns away from his adversaries to his God, and finds a deep unbroken joy in Jehovah; and in that joy his spirit revels. We do not triumph in the destruction of others, but in the salvation given to us of God. Prayer heard should always suggest praise. It would be well if we were more demonstrative in our holy rejoicing. We rob God by suppressing grateful emotions.

God is the champion, the true knight-errant of all those who are oppressed. Where there is so much condescension, justice, kindness, power and compassion, the loftiest songs should be rendered. Come, dear reader, have you not been delivered from sin, Satan and death, and will you not bless the Redeemer? You were poor and weak, but in due time Christ sought you, and set you free. Oh, magnify the Lord today, and speak well of his name!

Meditation: *Whatever strength and vigour is in me it shall be spent in celebrating your praises* (John Trapp).

Psalm 35:11-18

Suggested further reading: Acts 7:54-60

David had been a man of sympathy; he had mourned when Saul was in ill health, putting on the weeds of sorrow for him as though he were a near and dear friend. His heart went into mourning for his sick master. He prayed for his enemy, and made the sick man's case his own, pleading and confessing as if his own personal sin had brought on the evil. This showed a noble spirit in David, and greatly aggravated the baseness of those who now so cruelly persecuted him.

Prayer is never lost: if it does not bless those for whom intercession is made, it shall bless the intercessors. Clouds do not always descend in showers upon the same spot from which the vapours ascended, but they come down somewhere; and in the same way, supplications yield their showers of mercy in some place or other. If our dove finds no rest for the sole of her foot among our enemies, it shall fly into our bosoms and bring an olive branch of peace in its mouth. How sharp is the contrast all through this psalm between the righteous and his enemies! We must be earnest in keeping the line of demarcation broad and clear.

The strongest natural grief was just what David felt when his former companions were in trouble. The mother usually wins the deepest love, and her loss is most keenly felt; such was David's grief. How few professors in these days have such a heart of compassion; and yet under the gospel there should be far more tender love than under the law.

Had we more hearty love to manhood, and care for its innumerable ills, we might be far more useful; certainly we should be infinitely more Christlike. He who loves best prays best.

David cried out, 'Lord, how long will you look on?' Why be a mere spectator? Why so neglectful of your servant? Are you indifferent? Do you not care that we perish? We may thus reason with the Lord. He permits us this familiarity. There is a time for our salvation, but to our impatience it often seems to be very slow in coming; yet wisdom has ordained the hour, and nothing shall delay it. His enemies were fierce, cunning, and strong as young lions; only God could deliver him from their jaws, to God he therefore addresses himself.

Notable deliverances must be recorded, and their fame emblazoned. All the saints should be informed of the Lord's goodness. The theme is worthy of the largest assembly; the experience of a believer is a subject fit for an assembled universe to hear about. Most men publish their grief; good men should proclaim their mercies. Among friends and foes will I glorify the God of my salvation! Praise, personal praise, public praise, perpetual praise, should be the daily revenue of the King of heaven. Thus, for the second time, David's prayer ends in praise, as indeed all prayer should.

Meditation: *The wicked would strip the righteous naked to their very souls: they know no pity. There are only such limits to human malice as God himself may see fit to place* (C. H. Spurgeon).

Psalm 35:19-28

Suggested further reading: Luke 20:20-26

David would have been an orderly citizen, but his adversaries laboured to make him a rebel. He could do nothing right, all his dealings were misrepresented. It is an old trick of the enemy to brand good men with S.S. on their cheeks, as sowers of sedition, though they have always been a harmless race, like sheep among wolves. When mischief is meant, mischief is soon made. Unscrupulous partisans could even charge Jesus with seeking to overturn Caesar. How much more will they accuse his household in this way!

Our heavenly Father knows all our sorrow. Here is comfort. Omniscience is the saint's candle, which never goes out. A father will not endure seeing his child abused for long. Shall not God avenge his own elect? Rebuke your enemies and mine, O Lord. A word will do it. Clear my character, comfort my heart. Walk the furnace with me. Stand in the pillory at my side. The sweet presence of God is the divine cordial of the persecuted; his painful absence would be their deepest misery. David claims a nearness to his God, he holds him with both hands; he leaves his case with the righteous Judge. He begs that the suit may be brought on, heard, tried, and verdict given. It is good for a man when his conscience is so clear that he dares to make such an appeal.

What is the eternal result of all the laborious and crafty devices of the Lord's enemies? God will make little of them, though they 'magnify themselves'. He will shame them for shaming his people, bring them to confusion for making confusion, pull off their fine apparel and give them a beggarly suit of dishonour, and turn all their rejoicing into weeping and wailing, and gnashing of teeth. Truly, the saints can afford to wait.

Those who could not render him active aid, but in their hearts favoured him, David would have the Lord reward most abundantly. Men of tender heart set great store by the good wishes and prayers of the Lord's people. Jesus also prizes those whose hearts are with his cause. The day is coming when shouts of victory shall be raised by all who are on Christ's side, for the battle will turn, and the foes of truth will be routed. He would have their gladness contribute to the divine glory; they are not to shout to David's praise, but for the honour of Jehovah. Such acclamations may rightly be continued throughout time and eternity. Unceasing praise is vowed to the just and gracious God. From morning till evening the grateful tongue would talk and sing, and glorify the Lord. Oh, for such a resolve carried out by us all!

Meditation: *In the innocence of your works prepare yourself to praise God all the day long* (Augustine).

Psalm 36:1-4

Suggested further reading: Proverbs 4:14-19

Men's sins have a voice to godly ears. They are the outer index of an inner evil. Despite the professions of unrighteous men, when we see their unhallowed actions our heart is driven to the conclusion that they have no religion whatever. Unholiness is clear evidence of ungodliness. Wickedness is the fruit of an atheistic root. This may be made clear to the candid head by cogent reasoning, but it is clear already and intuitively to the pious heart. If God is everywhere, and I fear him, how can I dare to break his laws in his very presence? He must be a desperate traitor who will rebel in the monarch's own halls. Whatever theoretical opinions bad men may avow, they can only be classed with atheists, since, practically, this is what they are. Those eyes that have no fear of God before them now shall have the terrors of hell before them for ever.

David runs over the process of reasoning by which he had become convinced that wicked men have no proper idea of God or respect for him. God-fearing men see their sins and bewail them; where the reverse is the case we may be sure there is no fear of God. The sinner counts himself a fine fellow, worthy of great respect. He quiets his conscience, and so deceives his own judgement that he reckons he is a pattern of excellence; if not for morality, yet for having sense enough not to be enslaved by rules which are bonds to others. He is the freethinker, the man of strong mind, the philosopher; and the servants of God are, in his esteem, mean-spirited and narrow-minded. Of all flatteries this is the most absurd and dangerous. The descent to eternal ruin is easy enough, without making a sliding step of it, as self-flatterers do. In the end, he is found out and detested, despite his self-conceit. There is a limit to a man's self-congratulation; he is found out amid general scorn, and can no longer keep up the farce that he played so well. If this does not happen in this life, the hand of death will let light in upon the covered character, and expose the sinner to shame and contempt.

The self-flattering process plainly proves the atheism of sinners, since the bare reflection that God sees them would render such self-flatteries extremely difficult, if not impossible. Belief in God, like light, reveals, and then our sin and evil are perceived; but wicked men are in the dark, for they cannot see what is so clearly within them and around them that it stares them in the face.

What a portrait of a graceless man these few verses afford us! His jauntiness of conscience, his licentiousness of speech, his intent upon wrongdoing, his deliberate and continued preference of iniquity, and his atheistic heart as well, are all photographed to life. Lord, save us from being like this.

Meditation: *The wicked man has no regard to the oracles of God: he has one in his own heart, which dictates nothing but rebellion* (Zachary Mudge).

Psalm 36:5-12

Suggested further reading: John 8:12-20

Far, far above all comprehension is the truth and faithfulness of God. He never fails, nor forgets, nor falters, nor forfeits his word. Afflictions are like clouds, but the divine truthfulness is all around them. While we are under the cloud we are in the region of God's faithfulness; when we mount above it we shall not need such an assurance. To every word of threat, or promise, prophecy or covenant, the Lord has exactly adhered, for he is not a man that he should lie, nor the son of man that he should repent. Who can bribe the Judge of all the earth, or who can, by threatening, compel him to pervert judgement? Not even to save his elect would the Lord allow his righteousness to be set aside. All the myriads of creatures, rational and irrational, are fed by Jehovah's hand. The countless beasts, the innumerable birds, the inconceivable abundance of fishes, the all but infinite armies of insects, all owe their continuance in life to the unceasing outgoings of the divine power. What a view of God this presents to us! What a debased creature must he be who sees no trace of such a God, and feels no awe of him!

Benevolence, and mercy, and justice, are everywhere, but the excellence of that mercy is known only by those whose faith has lifted the veil and passed into the brighter presence of the Lord; these behold the excellence of the Lord's mercy. No gem or pearl can ever equal in value a sense of the Lord's love. Kings' regalia are a beggarly collection of worthless pebbles when compared with the tender mercy of Jehovah. David could not estimate it, and therefore, after putting a note of admiration, he left our hearts and imagination, and, better still, our experience, to fill up the rest.

Light is the glory of life. Life in the dark is misery, and rather death than life. The Lord alone can give natural, intellectual and spiritual life; he alone can make life bright and lustrous. In spiritual things the knowledge of God sheds a light on all other subjects. We need no candle to see the sun, we see it by its own radiance, and then see everything else by the same lustre. We never see Jesus by the light of self, but self in the light of Jesus. No inward intelligence of ours leads us to receive the Spirit's light, but rather, it often helps to quench the sacred beam; purely and only by his own illumination, the Holy Ghost lights up the dark recesses of our heart's ungodliness. Vain are those who look to learning and human wit; one ray from the throne of God is better than the noonday splendour of created wisdom. Lord, give me the sun, and let those who wish to, delight in the wax candles of superstition and the phosphorescence of corrupt philosophy. Faith derives both light and life from God, and so she neither dies nor darkens.

Meditation: *The light of nature is like a spark, the light of the gospel a lamp, the light of grace a star, but the light of glory the sun itself* (Thomas Adams).

Psalm 37:1-8

Suggested further reading: Psalm 73:1-9

It is, alas, too common for believers in their hours of adversity to think themselves harshly dealt with when they see persons utterly destitute of religion and honesty rejoicing in abundant prosperity! To fret is to worry, to have the heart burn, to fume, to become vexed. Nature is very apt to kindle a fire of jealousy when it sees law-breakers riding on horses, and obedient subjects walking in the mire. It is a lesson learned only in the school of grace, when one comes to view the most paradoxical providences with the devout complaisance of one who is sure that the Lord is righteous in all his acts. Faith cures fretting. Sight is cross-eyed, and views things only as they seem, hence her envy; faith has clearer optics to behold things as they really are, hence her peace. True faith is actively obedient. Doing good is a fine remedy for fretting. There is a joy in holy activity that drives away the rust of discontent.

He who was first bidden not to fret was next commanded actively to trust, and then is told with holy desire to delight in God. Make Jehovah the joy and rejoicing of your spirit. Bad men delight in carnal objects; do not envy them if they are allowed to take their fill in such vain idols; look to your better delight, and fill yourself to the full with your nobler portion. In a certain sense imitate the wicked; they delight in their portion — take care to delight in yours, and so, far from envying, you will pity them. There is no room for fretting if we remember that God is ours, but there is every incentive to sacred enjoyment of the most elevated and ecstatic kind. Every name, attribute, word, or deed of Jehovah should be delightful to us, and in meditating upon it our soul should be as glad as the epicure who feeds delicately with a profound relish for his dainties.

In the matter of personal reputation we may especially be content to be quiet, and leave our vindication with the Judge of all the earth. The more we fret in this case, the worse for us. Our strength is to sit still. The Lord will clear the slandered. If we look to his honour, he will see to ours. To hush the spirit, to be silent before the Lord, to wait with holy patience the time for clearing up the difficulties of providence — this is what every gracious heart should aim at. A silent tongue in many cases not only shows a wise head, but a holy heart. Time is nothing to him; let it be nothing to you. God is worth waiting for.

Fretfulness lies upon the verge of great sin. Many who have indulged a murmuring disposition have in the end come to sin, in order to gain their fancied rights. Beware of carping at others, take care that you yourself are on the right path; and as you would dread outward sin, tremble at inward repining.

Meditation: *The desires of God and the desires of the righteous agree in one; they are of one mind in their desires* (John Bunyan).

Psalm 37:9-15

Suggested further reading: Hebrews 10:26-31

Those who in patient faith expect their portion in another life 'shall inherit the earth'. Even in this life they have the most of real enjoyment, and in the ages to come theirs shall be the glory and the triumph. Passion, according to Bunyan's parable, has his good things first, and they are soon over. Patience has his good things last, and they last for ever. Even if they suffer, their consolations shall exceed their tribulations. By inheriting the land is meant obtaining covenant privileges and the salvation of God. Those who are truly humble shall take their lot with the rest of the heirs of grace, to whom all good things come by a sacred birthright.

Why cannot the wicked let the good man alone? Because there is enmity between the serpent's seed and the seed of the woman. Why not attack him fairly? Why plot and scheme? Because it is according to the serpent's nature to be very subtle. The godly man need not trouble himself, but leave well-deserved vengeance to be dealt out by the Lord, who will utterly deride the malice of the good man's enemies. Let the proud scorner gnash his teeth and foam at the mouth; he has one to deal with who will look down upon him and his ravings with serene contempt. The evil man does not see how close his destruction is upon his heels; he boasts of crushing others when the foot of justice is already uplifted to trample him as the mire of the streets. Sinners, in the hand of an angry God, and yet plotting against his children! Poor souls, to run like this upon the point of Jehovah's spear.

The unrighteous hold their weapon out of its sheath, and watch for a time to use it. One weapon is not enough, they carry another ready for action. The poor and needy are their game, the objects of their accursed malice. These cowards do not attack their equals, but seek out those excellent ones who, from the gentleness of their spirits and the poverty of their estates, are not able to defend themselves. But like Haman they shall be hanged upon the gallows built by themselves for Mordecai. This has been the case hundreds of times. Saul, who sought to slay David, fell on his own sword; and the bow, his favourite weapon, which he taught the children of Israel to use, was not able to deliver him on Gilboa. Their inventions of evil shall be rendered useless. Malice outwits itself. It drinks the poisoned cup that it mixed for another, and burns itself in the fire which it kindled for its neighbour. Why need we fret at the prosperity of the wicked when they are so industriously ruining themselves while they fancy they are injuring the saints?

Meditation: *When the wicked are most near to do a mischief to the Lord's people, then is a mischief most near unto them* (David Dickson).

Psalm 37:16-24

Suggested further reading: Proverbs 15:14-19

These nine verses mainly describe the character and blessedness of the godly, and the light is brought out with a few black touches descriptive of the wicked and their doom.

The little of one good man is contrasted with the riches of many wicked, and so the expression has greater impact. There is more happiness in the godly dinner of herbs than in the stalled ox of profane rioters. In the original there is an allusion to the noise of a multitude, as if to hint at the turmoil and hurly-burly of riotous wealth, and to contrast it with the quiet of the humbler portion of the godly. We would sooner hunger with John than feast with Herod; better to feed on scant fare with the prophets in Obadiah's cave than riot with the priests of Baal. A man's happiness does not consist in the heaps of gold that he has in store.

God's foreknowledge made him laugh at the proud, but in the case of the upright he sees a brighter future, and treats them as heirs of salvation. It is ever our comfort that our God knows all events, and that nothing in our future can take him unawares. No arrow can pierce us by accident, no dagger smite us by stealth; neither in time nor in eternity can any unforeseen ill occur to us. Futurity shall be but a continual development of the good things that the Lord has laid up in store for us. God's benediction is true wealth after all. True happiness, such as the covenant secures to all the chosen of heaven, lies wrapped up in the divine favour. His frown is death, no, more, 'tis hell.

The whole course of life of a good man is graciously ordained, and in loving-kindness all is fixed, settled and maintained. No reckless fate, no fickle chance rules us; our every step is the subject of divine decree. All that concerns a saint is interesting to his heavenly Father. God loves to view the holy strivings of a soul pressing forward to the skies. In the trials and the joys of the faithful, Jesus has fellowship with them, and delights to be their sympathizing companion. No saint shall fall finally or fatally. Sorrow may bring us to the earth, and death may bring us to the grave, but lower we cannot sink, and out of the lowest of all we shall arise to the highest of all. Condescendingly, with his own hand, God upholds his saints; he does not leave them to mere delegated agency, he affords personal assistance. Even in our falls the Lord gives a measure of sustaining. Where grace does not keep from going down, it shall save from keeping down. Job had double wealth in the end, Joseph reigned over Egypt, and Jonah was safely landed.

Meditation: *It is not that the saints are strong, or wise, or meritorious, that therefore they rise after every fall, but because God is their helper, and therefore none can prevail against them* (C. H. Spurgeon).

Psalm 37:25-33

Suggested further reading: 2 Samuel 23:1-7

David's observation is not my observation just as it stands, for I have relieved the children of undoubtedly good men, who have appealed to me as common beggars. But this does not cast a doubt upon David's observation. He lived under a more outward dispensation, and more of this world than the present rule of personal faith. The righteous are never forsaken; that is a rule without exception. Seldom indeed do their descendants beg bread; and although it does occasionally occur, through dissipation, idleness, or some such causes on the part of their sons, yet doubtless it is so rare that there are many alive who never saw it. Poor ministers' sons often become rich. I am not old, but I have seen the families of the poor godly become rich, and have seen the Lord reward the faithfulness of the father in the success of the son. So I have often thought that the best way to endow one's children with wealth is to become poor for Christ's sake.

The righteous are constantly under generous impulses; they do not prosper through parsimony, but through bounty. Like the bounteous giver of all good, of whom they are the beloved sons, they delight in doing good. How stingy, covetous professors can hope for salvation is a wonder to those who read such verses as this in the Bible. God pays back with interest in the next generation. Where the children of the righteous are not godly, there must be some reason for it in parental neglect, or some other guilty cause. The friend of the father is the friend of the family. The God of Abraham is the God of Isaac and of Jacob.

We must not envy the doers of evil, but depart altogether from their spirit and example. As Lot left Sodom without casting a look behind, so must we leave sin. No truce or parley is to be held with sin, we must turn away from it without hesitation, and set ourselves practically to work in the opposite direction. He who neglects to do good will soon fall into evil. The awarding of honour to whom honour is due is God's delight, especially when the upright man has been slandered by his fellow men. It must be a divine pleasure to right wrongs, and to defeat the machinations of the unjust.

God often appears to deliver his servants, and when he does not do so in this life with regard to their bodies, he gives their souls such joy and peace that they triumphantly rise beyond their tormentor's power. We may be in the enemy's hand for a while, as Job was, but we cannot be left there. Time shall reverse the verdict of haste, or else eternity shall clear away the condemnation of time. In due season just men will be justified.

Meditation: *A good man may fall into wants, but good men are rarely, if ever or at all, left in them* (Joseph Caryl).

Psalm 37:34-40

Suggested further reading: 1 Kings 21:17-26

'Wait on the Lord.' We have here another precept, and it is a lofty eminence to attain. Tarry in obedience as a servant, in hope as an heir, in expectation as a believer. This little word 'wait' is easy to say, but hard to carry out; yet faith must do it. Continue in the narrow path; let no haste for riches or ease cause unholy action. Let your motto be, 'On, on, on.' Never flag, or dream of turning aside. You shall have all of earthly good which is really good, and of heavenly good there shall be no limit. Exaltation shall be the lot of the excellent.

If, moved by curiosity, we enquire after the ungodly, they have left no trace; like birds of ill omen none desire to remember them. Some of the humblest of the godly are immortalized, their names are imperishably fragrant in the church, while the names of the most able infidels and blasphemers will hardly be remembered beyond a few years. Men who were in everybody's mouths only yesterday will be forgotten tomorrow, for only virtue is immortal. After having watched with surprise the downfall of the wicked, give your attention to the sincerely godly man, and observe the blessed contrast. Good men are men of note, and are worth our study. Upright men are marvels of grace, and worth beholding. The man of peace has an end of peace. Peace without end comes in the end to the man of God. His way may be rough, but it leads home. With believers it may rain in the morning, thunder at midday, and pour in torrents in the afternoon, but it must clear up before the sun goes down. War may last till our last hour, but then we shall hear the last of it. 'The salvation of the righteous is of the Lord.' Sound doctrine this, the very marrow of the gospel of free grace. By salvation is meant deliverance of every kind; not only the salvation which finally lands us in glory, but all the minor rescues along the way; these are all to be ascribed to the Lord, and to him alone. Let him have glory from those to whom he grants salvation.

Faith shall ensure the safety of the elect. It is the mark by which the sheep shall be separated from the goats. Not their merit, but their believing, shall distinguish them. Who would not try the walk of faith? Whoever truly believes in God will be no longer fretful against the apparent irregularities of this present life, but will rest assured that what is mysterious is nevertheless just, and what seems hard is, beyond a doubt, ordered in mercy. So the psalm ends with a note which is the death-knell of the unholy anxiety with which the psalm commenced. Happy are they who can thus sing themselves out of an ill frame of mind into a more gracious condition.

Meditation: *While we are waiting let us take heed of wavering. Go not a step out of God's way* (Thomas Watson).

Psalm 38:1-8

Suggested further reading: Job 6:1-7

David felt as if he had been forgotten by his God, and, therefore, he recounted his sorrows and cried mightily for help under them: 'Rebuked I must be, for I am an erring child and you a careful Father, but do not throw too much anger into the tones of your voice; deal gently, although I have sinned grievously. The anger of others I can bear, but not yours. As your love is most sweet to my heart, so your displeasure is most cutting to my conscience. Chasten me if you will, it is a Father's prerogative, and to endure it obediently is a child's duty; but, oh, do not turn the rod into a sword, do not smite so as to kill. True, my sins might well inflame you, but let your mercy and long-suffering quench the glowing coals of wrath. Oh, let me not be treated as an enemy or dealt with as a rebel. Remember your covenant, your fatherhood, and my feebleness, and spare your servant.'

God's law, applied by the Spirit to the conviction of the soul of sin, wounds deeply and rankles long; it is an arrow not to be brushed out lightly by careless mirthfulness, or to be extracted by the flattering hand of self-righteousness. The Lord knows how to shoot so that his bolts not only strike but stick. He can make convictions sink into the innermost spirit like arrows driven in up to the head. It seems strange that the Lord should shoot at his own beloved ones, but in truth he shoots at their sins rather than them, and those who feel his sin-killing shafts in this life shall not be slain with his hot thunderbolts in the next world. The Holy

Spirit reminds us again and again of humiliating truth, tears away every ground of glorying, and makes us know that in us, that is, in our flesh, there dwells no good thing.

The voice of sorrow is deep and hoarse, and often inarticulate and terrible. The heart learns groanings that cannot be uttered, and the voice fails to tone and tune itself to human speech. When our prayers appear to be animal rather than spiritual, they are none the less prevalent with the compassionate Father of mercy. He hears the murmur of the heart and the roaring of the soul because of sin, and in due time he comes to relieve his afflicted.

The more closely the preceding portrait of an awakened soul is studied in the light of experience, the more will its striking accuracy appear. It cannot be a description of merely outward disorder, graphic as it might then be; it has a depth and pathos in it which only the soul's mysterious and awful agony can fully match.

Meditation: *Christ is the centre of the soul; the needle of the compass trembles till it comes to the North Pole* (Thomas Watson).

Psalm 38:9-15

Suggested further reading: Job 6:14-23

Blessed be God, he reads the longings of our hearts; nothing can be hidden from him; what we cannot tell him he perfectly understands. The psalmist is conscious that he has not exaggerated, and therefore appeals to heaven for a confirmation of his words. The good Physician understands the symptoms of our disease and sees the hidden evil that they reveal; hence our case is safe in his hands. Sorrow and anguish hide themselves from the observation of man, but God spies them out. There is none more lonely than the broken-hearted sinner, yet he has the Lord for his companion.

Verse ten begins another tale of woe. He was so dreadfully pained by the unkindness of friends, that his heart was in a state of perpetual palpitation. The soul seeks sympathy in sorrow, and if it finds none, its sorrowful heartthrobs become incessant. Whatever affection his friends might pretend to, they kept out of his company, lest as a sinking vessel often draws down boats with it, they might be made to suffer through his calamities. It is very hard when those who should be the first to come to the rescue are the first to desert us. In times of deep soul trouble even the most affectionate friends cannot enter into the sufferer's situation: anxious though they may be, they cannot bind up the sores of a tender conscience. Oh, the loneliness of a soul passing under the convincing power of the Holy Ghost!

Alas! for us when in addition to inward griefs, we are beset by outward temptations. David's foes endeavoured basely to ensnare him. If fair means would not overthrow him, foul should be tried. This snaring business is a vile one, the devil's own poachers alone condescend to it; but prayer to God will deliver us, for the craft of the entire college of tempters can be met and overcome by those who are led of the Spirit. Lies and slanders poured from them like water from the town pump. When they could not act they talked, and when they could not talk they imagined, and schemed, and plotted. Our comfort is that our glorious Head knows the stubborn malignity of our foes, and will in due season put an end to it; even now he is setting a limit upon it.

David committed himself to the one who judges right-eously, and so in patience was able to possess his soul. Hope in God's intervention, and belief in the power of prayer, are two most blessed supports to the soul in time of adversity. Turning right away from the creature to the sov-ereign Lord of all, and to him as our own covenant God, we shall find the richest solace in waiting upon him. Reputa-tion, like a fair pearl, may be cast into the mire, but in due time when the Lord makes up his jewels, the godly charac-ter shall shine with unclouded splendour. Rest then, O slandered one, and let not your soul be tossed to and fro with anxiety.

Meditation: *Secret tears for secret sins are an excellent sign of a holy heart, and a healing balsam for broken spirits* (Samuel Lee).

Psalm 38:16-22

Suggested further reading: Job 6:24-30

The least flaw in a saint is sure to be noticed; long before it comes to a fall the enemy begins to rail, the merest trip of the foot sets all the dogs of hell barking. How careful ought we to be, and how importunate in prayer for upholding grace! We do not wish, like blind Samson, to make sport for our enemies; let us then beware of the treacherous Delilah of sin, by whose means our eyes may soon be put out.

Some of us are painfully aware of what it is to be like dry tinder for the sparks of sorrow; ready to halt, ready to mourn, and sigh and cry upon any occasion, and for any cause. David did not need to look out of a window to find sorrow, he felt it within, and groaned under a body of sin which was an increasing plague to him. Deep conviction continues to irritate the conscience; it will not endure a patched-up peace, but cries war to the knife till the enmity is slain. Until the Holy Ghost applies the precious blood of Jesus, a truly awakened sinner is covered with raw wounds that cannot be healed nor bound up, nor mollified with ointment.

Open confession is good for the soul. When sorrow leads to hearty and penitent acknowledgement of sin it is blessed sorrow, something to thank God for most devoutly. My confession will be salted with briny tears. It is good not so much to bewail our sorrows as to denounce the sins that lie at the root of them. To be sorry for sin is no atonement for it, but it is the right spirit in which to turn to Jesus, who is the reconciliation and the Saviour. A man is near to the end of his trouble when he comes to an end with his sins.

The poor pleader was far gone and ready to expire; only speedy help would serve his turn. See how sorrow quickens the importunity of prayer! Here is one of the sweet results of affliction: it gives new life to our pleading, and drives us with eagerness to our God. 'O Lord my salvation'; not only my Saviour, but also my salvation. He who has the Lord on his side has salvation in present possession. Faith foresees the blessed outcome of all her pleas, and in the final verse begins to ascribe to God the glory of the expected mercy. The Lord shall not leave us. His grace will be a most timely help to us, and in heaven we shall see that we did not have one trial too many, or one pang too severe. A sense of sin shall melt into the joy of salvation; grief shall lead on to gratitude, and gratitude to joy unspeakable and full of glory.

Meditation: *It is only the heart broken with godly sorrow that sends forth a true confession* (Nathanael Hardy).

Psalm 39:1-6

Suggested further reading: James 3:5-12

In his great perplexity his greatest fear was that he should sin. So he searched around for the most likely method of avoiding it, and he determined to be silent. It is excellent when a man can strengthen himself upon a good course by remembering a well and wisely formed resolve. To avoid sin one needed to be very circumspect, and keep one's actions as with a guard or garrison. Unguarded ways are generally unholy ones.

Neither bad nor good escaped his lips. Perhaps he feared that if he began to talk at all, he would be sure to speak amiss, and, therefore, he totally abstained. A sound course of action may be pushed to the extreme, and become a fault. Inward grief was allowed to work and ferment by lack of expression. The pent-up floods were swollen and agitated. Utterance is the natural outlet for the heart's anguish, and silence, therefore, both aggravates the evil and is a barrier against its cure. In such a case the resolve to hold one's peace needs powerful backing, and even this is most likely to give way when grief rushes upon the soul. The strongest banks are likely to be swept away before a flood that is gathering in force and foaming for outlet. Nature may do her best to silence the expression of discontent, but unless grace comes to her rescue, she will be sure to succumb.

The friction of inward thoughts produced an intense mental heat. The door of his heart was shut, and with the fire of sorrow burning within, the chamber of his soul soon grew unbearable with heat. Silence is an awful thing for a sufferer; it is the surest method to produce madness. As he thought upon the ease of the wicked and his own daily affliction, he could not unravel the mystery of providence, and therefore he became greatly agitated.

It is well that the vent of his soul was Godward and not towards man. He rashly and petulantly desired to know when his wretched life would end, so that he might begin to reckon the days till death, which would put an end to his woe. Impatience would pry between the folded leaves. As if there were no other comfort to be had, unbelief would hide itself in the grave and sleep itself into oblivion. David was neither the first nor the last who had spoken unadvisedly in prayer. Alas! poor human nature, dear as life is, man quarrels with God at such a rate that he would sooner cease to be than bear the Lord's appointment. Such pettishness in a saint! Let us wait till we are in a similar position, and we shall do no better. The ship on the stocks wonders why the barque springs a leak, but when it has tried the high seas, it marvels that its timbers hold together in such storms.

Meditation: *David's case is not recorded for our imitation, but for our learning* (C. H. Spurgeon).

Psalm 39:7-13

Suggested further reading: Hebrews 11:32-40

The psalmist turns to his God, disgusted by everything else; he has thought of the world and all things in it, and is relieved to know that such vain things are all passing away; he has cut all cords which bound him to earth. The Lord is self-existent and true, and therefore worthy of the confidence of men; he will live when all the creatures die, and his fulness will remain when all second causes are exhausted. To him, therefore, let us direct our expectation, and on him let us rest our confidence. Let all wise builders turn themselves away from sand to rock, for if not today, surely before long, a storm will rise before which nothing will be able to stand but that which has the lasting element of faith in God to cement it. David had but one hope, and that hope entered within the veil; hence he brought his vessel to safe anchorage, and after a little drifting all was peace.

How fair a sign it is when the psalmist no longer harps upon his sorrows, but begs freedom from his sins! What is sorrow when compared with sin! Once the poison of sin has gone from the cup, we need not fear its gall, for the bitter will act medicinally. No one can deliver a man from his transgressions but the blessed one who is called Jesus, because he saves his people from their sins; and once he works this great deliverance for a man from the cause, the consequences are sure to disappear too. The thorough cleansing desired is well worthy of note: to be saved from some transgressions would be of small benefit; total and perfect deliverance is needed.

God does not trifle with his rod; he uses it because of sin, and with a view to whip us from it; hence he means his strokes to be felt, and felt they are. As the moth frets the substance of the fabric, mars all its beauty, and leaves it worn out and worthless, so the chastisements of God expose our folly, weakness, and nothingness, and make us feel like worn-out vestures, worthless and useless.

'Hear my prayer, O Lord.' Do not drown my pleadings with the sound of your strokes. You have heard the clamour of my sins, Lord, hear the laments of my prayers. Here is an increase in intensity: a cry is more vehement, pathetic and impassioned than a prayer. The main thing was to have the Lord's ear and heart. When our sorrows pull up the sluices of our eyes, God will intervene before long and turn our mourning into joy. He may be quiet for a long time, as though he did not care, but the hour of deliverance will come, and come like the morning when the dewdrops are plentiful.

Meditation: We may, in all humility, plead our heartbreakings and weepings in sense of want of mercies which we crave, and our pantings and faintings after the same (Thomas Cobbett).

Psalm 40:1-5

Suggested further reading: Matthew 26:36-46

Jesus is evidently here, and although it might not be a violent wresting of language to see both David and his Lord,
both Christ and the church, the double comment might
obscure the fact, and therefore we shall let the sun shine
even though this may conceal the stars. Even if the New
Testament were not so express upon it, we should have
concluded that David spoke of our Lord in verses 6-9. However, in Hebrews 10:5-9 the apostle puts all conjecture out
of court, and confines the meaning to he who came into
the world to do the Father's will.

Patient waiting upon God was a special characteristic of
our Lord Jesus. Impatience never lingered in his heart, much
less escaped his lips. All through his agony in the garden,
his trial of cruel mocking before Herod and Pilate, and his
passion on the tree, he waited with omnipotent patience.
No glance of wrath, no word of murmuring, no deed of
vengeance came from God's patient Lamb; he waited and
waited on; was patient, and patient to perfection, far excel-
ling all others who have, according to their measure, glorified God in the fires. The Christ of God wears the imperial
crown among the patient. If the Only Begotten waits, shall
we be petulant and rebellious? Neither Jesus the head, nor
any one of the members of his body, shall ever wait upon
the Lord in vain.

When our Lord bore in his own person the terrible curse
which was due to sin, he was cast down like a prisoner in a

deep, dark, tearful dungeon, amid whose horrible gloom the captive heard a noise as of rushing torrents, while overhead resounded the tramp of furious foes. Reader, with humble gratitude, adore the dear Redeemer who, for your sake, was deprived of all consolation while surrounded with every form of misery. Mark his gratitude at being borne up amid his arduous labours and sufferings, and if you too have experienced the divine help, be sure to join your Lord in this song. The Redeemer's work is done. He rests on the firm ground of his accomplished engagements; he can never suffer again; he reigns in glory for ever.

This passage draws our attention especially to the marvels that cluster around the cross and flash from it. The accomplished redemption achieves many ends, and compasses a variety of designs; the outgoings of the atonement are not to be reckoned up, the influences of the cross reach further than the beams of the sun. Innumerable wonders of grace rise up from the cross: adoption, pardon, justification, and a long chain of godlike miracles of love proceed from it. Note that our Lord speaks of the Lord as 'my God'. The man Christ Jesus claimed for himself and us a covenant relationship with Jehovah. Let our interest in our God always be a peculiar treasure to us.

Meditation: *Our Lord's patience under suffering was an element of perfection in his work. Well may we rejoice that in the midst of all his temptations, and in the thickest of the battle against sin and Satan, he remained patient and willing to finish the work which his Father had given him to do* (James Frame).

Psalm 40:6-10

Suggested further reading: Hebrews 10:5-10

Our Lord was quick to hear and perform his Father's will. We learn from this that Jehovah values far more the obedience of the heart than all the imposing performances of ritualistic worship; and that our expiation from sin does not come to us as the result of an elaborate ceremonial, but as the effect of our great Substitute's obedience to the will of Jehovah.

Behold, O heavens, and earth, and you places under the earth! Sit down and watch with earnestness, for the invisible God comes in the likeness of sinful flesh, and as an infant the Infinite hangs at a virgin's breast! Immanuel did not send but come; he came in his own personality, in all that constituted his essential self he came forth from the ivory palaces to the abodes of misery; he came promptly at the destined hour; he came with sacred alacrity as one freely offering himself. It is thus recorded in the eternal decree. The mystic roll of predestination which providence gradually unfolds, contained within it, to the Saviour's knowledge, a written covenant, that in the fulness of time the divine one should descend to earth to accomplish a purpose which hundreds of sacrifices of bullocks and rams could not achieve. What a privilege to find our names written in the book of life, and what an honour, since the name of Jesus heads the page! Our Lord had respect to his ancient covenant engagements, and in this he teaches us to be scrupulously just in keeping our word. Have we so promised, is it so written in the book of remembrance? Then let us never default.

Our blessed Lord alone could completely do the will of God. The law is too broad for such poor creatures as we are to hope to fulfil it to the uttermost. However, Jesus not only did the Father's will, but also found delight in doing so. From all eternity he had desired the work set before him; in his human life he was constrained till he reached the baptism of agony in which he magnified the law, and even in Gethsemane itself he chose the Father's will, and set aside his own. Here is the essence of obedience, namely, in the soul's cheerful devotion to God: and our Lord's obedience, which is our righteousness, is in no measure lacking in this eminent quality. Notwithstanding his measureless grief, our Lord found delight in his work, and for 'the joy that was set before him he endured the cross, despising the shame'. No outward, formal devotion was rendered by Christ; his heart was in his work, holiness was his element, the Father's will his meat and drink. We must each of us be like our Lord in this, or we shall lack the evidence of being his disciples. Where there is no heart work, no pleasure, and no delight in God's law, there can be no acceptance. Let the devout reader adore the Saviour for the spontaneous and hearty manner in which he undertook the great work of our salvation.

Meditation: *The true way of justification of sinners by faith is a jewel so precious and necessary for poor souls that it should not be concealed* (David Dickson).

Psalm 40:11-17

Suggested further reading: Luke 22:39-46

Jesus was beset with evils on every side; countless woes surrounded the great Substitute for our sins. Our sins were innumerable, and so was his grief. There was no escape for us from our iniquities, and there was no escape for him from the woes that we deserved. Evils accumulated around the blessed one from every quarter, although in his heart evil found no place. He had no sin, but sins were laid on him, and he took them as if they were his. 'He was made sin for us.' The transfer of sin to the Saviour was real, and produced in him as man the horror that forbade him to look into the face of God, bowing him down with crushing anguish and intolerable woe. O my soul, what would your sins have done for you eternally if the Friend of sinners had not condescended to take them all upon himself? Oh, blessed Scripture! 'The Lord has laid upon him the iniquity of us all.' Oh, marvellous depth of love, which could lead the perfectly immaculate to stand in the sinner's place, and bear the horror of great trembling which sin must bring upon those conscious of it.

In the sixteenth verse, our Lord pronounces benedictions on his people. Note who the blessed objects of his petitions are: not all men, but some men. He pleads for seekers: the lowest in the kingdom, the babes of the family; those who have true desires, longing prayers, and consistent endeavours after God. Let seeking souls pluck up heart when they hear of this. What riches of grace, that in his bitterest hour Jesus should remember the lambs of the flock! And what does he entreat for them? It is that they may be intensely happy, emphatically joyful, for this is what the repetition of terms implies. Jesus would have all seekers made happy by finding what they seek after, and by winning peace through his grief. As deep as his sorrows were, so high would he have their joys. He groaned that we might sing, and was covered with a bloody sweat that we might be anointed with the oil of gladness. The Redeemer's passion resulted in the promotion of the glory of God by those who gratefully delight in his salvation. Our Lord's desire should be our directory; we love his great salvation with all our hearts. Let us then, with all our tongues, proclaim the resplendent glory of God. Never let his praises cease.

The man of sorrows closes with another appeal, based upon his affliction and poverty. This was sweet comfort to the holy heart of the great sufferer. The Lord's thoughts of us are a cheering subject of meditation, for they are ever kind and never cease. His disciples forsook him, and his friends forgot him, but Jesus knew that Jehovah never turned his heart away from him, and this upheld him in the hour of need. His unmoved confidence rested on God alone.

Meditation: *Lord Jesus, grant that in all our adversities we may possess like precious faith, and be found like you, more than conquerors* (C. H. Spurgeon).

Psalm 41:1-6

Suggested further reading: James 1:19-27

This is the third psalm opening with a benediction, and there is a growth in it beyond the first two. To search the Word of God comes first, pardoned sin is second, and now the forgiven sinner brings forth fruit unto God available for the good of others. The word used is as emphatic as in the previous cases, and so is the blessing that follows it.

The compassionate lover of the poor thought of others, and therefore God will think of him. God gives to us according to our own measure. Days of trouble come even to the most generous, and those who have lent shelter to others when times were better with them have made the wisest provision for rainy days. The promise is not that the generous saint shall have no trouble, but that he shall be preserved in it, and in due time brought out of it. The joy of doing good, the sweet reaction of another's happiness, the approving smile of heaven upon the heart, if not upon the estate; all these the niggardly soul knows nothing of. Selfishness bears in itself a curse, it is a cancer in the heart; while liberality is happiness, and makes the bones fat. In dark days we cannot rest upon the supposed merit of almsgiving, but still the music of memory brings with it no mean solace when it reminds us of widows and orphans we have helped, and prisoners and sick folk to whom we have ministered.

Here is the portion of all those who are made like their Lord, they bless and they shall be blessed, they preserve and shall be preserved, they watch over the lives of others and they themselves shall be precious in the sight of the Lord. The miser, like the hog, is of no use till he is dead — then let him die; the righteous, like the ox, is of service during life — then let him live. We must not imagine that the benediction pronounced in these verses belongs to all who casually give money to the poor, or leave it in their wills, or contribute to societies. Such do well, or act from mere custom, as the case may be, but they are not alluded to here. The blessing is for those whose habit it is to love their neighbour as themselves, and who for Christ's sake feed the hungry and clothe the naked. To imagine a man to be a saint who does not consider the poor whenever he can is to perceive the fruitless fig tree as acceptable; there will be sharp dealing with many professors on this point in the day when the King comes in his glory.

Meditation: *None of the godly man's afflictions shall hinder or take away his begun blessedness, even in this world* (David Dickson).

Psalm 41:7-13

Suggested further reading: John 13:12-20

Judas was an apostle, admitted to the privacy of the Great Teacher, hearing his secret thoughts, and, as it were, allowed to read his very heart. The kiss of the traitor wounded our Lord's heart as much as the nail wounded his hand. Judas was the treasurer of the apostolic college. Where we place great confidence an unkind act is felt more severely. Judas dipped in the same dish with his Lord and hence his treachery in selling his Master for a slave's price was so much more accursed. It is hard to be spurned in our need by those who formerly fed at our table. It is noteworthy that the Redeemer applied only the last words of this verse to Judas, perhaps because, knowing his duplicity, he had never made a familiar friend of him in the fullest sense, and had not placed implicit trust in him. Infernal malice so planned it that every circumstance in Jesus' death should add wormwood to it; and the betrayal was one of the bitterest drops of gall. We are indeed wretched when our former friend becomes our relentless foe, when confidence is betrayed, when all the rites of hospitality are perverted, and ingratitude is the only return for kindness. Yet in such a deplorable situation we may cast ourselves upon the faithfulness of God, who, having delivered our Covenant Head, is truly engaged to be the very present help of all for whom that covenant was made.

We all are cheered by tokens for good, and the psalmist felt it to be an auspicious omen, that after all his deep depression he was not utterly given over to his enemy. What if the believer has no triumph over his foes? He must be glad that they do not triumph over him. If we do not have all we wish, we should praise God for all we have. There is much in us the ungodly might exult over, and if God's mercy keeps the dogs' mouths closed when they might be opened, we must give him our heartiest gratitude. What a wonder it is that when the devil enters the fray with a poor, erring, bedridden, deserted, slandered saint, and has a thousand evil tongues to aid him, he still cannot win the day, but in the end slinks off without renown.

The psalm ends with a doxology. The blessing at the beginning from the mouth of God is returned from the mouth of his servant. We cannot add to the Lord's blessedness, but we can pour out our grateful wishes, and these he accepts, as we receive little presents of flowers from children who love us. The last verse may serve for the prayer of the universal church in all ages, but none can sing it so sweetly as those who have experienced as David did the faithfulness of God in times of extremity.

Meditation: *God preserves his own, and brings their foes to nought — after Passion week comes Easter* (J. P. Lange's Commentary).

Psalm 42:1-5

Suggested further reading: 2 Samuel 15:30-37

As after a long drought the poor fainting hind longs for the streams, or rather, as the hunted hart instinctively seeks after the river to bathe its smoking flanks and to escape the dogs, so his weary, persecuted soul pants after the Lord his God. Debarred from public worship, David was heartsick. Ease he did not seek, honour he did not covet, but the enjoyment of communion with God was an urgent need of his soul; he viewed it not merely as the sweetest of all luxuries, but as an absolute necessity, like water to a stag. Like the parched traveller in the wilderness, whose skin bottle is empty, and who finds the wells dry, he must drink or die; he must have his God or faint. His soul, his very self, his deepest life, was insatiable for a sense of the divine presence.

He who loves the Lord loves also the assemblies where his name is adored. Vain are all pretences to religion where the outward means of grace have no attraction. David was never so much at home as in the house of the Lord; he was not content with private worship; he did not forsake the place where saints assemble, as some do. See how pathetically he questions the prospect of uniting again in the joyous gathering! How he repeats and reiterates his desire! It would be well if all our acts of public worship were viewed as appearances before God; it would then be a sure mark of grace to delight in them. Alas, how many appear before the minister, or their fellow men, and think that enough!

The psalmist talks to himself as though he were two men. His faith reasons with his fears, his hope argues with his sorrows. These present troubles, are they to last for ever? The rejoicing of my foes, is it more than empty talk? My absence from the solemn feasts, is that a perpetual exile? Why this deep depression, this faithless fainting, this chicken-hearted melancholy? To search out the cause of our sorrow is often the best surgery for grief. Self-ignorance is not bliss; in this case it is misery. Salvation comes from the propitious face of God, and he will yet lift up his countenance upon us. Note well that the main hope and chief desire of David rest in the smile of God. His face is what he seeks and hopes to see, and this will recover his low spirits, this will put to scorn his laughing enemies, this will restore to him all the joys of those holy and happy days which linger in his memory. This is grand cheer. This verse, like the singing of Paul and Silas, looses chains and shakes prison walls. He who can use such heroic language in his gloomy hours will surely conquer. In the garden of hope grow the laurels for future victories, the roses of coming joy, the lilies of approaching peace.

Meditation: *Little do the drunkards think that take so much pleasure in frequenting the houses of Bacchus that the godly take a great deal more, and have a great deal more joy in frequenting the houses of God* (Zachary Bogan).

Psalm 42:6-11

Suggested further reading: Job 1:13-22

Here the song begins again upon the brass. Perhaps the psalmist's dejection continued, the spasm of despondency returned; well, then, he will put down his harp, and try its power upon himself again, as in his younger days he saw its influence upon Saul when the evil spirit came upon him. The song begins the second time with God more closely than at first. The singer was also a little more tranquil. Outward expression of desire was gone; there was no visible panting; the sorrow was now all restrained within doors. Within or upon himself he was cast down; and truly, while our thoughts look more within than upward, it may well be so. If self were to furnish comfort, we should have but poor provender. There is no solid foundation for comfort in such fickle frames as our heart is subject to. It is good to tell the Lord how we feel, and the more plain the confession the better: David talks like a sick child to its mother, and we should learn to imitate him.

As in a waterspout, the deeps above and below clasp hands, so it seemed to David that heaven and earth united to create a tempest around him. His woes were incessant and overwhelming. Billow followed billow, one sea echoed the roaring of another; bodily pain aroused mental fear, Satanic suggestions chimed in with mistrustful foreboding, outward tribulation thundered in awful harmony with inward anguish. His soul seemed drowned as in a universal deluge of trouble, over whose waves the providence of the Lord moved as a watery pillar, in dreadful majesty inspiring the utmost terror. The day may darken into a strange and untimely midnight, but the love of God ordained of old to be the portion of the elect shall be meted out to them by sovereign decree. He who is the living God is the God of our life, from him we derive it, with him in prayer and praise we spend it, to him we devote it, in him we shall perfect it. To be assured that our sighs and songs shall both have free access to our glorious Lord is to have reason for hope in the most deplorable condition. No day shall ever dawn on an heir of grace and find him altogether forsaken of his Lord: the Lord reigns, and as a sovereign he will with authority command mercy to be reserved for his chosen. Looked in the face, his fears were not so overwhelming as they seemed when shrouded in obscurity. Let the anchor still keep its hold. God is faithful, God is love; therefore there is room and reason for hope.

Meditation: *Your song and your prayer must be directed to God as the God of your life* (John Howe).

Psalm 43

Suggested further reading: Proverbs 22:22-23

'Vindicate me, O God.' Others are unable to understand my motives, and unwilling to give me a just verdict. My heart is clear as to its intent, and therefore I bring my case before you, content that you will impartially weigh my character, and right my wrongs. One such advocate as the Lord will more than suffice to answer a nation of brawling accusers. When people are ungodly no wonder that they are unjust: those who are not true to God himself cannot be expected to deal rightly with his people.

Here is argument, which is the very sinew of prayer. If we reasoned more with the Lord we should have more victories in supplication. All my strength belongs to you — I will not, therefore, use it on my own behalf against my personal foes. All my strength comes from you, I therefore seek help from you, for you are able to bestow it. All my strength is in you. I therefore leave this task of combating my foes entirely in your hands. Faith that leaves such things alone is wise faith.

We do not seek light to sin by, nor truth to be exalted by it, but that they may become our practical guides to the nearest communion with God. Only such light and truth as are sent us from God will do this. Common light is not strong enough to show the road to heaven, nor will mere moral or physical truths assist to the holy hill; but the light of the Holy Spirit, and the truth as it is in Jesus, these are elevating, sanctifying, perfecting; and hence their virtue in

leading us to the glorious presence of God. It is beautiful to
observe how David's longing to be away from the oppression of man always leads him to sigh more intensely for
communion with God.

It was not the altar as such that the psalmist cared for,
he was no believer in the heathenism of ritualism: his soul
desired spiritual fellowship, fellowship with God himself
in very deed. What are all the rites of worship unless the
Lord be in them; what, indeed, but empty shells and dry
husks? Note the holy rapture with which David regards his
Lord! He is not his joy alone, but his exceeding joy; not the
fountain of joy, the giver of joy, or the maintainer of joy, but
that joy itself. When God fills us with joy we ought ever to
pour it out at his feet in praise, and all the skill and talent
we have should be laid under contribution to increase the
divine revenue of glory. To have God in possession, and to
know it by faith, is the heart's heaven — here is where
fulness of bliss lies. 'Why are you cast down, O my soul? ...
Hope in God.'

Meditation: *Hope in God. The more terrible the storm, the
more necessary is the anchor* (William S. Plumer).

Psalm 44:1-8

Suggested further reading: Exodus 12:21-28

Among the godly Israelites the biography of their nation was preserved by oral tradition, with great diligence and accuracy. This mode of preserving and transmitting history has its disadvantages, but it certainly produces a more vivid impression on the mind than any other: to hear with the ears affects us more sensitively than to read with the eyes.

'Our fathers have told us.' They could not have had better informants. Schoolmasters are well enough, but, both by the order of nature and grace, godly fathers are the best instructors of their sons. It is to be feared that many children of professing believers could plead very little before God of what their fathers have told them. When fathers are tongue-tied religiously with their offspring, need they wonder if their children's hearts remain sin-tied? Just as in all free nations men delight to gather around the hearth, and tell the deeds of valour of their forefathers 'in the brave days of old', so the people of God under the old dispensation encouraged their families around the table, by recounting the wondrous doings of the Lord their God. Religious conversation need not be dull, and indeed it could not be if, as in this case, it dealt more with facts and less with opinions.

Note that the main point of the history transmitted from father to son was the work of God; this is the core of history, and therefore no man who is a stranger to the Lord's work can write history accurately. It is delightful to see the footprints of the Lord on the sea of changing events, to behold him riding on the whirlwind of war, pestilence and famine, and above all to see his unchanging care for his chosen people. Those who are taught to see God in history have learned a good lesson from their fathers, and no son of believing parents should be left in ignorance of so holy an art. A nation tutored as Israel was in a history so marvellous as their own, always had an available argument in pleading with God for aid in trouble, since he who never changes gives in every deed of grace a pledge of mercy yet to come. The traditions of our past experience are powerful pleas for present help.

We have abundant reason for boasting in God all the day long while we recount his mighty acts. What blessed boasting is this! It is the only sort of boasting that is bearable. Praise should be perpetual. If there were no new acts of love, the Lord still ought to be praised for what he has done for his people. Let the song be lifted up high as we remember the eternal love which chose us, predestinated us to be sons, redeemed us with a price, and then enriched us with all the fulness of God.

Meditation: *While the songs of other nations sing of the heroism of their ancestors, the songs of Israel celebrate the works of God* (Augustus F. Tholuck).

Psalm 44:9-16

Suggested further reading: Deuteronomy 4:25-31

Here the patriot bard begins to contrast the past glories of
the nation's history with its present sadness and distress,
which he does not ascribe to the death of some human champion, or to the accidents of war, but solely and alone to the
withdrawal of Israel's God. It seemed to the mourner that
Jehovah had grown weary of his people and put them away
in abhorrence, as men lay aside leprous garments, loathing
the sight of them. To show his displeasure he had caused
his people to be ridiculed by the heathen, whose easy victories over their largest armies covered Israel with disgrace.
Alas! for a church and people when the Lord in the active
energy of his Spirit withdraws from them, they want no
greater shame or sorrow. He will not cast away his people
finally and totally, but many a church has been left to defeat and disgrace on account of sin, and therefore all
churches should be exceedingly watchful lest the same
should happen to them. Poverty and distress bring no shame
on a people, but the Lord's absence takes from a church
everything that can exalt and ennoble.

The humiliating consciousness that the Lord has left
them soon makes men cowards. Flight ends the fight of
those who do not have the Lord in the vanguard. After defeat and retreat comes destruction. The poor, vanquished
nation paid a terrible penalty for being overcome: plunder
and murder desolated the conquered land, and the invaders loaded themselves with every precious thing that they

could carry away. In spiritual experience we know what it is to be despoiled by our enemies: doubts and fears rob us of our comforts, and terrible foreboding spoils us of our hopes; and all because the Lord, for wise purposes, sees fit to leave us to ourselves. Alas! for the deserted soul; no calamity can equal the sorrow of being left by God, even if it is just for a small moment.

The psalmist sets forth the brutality of the enemy in many words in order to move the pity of the Lord, to whose just anger he traced all the sorrows of his people. He used the very best of arguments, for the suffering of his chosen touches the heart of God far more readily than any other reasoning. Blessed be his name, our great Advocate above knows how to avail himself of this powerful plea, and if we are at this hour enduring reproach for truth's sake, he will urge it before the eternal throne; and shall not God avenge his own elect? A father will not endure to see his children spitefully entreated for long; he may put up with it for a little, but his love will speedily arouse his anger, and then the persecutor and reviler will suffer badly.

Meditation: *When the visible church is visited with sad calamities, its true members are partakers of the trouble, and sorrow, and shame of that condition* (David Dickson).

Psalm 44:17-26

Suggested further reading: Deuteronomy 6:10-15

Here the psalmist pleads the fact that Israel had not turned away from her allegiance to Jehovah. When in the midst of much grief we can still cling to God in loving obedience, it must be well with us. True fidelity can endure rough usage. Those who follow God for what they get will leave him when persecution is stirred up, but not so the sincere believer; he will not forget his God, even though the worst come to the worst.

It was a healthy sign for the nation that her prophet-poet could testify to her uprightness before God, both in heart and act. Far more often the case would have worn quite another colour, for the tribes were all too apt to set up other gods and forsake the rock of their salvation. The nation is described as completely enveloped in the dense darkness of despair and death, covered up as though coffined in hopelessness. Yet the claim is made that they still remained mindful of their God, and it is a glorious plea. Better death than false of faith. Those who are true to God shall never find him false to them. The reasoning is that the Lord himself knew the people to be sincerely his followers, and therefore was not visiting them because of sin; hence, then, affliction evidently came from quite another cause.

'For your sake', not for our offences, but for obeying you; the trials of these suppliants came upon them because they were loyal to their God. Persecution never ceased to hound

them to the death, they had no respite and found no door
of escape; and all on God's behalf, because they would not
forsake their covenant God and King. In this and following
verses we clearly hear the martyr's cry. From Piedmont and
Smithfield, from St Bartholomew's massacre and the
dragonnades of Claverhouse, this appeal goes up to heaven,
while the souls under the altar continue their solemn cry
for vengeance. The church shall not plead in this fashion
for long, her shame shall be recompensed, her triumph shall
dawn.

Why, Lord, do you become oblivious of your children's
woes? This question is far more easily asked than answered;
it is hard, indeed, in the midst of persecution to see the
reason why we are left to suffer so severely. Here is the
final plea. The favour is redemption, the plea is mercy; and
this, too, in the case of faithful sufferers who had not forgotten their God. Mercy is always a safe plea, and never
will any man find one better. Here ends this memorable
psalm, but in heaven its power does not end, it brings down
deliverance for the tried people of God.

Meditation: *A godly man dares not sin secretly. He knows
that God sees in secret. As God cannot be deceived by our
subtlety, so he cannot be excluded by our secrecy* (Thomas
Watson).

Psalm 45:1-9

Suggested further reading: Luke 4:16-22

Well-focused spiritual eyes see only Jesus here. This is no wedding song of earthly nuptials, but an ode for the heavenly Bridegroom and his elect spouse.

As though the King himself had suddenly appeared before him, the psalmist, lost in admiration for him, turns to address his Lord. In person, but especially in mind and character, the King of saints is peerless in beauty. The Hebrew word is doubled, 'Beautiful, beautiful are you'; Jesus is so emphatically lovely that words must be doubled, strained, indeed, exhausted before he can be described. Grace of person and grace of speech reach their highest point in him. Grace has in the most copious manner been poured upon Christ, for it pleased the Father that in him should all fulness dwell, and now grace is in superabundance, poured forth from his lips to cheer and enrich his people. Christ is blessed, blessed of God, blessed for ever, and this is to us one great reason for his beauty, and the source of the gracious words which proceed out of his lips. The rare endowments of the man Christ Jesus are given him by the Father, and by them his people may be blessed with all spiritual blessings in union with himself. Whom God blesses we should bless, and the more so because all his blessedness is communicated to us.

The psalmist cannot restrain his adoration. His enlightened eye sees in the royal Husband of the church, God, God to be adored, God reigning, God reigning everlastingly.

Blessed sight! Blind are the eyes that cannot see God in Christ Jesus! We never appreciate the tender condescension of our King in becoming one flesh with his church, and placing her at his right hand, until we have fully rejoiced in his essential glory and deity. What a mercy for us that our Saviour is God, for who but a God could execute the work of salvation? What a glad thing it is that he reigns on a throne that will never pass away, for we need both sovereign grace and eternal love to secure our happiness. If Jesus could cease to reign we should cease to be blessed, and were he not God, and therefore eternal, this must be the case. No throne can endure for ever, but that on which God himself sits. He is the lawful monarch of all things that exist. His rule is founded in right, its law is right, its result is right. Our King is no usurper and no oppressor. Even when he breaks his enemies with a rod of iron, he will do no man wrong; his vengeance and his grace both conform with justice. Hence we trust him without suspicion; he cannot err; no affliction is too severe, for he sends it; no judgement too harsh, for he ordains it. O blessed hands of Jesus! The reigning power is safe with you. All the just rejoice in the government of the King who reigns in righteousness.

Meditation: *God was the God of Christ in covenant, that he might be our God in covenant* (William Troughton).

Psalm 45:10-17

Suggested further reading: Ephesians 5:25-32

To renounce the world is not easy, but it must be done by
all who are betrothed to the great King, for a divided heart
he cannot endure; it would be misery to the beloved one as
well as dishonour to her Lord. Wholehearted love is the
duty and bliss of the marriage state in every case, but especially so in this lofty, mystic marriage. The church must
forsake all others and cleave to Jesus only, or she will not
please him nor enjoy the full manifestation of his love. What
less can he ask, what less may she dare propose than to be
wholly his? Jesus sees a beauty in his church, a beauty that
he delights in most when it is not marred by worldliness.
He has always been most near and precious to his saints
when they have cheerfully taken up his cross and followed
him outside the camp. His Spirit is grieved when they mingle themselves among the people and learn their ways.

The King has royal rights; his condescending grace does
not lessen but rather enforce his authority. Our Saviour is
also our Ruler. The husband is the head of the wife; the
love he bears her does not lessen but strengthen her obligation to obey. The church must reverence Jesus, and bow
before him in prostrate adoration; his tender union with
her gives her liberty, but not licence; it frees her from all
other burdens, but places his easy yoke upon her neck. Who
would wish it to be otherwise? The service of God is heaven
in heaven, and perfectly carried out it is heaven upon earth.
Jesus, you are the one whom your church praises in her

unceasing songs, and adores in her perpetual service. Teach us to be wholly your own. Bear with us, and work by your Spirit in us till your will is done by us on earth as it is in heaven.

The fame of Messiah is not left to human guardianship; the Eternal guarantees it, and his promise never fails. All down the ages the memories of Gethsemane and Calvary shall glow with inextinguishable light; nor shall the lapse of time, the smoke of error, or the malice of hell be able to dim the glory of the Redeemer's fame. Praise is due from every heart to him who loved us, and redeemed us by his blood; this praise will never be fully paid, but will be a standing and growing debt for ever. His daily benefits enlarge our obligations, let them increase the number of our songs. Age to age reveals more of his love. Let every year swell the volume of the music of earth and heaven, and let thunders of song roll up in full diapason to the throne of him that lives, and was dead, and is alive for evermore, and has the keys of hell and of death.

Meditation: *When the children of God recollect their glorious and heavenly pedigree, they endeavour to excel other, both in the beautiful disposition of soul, and manner of life* (Hermann Witsius).

Psalm 46:1-3

Suggested further reading: Isaiah 43:1-7

Israel's boast is in Jehovah, the only living and true God. Others vaunt their impregnable castles, placed on inaccessible rocks and secured with gates of iron, but God is a far better refuge from distress than all these. When the time comes to carry the war into the enemy's territories, the Lord stands his people in better stead than all the valour of legions or the boasted strength of chariot and horse. Soldiers of the cross, remember this, count yourselves safe, and make yourselves strong in God. Do not forget the personal possessive word 'our'; make sure, each one, of your portion in God, that you may say, 'He is my refuge and strength.' Neither forget the fact that God is our refuge just now, in the immediate present, as truly as when David penned the word. God alone is our all in all. All other refuges are refuges of lies, all other strength is weakness, for power belongs to God: but as God is all sufficient, our defence and might are equal to all emergencies. He never withdraws himself from his afflicted. He is their help, truly, effectually and constantly. He is present or near them, close at their side and ready for their succour, and this is emphasized by the word 'very' in our version. He is more present than friend or relative can be, indeed, more nearly present than even the trouble itself. To all this comforting truth is added the consideration that his assistance comes at the needed time. He is not as the swallows that leave us in the winter; he is a friend in need and a friend indeed.

The two phrases of verse two set forth the most terrible commotion within the range of imagination, and include the overthrow of dynasties, the destruction of nations, the ruin of families, the persecutions of the church, the reign of heresy, and whatever else may at any time try the faith of believers. Let the worst come to the worst, the child of God should never give way to mistrust; since God remains faithful there can be no danger to his cause or people. When the elements shall melt with fervent heat, and the heavens and the earth shall pass away in the last general conflagration, we shall serenely behold 'the wreck of matter, and the crash of worlds', for even then our refuge shall preserve us from all evil, our strength shall prepare us for all good.

When all things are excited to fury, and reveal their utmost power to disturb, faith smiles serenely. She is not afraid of noise, or even of real force; she knows that the Lord stills the raging of the sea, and holds the waves in the hollow of his hand. Great men who are like mountains may quake for fear in times of great calamity, but the man whose trust is in God need never be dismayed.

Meditation: *When it is very dark with us, let brave spirits say, 'Come, let us sing the forty-sixth psalm'* (C. H. Spurgeon).

Psalm 46:4-7

Suggested further reading: Revelation 22:1-5

Divine grace, like a smoothly flowing, fertilising, full, and never-failing river, yields refreshment and consolation to believers. This is the river of the water of life, of which the church above as well as the church below partakes evermore. It is no boisterous ocean, but a placid stream; it is not stayed in its course by earthquakes or crumbling mountains, it follows its serene course without disturbance. Happy are they who know from their own experience that there is such a river of God.

The peculiar glory of Jerusalem was that the Lord had a place within her walls where he peculiarly revealed himself. This is the choice privilege of the saints, concerning which we may cry with wonder, 'Lord, how is it that you will manifest yourself to us, and not to the world?' To be a temple for the Holy Spirit is the delightful portion of each saint, to be the living temple for the Lord our God is also the high honour of the church in her corporate capacity. Our God is here called by a worthy title, indicating his power, majesty, sublimity and excellency; and it is worthy of note that under this character he dwells in the church. We do not have a great God in nature, and a little God in grace; no, the church contains as clear and convincing a revelation of God as the works of nature. Even more amazing is the excellent glory that shines between the cherubim, overshadowing that mercy seat which is the centre and gathering place of the people of the living God. To have the Most High dwelling within her members is to make the church on earth like the church in heaven.

'The Lord of Hosts is with us.' This is the reason for all Zion's security, and for the overthrow of her foes. The Lord rules the angels, the stars, the elements, and all the hosts of heaven; and the heaven of heavens are under his sway. The armies of men, though they do not know it, are made to subserve his will. This great General of the forces of the land, and the Lord High Admiral of the seas, is on our side — our august ally; woe unto those who fight against him, for they shall fly like smoke before the wind when he gives the word to scatter them. Immanuel is Jehovah of Hosts, and Jacob's God is our high place of defence.

Meditation: *It is the real presence of Christ, and the supernatural power of his Spirit, which makes the church mighty to the conquest of souls. The church spreads because her 'God is in the midst of her'* (William Binnie).

Psalm 46:8-11

Suggested further reading: Isaiah 11:6-10

The joyful citizens of Jerusalem are invited to go forth and view the remains of their enemies, that they may mark the prowess of Jehovah and the spoil that his right hand has won for his people. It would do us good if we also carefully noted the providential dealings of our covenant God, and were quick to perceive his hand in the battles of his church. Whenever we read history it should be with this thought sounding in our ears. We should read the newspaper in the same spirit, to see how the Head of the church rules the nations for his people's good, as Joseph governed Egypt for the sake of Israel. The destroyers he destroys, the desolators he desolates. How forceful is the verse at this point! The ruined cities of Assyria, Babylon, Petra, Bashan and Canaan are our instructors, and in tables of stone record the doings of the Lord. In every place where his cause and crown have been disregarded ruin has surely followed; sin has been a blight on nations, and left their palaces to lie in heaps. In the days of the writer of this psalm, there had probably occurred some memorable interposition of God against his Israel's foes; and as he saw their overthrow, he called on his fellow citizens to come forth and attentively consider the terrible things which had been wrought on their behalf in righteousness. Dismantled castles and ruined abbeys in our own land stand as memorials of the Lord's victories over oppression and superstition. May there soon be more of such desolation.

The boasts of the ungodly and the timorous foreboding of the saints should certainly be hushed by a sight of what the Lord has done in past ages. The heathen forget God, they worship idols, but they will yet honour Jehovah. Reader, the prospects of missions are bright, bright as the promises of God. Let no man's heart fail him; the solemn declarations of the tenth verse must be fulfilled. The whole round earth shall yet reflect the light of his majesty. All the more because of the sin, and obstinacy, and pride of man shall God be glorified when grace reigns unto eternal life in all corners of the world.

'The Lord of hosts is with us; the God of Jacob is our refuge.' It was fitting to sing this twice over. It is a truth of which no believer wearies, it is a fact too often forgotten, it is a precious privilege that cannot be considered too often. Reader, is the Lord on your side? Is Emmanuel, God with us, your Redeemer? Is there a covenant between yourself and God as between God and Jacob? If so, thrice happy are you. Show your joy in holy song, and in times of trouble play the man by still making music for your God.

Meditation: *The bare consideration that God is God may well be sufficient to still all objections and oppositions against the divine sovereign dispensation* (Jonathan Edwards).

Psalm 47:1-4

Suggested further reading: Daniel 7:9-14

The most natural and most enthusiastic tokens of exultation are to be used in view of the victories of the Lord, and
his universal reign. Our joy in God may be demonstrative,
and yet he will not censure it. The joy is to extend to all
nations. Even now if they did but know it, it is the best
hope of all nations that Jehovah rules over them. All people
will be ruled by the Lord in the latter days, and will exult
in that rule; were they wise they would submit to it now,
and rejoice to do so; indeed, they would clap their hands
in rapture at the thought.

JEHOVAH, the self-existent and only God, 'most high', most
great in power, lofty in dominion, eminent in wisdom, elevated in glory, is terrible. None can resist his power or stand
before his vengeance; yet as these terrors are wielded on
the behalf of his subjects, they are fit reasons for rejoicing.
Omnipotence, which is terrible to crush, is almighty to protect. 'He is a great King over all the earth.' Not over Judea
only, but even to the utmost isles his reign extends. Our
God is no local deity, no petty ruler of a tribe; in infinite
majesty he rules the mightiest realms as absolute arbiter of
destiny, sole monarch of all lands, King of kings and Lord
of lords. Not a hamlet or an islet is excluded from his
dominion. How glorious will that era be when this is seen
and known of all; when in the person of Jesus all flesh shall
behold the glory of the Lord!

While as yet we do not see all things put under him, we are glad to put ourselves and our fortunes at his disposal. We feel his reign to be so gracious that even now we ask to be subject to it to the fullest degree. We submit our will, our choice and our desire wholly to him. Our heritage here and hereafter we leave to him; let him do with us as seems good to him. He gave his ancient people their portion, he will give us ours, and we ask nothing better. This is the most spiritual and real manner of clapping our hands because of his sovereignty, namely, to leave all our affairs in his hands, for then our hands are empty of all care for self, and free to be used in his honour. He was the boast and glory of Israel; he is and shall be ours. He loved his people and became their greatest glory; he loves us, and he shall be our exceeding joy. As for the latter days, we ask nothing better than to stand in our appointed lot, for if we have but a portion in our Lord Jesus, it is enough for our largest desires. Our beauty, our boast, our best treasure, lies in having such a God to trust in, such a God to love us.

Meditation: *The church celebrates the ascension of Christ, because then he was 'highly exalted'. Then he became 'terrible' to his enemies, all power in heaven and in earth being committed to him; and then he began to display the excellent majesty of his universal kingdom, to which he was then inaugurated, being crowned 'King of kings, and Lord of lords'* (George Horne).

Psalm 47:5-9

Suggested further reading: Zechariah 14:1-11

Faith hears the people already shouting. The command of the first verse is here regarded as a fact. The fight is over, the conqueror ascends to his triumphal chariot, and rides up to the gates of the city which is made resplendent with the joy of his return. The words are fully applicable to the ascension of the Redeemer. We do not doubt that angels and glorified spirits welcomed him with acclamations. He did not come without song, shall we imagine that he returned in silence?

What jubilation is here, when five times over the whole earth is called upon to sing to God! He is worthy, he is Creator, he is goodness itself. He never ceases to be good, let us never cease to be grateful. Strange that we should need so much urging to attend to so heavenly an exercise. Let him have all our praise; no one ought to have even a particle of it. Jesus shall have it all. Let his sovereignty be the fount of gladness. It is a sublime attribute, but full of bliss to the faithful. Let our homage be paid not in groans but in songs. He does not ask slaves to grace his throne; he is no despot; singing is fit homage for a monarch so blessed and gracious. Let all hearts that own his sceptre sing and sing on for ever, for there is everlasting reason for thanksgiving while we dwell under the shadow of such a throne.

Now at this moment, over the most debased idolaters, God holds a secret rule; here is work for faith. How we ought to long for the day when this view of truth shall be changed, and the rule now unrecognized shall be delighted in! The great truth that 'God reigns' in providence is the guarantee that in a gracious gospel sense his promise shall be fulfilled, and his kingdom shall come. Unmoved he occupies an undisputed throne, whose decrees, acts and commands are holiness itself. What other throne is like this? Never was it stained with injustice, or defiled with sin. Neither is he who sits upon it dismayed, or in a dilemma. He sits in serenity, for he knows his own power, and sees that his purposes will not miscarry. Here is reason enough for holy song.

All principalities and powers must be subject to Jehovah and his Christ, for 'He is greatly exalted.' In nature, in power, in character, in glory, there is none to compare with him. Oh, glorious vision of a coming era! Make haste, you wheels of time! Meanwhile, saints, 'Be steadfast, immovable, always abounding in the work of the Lord, knowing that your labour is not in vain in the Lord.'

Meditation: *An understanding enlightened of the Holy Spirit is only fully capable of offering worthy praise* (C. H. Spurgeon).

Psalm 48:1-8

Suggested further reading: 2 Chronicles 20:14-21

How great Jehovah is essentially none can conceive; but we can all see that he is great in the deliverance of his people, great in their esteem who are delivered, and great in the hearts of those enemies whom he scatters by their own fears. There is none great in the church but the Lord. Jesus is 'the great Shepherd', he is 'a Saviour, and a great one', our great God and Saviour, our great High Priest; his Father has divided him a portion with the great, and his name shall be great unto the ends of the earth. His worship should be according to his nature; it cannot be too constant, too laudatory, too earnest, too reverential, too sublime. There is none like the Lord, and there should be no praises like his praises.

We worship no unknown god. We know him as our refuge in distress, we delight in him as such, and run to him in every time of need. We know nothing else as our refuge. Though we are made kings, and our houses are palaces, yet we have no confidence in ourselves, but trust in the Lord Protector, whose well-known power is our bulwark. 'The kings' came and they went. No sooner together than scattered. They came one way and fled twenty ways: boastful the gathering hosts with their royal leaders, despairing the fugitive bands, with their astonished captains. They came like foam on the angry sea, like foam they melted away. They came, they saw, but they did not conquer. No sooner did they perceive that the Lord was in the Holy City, than they took to their heels. Before the Lord came to blows with them, they were faint-hearted, and beat a retreat. The troublers were troubled. Their haste in coming was nothing to their hurry in going. Panic seized them, horses were not swift enough; they would have borrowed the wings of the wind. They fled ignominiously, like children in a fright. Glory be to God, it shall even be like this with the foes of his church; when the Lord comes to our help, our enemies shall be as nothing. Could they foresee their ignominious defeat, they would not advance to the attack. When the Lord arises for the help of his church, the proudest of his foes shall be like trembling women and their dismay shall be but the beginning of eternal defeat. The church too often relies on the wisdom of men, and these human helps are soon shipwrecked; yet the church itself is safe beneath the care of her God and King. The true church can never be disestablished. That which kings establish can last for time only, that which God establishes endures to all eternity.

Meditation: *The temporal Zion is now in the dust, but the true Zion is rising and shaking herself from it, and putting on her beautiful garments to welcome her King when he comes to reign over the whole earth* (W. M. Thomson).

Psalm 48:9-14

Suggested further reading: 2 Chronicles 20:22-37

Holy men are thoughtful men; they do not allow God's wonders to pass before their eyes and melt into forgetfulness,
but they meditate deeply upon them. Devout minds never
tire of so divine a theme. It is good to think of past loving-
kindness in times of trial, and equally profitable to remember it in seasons of prosperity. Grateful memories sweeten
sorrows and sober joys.

Where God is most seen he is best loved. The assembled
saints constitute a living temple, and our deepest musings
when so gathered together should have regard to the loving-
kindness of the Lord, exhibited in the varied experiences
of each of the living stones. Memories of mercy should be
associated with continuance of praise. The glory of
Jehovah's exploits overleaps the boundaries of earth; angels behold with wonder, and from every star delighted
intelligences proclaim his fame beyond the ends of the
earth. What if men are silent, yet the woods, and seas, and
mountains, with all their countless tribes, and all the unseen spirits that walk them, are full of the divine praise.

We cannot too frequently or too deeply consider the origin, privileges, history, security and glory of the church.
Some subjects deserve but a passing thought; this is worthy of the most patient consideration. Is the church of God
what she was in doctrine, in strength and in beauty? Her
foes counted her towers in envy first, and then in terror; let
us count them with sacred exultation. Consider most

attentively how strong are her ramparts, how safely her inhabitants are entrenched behind successive lines of defence. The security of the people of God is not a doctrine to be kept in the background, it may be safely taught, and frequently pondered: only to base hearts will that glorious truth prove harmful. The sons of perdition make a stumbling stone even of the Lord Jesus himself; it is little wonder that they pervert the truth of God concerning the final perseverance of the saints. We are not to turn away from inspecting Zion's ramparts because idlers skulk behind them. Would to God professors were more considerate of the condition of the church; so far from telling the towers, some of them scarcely know what or where they are; they are too busy counting their money, and considering their ledgers.

'God is our God for ever', a good reason for preserving a record of all that he has wrought. Israel will not change her God so as to wish to forget, nor will the Lord change so as to make the past mere history. He will be the covenant God of his people world without end. There is no other God, we wish for no other, we would have no other even if there were another. Throughout life, and to our dying couch, he will graciously conduct us, and even after death he will lead us to the living fountains of waters. We look to him for resurrection and eternal life.

Meditation: *This glorious God with all his divine perfection is my God, for ever and ever, and even death itself shall not separate me from his love* (George Burder).

Psalm 49:1-12

Suggested further reading: Matthew 16:24-28

The man of God calmly looks forward to dark times when those evils that have dogged his heels shall gain a temporary advantage over him. Iniquitous men, called in the abstract 'iniquity', lie in wait for the righteous, as serpents that aim at the heels of travellers: the iniquity of our heels is that evil which aims to trip us up or impede us. It was an old prophecy that the serpent should wound the heel of the woman's seed, and the enemy of our souls is diligent to fulfil that premonition. In some dreary part of our road it may be that evil will wax stronger and bolder, and gaining upon us will openly assail us; those who followed at our heels, like a pack of wolves, may perhaps overtake us, and surround us. What then? Shall we yield to cowardice? Shall we be a prey to their teeth? God forbid. No, we will not even fear, for what are these foes? What indeed, but mortal men who shall perish and pass away? There can be no real ground of alarm to the faithful. Their enemies are too insignificant to be worthy of one thrill of fear.

What if the good man's foes are numbered among those considered great on the earth! Still he need not fear them. Poor fools, to be content with such a rotten confidence. When we set our rock in contrast with theirs, it would be folly to be afraid of them. Even though they are loud in their brags, we can afford to smile. What if they glory 'and boast in the multitude of their riches'? Yet while we glory in our God we are not dismayed by their proud threatening. Great strength, position and estate make wicked men very lofty in their own esteem, and tyrannical towards others; but the heir of heaven is not overawed by their dignity, nor cowed by their haughtiness. He sees the small value of riches, and the helplessness of their owners in the hour of death, and therefore he is not so mean as to be afraid of an ephemera, a moth, a bubble.

Man is but a lodger for the hour, and does not stay a night: even when he dwells in marble halls his notice to quit is written out. He is not like the sheep that are preserved by the Great Shepherd, but like the hunted beast which is doomed to die. He lives a brutish life and dies a brutish death. Wallowing in riches, surfeited with pleasure, he is fatted for the slaughter, and dies like the ox in the shambles. Alas! that so noble a creature should use his life so unworthily, and end it so disgracefully. So far as this world is concerned, how does the death of many men differ from the death of a dog? What room is there, then, for fear to the godly when such natural brute beasts assail them? Should they not in patience possess their souls?

Meditation: *Who knocks more boldly at heaven-gate to be let in than they whom Christ will reject as workers of iniquity? Oh, what delusion is this!* (William Gurnall).

Psalm 49:13-20

Suggested further reading: Luke 16:19-31

Grace is not hereditary, but sordid worldliness goes from generation to generation. The race of fools never dies out. No need of missionaries to teach men to be earthworms, they crawl naturally to the dust.

The righteous are led by the Good Shepherd, but the ungodly have death for their shepherd, and he drives them onward to hell. As the power of death rules them in this world, for they have not passed from death to life, so the terrors of death shall devour them in the world to come. As grim giants, in old stories, are said to feed on men whom they entice to their caves, so death, the monster, feeds on the flesh and blood of the mighty. The poor saints were once the tail, but at daybreak they shall be the head. Sinners rule till nightfall; their honours wither in the evening, and in the morning they find their position utterly reversed. The sweetest reflection to the upright is that 'the morning' intended here begins an endless, changeless day. How the spirit of the proud worldling is vexed, when the Judge of all the earth holds his morning session, to see the man whom he despised, exalted high in heaven, while he himself is cast away! Whatever the ungodly had of glory shall disappear in the tomb. Form and comeliness shall vanish from them, the worm shall make sad havoc of all their beauty. Even their last dwelling-place, the grave, shall not be able to protect the relics committed to it; their bodies shall dissolve, no trace shall remain of all their strong limbs and lofty heads, no vestige of remaining beauty will be traceable. The beauty of the righteous is not yet revealed, it awaits its manifestations; but all the beauty the wicked will ever have is in full bloom in this life; it will wither, fade, decay, rot, and utterly pass away. Who, then, would envy or fear the proud sinner? Saddest of all is the reflection that though men are like beasts in all the degradation of perishing, yet not in the rest which animal perishing secures, for, alas! it is written, 'These shall go away into everlasting punishment.'

'But God will redeem my soul from the power of the grave.' Like our risen Head we cannot be held by the bands of the grave; redemption has set us free from the slavery of death. No redemption could man find in riches, but God has found it in the blood of his dear Son. Our Elder Brother has given to God a ransom, and we are the redeemed of the Lord; because of this redemption by price we shall assuredly be redeemed by power out of the hand of the last enemy.

Meditation: *Take any beast, or all beasts, the worst of beasts, man is the picture of them all, and he daily exemplifies the vilest of their qualities in his own* (Joseph Caryl).

Psalm 50:1-6

Suggested further reading: Deuteronomy 33:1-5

To render the address more impressive, three august titles
are mentioned, just as in royal decrees the names and dig-
nities of monarchs are placed in the forefront. Here the true
God is described as Almighty, as the only and perfect object of adoration and as the self-existent one. The dominion of Jehovah extends over the whole earth, and therefore
to all mankind is his decree directed. The east and the west
are bidden to hear the God who makes his sun to rise on
every quarter of the globe. Shall the summons of the great
King be despised? Will we dare provoke him to anger by
slighting his call?

The Lord is represented not only as speaking to the earth,
but also as coming forth to reveal the glory of his presence
to an assembled universe. God of old dwelt in Zion among
his chosen people, but here the beams of his splendour are
described as shining forth upon all nations. The sun was
spoken of in the first verse, but here is a far brighter sun.
The majesty of God is most conspicuous among his own
elect, but it is not confined to them; the church is not a
dark lantern, but a candlestick. God shines not only in Zion,
but also out of her. She is made perfect in beauty by his
indwelling and that beauty is seen by all observers when
the Lord shines forth from her.

The psalmist speaks of himself and his brethren as standing in immediate anticipation of the Lord's appearance upon
the scene. 'He comes,' they say, 'our covenant God is

coming'; they can hear his voice from afar, and perceive the splendour of his attending train. This is how we should await the long-promised appearing of the Lord from heaven. What a moment of awe when the Omnipotent is expected to reveal himself! What will be the reverent joy and solemn expectation when the poetic scene of this psalm becomes in the last great day an actual reality! Fire is the emblem of justice in action, and the tempest is a token of his overwhelming power. Who will not listen in solemn silence when such is the tribunal from which the judge pleads with heaven and earth?

'For God is judge himself.' This is the reason for the correctness of the judgement. Priests of old, and churches of later times, were readily deceived, but not so the all-discerning Lord. No deputy-judge sits on the great white throne; the injured Lord of all himself weighs the evidence and allots the vengeance or reward. The scene in the psalm is a grand poetical conception but it is also an inspired prophecy of that day which shall burn as an oven, when the Lord shall discern between him that fears him and him that fears him not.

Meditation: *We are not Christians till we have subscribed to God's covenant, and that without any reservation* (William Gurnall).

Psalm 50:7-15

Suggested further reading: 1 Samuel 12:19-25

This address is directed to the professed people of God. It is clearly, in the first place, meant for Israel; but is equally applicable to the visible church of God in every age. It declares the futility of external worship when spiritual faith is absent and the mere outward ceremonial is relied upon.

God had taken them to be his peculiar people above all other nations, and they had in the most solemn manner avowed that he was their God. Hence the special reason for calling them to account. The law began with, 'I am the Lord your God, which brought you up out of the land of Egypt,' and now the session of their judgement opens with the same reminder of their singular position, privilege and responsibility. It is not merely that Jehovah is God, but your God, O Israel; it is this that makes you so amenable to his searching reproofs.

Though they had not failed in maintaining his outward worship, or even if they had, he was not about to call them to account for this, a more weighty matter was now under consideration. They thought the daily sacrifices and the abounding burnt offerings to be everything: he counted them nothing if the inner sacrifice of heart devotion had been neglected. What was greatest with them was least with God. It is even so today. Sacraments (so called) and sacred rites are the main concern with unconverted but religious men, but with the Most High the spiritual worship which they forget is the sole matter. Let the external be maintained by all means according to the divine command, but if the secret and spiritual is not in them, they are a vain oblation, a dead ritual, and even an abomination before the Lord. The sacrifices, considered by themselves, are contemned, but the internal emotions of love resulting from a remembrance of divine goodness, are commended as the substance, meaning and soul of sacrifice.

'Call upon me in the day of trouble.' Oh, blessed verse! Is this then true sacrifice? Is it an offering to ask an alms of heaven? It is even so. The King himself so regards it. For here is faith manifested, here is love proved, for in the hour of peril we fly to those we love. It seems a small thing to pray to God when we are distressed, yet it is a more acceptable worship than the mere heartless presentation of bullocks and he-goats. Thus we see what is true ritual. Here we read inspired rubrics. Spiritual worship is the great, the essential matter; all else without it is rather provoking than pleasing to God. As help to the soul, outward offerings were precious, but when men did not go beyond them, even their hallowed things were profaned in the view of heaven.

Meditation: *The Lord has promised his children supply of all good things, yet they must see the means of entreaty, by prayer* (Thomas Adams).

Psalm 50:16-23

Suggested further reading: 1 Kings 14:7-16

He now addresses the breakers of the second table; he had previously spoken to those who had neglected the first. You openly violate my moral law, and yet are great sticklers for my ceremonial commands! What have you to do with them? What interest can you have in them? Do you dare to teach my law to others, and profane it yourselves? What impudence, what blasphemy is this! Even if you claim to be sons of Levi, what of that? Your wickedness disqualifies you, disinherits you and puts you out of the succession. It should silence you, and would if my people were as spiritual as I would have them, for they would refuse to hear you, and to pay you the portion of temporal things which is due to my true servants. You count up your holy days, you contend for rituals, you fight for externals, and yet the weightier matters of the law you despise! How horrible an evil it is, that to this day we see men who despise precepts explaining doctrines! They make grace a coverlet for sin, and even judge themselves to be sound in the faith, while they are rotten in life. We need the grace of the doctrines as much as the doctrines of grace, and without it an apostle is but a Judas, and a fair-spoken professor is an arrant enemy of the cross of Christ.

One by one the moral precepts are broken by the sinners in Zion. Under the cloak of piety, those who live unclean lives conceal themselves. We may do this by smiling at unchaste jests, listening to indelicate expressions, and conniving at licentious behaviour in our presence; and if we act in this way, how dare we preach, or lead public prayer, or wear the Christian name? See how the Lord lays righteousness to the plummet! How plainly all this declares that without holiness no man shall see the Lord! No amount of ceremonial or theological accuracy can cover dishonesty and fornication; these filthy things must be either purged from us by the blood of Jesus, or they will kindle a fire in God's anger which will burn even to the lowest hell.

'Now' is a word of entreaty, for the Lord is reluctant even to let the most ungodly run on to destruction. 'Consider this'; take these truths to heart, you who trust in ceremonies and you who live in vice, for both of you sin in that 'you forget God'. Consider how unaccepted you are, and turn to the Lord. See how you have mocked the eternal, and repent of your iniquities. You reject the Mediator: beware, for you will sorely need one in the day of wrath, and none will be near to plead for you. How terrible, how complete, how painful, how humiliating, will be the destruction of the wicked! God uses no soft words, or velvet metaphors, nor may his servants do so when they speak of the wrath to come. O reader, consider this.

Meditation: *Atheists mock those Scriptures which tell us that we shall give account of all our deeds; but God shall make them find the truth of it in that day of their reckoning* (William Struther).

Psalm 51:1-6

Suggested further reading: 2 Samuel 11:1-13

David appeals at once to the mercy of God, even before he mentions his sin. The sight of mercy is good for eyes that are sore with penitential weeping. Pardon of sin must ever be an act of pure mercy, and therefore to that attribute the awakened sinner flies.

It is not enough to blot out the sin; his person is defiled, and he must be purified. He would have God himself cleanse him, for none but he could do it effectually. The hypocrite is content if his garments are washed; but the true suppliant cries, 'Wash me.' The careless soul is content with a nominal cleansing, but the truly awakened conscience desires a real and practical washing, one which was most complete and efficient. His sin is viewed as one great pollution, affecting the entire nature, and as all his own; as if nothing were so much his own as his sin. The one sin against Bathsheba served to show the psalmist the whole mountain of his iniquity, of which that foul deed was but one falling stone. He desires to be rid of the whole mass of his filthiness, which, though once so little observed, had then become a hideous and haunting terror to his mind.

God desires not merely outward virtue, but inward purity, and the penitent's sense of sin is greatly deepened as with astonishment he discovers how far he is from satisfying the divine demand. Reality, sincerity, true holiness, heart-fidelity, these are the demands of God. He does not care for the pretence of purity, he looks to the mind, heart and soul. The Holy One of Israel has always estimated men by their inner nature, and not by their outward professions; to him the inward is as visible as the outward, and he rightly judges that the essential character of an action lies in the motive of the one who works it. The penitent feels that God is teaching him truth concerning his nature, which he had not before perceived. The love of the heart, the mystery of its fall, and the way of its purification — this hidden wisdom we must all attain; and it is a great blessing to be able to believe that the Lord will 'make us to know it'. No one can teach our innermost nature but the Lord, but he can instruct us to profit. The Holy Spirit can write the law on our heart, and that is the sum of practical wisdom. He can put the fear of the Lord within, and that is the beginning of wisdom. He can reveal Christ in us, and he is essential wisdom. Such poor, foolish, disarranged souls as ours shall yet be ordered aright, and truth and wisdom shall reign within us.

Meditation: *There is a godly sorrow which leads a man to life; and this sorrow is wrought in a man by the Spirit of God, and in the heart of the godly; that he mourns for sin because it has displeased God, who is so dear and so sweet a Father to him. And suppose he had neither a heaven to lose, nor a hell to gain, yet he is sad and sorrowful in heart because he has grieved God* (John Welch).

Psalm 51:7-12

Suggested further reading: 2 Samuel 11:14-27

Scarcely does Holy Scripture contain a verse more full of
faith than the seventh. Considering the nature of the sin,
and the deep sense the psalmist had of it, it is a glorious
faith to be able to see in the blood sufficient, no, all-
sufficient merit to purge it away entirely. Considering also
the deep, natural inbred corruption which David saw and
experienced within, it is a miracle of faith that he could
rejoice in the hope of perfect purity in his inward being.
Yet, it must be added, the faith is no more than the word
warrants, than the blood of atonement encourages, than
the promise of God deserves. Oh, that some reader may
take heart, even now while smarting under sin, to do the
Lord the honour to rely as confidently as this on the finished sacrifice of Calvary and the infinite mercy revealed
there.

David's face was ashamed with looking on his sin, and
no diverting thoughts could remove it from his memory;
but he prays the Lord to do with his sin what he himself
cannot. If God does not hide his face from our sin, he must
hide it for ever from us; and if he does not blot out our sins,
he must blot our names out of his book of life. In the seventh
verse he asked to be clean; in the tenth he seeks a heart
suitable to that cleanliness; but he does not say, 'Make my
old heart clean'; he is too experienced in the hopelessness
of the old nature. He would have the old man buried as a
dead thing, and a new creation brought in to fill its place.

None but God can create either a new heart or a new earth. Salvation is a marvellous display of supreme power; the work in us as much as that for us is wholly of Omnipotence. The affections must be rectified first, or all our nature will go amiss. The heart is the rudder of the soul, and till the Lord takes it in hand we steer in a false and foul way. O Lord, who once made me, be pleased to make me new, and in my most secret parts renew me.

Conscious of weakness, mindful of having so lately fallen, David seeks to be kept on his feet by power superior to his own. That royal Spirit, whose holiness is true dignity, is able to make us walk as kings and priests, in all the uprightness of holiness; and he will do so if we seek his gracious upholding. Such influences will not enslave but emancipate us; for holiness is liberty, and the Holy Spirit is a free Spirit. The praying for joy and upholding go well together; it is all over with joy if the foot is not kept; and, on the other hand, joy is a very upholding thing, and greatly aids holiness. However, the free, noble, loyal Spirit is at the bottom of both.

Meditation: *He used the word create, a word only used of the work of God, and showing that the change in him could be wrought only by God* (Christopher Wordsworth).

Psalm 51:13-19

Suggested further reading: 2 Samuel 12:1-15

It was David's fixed resolve to be a teacher of others; and assuredly none instruct others so well as those who, themselves, have been experimentally taught of God. Reclaimed poachers make the best gamekeepers. The pardoned sinner's matter will be good, for he has been taught in the school of experience, and his manner will be telling, for he will speak sympathetically, as one who has felt what he declares. The audience the psalmist would choose is memorable; he would instruct transgressors like himself. Others might despise them, but, 'a fellow feeling makes us wondrous kind'. If unworthy to edify saints, he would creep in along with the sinners, and humbly tell them of divine love.

He is so afraid of himself that he commits his whole being to the divine care, and fears to speak till the Lord unstops his shame-silenced mouth. How marvellously the Lord can open our lips, and what divine things we poor simpletons pour forth under his inspiration! This prayer of a penitent is a golden petition for a preacher. Lord, I offer it for my brethren and myself. But it may stand in good stead any one whose shame for sin makes him stammer in his prayers, and when it is fully answered, the tongue of the dumb begins to sing.

The psalmist was so illuminated as to see far beyond the symbolic ritual; his eye of faith gazed with delight upon the actual atonement. He would have been glad enough to present tens of thousands of victims if these would have met the case. Indeed, anything which the Lord prescribed he would cheerfully have rendered. We are ready to give up all we have if we may but be cleared of our sins; and when sin is pardoned our joyful gratitude is prepared for any sacrifice. He knew that no form of burnt sacrifice was a satisfactory propitiation. His deep soul-need made him look from the type to the antitype, from the external rite to the inward grace.

When the heart mourns for sin, God is better pleased than when the bullock bleeds beneath the axe. 'A broken heart' is an expression implying deep sorrow, embittering the very life; it carries in it the idea of all but killing anguish in that region which is so vital as to be the very source of life. So excellent is a spirit humbled and mourning for sin, that it is not only a sacrifice, but also it has a plurality of excellence, and is pre-eminently God's sacrifices. A heart crushed is a fragrant heart. Men contemn those who are contemptible in their own eyes, but the Lord does not see as man sees. He despises what men esteem, and values that which they despise. Never yet has God spurned a lowly, weeping penitent, and never will he while God is love, and while Jesus is called the man who receives sinners.

Meditation: *Bullocks and rams God desires not, but contrite hearts he seeks after; indeed, but one of them is better to him than all the varied offerings of the old Jewish sanctuary* (C. H. Spurgeon).

Psalm 52:1-5

Suggested further reading: 1 Samuel 21:1-9

Doeg had small matter for boasting in having procured the slaughter of a band of defenceless priests. A mighty man indeed to kill men who never touched a sword! He ought to have been ashamed of his cowardice. He had no room for exultation! Honourable titles are but irony where the wearer is mean and cruel. The tyrant's fury cannot dry up the perennial stream of divine mercy. If priests are slain, their Master lives. If Doeg triumphs for a while the Lord will outlive him, and right the wrongs that he has done. This ought to modify the proud exultation of the wicked, for after all, while the Lord lives, iniquity has little cause to exalt itself.

David represents the false tongue as being effectual for mischief, like a razor which, unawares to the person operated on, is making him bald; so softly and deftly do Oriental barbers perform their work. Or he may mean that as with a razor a man's throat may be cut very speedily, under the pretence of shaving him, even thus keenly, basely, but effectually Doeg destroyed the band of the priests. Whetted by malice, and guided by craft, he did his cruel work with accursed thoroughness.

Men can manage to say a great many furious things, and yet cover all over with the pretext of justice. They claim that they are jealous for the right, but the truth is they are determined to put down truth and holiness, and craftily go about it under this transparent pretence.

The persecutor would gladly destroy the church, and therefore God shall destroy him, pull down his house, pluck up his roots, and make an end of him. God shall extinguish his coal and sweep him away like the ashes of the hearth; he would have quenched the truth, and God shall quench him. Like a plant torn from the place where it grew or a captive dragged from his home, God will 'pluck him out of his dwelling place'. Ahimelech and his brother priests were cut off from their abode, and so should be those who compassed and contrived their murder. The persecutor shall be eradicated, stubbed up by the root, cut up root and branch. He sought the death of others and death shall fall upon him. He troubled the land of the living, and he shall be banished to that land where the wicked cease from troubling. Those who will not 'let live' have no right to 'live'. God will turn the tables on malicious men, and mete to them a portion with their own measure.

Meditation: *The smooth, adroit manner of executing a wicked device neither hides nor abates its wickedness. Murder with 'a sharp razor' is as wicked as murder with a meat-axe or a bludgeon. A lie very ingeniously framed and rehearsed in an oily manner is as great a sin, and in the end will be seen to be as great a folly as the most bungling attempt at deception* (William S. Plumer).

Psalm 52:6-9

Suggested further reading: 1 Samuel 22:9-23

'The righteous' — the object of the tyrant's hatred — shall outlive his enmity, and 'also shall see', before his own face, the end of the ungodly oppressor. God permits Mordecai to see Haman hanging on the gallows. David had brought to him the tokens of Saul's death on Gilboa. Holy awe shall sober the mind of the good man; he shall reverently adore the God of providence. Schemes so far-reaching all baffled, plans so deep, so politic, all thwarted. This is a goodly theme for that deep-seated laughter which is more akin to solemnity than merriment.

Look here, and read the epitaph of a mighty man, who lorded it proudly during his little hour, and set his heel upon the necks of the Lord's chosen. Behold the man, the great vainglorious man! He found a fortress, but not in God; he gloried in his might, but not in the Almighty. Where is he now? How has it fared with him in the hour of his need? Behold his ruin, and be instructed. The substance he had gathered, and the mischief he had wrought, were his boast and glory. Wealth and wickedness are dreadful companions; when combined they make a monster. When the devil is master of moneybags, he is a devil indeed. Beelzebub and Mammon together heat the furnace seven times hotter for the child of God, but in the end they shall work out their own destruction. Wherever we see today a man great in sin and substance, we shall do well to anticipate his end and view this verse as the divine memorial.

'But I', hunted and persecuted though I am, 'am like a green olive tree.' I am not plucked up or destroyed, but am like a flourishing olive, which out of the rock draws oil, and amid the drought still lives and grows. He was one of the divine family, and could not be expelled from it; his place was near his God, and there was he safe and happy, despite all the machinations of his foes. He was bearing fruit, and would continue to do so when all his proud enemies were withered like branches lopped from the tree. Eternal mercy is my present confidence. David knew God's mercy to be eternal and perpetual, and in that he trusted. What a rock to build on! What a fortress to fly to! David views his prayers as already answered, the promises of God as already fulfilled, and therefore he at once lifts up the sacred psalm. God shall still be the psalmist's hope; he will not in future look elsewhere. Let the mighty ones boast, we will wait on the Lord; and if their haste brings them present honour, our patience will have its turn by and by, and bring us the honour that excels.

Meditation: *While others trust in the riches of their own righteousness and services, and do not make Christ their strength, you renounce all, and trust in the mercy of God in Christ, and you shall be like a green olive when they fade and wither* (William Gurnall).

Psalm 53

Suggested further reading: Psalm 14

Being a fool the atheist speaks according to his nature; being a great fool he meddles with a great subject, and comes to a wild conclusion. He is, morally as well as mentally, a fool, a fool in the heart as well as in the head: a fool in morals as well as in philosophy. With the denial of God as a starting point, we may well conclude that the fool's progress is a rapid, riotous, raving, ruinous one. He who begins at impiety is ready for anything. 'No God', being interpreted, means no law, no order, no restraint to lust, no limit to passion. Who but a fool would be of this mind?

Bad principles soon lead to bad lives. One does not find virtue promoted by the example of your Voltaires and Tom Paines. Those who talk so abominably as to deny their Maker will act abominably when it serves their turn. It is the abounding denial and forgetfulness of God among men that is the source of the unrighteousness and crime that we see around us. If all men are not outwardly vicious it is to be accounted for by the power of other and better principles, but left to itself the 'No God' spirit so universal in mankind would produce nothing but the most loathsome actions. The one typical fool is reproduced in the whole race; without a single exception men have forgotten the right way. This accusation made twice in the psalm, and repeated a third time by the inspired apostle Paul, is an indictment most solemn and sweeping, but he who makes it cannot err, he knows what is in man; neither will he lay more to man's charge than he can prove.

Had there been one understanding man, one true lover of his God, the divine eye would have discovered him. Those pure heathens and admirable savages, that men talk so much of, do not appear to have been visible to the eye of Omniscience, the fact being that they live nowhere but in the realm of fiction. The Lord did not look for great grace, but only for sincerity and right desire, but these he found not. He saw all nations, and all men in all nations, and all hearts in all men, and all motions of all hearts, but he saw neither a clear head nor a clean heart among them all. Where God's eyes see no favourable sign we may rest assured there is none.

David sees the end of the ungodly and the ultimate triumph of the spiritual seed. God's people may well look with derision upon their enemies since they are the objects of divine contempt. They scoff at us, but we may with far greater reason laugh them to scorn, because the Lord our God considers them as vanity and less than nothing.

Meditation: *God, in this psalm, 'speaks twice', for this is the same almost verbatim with the fourteenth psalm. The scope of it is to convince us of our sins, to set us a-blushing, and to set us a-trembling because of them; there is need of 'line upon line' to this purpose* (Matthew Henry).

Psalm 54

Suggested further reading: 1 Samuel 26:1-4

Vocal prayer helps the supplicant, and we keep our minds more fully awake when we can use our tongues as well as our hearts. But what is prayer if God does not hear? It is all one whether we babble nonsense or plead arguments if our God does not grant us a hearing. When his situation had become dangerous, David could not afford to pray out of mere custom, he must succeed in his pleadings, or become the prey of his adversary.

Kings generally coin their own likeness. Saul led the way, and others followed seeking David's soul, his blood, his life and his very existence. Cruel and intense were they in their malice, they would utterly crush the good man; no half measures would content them. They had no more regard for right and justice than if they knew no God, or cared for none. Had they regarded God they would not have betrayed the innocent to be hunted down like a poor harmless stag. David felt that atheism lay at the bottom of the enmity that pursued him. Good men are hated for God's sake, and this is a good plea for them to urge in prayer.

He saw enemies everywhere, and now to his joy as he looks upon the band of his defenders he sees one whose aid is better than all the help of men; he is overwhelmed with joy at recognizing his divine champion, and cries, 'Behold'. And is not this a theme for pious exultation in all time, that the great God protects us, his own people? What does the number or violence of our foes matter when he uplifts the shield of his omnipotence to guard us, and the sword of his power to aid us?

Our covenant God is pledged to bring us out of all trouble, and therefore even now let us lift up the note of triumph to Jehovah, the faithful preserver of those who put their trust in him. Thus far we have proved his promise good; he does not change, and therefore in all the unknown future he will be equally our guardian and defence, 'showing himself strong on behalf of those whose heart is perfect toward him'. He knew that he should yet look on his haughty foes, gazing down on them in triumph as now they looked on him in contempt. He desired this as a matter of justice, and not of personal pique. His righteous soul exulted because he knew that unprovoked and gratuitous malice would meet with a righteous punishment. If we could keep out of our hearts all personal enmity as fully as the psalmist did in this psalm, we might yet equally feel with him a sacred acquiescence and delight in that divine justice which will save the righteous and overthrow the malicious.

Meditation: *Particular difficulties and particular deliveries should be particularly remarked* (David Dickson).

Psalm 55:1-8

Suggested further reading: 2 Samuel 16:1-8

The fact is so commonly before us, otherwise we should be surprised to observe how universally and constantly the saints resort to prayer in seasons of distress. From the Great Elder Brother down to the very least of the divine family, all of them delight in prayer. They run as naturally to the mercy seat in time of trouble as the little chickens to the hen in the hour of danger. But note well that it is never the bare act of prayer that satisfies the godly, they crave an audience with heaven, an answer from the throne, and nothing less will content them.

What a comfort that we may be familiar with our God! We may not complain of him, but we may complain to him. When we are distracted with grief we may bring before him our rambling thoughts, and that too in utterances rather to be called a noise than language. He will attend so carefully that he will understand us, and he will often fulfil desires that we ourselves could not have expressed in intelligible words. 'Groaning that cannot be uttered,' are often prayers that cannot be refused. Our Lord himself used strong crying and tears, and was heard in that he feared.

His spirit writhed in agony, like a poor worm; he was mentally as much in pain as a woman in travail physically. His inmost soul was touched; and a wounded spirit who can bear? If this was written when David was attacked by his own favourite son, and ignominiously driven from his capital, he had reason enough for using these expressions.

He said, 'Oh that I had wings like a dove! For then I would fly away, and be at rest'. If he could not resist as an eagle, he would escape as a dove. Swiftly and unobserved, on strong, untiring pinions would he hasten away from the abodes of slander and wickedness. His love of peace made him sigh for an escape from the scene of strife. We are all too apt to utter this vain desire, for vain it is; no wings of doves or eagles could bear us away from the sorrows of a trembling heart. Inward grief knows nothing of place. Moreover, it is cowardly to shun the battle that God would have us fight. We had better face the danger, for we have no armour for our backs. He needed a swifter conveyance than doves' pinions who would out-fly slander; he may be at rest who does not fly, but commends his case to his God. Even the dove of old found no rest till she returned to her ark, and amid all our sorrow we may find rest in Jesus. We need not depart; all will be well if we trust in him.

Meditation: *A mourning suppliant shall neither lose his prayers nor his tears; for, 'I mourn,' is brought for a reason of his hope that God shall attend and hear him* (David Dickson).

Psalm 55:9-15

Suggested further reading: 2 Samuel 15:10-14

The rabble and their leaders were plotting and planning, raging and contending against their king, running wild with a thousand mad projects. Anarchy had fermented among them, and the king hoped that now the very lawlessness that had exiled him might create weakness among his foes. Revolution devours its own children. They who are strong through violence will sooner or later find that their strength is their death. Absalom and Ahithophel may raise the mob, but they cannot so easily rule it, nor so readily settle their own policy to remain firm friends. The prayer of David was heard, the rebels were soon divided in their councils; Ahithophel went his way to be hanged with a rope and Absalom to be hanged without one.

It was not an open foe, but a pretended friend; he went over to the other camp and tried to prove the reality of his treachery by slandering his old friend. None are such real enemies as false friends. Reproaches from those who have been intimate with us, and trusted by us, cut us to the quick; and they are usually so well acquainted with our peculiar weaknesses that they know how to touch us where we are most sensitive, and to speak so as to do us most damage. We can find a hiding-place from open foes, but who can escape from treachery? If our enemies proudly boast over us we nerve our souls for resistance, but when those who pretended to love us leer at us with contempt, where shall we go? Our blessed Lord had to endure the deceit and faithlessness of a favoured disciple at its worst; let us not marvel when we are called to tread the road that is marked by his pierced feet.

It was not merely the counsel that men take together in public or upon common themes, their fellowship had been tender and confidential. Soul had been in converse with soul, at least on David's part. However feigned might have been the affection of the treacherous one, the betrayed friend had not dealt with him coldly, or guarded his utterance before him. Shame on the wretch who could belie such fellowship and betray such confidence! Religion had rendered their fellowship sacred, they had mingled their worship, and communed on heavenly themes. If ever any bonds ought to be held inviolable, religious connection should be. There is a measure of impiety, of a detestable sort, in the deceit that debases the union of men who make professions of godliness. Shall the very altar of God be defiled with hypocrisy? Shall the gatherings of the temple be polluted by the presence of treachery? All this was true of Ahithophel. Of the serpent's brood some vipers still remain, who will sting the hand that cherished them, and sell for silver those who raised them to the position which rendered it possible for them to be so abominably treacherous.

Meditation: *This prayer is a prophecy of the utter, the final, the everlasting ruin of all those who, whether secretly or openly, oppose and rebel against the Lord's Messiah* (Matthew Henry).

Psalm 55:16-23

Suggested further reading: 1 Peter 5:5-11

The psalmist would not endeavour to meet the plots of his adversaries by counterplots, or imitate their incessant violence, but in direct opposition to their godless behaviour would continually resort to his God. Thus Jesus did, and it has been the wisdom of all believers to do the same. As this exemplifies the contrast of their character, so it will foretell the contrast of their end — the righteous shall ascend to their God, the wicked shall sink to ruin.

Seasons of great need call for frequent seasons of devotion. The three periods chosen are most fitting; to begin, continue, and end the day with God is supreme wisdom. Where time has naturally set up a boundary, there let us set up an altar-stone. The psalmist means that he will always pray: he will run a line of prayer right along the day and track the sun with his petitions. Day and night he saw his enemies busy (v. 10), and therefore he would meet their activity by continuous prayer. He is confident that he will prevail; he makes no question that he would be heard, he speaks as if he were already answered. When our window is opened towards heaven, the windows of heaven are open to us. Have but a pleading heart and God will have a plenteous hand.

His own reverential feeling causes him to remember the daring godlessness of the wicked. He feels that his trials have driven him to his God, and he declares that their uninterrupted prosperity was the cause of their living in such neglect of the Most High. It is a very manifest fact that long-continued ease and pleasure are sure to produce the worst influences upon graceless men: though troubles do not convert them, yet their absence makes their corrupt nature develop more readily. Stagnant water becomes putrid. Summer heat breeds noxious insects. He who is without trouble is often without God. It is a forcible proof of human depravity that man turns the mercy of God into nutriment for sin: the Lord save us from this.

For the ungodly a sure, terrible, and fatal overthrow is appointed. Climb as they may, 'the pit' yawns for them, God himself will cause them to descend into it, and 'destruction' there shall be their portion. They were in heart murderers of others, and they became in reality self-murderers. Do not doubt that virtue lengthens life, and that vice tends to shorten it. A very wise, practical conclusion is found in the words 'I will trust in you.' We can have no better ground of confidence. The Lord is all, and more than all that faith can need as the foundation of peaceful dependence. Lord, increase our faith evermore.

Meditation: *Many would destroy the saints, but God has not suffered it, and never will. Like pillars, the godly stand immovable, to the glory of the Great Architect* (C. H. Spurgeon).

Psalm 56:1-7

Suggested further reading: 1 Samuel 21:10-14

It is sweet to see how the tender dove-like spirit of the psalm-ist flies to the most tender attribute for succour in the hour of peril. The open mouths of sinners when they rage against us should open our mouths in prayer. We may plead the cruelty of men as a reason for the divine interposition; a father is soon aroused when his children are shamefully entreated. David has his eye on the leader of his foes, and lays his complaint against him in the right place. If we may plead in this way against man, much more against that great enemy of souls, the devil. We ask the Lord to forgive us our trespasses, which is another way of saying, 'Be merciful to me, O God,' and then we say, 'Lead us not into temptation, but deliver us from the evil one.' The more violent the at-tack of Satan, the stronger our plea for deliverance.

David was no braggart, he does not claim never to be afraid, and he was no brutish Stoic free from fear because of the lack of tenderness. David's intelligence deprived him of the stupid heedlessness of ignorance; he saw the imminence of his peril, and was afraid. We are men, and therefore liable to overthrow; we are feeble, and therefore unable to prevent it; we are sinful men, and therefore de-serving it, and for all these reasons we are afraid. But the condition of the psalmist's mind was complex — he feared, but that fear did not fill the whole area of his mind, for he adds, 'I will trust in you.' It is possible, then, for fear and faith to occupy the mind at the same moment. We are strange beings, and our experience in the divine life is stranger still. We are often in a twilight, where light and darkness are both present, and it is hard to tell which predominates. It is a blessed fear that drives us to trust. Unregenerate fear drives from God, gracious fear drives to him. If I fear man I have only to trust God, and I have the best antidote. To trust when there is no cause for fear is but the name of faith, but to be reliant upon God when occasions for alarm are abundant and pressing is the conquering faith of God's elect. Though the verse is in the form of a resolve, it became a fact in David's life: let us make it so in ours. Whether the fear arise from without or within, from past, present, or future, from men or devils, let us maintain faith, and we shall soon recover courage.

Altogether and alone we should rest ourselves on God. Faith exercised, fear is banished, and holy triumph ensues, so that the soul asks, 'What can flesh do to me?' What, indeed? He can do me no real injury; all his malice shall be overruled for my good.

Meditation: *Man is flesh, flesh is grass — Lord, in your name I defy its utmost wrath* (C. H. Spurgeon).

Psalm 56:8-13

Suggested further reading: Romans 8:31-39

The machinery of prayer is not always visible, but it is most efficient. God inclines us to pray, we cry in anguish of heart, he hears, he acts, the enemy is turned back. What a God is this who hearkens to the cry of his children, and in a moment delivers them from the mightiest adversaries! This is one of the believer's certainties, his axioms, his infallible, indisputable verities. 'God is for me.' This we know; and we know, therefore, that none can be against us who are worth a moment's fear. 'If God is for us, who can be against us?' Who will restrain prayer when it is so potent? Who will seek any other ally than God, who is instantly present so soon as we give the ordained signal, by which we testify both our need and our confidence?

Now comes the thanksgiving. He is a wretch who, having obtained help, forgets to return a grateful acknowledgement. The least we can do is to praise him from whom we receive such distinguished favours. The Lord is to be praised under every aspect, and in all his attributes and acts, but certain mercies more peculiarly draw out our admiration towards special portions of the great whole. The praise that is never specially directed cannot be very thoughtful, and it is to be feared cannot be very acceptable. He delights to dwell on his praise, therefore he repeats his song. The change by which he brings in the glorious name of Jehovah is doubtless meant to indicate that under every aspect he delights in his God and in his word.

Faith has banished fear. He views his foes in their most forcible character, calling them not flesh, but indicating them as man, yet he does not dread them. Though the whole race was his enemy he would not be afraid now that his trust is stayed on God. He is not afraid of what they threaten to do, for much of that they cannot do; and even what is in their power, what they can do, he defies with holy daring. He speaks for the future, 'I will not', for he is sure that the security of the present will suffice for days to come. His enemies were defeated in their attempts upon his life, and therefore he vowed to devote his life to God. One mercy is a plea for another, for indeed it may happen that the second is the necessary complement of the first. Walking at liberty, in holy service, in sacred communion, in constant progress in holiness, enjoying the smile of heaven — this I seek after. Here is the loftiest reach of a good man's ambition, to dwell with God, to walk in righteousness before him, to rejoice in his presence, and in the light and glory that it yields.

Meditation: *By the assistance of God I shall be enabled to praise him for the performance of his promises* (Symon Patrick).

Psalm 57:1-6

Suggested further reading: 1 Samuel 22:1-5

The repetition of the cry suggests urgent need, for thus intense urgency of desire is expressed. If 'he gives twice who gives quickly', so he who would receive quickly must ask twice. The psalmist pleads for mercy at first, and he feels he cannot improve upon his plea, and therefore returns to it. God is the God of mercy, and the Father of mercies; it is most fit therefore that in distress we should seek mercy from him in whom it dwells. Faith urges her suit right well. How can the Lord be unmerciful to a trustful soul? Our faith does not deserve mercy, but it always wins it from the sovereign grace of God when it is sincere, as in this case where 'the soul' of the man believed.

David has cogent reason for praying, for he sees God performing. Saul hunted David, but David caught him more than once and might have slain him on the spot. Evil is a stream which one day flows back to its source. We may sit down at the pit's mouth and view with wonder the just retaliations of providence. If there are no fit instruments on earth, heaven shall yield up its legions of angels for the succour of the saints. We may in times of great straits expect mercies of a remarkable kind; like the Israelites in the wilderness, we shall have our bread hot from heaven, new every morning; and for the overthrow of our enemies God shall open his celestial batteries, and put them to utter confusion. Wherever the battle is more fierce than usual, help shall come from headquarters, for the Commander-in-chief sees all. He asked for mercy, and truth came with it. Thus God always gives us more than we ask or think. His attributes, like angels on the wing, are ever ready to come to the rescue of his chosen.

The believer waits and God works. The Lord has undertaken for us, and he will not draw back, he will go through with his covenant engagements. Whatsoever the Lord takes in hand he will accomplish; hence past mercies are guarantees for the future, and admirable reasons for continuing to cry unto him. Before he has quite concluded his prayer the good man interjects a verse of praise; and glorious praise too, seeing it comes up from the lion's den and from amid the coals of fire. Higher than the heavens is the Most High, and so high ought our praises to rise. Above even the power of cherubim and seraphim to express it, the glory of God is revealed and is to be acknowledged by us. As above, so below, let your praises, O great Jehovah, be universally proclaimed. As the air surrounds all nature, so let your praises gird the earth with a zone of song.

Meditation: *It is observable that David uses the same expression of praising God here when he was in the cave, hiding himself to save his life as he did when he triumphed over his enemies* (Jeremiah Burroughs).

Psalm 57:7-11

Suggested further reading: Revelation 15:3-4

One would have thought he would have said, 'My heart is fluttered'; but no, he is calm, firm, happy, resolute, established. When the central axle is secure, the whole wheel is right. I am resolved to trust you, to serve you, and to praise you. Twice he declares this to the glory of God who thus comforts the souls of his servants. Reader, it is surely well with you, if your once roving heart is now firmly fixed upon God and the proclamation of his glory. David would make Adullam ring with music, and all its caverns echo with joyous song. Believer, make a firm decree that in all seasons your soul shall magnify the Lord.

David says, 'I will awaken the dawn', with his joyous notes. No sleepy verses and weary notes shall be heard; he will thoroughly arouse himself for this high employment. When we are at our best we fall far short of the Lord's deserts; let us, therefore, make sure that what we bring him is our best, and, if marred with infirmity, at least let it not be deteriorated by indolence. Three times the psalmist calls upon himself to awake. Do we need so much arousing, and for such work? Then let us not spare it, for the engagement is too honourable, too needful to be left undone or ill done for want of arousing ourselves.

'I will praise you, O Lord, among the peoples.' Gentiles shall hear his praise. Here is an instance of the way in which the truly devout evangelic spirit overleaps the boundaries which bigotry sets up. The ordinary Jew would never wish the Gentile dogs to hear Jehovah's name, except to tremble at it; but this grace-taught psalmist has a missionary spirit, and would spread the praise and fame of his God.

Imagination fails to guess the height of heaven, and even thus the riches of mercy exceed our highest thoughts. The psalmist, as he sits at the cave's mouth and looks up to the firmament, rejoices that God's goodness is vaster and more sublime than even the vaulted skies. Upon the cloud he sets the seal of his truth, the rainbow, which ratifies his covenant; in the cloud he hides his rain and snow, which prove his truth by bringing to us seedtime and harvest, cold and heat. Creation is great, but the Creator far greater. Heaven cannot contain him; above clouds and stars his goodness far exceeds.

'Be exalted, O God, above the heavens.' This is a grand chorus. Take it up, angels and you spirits made perfect, and join in it, sons of men below, as you say, 'Let your glory be above all the earth.' The prophet in the previous verse spoke of mercy 'unto the heavens', but here his song flies 'above the heavens'; praise rises higher and higher, and knows no bound.

Meditation: *Heaven and earth have a mutually interwoven history, and the blessed, glorious end of this is in the sunrise of the Divine glory over both* (Franz Delitzsch).

Psalm 58:1-5

Suggested further reading: Isaiah 10:1-4

The enemies of David were a numerous and united band, and because they so unanimously condemned the persecuted one, they were apt to take it for granted that their verdict was a right one. 'What everybody says must be true' is a lying proverb based upon the presumption that comes of large combinations. Have we not all agreed to hound the man to death, and who dare hint that so many great ones can be mistaken? Yet he who is persecuted lays the axe at the root by requiring his judges to answer the question as to whether or not they were acting according to justice. Men would do well to sometimes pause, and candidly consider this. Some of those who surrounded Saul were rather passive than active persecutors; they held their tongues when the object of royal hate was slandered. Silence gives consent. He who refrains from defending the right is himself an accomplice in the wrong.

It is small wonder that some men persecute the righteous seed of the woman; since all of them are of the serpent's brood, an enmity is set between them. No sooner born than alienated from God — what a condition to be found in! Do we leave the right track so early? Do we at the same moment begin to be both men and sinners? Every observer may see how very soon infants act lies. Before they can speak they practise little deceptive arts. He who starts early in the morning will go far before night. To be untruthful is one of the surest proofs of a fallen state, and since falsehood is universal, so also is human depravity. Is man also a poisonous reptile? Yes, and his venom is even as that of a serpent. The viper has but death for the body in his fangs; but unregenerate man carries poison under his tongue, destructive to the nobler nature. Man, in his natural corruption, appears to have all the ill points of a serpent without its excellence. O sin, what have you done!

Ungodly men are not to be won to right by the most logical arguments, or the most pathetic appeals. Try all your arts, preachers of the word! Lay yourselves out to meet the prejudices and tastes of sinners, and you shall yet have to cry, 'Who has believed our report?' It is not in your music, but in the sinner's ear that the cause of failure lies, and it is only the power of God that can remove it. No, we call and call, and call in vain, till the arm of the Lord is revealed. This is at once the sinner's guilt and danger. He ought to hear but will not, and because he will not hear, he cannot escape the damnation of hell.

Meditation: *The principles of the wicked are even worse than their practices* (George Rogers).

Psalm 58:6-11

Suggested further reading: Deuteronomy 32:36-43

So sudden is the overthrow of the wicked, so great a failure is their life, that they never see joy. In the very midst of the man's life, and in the fury of his rage against the righteous, the persecutor is overwhelmed with a tornado, his designs are baffled, his contrivances defeated, and himself destroyed. The malicious wretch puts on his great seething pot, he gathers his fuel, he means to play the cannibal with the godly; but he reckons without his host, or rather without the Lord of hosts, and the unexpected tempest removes all trace of him, and his fire, and his feast, and all in a moment.

There is nothing in Scripture of that sympathy with God's enemies which modern traitors are so fond of parading as the finest species of benevolence. We shall at the last say, 'Amen', to the condemnation of the wicked, and feel no disposition to question the ways of God with the impenitent. Remember how John, the loving disciple, puts it: 'After these things I heard a loud voice of a great multitude in heaven, saying, "Alleluia! Salvation and glory and honour and power to the Lord our God! For true and righteous are his judgements, because has judged the great harlot who corrupted the earth with her fornication; and he has avenged on her the blood of his servants shed by her." Again they said, "Alleluia! And her smoke rises up forever and ever."' He shall triumph over them, they shall be so utterly vanquished that their overthrow shall be final and fatal, and his deliverance complete and crowning. The damnation of sinners shall not mar the happiness of saints.

Every man, however ignorant, shall be compelled to say, 'Surely, there is a reward for the righteous.' If nothing else is true, this is. The godly are not after all forsaken and given over to their enemies; the wicked are not to have the best of it, truth and goodness are recompensed in the long run. All men shall be forced by the sight of the final judgement to see that there is a God, and that he is the righteous ruler of the universe. Two things will come out clearly after all — there is a God and there is a reward for the righteous. Time will remove doubts, solve difficulties and reveal secrets; meanwhile faith's foreseeing eye discerns the truth even now, and is glad at this.

Meditation: *The righteous shall be glad when he sees the vengeance of God, as it is a fulfilling of the threatening of God against the sin of man, and an evidence of his own holiness* (Joseph Caryl).

Psalm 59:1-5

Suggested further reading: 1 Samuel 19:1-7

Saul was a king, and therefore sat in high places and used all his authority to crush David; the persecuted one therefore beseeches the Lord to set him on high also, only in another sense. He asks to be lifted up, as into a lofty tower, beyond the reach of his adversary. Note how he sets the title 'My God', over against the word 'my enemies'. This is the right method of effectually catching and quenching the fiery darts of the enemy upon the shield of faith. God is our God, and therefore deliverance and defence are ours.

Saul was treating him very unjustly, and, besides that, was pursuing a tyrannical and unrighteous course towards others, therefore David appeals against him more vehemently. Evil men were in prominence at court, and were the ready tools of the tyrant — against these also he prays. Bad men in a bad cause may be pleaded against without question. When a habitation is beset by thieves, the good man of the house rings the alarm bell; and in these verses we may hear it ring out loudly, 'Deliver me ... defend me ... deliver me ... save me.' Saul had more cause to fear than David had, for the invincible weapon of prayer was being used against him, and heaven was being aroused to give him battle.

It is the mark of a thoughtful prayer that the titles that are applied to God in it are appropriate, and are, as it were, congruous to the matter, and fitted to add force to the argument. Shall Jehovah endure to see his people oppressed?

Shall the God of hosts permit his enemies to exult over his servant? Shall the faithful God of a chosen people leave his chosen to perish? The name of God is, even in a literal sense, a fortress and high tower for all his people. What a forceful petition is contained in the words 'awake to punish'. Actively smite, in wisdom judge, with force chastise. 'Do not be merciful to any wicked transgressors.' Be merciful to them as men, but not as transgressors; if they continue hardened in their sin, do not wink at their oppression. To wink at sin in transgressors will be to leave the righteous under their power, therefore do not pass by their offences but deal out the due reward. The psalmist feels that the overthrow of oppression which was so needful for himself must be equally desirable for multitudes of the godly placed in like positions, and therefore he prays for the whole company of the faithful, and against the entire brotherhood of traitors.

Meditation: *If we ourselves are conscious of our innocence, we may with humble confidence appeal to God, and beg of him to plead our injured cause, which he will do in due time* (Matthew Henry).

Psalm 59:6-13

Suggested further reading: 1 Samuel 19:8-17

David speaks to God as to one who is close at hand. He points to those who wait in ambush and speaks to God about them. They are laughing at me, and longing for my destruction, but you have the laugh of them seeing you have determined to send them away without their victim, and made fools of by Michal. The greatest, cleverest and most malicious of the enemies of the church are only objects of ridicule to the Lord; their attempts are utterly futile, they need give no concern to our faith, as if David had said, 'What are these fellows who lie in ambush? And what is the king their master, if God is on my side?' If not only these but all the heathen nations were besetting the house, still Jehovah would easily enough disappoint them and deliver me. In the end of all things it will be seen how utterly contemptible and despicable are all the enemies of the cause and kingdom of God. He is a brave man who sees this today when the enemy is in great power, and while the church is often as one shut up and besieged in his house.

Is my persecutor strong? Then, my God, for this very reason I will turn myself to you, and leave my matters in your hand. It is a wise thing to find in the greatness of our difficulties a reason for casting ourselves upon the Lord. 'God is my defence', my high place, my fortress, the place of my resort in the time of my danger. If the foe is too strong for me to cope with him, I will retreat into my castle, where he cannot reach me.

God, who is the giver and fountain of all the undeserved goodness I have received, will go before me and lead my way as I march onward. He will meet me in my time of need. Not alone shall I have to confront my foes, but he whose goodness I have long tried and proved will gently clear my way, and be my faithful protector. How frequently have we met with preventing mercy — the supply prepared before the need occurred, the refuge built before the danger arose. Far ahead into the future the foreseeing grace of heaven has projected itself, and forestalled every difficulty. God will enable his servant to gaze steadily upon the foe without trepidation; he shall be calm, and self-possessed, in the hour of peril; and before long he shall look down on the same foes defeated, overthrown, destroyed. When Jehovah leads the way victory follows at his heels. See God, and you need not fear to see your enemies. Thus the hunted David, besieged in his own house by traitors, looks only to God, and exults over his enemies.

Meditation: *Every saint may apply to God, as the God of every mercy that he needs* (John Hill).

Psalm 59:14-17

Suggested further reading: 1 Samuel 19:18-24

Verse 6 is repeated, as if the songster defied his foes and revelled in the thought of their futile search, their malice, their disappointment, their rage, their defeated vigilance, and their wasted energy. He laughs at the thought that the entire city would know how they were deceived, and all Israel would ring with the story of the image and the goats' hair in the bed. Nothing was more a subject of Oriental merriment than a case in which the crafty are deceived, and nothing makes a man more the object of derision than to be outwitted by a woman, as in this instance Saul and his base minions were by Michal. The warrior poet can imagine the howl of rage in the council of his foes when they found their victim clean escaped from their hands.

What a blessed morning will soon break for the righteous, and what a song will be theirs! Sons of the morning, you may sigh tonight, but joy will come on the wings of the rising sun. Tune your harps even now, for the signal to commence the eternal music will soon be given; the morning comes and your sun shall go down no more for ever. The song is for God alone, and it is one which none can sing but those who have experienced the loving-kindness of their God. Looking back upon a past completely full of mercy, the saints will bless the Lord with their whole hearts, and triumph in him as the high place of their security. The greater our present trials the louder will our future songs be, and the more intense our joyful gratitude. If we had no day of trouble, where was our season of retrospective thanksgiving? David's entrapment by Saul's bloodhounds creates an opportunity for divine interposition and so for triumphant praise.

Strength has been overcome by strength; not by the hero's own prowess, but by the might of God alone. See how the singer girds himself with the almightiness of God, and calls it all his own by faith. Sweet is the music of experience, but it is all for God; there is not even a stray note for man, for self, or for human helpers. With full assurance he claims possession of the Infinite as his protection and security. He sees God in all, and all his own. Mercy rises before him, conspicuous and manifold, for he feels he is undeserving; and security is with him, undisturbed and impregnable, for he knows that he is safe in divine keeping. Oh, choice song! My soul would sing it now in defiance of all the dogs of hell. Away, away, adversaries of my soul, the God of my mercy will keep you all at bay!

Meditation: *Reader, take care to avoid such sins, and cultivate a spirit of lively devotion; that, instead of receiving your portion where there is weeping, wailing, and gnashing of teeth, you may sing to the God of your mercy for ever* (Benjamin Boothroyd).

Psalm 60:1-5

Suggested further reading: 2 Samuel 1:17-27

Before the days of Saul, Israel had been brought very low; during his government it had suffered from internal strife, and his reign was closed by an overwhelming disaster at Gilboa. David found himself the possessor of a tottering throne, troubled with the double evil of faction at home, and invasion from abroad. He immediately traced the evil to its true source, and began at the fountainhead. His were the politics of piety, which after all are the wisest and most profound. He knew that the displeasure of the Lord had brought calamity upon the nation, and he set himself by earnest prayer to remove that displeasure.

David clearly sees the fruits of the divine anger. He traces the flight of Israel's warriors, the breaking of her power, the division in her body politic, to the hand of God. Whoever might be the secondary agent of these disasters, he beholds the Lord's hand as the prime moving cause, and pleads with the Lord concerning the matter. Israel was like a city with a breach made in its wall, because her God was angry with her. The first two verses, with their depressing confession, must be regarded as greatly enhancing the power of the faith that in the following verses rejoices in better days, through the Lord's gracious return to his people. There was more need for God to turn to his people than for Judah's troops to be brave, or Joab and the commanders wise. God with us is better than strong battalions; God displeased is more terrible than all the Edomites that ever marched into the valley of salt, or all the devils that ever opposed the church. If the Lord turns to us, what care we for Aram-naharaim or Aram-zobah, or death, or hell? But if he withdraws his presence, we tremble at the fall of a leaf.

In the fourth verse the strain takes a turn. The Lord has called back to himself his servants, and commissioned them for his service, presenting them with a standard to be used in his wars. Their afflictions had led them to exhibit holy fear, and then, being fitted for the Lord's favour, he gave them an ensign, which would be a rallying point for their hosts, a proof that he had sent them to fight, and a guarantee of victory. The bravest men are usually entrusted with the banner, and it is certain that those who fear God most have less fear of man than any others. The Lord has given us the standard of the gospel, let us live to uphold it, and if needful die to defend it. Our right to contend for God, and our reason for expecting success, are found in the fact that the faith has been once committed to the saints, and that by the Lord himself.

Meditation: *God will be sure to plough his own ground, whatsoever becomes of the waste; and to weed his own garden, though the rest of the world should be let alone to grow wild* (John Trapp).

Psalm 60:6-12

Suggested further reading: 2 Samuel 8:3-14

Faith is never happier than when it can fall back upon the promise of God. She sets this over against all discouraging circumstances; let outward providence say what it will, the voice of a faithful God drowns every sound or tear. God had promised Israel victory and David the kingdom: the holiness of God secured the fulfilment of his own covenant, and therefore the king spoke confidently. The good land had been secured to the tribes by the promise made to Abraham, and that divine grant was an abundantly suffi- cient warrant for the belief that Israel's arms would be successful in battle. Believer, make good use of this, and banish doubts while promises remain.

When God has spoken, his divine 'shall', our 'I will', becomes no idle boast, but the fit echo of the Lord's decree. Believer, up and take possession of covenant mercies. Let not Canaanitish doubts and legalisms keep you out of the inheritance of grace. Live up to your privileges, take the good which God provides you. O proud Philistia, where are your vaunts? Where now your haughty looks, and prom- ised conquests? Thus dare we defy the last enemy, 'O death, where is your sting? O grave, where is your victory?' So utterly hopeless is the cause of hell when the Lord comes forth to the battle, that even the weakest daughter of Zion may shake her head at the enemy, and laugh him to scorn. Oh, the glorying of faith! There is not a grain of vainglory in it, yet her holy boastings none can hinder. When the Lord speaks the promise, we will not be slow to rejoice and glory in it.

The chastising God is our only hope. He loves us still. For a small moment he forsakes, but with great mercy he gathers his people. Strong to smite, he is also strong to save. He, who proved to us our need of him by showing us what poor creatures we are without him, will now reveal the glory of his help by conducting great enterprises to a noble issue. From God all power proceeds, and all we do well is done by divine operation; but still we, as soldiers of the great king, are to fight, and to fight valiantly too. Divine working is not an argument for human inaction, but rather is it the best excitement for courageous effort. Helped in the past, we shall also be helped in the future, and being assured of this we resolve to play the man. The Lord is with us, omnipotence sustains us, and we will not hesitate, we dare not be cowards. Oh, that our King, the true David, were come to claim the earth, for the kingdom is the Lord's, and he is the governor among the nations!

Meditation: *So long as sight and reason find footing in matters, there is no place for faith and hope; the abundance of human helps puts not grace to proof, but the strength of faith is in the absence of them all* (William Struther).

Psalm 61:1-4

Suggested further reading: 2 Samuel 21:15-22

David was in terrible earnest; he shouted, he lifted up his voice on high. He is not, however, content with the expression of his need: to give vent to his sorrows is not enough for him, he wants actual audience of heaven, and manifest succour as the result. Pharisees may rest in their prayers; true believers are eager for an answer to them. Ritualists may be satisfied when they have 'said or sung' their litanies and formal prayers, but living children of God will never rest till their supplications have entered the ears of the Lord God of Hosts.

Observe that David never dreamed of seeking any other God; he did not imagine the dominion of Jehovah to be local. He was at the end of the promised land, but he knew he was still in the territory of the Great King; to him only does he address his petitions. It is hard to pray when the very heart is drowning, yet gracious men plead best at such times. Tribulation brings us to God, and brings God to us. Faith's greatest triumphs are achieved in her heaviest trials. Mark how our psalmist tells the Lord, as if he knew he was hearing him, that he intended to call upon him. Our prayer by reason of our distress may be like a call upon a far-off friend, but our inmost faith has its quiet heart-whispers to the Lord as to one who is assuredly our very present help.

How infinitely higher is the salvation of God than we are. We are low and grovelling, but it towers like some tall cliff far above us. This is its glory, and is our delight when once we have climbed into the rock, and claimed an interest in it; but while we are as yet trembling seekers, the glory and sublimity of salvation appal us, and we feel that we are too unworthy even to partake of it. Hence we are led to cry for grace upon grace, and to see how dependent we are for everything, not only for the Saviour, but also for the power to believe on him.

He who communes with God is always at home. The divine omnipresence surrounds such a person consciously; his faith sees all around him the palace of the King, in which he walks with exulting security and overflowing delight. Happy are the indoor servants who do not go out from his presence. Hewers of wood and drawers of water in the tents of Jehovah are more to be envied than the princes who riot in the pavilions of kings. The best of all is that our residence with God is not for a limited period of time, but for ages; indeed, for ages of ages, for time and for eternity: this is our highest and most heavenly privilege.

Meditation: *It is the great work of faith to cry out after God, at a distance, when you are afraid lest at the next turn he should be quite out of sight* (John Owen).

Psalm 61:5-8

Suggested further reading: Deuteronomy 17:14-20

Proofs of divine faithfulness are to be remembered, and to be mentioned to the Lord's honour. The prayer of verse 1 is certain of an answer because of the experience of verse 5, since we deal with an immutable God.

We are made heirs, joint-heirs with all the saints, partakers of the same portion. With this we ought to be delighted. If we suffer, it is the heritage of the saints; if we are persecuted, are in poverty, or in temptation, all this is contained in the title-deeds of the heritage of the chosen. Those we are to sup with we may well be content to dine with. We have the same inheritance as the First-born himself; what better is conceivable? Saints are described as fearing the name of God; they are reverent worshippers; they stand in awe of the Lord's authority; they are afraid of offending him; they feel their own nothingness in the sight of the Infinite One. To share with such men, to be treated by God with the same favour as he metes out to them, is matter for endless thanksgiving. All the privileges of all the saints are also the privilege of each one.

David, considering his many perils, enjoyed a long and prosperous reign. He lived to see generation after generation personally; in his descendants he lived as king through a very long period; his dynasty continued for many generations; and in Christ Jesus, his seed and son, spiritually David reigns on evermore. Thus he who began at the foot of the rock, half drowned, and almost dead, is here led to the summit, and sings as a priest abiding in the tabernacle, a king ruling with God for ever, and a prophet foretelling good things to come. The King 'shall abide before God for ever'. Though this is true of David in a modified sense, we prefer to view the Lord Jesus as here intended as the lineal descendant of David, and the representative of his royal race. Jesus is enthroned before God to eternity; here is our safety, dignity and delight. We reign in him; in him we are made to sit together in the heavens. David's personal claim to sit enthroned for ever is but a foreshadowing of the revealed privilege of all true believers. As men cry, 'Long live the king,' so we hail with acclamation our enthroned Immanuel, and cry, 'Let mercy and truth preserve him.' Eternal love and immutable faithfulness are the bodyguards of Jesus' throne, and they are both the providers and the preservers of all those who in him are made kings and priests unto God. We cannot keep ourselves, and nothing short of divine mercy and truth can do it; but these both can and will, nor shall the least of the people of God be allowed to perish.

Meditation: *Here David foretells the uninterrupted succession of the kingdom down to the time of Christ* (John Calvin).

Psalm 62:1-4

Suggested further reading: Isaiah 30:8-14

The faith that rests on God alone is alone true; the confidence that relies only partly on the Lord is vain confidence. To wait upon God, and for God, is the habitual position of faith; to wait on him truly is sincerity; to wait on him only is spiritual chastity. The original states 'only to God is my soul silence'. The presence of God alone could awe his heart into quietude, submission, rest and acquiescence; but when that was felt, not a rebellious word or thought broke the peaceful silence. The proverb that speech is silver but silence is gold, is more than true in this case. No eloquence in the world is half so full of meaning as the patient silence of a child of God. It is an eminent work of grace to bring down the will and subdue the affections to such a degree that the whole mind lies before the Lord like the sea beneath the wind, ready to be moved by every breath of his mouth, but free from all inward and self-caused emotion, and also from all power to be moved by anything other than the divine will. If to wait on God is worship, to wait on the creature is idolatry; if to wait on God alone is true faith, to associate an arm of flesh with him is audacious unbelief.

It is always best to begin with God, and then may we confront our enemies. Make all sure with heaven, then may you grapple with earth and hell. It is a marvel that men will readily enough continue in vain and sinful courses, and yet to persevere in grace is so great a difficulty as to be an impossibility, were it not for divine assistance. The persistence of those who oppose the people of God is so strange that we may well expostulate with them and say, 'How long will you display such malice?'

The excellence of the righteous is obnoxious to the wicked, and the main object of their fury. The elevation that God gives to the godly in providence, or in repute, is also the envy of the baser sort, and they labour to pull them down to their own level. Observe the concentration of malice upon one point only, as here set in contrast with the sole reliance of the gracious one upon his Lord. If the wicked could but ruin the work of grace in us, they would be content; to crush our character, to overturn our influence, is the object of their consultation.

Meditation: *Grace makes the heart move leisurely to all things except God* (Alexander Carmichael).

Psalm 62:5-12

Suggested further reading: Luke 12:13-21

The soul is apt to be dragged away from its anchorage, or is readily tempted to add a second confidence to the one sole and sure ground of reliance; we must, therefore, stir ourselves up to maintain the holy position which we were at first able to assume. We expect from God because we believe in him. Expectation is the child of prayer and faith, and is owned of the Lord as an acceptable grace. We should desire nothing but what it would be right for God to give, then our expectation would be all from God; and concerning truly good things we should not look to second causes, but to the Lord alone, and so again our expectation would be all from him. The vain expectations of worldly men do not come; they promise, but there is no performance; our expectations are on the way, and in due season will arrive to satisfy our hopes. Happy is the man who feels that all he has, all he wants, and all he expects are to be found in his God. To bow an immortal spirit to the constant contemplation of fading possessions is extreme folly. Shall those who call the Lord their glory, glory in yellow earth? Shall the image and superscription of Caesar deprive them of communion with the one who is the image of the invisible God? As we must not rest in men, so neither must we repose in money. Gain and fame are only so much foam of the sea. All the wealth and honour the whole world can afford would be too slender a thread to bear up the happiness of an immortal soul.

In what should we glory but in him who saves us? Our honour may well be left with him who secures our souls. To find all in God, and to glory that it is so, is one of the sure marks of an enlightened soul. Observe how the psalmist brands his own initials upon every name which he rejoicingly gives to his God — my expectation, my rock, my salvation, my glory, my strength, my refuge. He is not content with knowing that the Lord is all these things; he acts faith towards him, and lays claim to him under every character. It is the word 'my' that puts the honey into the comb. If our experience has not yet enabled us to realize the Lord under any of these consoling titles, we must seek grace that we may yet be partakers of their sweetness. The bees in some way or other penetrate the flowers and collect their juices; it must be hard for them to enter the closed cups and mouthless bags of some of the favourites of the garden, yet the honey-gatherers find or make a passage. In this they are our instructors, for into each delightful name, character and office of our covenant God our persevering faith must find an entrance, and from each it must draw delight.

Meditation: *See that you do not expect happiness in money, nor anything that is purchasable by it; in gratifying either the desire of the flesh, the desire of the eyes, or the pride of life* (John Wesley).

Psalm 63:1-5

Suggested further reading: 1 Samuel 23:14-23

The straightforward, clear language of the opening sentence would be far more becoming in Christians than the timorous and doubtful expressions so usual among believers. Possession breeds desire. Full assurance is no hindrance to diligence, but is the mainspring of it. How can I seek another man's God? But it is with ardent desire that I seek after him whom I know to be my own. Observe the eagerness implied in the time mentioned; he will not wait for noon or the cool eventide; he is up at dawn to meet his God. Communion with God is so sweet that the chill of the morning is forgotten, and the luxury of the couch is despised. The morning is the time for dew and freshness, and the psalmist consecrates it to prayer and devout fellowship. The best of men have been on their knees at such times. The word 'early' has not only the sense of early in the morning, but also that of eagerness, immediateness. He who truly longs for God longs for him now. Holy desires are among the most powerful influences that stir our inner nature; hence the next sentence, 'My soul thirsts for you.' Thirst is an insatiable longing after that which is one of the most essential supports of life; there is no reasoning with it, no forgetting it, no despising it, no overcoming it by stoical indifference. Thirst will be heard; the whole man must yield to its power. This is how it is with that divine desire which the grace of God creates in regenerate men; only God himself can satisfy the craving of a soul really aroused by the Holy Spirit.

He longed not so much to see the sanctuary as to see his God; he looked through the veil of ceremonies to the Invisible One. His heart had often been gladdened by communion with God in the outward ordinances, and for this great blessing he sighs again; as well he might, for it is the weightiest of all earth's sorrows for a Christian man to lose the conscious presence of his covenant God. Our misery is that we thirst so little for these sublime things, and so much for the mocking trifles of time and sense. We are truly always in a weary land, for this is not our rest. It is marvellous that believers do not thirst more continuously after their portion far beyond the river where they shall hunger no more, neither thirst any more, but shall see the face of their God, and his name shall be on their foreheads. David did not thirst for water or any earthly thing, only for spiritual manifestations. The sight of God was enough for him, but nothing short of that would content him. How great a friend is he, the very sight of whom is consolation! Oh, my soul, imitate the psalmist, and let all your desires ascend towards the highest good; longing here to see God, and having no higher joy even for eternity.

Meditation: *There is that in a gracious God and in communion with him, which gives abundant satisfaction to a soul. And there is that in a gracious soul, which takes abundant satisfaction in God, and in communion with him* (Matthew Henry).

Psalm 63:6-11

Suggested further reading: 1 Samuel 23:24-29

Night is congenial, in its silence and darkness, to a soul that would forget the world, and rise into a higher sphere. Absorption in the most hallowed of all themes makes watches, which would otherwise be weary, glide away all too rapidly; it causes the lonely and hard couch to yield the most delightful repose — repose more restful than even sleep itself. We read of beds of ivory, but beds of piety are better by far. Some revel in the night, but they are not a tithe so happy as those who meditate in God.

Meditation had refreshed his memory and recalled to him his past deliverance. It would be better if we read our own diaries more often, especially noting the hand of the Lord in helping us in suffering, want, labour or dilemma. This is the grand use of memory, to furnish us with proofs of the Lord's faithfulness, and lead us onward to a growing confidence in him. We follow close at the Lord's heel, because we are one with him. Who shall divide us from his love? If we cannot walk with him with equal footsteps, we will at least follow after with all the strength he lends us, earnestly panting to reach him and abide in his fellowship. The divine power, which has so often been dwelt upon in this and the preceding psalms, is mentioned here as the source of man's attachment to God. How strong we are when the Lord works in us by his own right hand, and how utterly helpless if he withheld his aid!

As David earnestly sought for God, so there were men of another order who as eagerly sought after his blood; these are whom he speaks of. At his life they aimed, at his honour, his best welfare; and this they would not merely injure but utterly ruin. The devil is a destroyer, and all his seed are greedy to do the same mischief. As he has mined himself by his crafty devices, so also shall they. Destroyers shall be destroyed. Those who hunt souls shall themselves be the victims. Into the pits that they dug for others they shall fall themselves. The slayers shall be slain, and the grave shall cover them. The hell, which they in their curse invoked for others, shall shut its mouth upon them. Every blow aimed against the godly will recoil on the persecutor; he who smites a believer drives a nail in his own coffin.

Usurpers shall fade, but David shall flourish; and his prosperity shall be publicly acknowledged as the gift of God. The Lord's anointed shall not fail to offer his joyful thanksgiving: his well-established throne shall own the superior lordship of the King of kings; his rejoicing shall be alone in God.

Meditation: *When the good man knows and enjoys most of God, he wants to know and enjoy more* (Benjamin Beddome).

Psalm 64:1-6

Suggested further reading: Exodus 14:10-18

It often helps devotion if we are able to use the voice and speak audibly; but even mental prayer has a voice with God that he will hear. We do not read that Moses had spoken with his lips at the Red Sea, and yet the Lord said to him, 'Why do you cry to me?' Prayers that are unheard on earth may be among the best heard in heaven. It is our duty to note how constantly David turns to prayer; it is his battleaxe and weapon of war; he uses it under every pressure, whether of inward sin or outward wrath, foreign invasion or domestic rebellion. We shall act wisely if we make prayer to God our first and best-trusted resource in every hour of need. David had but the one resource of prayer against the twofold weapons of the wicked, for defence against sword or arrow he used the one defence of faith in God. With all our sacrifices of prayer we should offer the salt of faith.

Slander has ever been the master weapon of the good man's enemies, and great is the care of the malicious to use it effectively. As warriors grind their swords, to give them an edge which will cut deep and wound desperately, so do the unscrupulous invent falsehoods which shall be calculated to inflict pain, to stab the reputation, to kill the honour of the righteous. What is there which an evil tongue will not say? What misery will it not labour to inflict?

Wicked men frequently have the craft to hasten slowly, to please in order to ruin, to flatter that before long they may devour, and to bow the knee that they may ultimately crush beneath their foot. He who deals with the serpent's seed has good need of the wisdom which is from above: the generation of vipers twist and turn, wind and wriggle, yet evermore they are set upon their purpose, and go the nearest way to it when they wander round about. Alas! How dangerous is the believer's condition, and how readily may he be overcome if left to himself. This is the complaint of reason and the moan of unbelief. When faith comes in, we see that even in all this the saints are still secure, for they are all in the hands of God. It is a good thing to conquer malicious foes, but a better thing still to be screened from all conflict with them, by being hidden from the strife. The Lord knows how to give his people peace, and when he wills to make quiet, he is more than a match for all disturbers, and can defeat their deep-laid plots and their overt hostilities alike.

Meditation: *The most mischievous weapons of the wicked are words, but the Word is the chief weapon of the Holy Spirit* ('J.L.K.').

Psalm 64:7-10

Suggested further reading: Jeremiah 50:21-28

'Vengeance is mine; I will repay,' says the Lord. The righteous need not learn the arts of self-defence or of attack,
their avenging is in better hands than their own. One of the
Lord's arrows shall be enough, for he never misses his aim.
He turns the tables on his adversaries, and defeats them
with their own weapons. They were looking to surprise the
saint, but, lo! they are taken unaware themselves; they desired to inflict deadly wounds, and are smitten themselves
with wounds which none can heal. While they were bend-
ing their bows, the great Lord had prepared his bow already,
and he let slip the shaft when least they looked for such an
unsparing messenger of justice.

Afraid, both of them and their overthrow, their former
friends shall give them wide space, lest they perish with
them. Who cares to go near to Herod when the worms are
eating him? Or to be in the same chariot with Pharaoh when
the waves roar round him? Those who crowded around a
powerful persecutor, and cringed at his feet, are among the
first to desert him in the day of wrath. Woe unto you, liars!
Who will desire fellowship with you in your seething lake
of fire? All men shall be filled with awe by the just judgements of God, as the Canaanites were by the overthrow of
Pharaoh at the Red Sea. Those who might have been bold
in sin shall be made to tremble and to stand in awe of the
righteous Judge. It shall become the subject of general conversation. So strange, so pointed, so terrible shall be the

Lord's overthrow of the malicious, that it shall be spoken of in all companies. They sinned secretly, but their punishment shall be wrought before the face of the sun. The judgements of God are frequently so clear and manifest that men cannot misread them, and if they have any thought at all, they must extract the true teaching from them. Some of the divine judgements are a great deep, but in the case of malicious persecutors the matter is plain enough, and the most illiterate can understand.

Admiring his justice and fully acquiescing in its displays, the righteous shall also rejoice at the rescue of injured innocence, yet their joy shall not be selfish or sensual, but altogether in reference to the Lord. Their observation of providence shall increase their faith, since he who fulfils his threatening will not forget his promises. The victory of the oppressed shall be the victory of all upright men; the whole host of the elect shall rejoice in the triumph of virtue. While strangers fear, the children are glad in view of their Father's power and justice. That which alarms the evil cheers the good.

Meditation: *Lord God of mercy, grant to us to be preserved from all our enemies, and saved in your Son with an everlasting salvation* (C. H. Spurgeon).

Psalm 65:1-4

Suggested further reading: Ephesians 1:3-14

Though Babylon adores Antichrist, Zion remains faithful
to her King; to him, and to him only, she brings her perpetual oblation of worship. Those who have seen the blood
of sprinkling in Zion, and know themselves to belong to
the church of the first-born, can never think of her without
presenting humble praise to Zion's God; his mercies are
too numerous and precious to be forgotten. The praises of
the saints wait for a signal from the divine Lord, and when
he shows his face they burst forth at once. Like a company
of musicians gathered to welcome and honour a prince,
who wait till he makes his appearance, so do we reserve
our best praises till the Lord reveals himself in the assembly of his saints; and, indeed, till he shall descend from
heaven in the day of his appearing. Praise attends the Lord's
pleasure, and continues to bless him, whether he shows
tokens of present favour or not; she is not soon wearied,
but all through the night she sings on in sure hope that the
morning comes. We shall continue to wait on, tuning our
harps, amid the tears of earth; but oh, what harmonies will
we pour forth, when the home-bringing comes, and the King
shall appear in his glory.

After cleansing comes benediction, and truly this is a
very rich one. It comprehends election, effectual calling,
access, acceptance and sonship. First, we are chosen of God,
according to the good pleasure of his will, and this alone is
blessedness. Then, since we cannot and will not come to

God of ourselves, he works graciously in us, and attracts us powerfully; he subdues our unwillingness, and removes our inability by the almighty workings of his transforming grace. This also is no slight blessedness. Furthermore, we, by his divine drawings, are made nigh by the blood of his Son, and brought near by his Spirit into intimate fellowship; so that we have access with boldness, and are no longer as those who are afar off by wicked works: here also is un-rivalled blessedness. To crown all, we do not come nigh in peril of dire destruction, but we approach as chosen and accepted ones, to become dwellers in the divine house-hold: this is heaped-up blessedness, vast beyond conception. But dwelling in the house we are treated as sons, for the servant does not abide in the house for ever, but the son does. Behold what manner of love and blessedness the Father has bestowed upon us that we may dwell in his house, and go out no more for ever. Happy are those who dwell at home with God. May both writer and reader be like this. Acceptance leads to abiding: God does not make a temporary choice, or give and take. His gifts and calling are without repentance. He who is once admitted to God's courts shall inhabit them for ever.

Meditation: *I am not murmuring, but rather stringing my harp and tuning my instrument with much patience and confidence, that I may be ready to strike up when the joyful news of my deliverance comes* (William Gurnall).

Psalm 65:5-8

Suggested further reading: Isaiah 48:8-13

God's memorial is that he hears prayer, and his glory is that he answers it in a manner fitted to inspire awe in the hearts of his people. The saints, in the commencement of the psalm, offered praise in reverential silence; and now, in the same awe-stricken spirit, they receive answers to their prayers. The direct allusion here is, no doubt, to the Lord's overthrow of the enemies of his people in ways calculated to strike terror into all beholders; his judgements in their severe righteousness were calculated to excite fear both among friends and foes. Who would not fear a God whose blows are so crushing? We do not always know what we are asking for when we pray; when the answer comes, the veritable answer, it is possible that we may be terrified by it. We seek sanctification, and trial will be the reply; we ask for more faith, and more affliction is the result; we pray for the spread of the gospel, and persecution scatters us. Nevertheless, it is good to ask on, for nothing that the Lord grants in his love can do us any harm. Terrible things will turn out to be blessed things after all, when they come in answer to prayer.

All men are equally dependent upon God: the seafaring man is usually most conscious of this, but in reality he is not more so than the farmer, nor the farmer than anyone else. There is no room for self-confidence on land or sea, since God is the only true confidence of men on earth or ocean. Faith is a plant of universal growth, it is a tree of life on shore and a plant of renown at sea; and, blessed be God, those who exercise faith in him anywhere shall find that he is swift and strong to answer their prayers. A remembrance of this should quicken our devotions when we approach the Lord our God. East and west are made happy by God's favour to its dwellers. Our rising hours are bright with hope, and our evening moments mellow with thanksgiving. Whether the sun goes forth or comes in we bless God and rejoice in the gates of the day. When the fair morning blushes with the rosy dawn we rejoice; and when the calm evening smiles restfully we rejoice still. We do not believe that the dew weeps the death of the day; we only see jewels bequeathed by the departing day for its successor to gather up from the earth. Faith, when she sees God, rounds the day with joy. She cannot fast, because the Bridegroom is with her. Night and day are alike to her, for the same God made them and blessed them. She would have no rejoicing if God did not make her glad; but, blessed be his name, he never ceases to make joy for those who find their joy in him.

Meditation: *The Scriptures, in viewing the works that God does through means, never lose sight of God himself* (Alexander Carson).

Psalm 65:9-13

Suggested further reading: Genesis 8:15-22

God's visits leave a blessing behind; this is more than can be said of every visitor. When the Lord goes on visitations of mercy, he has an abundance of necessary things for all his needy creatures. He is represented here as going round the earth, like a gardener surveying his garden, giving water to every plant that requires it, and not in small quantities, but until the earth is drenched and soaked with a rich supply of refreshment. O Lord, in this manner visit your church, and my poor, parched and withering piety. Make your grace overflow towards my graces; water me, for no plant of your garden needs it more.

The harvest is the plainest display of the divine bounty, and the crown of the year. The Lord himself conducts the coronation, and sets the golden coronal upon the brow of the year. Or, we may understand that God's love encircles the year as with a crown; each month has its gems, each day its pearl. Unceasing kindness girdles all time with a belt of love. The providence of God in its visitations makes a complete circuit, and surrounds the year. The footsteps of God, when he visits the land with rain, create fertility. It may be said that the march of Jehovah may be traced by the abundance which he creates. For spiritual harvests we must look to him, for he alone can give times of refreshing and feasts of Pentecost.

Not only where man is found do the showers descend, but away in the lonely places, where only wild animals

have their haunt, there the bountiful Lord makes the refreshing rain to drop. Ten thousand oases smile while the
Lord of mercy passes by. The birds of the air, the wild goats,
and the fleet stags rejoice as they drink from the pools, newly
filled from heaven. The most lonely and solitary souls God
will visit in love. The voice of nature is articulate to God; it
is not only a shout, but also a song. The sounds of animate
creation are well ordered as they combine with the equally
well-tuned ripple of the waters, and sighing of the wind.
Nature has no discords. Her airs are melodious, her chorus
is full of harmony. All, all is for the Lord; the world is a
hymn to the Eternal. Blessed is he who, hearing, joins in it,
and makes one singer in the mighty chorus.

Meditation: *When rain comes after a long drought, there is
melody made by all creatures in this lower world* (Ralph
Robinson).

Psalm 66:1-7

Suggested further reading: John 4:19-26

If praise is to be widespread, it must be vocal; exulting sounds stir the soul and cause a sacred contagion of thanksgiving. Composers of tunes for the congregation should see to it that their airs are cheerful: we need not so much noise, as joyful noise. God is to be praised with the voice, and the heart should go with it in holy exultation. All praise from all nations should be rendered unto the Lord. Happy the day when no shouts shall be presented to false gods, but all the earth shall adore its Creator. The languages of the lands are many, but their praises should be one, addressed to one only God.

Let not his praise be mean and grovelling: let it arise with grandeur and solemnity before him. The pomp of the ancient festivals is not to be imitated by us, under this dispensation of the Spirit, but we are to throw so much of heart and holy reverence into all our worship that it shall be the best we can render. Heart worship and spiritual joy render praise more glorious than vestments, incense and music could do. Turn all your praises to him. Devotion, unless it is resolutely directed to the Lord, is no better than whistling to the wind. The mind is usually first arrested by those attributes which cause fear and trembling; and, even when the heart has come to love God, and rest in him, there is an increase of worship when the soul is awed by an extraordinary display of the more dreadful of the divine characteristics. Looking upon the earthquakes which have shaken continents, the hurricanes which have devastated nations, the plagues which have desolated cities, and other great and amazing displays of divine working, men may well say: 'How awesome are your works.' Till we see God in Christ, the terrible predominates in all our apprehensions of him.

The nature and works of God will be the theme of earth's universal song, and he himself shall be the object of the joyful adoration of our emancipated race. Acceptable worship not only praises God as the mysterious Lord, but also is rendered fragrant by some measure of knowledge of his name or character. God would not be worshipped as an unknown God, nor have it said of his people, 'You worship what you do not know.' May the knowledge of the Lord soon cover the earth, so that intelligent worship may be universally possible! Such a consummation was evidently expected by the writer of this psalm; and, indeed, throughout all Old Testament writings there are intimations of the future general spread of the worship of God.

Meditation: *He does not sing praises well, who desires to sing alone* (Thomas Le Blanc).

Psalm 66:8-15

Suggested further reading: Hebrews 12:3-11

At any time the preservation of life, and especially the soul's life, is a great reason for gratitude, but much more when we are called to undergo extreme trials, which of themselves would crush our being. Blessed be God, who, having put our souls into possession of life, has been pleased to preserve that heaven-given life from the destroying power of the enemy! If God has enabled us not only to keep our life, but also our position, we are bound to give him double praise. Living and standing is the saint's condition through divine grace. Immortal and immovable are those whom God preserves. Satan is put to shame, for instead of being able to slay the saints, as he hoped, he is not even able to trip them up. God is able to make the weakest to stand fast, and he will do so.

David had his temptations. All the saints must go to the proving house; God had one Son without sin, but he never had a son without trial. Why ought we to complain if we are subjected to the rule that is common to all the family, and from which so much benefit has flowed to them? The Lord himself proves us. Who then shall raise a question as to the wisdom and the love that is displayed in its outworking? The day may come when, as in this case, we shall make hymns out of our grief, and sing all the more sweetly because our mouths have been purified with bitter draughts. Since trial is sanctified to so desirable an end, ought we not to submit to it with abounding resignation.

God's people and affliction are intimate companions. As in Egypt every Israelite was a burden-bearer, so is every believer while he is in this foreign land. As Israel cried to God because of their sore bondage, so also do the saints. We too often forget that God lays our afflictions upon us: if we remembered this fact, we should submit more patiently to the pressure that now pains us. The time will come when, for every ounce of present burden, we shall receive a far more exceeding and eternal weight of glory.

The child of God is so aware of his own personal indebtedness to grace, that he feels he must utter a song of his own. He joins in the common thanksgiving, but since the best public form must fail to meet each individual case, he makes sure that the special mercies received by him shall not be forgotten, for he records them with his own pen, and sings of them with his own lips. Even the thankful heart dares not come to God without a victim of grateful praise; of this as well as of every other form of worship, we may say, 'The blood is its life.' Reader, never attempt to come before God without Jesus, the divinely promised, given and accepted burnt offering.

Meditation: *It is truth, that all we have is in the hand of God* (Joseph Caryl).

Psalm 66:16-20

Suggested further reading: Isaiah 1:10-17

It is well when prayer and praise go together, like the horses in Pharaoh's chariot. Some, who do not sing, cry; and some, who do not cry, sing: both together are best. Since the Lord's answers so frequently follow close at the heels of our petitions, and even overtake them, it is fitting to let our grateful praises keep pace with our humble prayers. Notice that the psalmist both cried and spoke; the Lord has cast the dumb devil out of his children, and those of them who are least fluent with their tongues are often the most eloquent with their hearts.

Can I desire the Lord to connive at my sin, and accept me while I wilfully cling to any evil way? Nothing hinders prayer like iniquity harboured in the breast; as with Cain, so with us, sin lies at the door, and blocks the passage. If you listen to the devil, God will not listen to you. If you refuse to hear God's commands, he will surely refuse to hear your prayers. God will hear an imperfect petition for Christ's sake, but not one that is wilfully miswritten by a traitor's hand. For God to accept our devotions, while we are delighting in sin, would be to make himself the God of hypocrites, which is a fitter name for Satan than for the Holy One of Israel.

'But certainly God has heard me,' a sure sign that the petitioner was no secret lover of sin. The answer to his prayer was a fresh assurance that his heart was sincere before the Lord. See how sure the psalmist is that he has been heard; it is for him no hope, surmise, or fancy, but he seals it with a 'certainly'. Facts are blessed things when they reveal both God's heart as loving and our own heart as sincere. Love of sin is a plague spot, a condemning mark, a killing sign, but those prayers, which evidently live and prevail with God, most clearly arise from a heart which is free from dalliance with evil. Let the reader see to it that his inmost soul be rid of all alliance with iniquity, all toleration of secret lust, or hidden wrong.

'Blessed be God,' he has neither withdrawn his love nor my liberty to pray. He has neither cast out my prayer nor me. His mercy and my cries still meet each other. The psalm ends on its key note. Praise all through is its spirit and design. Lord, enable us to enter into it. Amen.

Meditation: *While we regard iniquity, how is it possible for us to regard spiritual things, the only lawful object of our prayers? And, if we regard them not, how can we be urgent with God for the giving of them? And where there is no fervency on our part, no wonder if there is no answer on God's* (Robert South).

Psalm 67:1-4

Suggested further reading: Numbers 6:22-27

This is a fit refrain to the benediction of the High Priest in
the name of the Lord, as recorded in Numbers 6:24, 25. It
begins at the beginning with a cry for mercy. Forgiveness of
sin is always the first link in the chain of mercies experienced by us. Mercy is a foundation attribute in our salvation. The best saints and the worst sinners may unite in
this petition. It is addressed to the God of mercy, by those
who feel their need of mercy, and it implies the death of all
legal hopes or claims of merit. Next, the church begs for a
blessing: 'Bless us;' a very comprehensive and far-reaching
prayer. When we bless God we do but little for our blessings are but words, but when God blesses he enriches us
indeed, for his blessings are gifts and deeds. But his blessing alone is not all his people crave, they desire a personal
consciousness of his favour, and pray for a smile from his
face. These three petitions include all that we need here or
hereafter.

This verse may be regarded as the prayer of Israel, and
spiritually of the Christian church. The largest charity is
shown in this psalm, but it begins at home. The whole
church, each church, and each little company, may rightly
pray, 'Bless us.' It would, however, be very wrong to let our
charity end where it begins, as some do; our love must make
long marches, and our prayers must have a wide sweep.
We must embrace the whole world in our intercessions.

As showers which first fall upon the hills afterwards run down in streams into the valleys, so the blessing of the Most High comes upon the world through the church. We are blessed for the sake of others as well as ourselves. God deals in a way of mercy with his saints, and then they make that way known far and wide, and the Lord's name is made famous on the earth. Ignorance of God is the great enemy of mankind, and the testimonies of the saints, experimental and grateful, overcome this deadly foe. God has a set way and method of dealing out mercy to men, and it is the duty and privilege of a revived church to make that way known everywhere. This all nations need, but many of them do not know it, desire it, or seek it; our prayer and labour should be that the knowledge of salvation may become as universal as the light of the sun. Despite the gloomy notions of some, we cling to the belief that the kingdom of Christ will embrace the whole habitable globe, and that all flesh shall see the salvation of God: for this glorious consummation we agonize in prayer.

Meditation: *God forgives, then he gives; till he be merciful to pardon our sins through Christ, he cannot bless or look kindly on us sinners* (William Gurnall).

Psalm 67:5-7

Suggested further reading: Leviticus 26:3-13

These words are no vain repetition, but are a chorus worthy to be sung again and again. The great theme of the psalm is the participation of the Gentiles in the worship of Jehovah; the psalmist is full of it, he hardly knows how to contain or express his joy.

Sin first laid a curse on the soil, and grace alone can remove it. Under tyrannical governments lands become unproductive, even the land that flowed with milk and honey is almost a wilderness under Turkish rule. However, when the principles of true religion shall have elevated mankind, and the dominion of Jesus shall be universally acknowledged, the science of tillage shall be perfected, men shall be encouraged to labour, industry shall banish penury, and the soil shall be restored to more than its highest condition of fertility.

'God, our own God, shall bless us.' He will make earth's increase to be a real blessing. Men shall see in his gifts the hand of that same God whom Israel of old adored, and Israel, especially, shall rejoice in the blessing, and exult in her own God. We never love God aright till we know him to be ours, and the more we love him the more we long to be fully assured that he is ours. What dearer name can we give to him than 'my own God'? The spouse in the song has no sweeter canticle than 'My beloved is mine and I am his.' Every believing Jew must feel a holy joy at the thought that the nations shall all be blessed by Abraham's God; but every

Gentile believer also rejoices that the whole world shall yet worship the God and Father of our Lord and Saviour Jesus Christ, who is our Father and our God.

The prayer of the first verse is the song of the last. We have the same phrase twice, and truly the Lord's blessing is manifold; he blesses and blesses and blesses again. How many are his beatitudes! How choice his benedictions! They are the peculiar heritage of his chosen. He is the Saviour of all men, but specially of them that believe. In this verse we find a song for all future time. God shall bless us is our assured confidence; he may smite us, or strip us, or even slay us, but he must bless us. He cannot turn away from doing good to his elect. The far-off shall fear. The ends of the earth shall end their idolatry, and adore their God. All tribes, without exception, shall feel a sacred awe of the God of Israel. Ignorance shall be removed, insolence subdued, injustice banished, idolatry abhorred, and the Lord's love, light, life and liberty shall be over all, the Lord himself being King of king and Lord of lords. Amen, and Amen.

Meditation: *Our unthankfulness is the cause of the earth's unfruitfulness. While man is blessing God for his mercies, He is blessing man with his mercies* (William Secker).

Psalm 68:1-6

Suggested further reading: Numbers 10:33-36

Moses spoke in similar words when the cloud moved onward, and the ark was carried forward. The ark would have
been a poor leader if the Lord had not been present with
the symbol. Israel beseeches him to arise, as elsewhere, to
'Awake,' put on his sword. We, also, may importunately cry
unto the Lord, that he would be pleased to make bare his
arm, and plead his own cause.

Wax is hard by itself, but put it to the fire, how soft it is.
Wicked men are haughty till they come into contact with
the Lord, and then they faint for fear; their hearts melt like
wax when they feel the power of his anger. Wax, also, burns
and passes away; the taper is utterly consumed by the flame:
so shall all the boastful power of the opposers of the gospel
be as a thing of nought. Rome, like the candles on her altars,
shall dissolve, and with equal certainty shall infidelity disappear. Israel saw, in the ark, God on the mercy seat —
power in connection with propitiation — and they rejoiced
in the omnipotence of such a manifestation. This is even
more clearly the confidence of the New Testament church,
for we see Jesus, the appointed atonement, clothed with
glory and majesty, and before his advance all opposition
melts like snow in the sun; the pleasure of the Lord shall
prosper in his hands. When he comes by his Holy Spirit,
conquest is the result; but when he arises in person, his
foes shall utterly perish.

The presence of God on the throne of grace is an over-flowing source of delight to the godly; and let them not fail to drink of the streams which are meant to make them glad. If any find the rule of Jehovah to be irksome, it is because their rebellious spirits kick against his power. Israel did not find the desert dry, for the smitten rock gave forth its streams; but even in Canaan itself men were consumed with famine, because they cast off their allegiance to their covenant God. Even where God is revealed on the mercy seat, some men persist in rebellion, and such need not wonder if they find no peace, no comfort, no joy, even where all these abound. Justice is the rule of the Lord's kingdom, and hence there is no provision for the unjust to indulge their evil lusting: a perfect earth, and even heaven itself, would be a dry land to those who can only drink of the waters of sin. Of the most soul-satisfying of sacred ordinances these witless rebels cry, 'What a weariness it is!' and, under the most soul-sustaining ministry, they complain of 'the foolishness of preaching'. When a man has a rebellious heart, he must of necessity find all around him a dry land.

Meditation: *The wicked flee from the presence of God, since it inspires them with terror; the righteous on the other hand rejoice in it, because nothing delights them more than to think that God is near them* (John Calvin).

Psalm 68:7-14

Suggested further reading: Deuteronomy 8:1-10

The Lord went before, and, therefore, whether the Red Sea or burning sand lay in the way, it mattered not; the pillar of cloud and fire always led them the right way. He was the Commander-in-chief of Israel, from whom they received all orders, and the march was therefore his march. We may speak, if we will, of the 'wanderings of the children of Israel', but we must not think of them straying aimlessly, they were in reality a well-arranged and well-considered march.

The march of God was not signalized solely by displays of terror, for goodness and bounty were also made conspicuous. Such rain as never fell before dropped on the desert sand, bread from heaven and winged fowls fell all around the host; good gifts were poured upon them; rivers leaped forth from rocks. The earth shook with fear, and in reply, the Lord, as from a cornucopia, shook out blessings upon it. As at the end of each stage, when they halted, weary with the march, they found such showers of good things awaiting them that they were speedily refreshed. Their foot did not swell all those forty years. When they were exhausted, God was not; when they were weary, he was not. They were his chosen heritage, and, therefore, although for their good he allowed them to be weary, yet he watchfully tended them and tenderly considered their distresses. In like manner, to this day, the elect of God in this wilderness state are apt to become tired and faint, but their ever-loving Jehovah comes in with timely succours, cheers the faint, strengthens the weak, and refreshes the hungry; so that once again, when the silver trumpets sound, the church militant advances with bold and firm step towards 'the rest which remains'. By this faithfulness, the faith of God's people is confirmed, and their hearts established; if fatigue and want made them waver, the timely supply of grace stays them again upon the eternal foundation.

The lords of hosts fled before the Lord of Hosts. No sooner did the ark advance than the enemy turned his back: even the princely leaders did not stay, but took to flight. The rout was complete, the retreat hurried and disorderly. The victory was due to the Almighty arm alone; he scattered the haughty ones who came against his people, and he did it as easily as snow is driven from the bleak sides of Salmon. It was intended to portray the glory and completeness of the divine triumph over the greatest foes. In this let all believers rejoice.

Meditation: *The Lord Jesus now comes, day by day, to load us with blessings, and at the last will carry us safely through death into life and glory* (Ridley H. Herschell).

Psalm 68:15-19

Suggested further reading: Ephesians 4:7-16

The priests on the summit of the chosen hill extol the Lord for his choice of Zion as his dwelling-place. Zion certainly was not a high hill comparatively; and it is here conceded that Bashan is a greater mount, but not so glorious, for in choosing Zion the Lord had exalted it above the loftier hills. He chooses as he pleases, and, according to the counsel of his own will, he selects Zion, and passes by the proud, uplifted peaks of Bashan. Thus he makes the base things of this world, and things that are despised, to become monuments of his grace and sovereignty. Spiritually the Lord abides eternally in Zion, his chosen church, and it was Zion's glory to be typical of that. What were Carmel and Sirion, with all their height, compared to Zion, the joy of the whole earth! God's election is a patent of nobility. They are choice men whom God has chosen, and the place that he honours with his presence is superlatively honoured.

The throne of grace on Zion is as holy as the throne of justice on Sinai. The displays of his glory may not be so terrible under the new covenant as under the old; but they are even more marvellous if seen by the spiritual eye. How joyful was it to a pious Hebrew to know that God was as truly with his people in the tabernacle and temple as amid the terrors of the Mount of Horeb! But it is even more heart-cheering to us to be assured that the Lord abides in his church, and has chosen it to be his rest for ever. May we be zealous for the maintenance of holiness in the spiritual house that God condescends to occupy: let a sense of his presence consume, as with flames of fire, every false way. The presence of God is the strength of the church; all power is ours when God is ours. Providence is on our side, and it 'has servants everywhere'. There is no room for a shade of doubt or discouragement, but every reason for exultation and confidence.

The ark was conducted to the summit of Zion; God himself took possession of the high places of the earth, being extolled and very high. The antitype of the ark, the Lord Jesus, has ascended into the heavens with signal marks of triumph. To do battle with our enemies, the Lord descended and left his throne; but now the fight is finished, he returns to his glory, high above all things is he now exalted. Paul's rendering is the gospel one: Jesus has 'received gifts for men', of which he makes plentiful distribution, enriching his church with the priceless fruits of his ascension, such as apostles, evangelists, pastors and teachers, and all their varied endowments. In him, the man who received gifts for man, we are endowed with priceless treasures, and, moved with gratitude, we return gifts to him, indeed, we give him ourselves, our all.

Meditation: *Christ received that he might give; received the spoil that he might distribute it* (Andrew Fuller).

Psalm 68:20-27

Suggested further reading: Deuteronomy 33:24-29

The Almighty who has entered into covenant with us is the source of our safety, and the author of our deliverance. As surely as he is our God he will save us. To be his is to be safe. He has ways and means of rescuing his children from death: when they are at their wit's end, and see no way of escape, he can find a door of deliverance for them.

The Preserver is also the Destroyer. He smites his foes on the crown of their pride. The seed of the woman crushes the serpent's head. There is no defence against the Lord, he can in a moment smite with utter destruction the lofty crests of his haughty foes. He covers the head of his servants, but he crushes the head of his foes. At the Second Coming of the Lord Jesus, his enemies will find his judgements to be terrible beyond belief. The powers of evil may flee to the utmost ends of the earth, but the Lord will arrest them, and lead them back in chains to adorn his triumph. The most complete and terrible vengeance shall be awarded to the oppressed people. So overwhelming should be the defeat of the foe that dogs should lick their blood.

In the song the marching of the Lord had been described; friends and foes had seen his goings forth with the ark and his people. We suppose that the procession was now climbing the hill, and entering the enclosure where the tabernacle of the ark was pitched; it was suitable at this moment to declare with song that the tribes had seen the glorious progress of the Lord as he led forth his people. The splendid procession of the ark, which symbolized the throne of the great King, was before the eyes of men and angels as it ascended to the holy place; and the psalmist points to it with exultation before he proceeds to describe it. All nature and providence are, as it were, a procession attending the great Lord, in his visitations of this lower globe. Winter and summer, sun and moon, storm and calm, and all the varied glories of nature swell the pomp of the King of kings, of whose dominion there is no end. Let the assembled company magnify the God whose ark they followed. United praise is like the mingled perfume that Aaron made; it should all be presented unto God. He blesses us: let him be blessed. O happy day, when all believers shall be one around the ark of the Lord, striving for nothing but the glory of the God of grace!

Meditation: *Part of our business must be to unite in prayer for future mercies. We are not so strong, either as individuals or assemblies, but that there is room for increase; and this is the proper object of prayer. God has wrought a great work for us in regeneration. God has wrought much for us as a church in giving us increase, respect, and room in the earth. Pray that each may be increased* (Andrew Fuller).

Psalm 68:28-35

Suggested further reading: Isaiah 19:18-25

As a commander-in-chief, the Lord made the valiant men pass in battle array, and bade them be strong in the day of conflict. As all power comes from God at first, so its continual maintenance is also from him. We who have life should pray to have it 'more abundantly'; if we have strength we should seek to be still more established. We expect God to bless his own work. He has never left any work unfinished yet, and he never will. 'When we were without strength, in due time Christ died for the ungodly'; and now, being reconciled to God, we may look to him to perfect that which concerns us, since he never forsakes the work of his own hands.

Before, he was described in his earthly manifestations as marching through the desert: now, in his celestial glory, as riding in the heavens of the primeval ages. Long before this heaven and earth were made, the loftier abodes of the Deity stood fast; before men or angels were created, the splendours of the Great King were as great as now, and his triumphs as glorious. Our knowledge reaches but to a small fragment of the life of God, whose 'goings forth were of old, even from everlasting'. When even his voice rends the rocks and uproots the cedars, what cannot his hand do? His finger shakes the earth; who can conceive the power of his arm? Let us never by our doubts or our daring defiance appear to deny power unto God; on the contrary, by yielding to him and trusting in him, let our hearts acknowledge his might. When we are reconciled to God, his omnipotence is an attribute of which we sing with delight. The favoured nation is protected by his majesty; his greatness is to them goodness, his glory is their defence. He does not confine his power to the sons of men, but makes it like a canopy to cover the skies. Rain, snow, hail and tempest are his artillery; he rules all nature with awe-inspiring majesty. Nothing is so high as to be above him, or too low to be beneath him; praise him, then, in the highest.

All the power of Israel's warriors is derived from the Lord, the fountain of all might. He is strong, and makes strong: blessed are those who draw from his resources, they shall renew their strength. While the self-sufficient faint, the All-Sufficient shall sustain the feeblest believer. 'Blessed be God!' A short but sweet conclusion, let our souls say Amen to it; and yet again, Amen.

Meditation: *When the enemies of God rise up against his church, it is time for the church to fall down to God, to implore his aid against those enemies. Holy prayers are more powerful than profane swords* (Thomas Wall).

Psalm 69:1-4

Suggested further reading: John 15:18-25

If any enquire, 'Of whom does the psalmist speak? Of himself, or of some other man?' we would reply, 'Of himself, and of some other man.' Who the other is, we need not be long in discovering; it is the Crucified alone who can say, 'In my thirst they gave me vinegar to drink.'

'Save me, O God!' Thus David had prayed, and here his Son and Lord utters the same cry. This is the second psalm that begins with a 'Save me, O God,' and the former (Ps. 54) is but a short summary of this more lengthy complaint. It is remarkable that such a scene of woe should be presented to us immediately after the jubilant ascension hymn of the last psalm, but this only shows how interwoven are the glories and the sorrows of our ever-blessed Redeemer. The head that now is crowned with glory is the same that wore the thorns; he, to whom we pray, 'Save us, O God,' is the selfsame person who cried, 'Save me, O God.'

In water one might swim, but in mud and mire all struggling is hopeless; the mire sucks down its victim. Everything gave way under the Sufferer; he could not get a foothold for support — this is a worse fate than drowning. Here our Lord pictures the close, clinging nature of his heart's woes. Sin is as mire for its filthiness, and the holy soul of the Saviour must have loathed even that connection with it which was necessary for its expiation. His pure and sensitive nature seemed to sink in it, for it was not his element, he was not, like us, born and acclimatized to this great dismal swamp. Let our hearts feel the emotions, both of contrition and gratitude, as we see in this simile the deep humiliation of our Lord. He was no faint-hearted sentimentalist; his were real woes, and though he bore them heroically, yet were they terrible even to him. His sufferings were unlike all others in degree, the waters were such as soaked into the soul; the mire was the mire of the abyss itself, and the floods were deep and overflowing. My soul, your Well-Beloved endured all this for you. Many waters could not quench his love, neither could the floods drown it; and, because of this, you have the rich benefit of that covenant assurance, 'As I have sworn that the waters of Noah should no longer cover the earth; so have I sworn that I would not be angry with you, nor rebuke you.' He stemmed the torrent of almighty wrath, that we might for ever rest in Jehovah's love.

Meditation: *In this psalm the whole Christ speaks; now in his own person, now crying with the voice of his members to God his father* (Gerhohus).

Psalm 69:5-12

Suggested further reading: Romans 15:1-6

'O God, you know my foolishness.' David might well say this, but not David's Lord; unless it is understood as an appeal to God concerning his freedom from folly which men imputed to him when they said he was mad. That which was foolishness to men was superlative wisdom before God. How often might we use these words in their natural sense, and if we were not such fools as to be blind to our own folly, this confession would be frequently on our lips. When we feel that we have been foolish we are not, therefore, to cease from prayer, but rather to be more eager and fervent in it.

David appealed to the Lord of hosts by his power to help him, and now to the God of Israel by his covenant faithfulness to come to the rescue. If the captain of the host fail, how will it fare with the rank and file? If David flees, what will his followers do? If the king of believers shall find his faith unrewarded, how will the feeble ones hold on their way? Our Lord's behaviour during his sharpest agonies is no cause of shame to us; he wept, for he was man, but he murmured not, for he was sinless man. He cried, 'My Father, if it is possible, let this cup pass from me'; for he was human, but he added, 'Nevertheless, not as I will, but as you will,' for his humanity was without taint of rebellion. In the depths of tribulation no repining word escaped him, for there was no repining in his heart. The Lord of martyrs witnessed a good confession. He was strengthened in the

hour of peril, and came off more than a conqueror, as we
also shall do, if we hold fast our confidence even to the
end.

Because he undertook to do the Father's will, and teach
his truth, the people were angry; because he declared himself to be the Son of God, the priesthood raved. They could
find no real fault in him, but were forced to hatch up a
lying accusation before they could commence their sham
trial of him. The basis of the quarrel was that God was with
him, and he with God, while the scribes and Pharisees
sought only their own honour. Reproach is at all times very
cutting to a man of integrity, and it must have come with
acute force upon one of so unsullied a character as our
Lord. Yet see how he turns to his God, and finds his consolation in the fact that he is enduring all for his Father's
sake. The same comfort belongs to all misrepresented and
persecuted saints.

Meditation: *The shame of the cross is more grievous than
the rest of the trouble of it* (David Dickson).

Psalm 69:13-18

Suggested further reading: Mark 14:32-42

There is to each of us an accepted time, and woe to us if we allow it to glide away unimproved. God's time must be our time, or it will come to pass that, when time closes, we shall look in vain for space for repentance. Our Lord's prayers were well timed, and always met with acceptance. Even the perfect one makes his appeal to the rich mercy of God; much more should we. To misery no attribute is sweeter than mercy, and when sorrows multiply, the multitude of mercy is much prized. When enemies are more than the hairs of our head, they are yet to be numbered, but God's mercies are altogether innumerable, and let it never be forgotten that every one of them is an available and powerful argument in the hand of faith. Our Lord teaches us here the sacred art of wrestling in prayer, and ordering our cause with arguments; and he also indicates to us that the nature of God is the great treasury of strong reasons, which shall be most prevalent to us in supplication.

He turns into prayer the very words of his complaint; and it is well if, when we complain, we neither feel nor say anything that we should fear to utter before the Lord as a prayer. We are allowed to ask for deliverance from trouble as well as for support under it; both petitions are combined here. How strange it seems to hear such language from the Lord of glory. Both from his foes, and the grief that they caused him, he seeks a rescue. God can help us in all ways, and we may, therefore, put up a variety of requests without

fear of exceeding our liberty to ask, or his ability to answer.
How appropriately may many of us use this prayer! We
deserve to be swept away as with a flood, to be drowned in
our sins, to be shut up in hell. Let us, then, plead the merits
of our Saviour, lest these things happen to us.

The near approach of God is all the sufferer needs; one
smile of heaven will still the rage of hell. It shall be my
redemption if you will appear to comfort me. This is a
deeply spiritual prayer, and one very suitable for a deserted
soul. It is in renewed communion that we shall find redemption realized. 'Deliver me because of my enemies',
lest they should, in their vaunting, blaspheme your name,
and boast that you are not able to rescue those who put
their trust in you. Jesus, in condescending to use such supplications, fulfils the request of his disciples: 'Lord, teach
us to pray.'

Meditation: *Faith in God gives hope to be helped, and is
half a deliverance before the full deliverance come; for the
psalmist is now with his head above the water, and not so
afraid as when he began the psalm* (David Dickson).

Psalm 69:19-28

Suggested further reading: Matthew 27:32-37

Here are three words piled up to express the Redeemer's keen sense of the contempt poured upon him; and his assurance that every form of malicious despite was observed by the Lord. The whole lewd and loud company is now present before your eyes: Judas and his treachery; Herod and his cunning; Caiaphas and his counsel; Pilate and his vacillation; Jews, priests, people, rulers, all, you see and will judge.

Intense mental suffering arises from slander; and, in the cage of the sensitive nature of the immaculate Son of Man, it was enough to lacerate the heart till it broke. Calumny and insult bowed him to the dust; he was sick at heart. The heaviness of our Lord in the garden is expressed by many forcible words in the four Gospels, and each term goes to show that the agony was great beyond measure; he was filled with misery, like a vessel which is full to the brim. A criminal's draught was offered to our innocent Lord, a bitter portion to our dying Master. How pitiful was the hospitality provided by earth for her King and Saviour! How often have our sins filled the gall-cup for our Redeemer? Let us not excuse ourselves.

What can be too severe a penalty for those who reject the incarnate God, and refuse to obey the commands of his mercy? They deserve to be flooded with wrath, and they shall be; for upon all who rebel against the Saviour, Christ the Lord, 'Wrath has come to the uttermost.' God's indignation is no trifle; the anger of a holy, just, omnipotent and infinite Being is to be dreaded above all things; even a drop of it consumes, but to have it poured upon us is inconceivably dreadful. O God, who knows the power of your anger? God is not to be insulted with impunity; and his Son, our ever-gracious Saviour, the best gift on infinite love, is not to be scorned and scoffed at for nothing. He that despised Moses' law died without mercy, but what shall be the 'sorer punishment' reserved for those who have trodden under foot the Son of God?

Death shall obliterate all recollection of the wicked; they shall no longer be held in esteem, even by those who paid them homage. Judas first, and Pilate, and Herod, and Caiaphas, all in due time, were speedily wiped out of existence; their names only remain as bywords, but among the honoured men who live after their departure they are not recorded. Man in his imperfect copy of God's book of life will have to make many emendations, both of insertion and erasure; but, as before the Lord, the record is for ever fixed and unalterable. Beware, O man, of despising Christ and his people, lest your soul should never partake in the righteousness of God, without which men are condemned already.

Meditation: *The very talking and venting of ill speeches, to the prejudice of Christ's cause and truth, and true holiness in his saints, especially when they are under suffering and afflictions, whatsoever, is a high provocation of God's wrath* (David Dickson).

Psalm 69:29-36

Suggested further reading: 1 Timothy 1:12-17

The psalmist was very much afflicted, but his faith was in God. The poor in spirit and mourners are both blessed under the gospel, so that here is a double reason for the Lord to smile on his suppliant. No man was ever poorer or more sorrowful than Jesus of Nazareth, yet his cry out of the depths was heard, and he was uplifted to the highest glory.

He who sang after the Passover sings yet more joyously after the resurrection and ascension. He is, in very truth, 'the sweet singer of Israel'. He leads the eternal melodies, and all his saints join in chorus. How sure was our Redeemer of ultimate victory, since he vows a song even while still in the furnace. In us, also, faith foresees the happy outcome of affliction, and makes us even now begin the music of gratitude which shall go on for ever increasing in volume, world without end. What clear shining after the rain we have in this and succeeding verses. The darkness is past, and the glory light shines forth as the sun. All the honour is rendered unto him to whom all the prayer was presented; he alone could deliver and did deliver, and therefore, to him only be the praise.

Grateful hearts are ever on the lookout for recruits, and the rejoicing psalmist discerns with joy the fact that other oppressed and lowly men observing the Lord's dealings with his servants are encouraged to look for a similar outcome to their own tribulations. The standing consolation of the godly is the experience of their Lord, for as he is, so are we also in this world. Indeed, moreover, his triumph has secured ours, and therefore, we may on the most solid grounds rejoice in him. This gave our great leader satisfaction as he foresaw the comforts that would flow to us from his conflict and conquest. The writer had fathomed the deeps, and had ascended to the heights; and, therefore, calls on the whole range of creation to bless the Lord. Our Well-Beloved here excites us all to grateful adoration: who among us will hold back? God's love to Christ argues good to all forms of life; the exaltation of the Head brings good to the members, and to all in the least connected with him. Inasmuch as the creation itself also is to be delivered from bondage by Christ's work, let all that have life and motion magnify the Lord. Glory be to you, O Lord, for the sure and all-including pledge of our Surety's triumph: we see in this the exaltation of all your poor and sorrowful ones, and our heart is glad.

Meditation: *The consolation is much greater when it is said, 'The Lord hears the poor,' than if it were written, 'He has heard poor David'* (Musculus).

Psalm 70

Suggested further reading: 2 Samuel 17:15-22

This is a copy with variations of Psalm 40:13-17. It is the second psalm that is a repetition of another. It is not forbidden us, in hours of dire distress, to ask for God to act speedily in coming to rescue us. As we have the words of this psalm twice in the letter, let them be doubly with us in spirit. It is most fitting that we should day by day cry to God for deliverance and help; our frailty and our many dangers render this a perpetual necessity.

The psalmist's enemies desired to put his faith to shame, and he eagerly entreats that they may be disappointed, and covered with confusion themselves. It shall certainly be so, at that dread day, if not sooner, when the wicked shall awake to shame and everlasting contempt. When men labour to turn others back from the right road, God retaliates by driving them back from the point they are aiming at.

They thought to shame the godly, but it was their shame, and shall be their shame for ever. How fond men are of taunts, and if they are meaningless 'Ahas', more like animal cries than human words, it matters nothing, so long as they are a vent for scorn and sting the victim. Rest assured, the enemies of Christ and his people shall have wages for their work; they shall be paid in their own coin; they loved scoffing, and they shall be filled with it — indeed, they shall become a proverb and a byword for ever.

Anger against enemies must not make us forget our friends, for it is better to preserve a single citizen of Zion, than to kill a thousand enemies. All true worshippers, though as yet in the humble ranks of seekers, shall have cause for joy. Even though the seeking commences in darkness, it shall bring light with it. Those who have tasted divine grace, and are, therefore, wedded to it, are a somewhat more advanced race, and these shall not only feel joy, but shall also with holy constancy and perseverance tell abroad their joy, and call upon men to glorify God. The doxology, 'Let God be magnified,' is infinitely more manly and ennobling than the dog's bark of 'Aha, aha.'

Psalm 40 sings of God's thoughts, and, therefore, ends with them; but the peculiar note of Psalm 70 is 'Make haste,' and, therefore, so it concludes. 'You are my help and my deliverer', my help in trouble, my deliverer out of it. 'O Lord, do not delay.' Here is the name of 'Jehovah' instead of 'my God'. We are warranted in using all the various names of God, for each has its own beauty and majesty, and we must reverence each by its holy use as well as by abstaining from taking it in vain.

Meditation: *He who deserved the hallelujahs of an intelligent universe, and the special hosannahs of all the children of men, had first to anticipate, and then to endure from the mouths of the very rebels whom he came to bless and to save, the malicious taunting of 'Aha, aha' (James Frame).*

Psalm 71:1-4

Suggested further reading: 2 Timothy 4:6-13

We have here 'The prayer of the aged believer', who in holy confidence of faith, strengthened by a long and remarkable experience, pleads against his enemies, and asks further blessings for himself. Anticipating a gracious reply, he promises to magnify the Lord exceedingly.

Every day must we guard against every form of reliance upon an arm of flesh, and hourly hang our faith upon the ever-faithful God. Not only on God must we rest, as a man stands on a rock, but in him must we trust, as a man hides in a cave. The more intimate we are with the Lord, the firmer will our trust be. God knows our faith, and yet he loves to hear us avow it; hence, the psalmist not only trusts in the Lord, but also tells him that he is so trusting. Be true, O God, to your word. It is a righteous thing in you to keep the promises that you have made to your servants. I have trusted you, and you will not be unrighteous to forget my faith. I am taken as in a net, but liberate me from the malice of my persecutors. Stoop to my feebleness, and hear my faint whispers; be gracious to my infirmities, and smile upon me: I ask salvation; listen to my petitions, and save me. Like one wounded and left for dead by my enemies, I need you to bend over me and bind up my wounds. These mercies are asked on the plea of faith, and they cannot, therefore, be denied.

This castle is fast shut against all adversaries, its gates they cannot burst open; the drawbridge is up, the portcullis

is down, the bars are fast in their places; but, there is a
secret door, by which friends of the great Lord can enter at
all hours of the day or night, as often as ever they please.
There is never an hour when it is unlawful to pray. Mercy's
gates stand wide open, and shall do so, till, at the last, the
Master of the house has risen up and shut the door. Believers
find their God to be their habitation, strong and accessible,
and this is for them a sufficient remedy for all the ills of
their mortal life.

God is on the same side with us, and those who are our
enemies are also his, for they are wicked. Therefore the
Lord will surely rescue his own confederates, and he will
not allow evil to triumph over the just. He who addresses
such a prayer as this to heaven does more injury to his
enemies than if he had turned a battery of cannon upon
them.

Meditation: *It is a good beginning, and a recommendation
to our prayers, when we can declare our faith and trust to be
in God alone* (Edward Walter).

Psalm 71:5-13

Suggested further reading: Isaiah 46:3-11

God, who gives us grace to hope in him, will assuredly fulfil our hope, and, therefore, we may plead it in prayer. His name is 'The Lord', the hope of Israel; and, as he cannot be a false or failing hope, we may expect to see our confidence justified.

Before the psalmist was able to understand the power that preserved him, he was sustained by it. God knows us before we know anything. The elect of old lay in the bosom of God before they were laid on their mothers' bosoms; and when their infantile weakness had no feet strong enough to carry it, the Lord upheld it. We do well to reflect upon divine goodness to us in childhood, for it is full of food for gratitude. The Amalekite in Bible history left his Egyptian servant to starve when he grew old and sick, but not so the Lord of saints; even to grey hairs he bears and carries us. Old age robs us of personal beauty, and deprives us of strength for active service; but it does not lower us in the love and favour of God.

'God has forsaken him.' O bitter taunt! There is no worse arrow in all the quivers of hell. Our Lord felt this barbed shaft and it is no wonder if his disciples feel the same. Were this exclamation the truth, it would indeed be an ill day for us; but, glory be to God, it is a barefaced lie. Nearness to God is our conscious security. A child in the dark is comforted by grasping its father's hand. To call God ours, as having entered into covenant with us, is a mighty plea in prayer, and a great stay to our faith. The cry of 'make haste' has occurred many times in this portion of the Psalms, and it was evoked by the sore pressure of affliction. Sharp sorrows soon put an end to procrastinating prayers.

Enemies shall be confounded as they enquire the reason for their overthrow; the men they seek to destroy seem so weak, and their cause so contemptible, that they will be filled with amazement as they see them not only survive all opposition, but even surmount it. How confounded must Pharaoh have been when Israel multiplied, despite his endeavours to exterminate the race; and how consumed with rage must the Scribes and Pharisees have become when they saw the gospel spreading from land to land by the very means which they used for its destruction. The Lord would have their shame made visible to all eyes, by their wearing it in their blushes as a mantle. They would have made a laughing-stock of the believer, if his God had forsaken him; therefore, let unbelief and atheism be made a public scoffing in their persons.

Meditation: *The psalmist has eyes for the daily miracles of the Lord; and, therefore, his mouth is daily full of the praise of the Lord* (Augustus F. Tholuck).

Psalm 71:14-18

Suggested further reading: Philippians 3:1-11

We are to bear testimony as experience enables us, and not withhold from others that which we have tasted and handled. The faithfulness of God in saving us, in delivering us out of the hand of our enemies, and in fulfilling his promises, is to be proclaimed everywhere by those who have proved it in their own history. How gloriously conspicuous is righteousness in the divine plan of redemption! It should be the theme of constant discourse. The devil rages against the substitutionary sacrifice, and those who are in error of every form make this the main point of their attack. May it be ours, therefore, to love the doctrine, and to spread its glad tidings on every side, and at all times. Mouths are never so usefully employed as in recounting the righteousness of God revealed in the salvation of believers in Jesus. Has our reader been silent upon this choice subject? Let us, then, press him to tell abroad what he enjoys within: he who keeps such glad tidings to himself does not do right.

As God himself fills all space, and is, therefore, the only God, leaving no room for another, so God's righteousness, in Christ Jesus, fills the believer's soul. He counts all other things but dross and dung 'that he may gain Christ, and be found in him, not having his own righteousness which is from the law, but that righteousness which is of God through faith'. What would be the use of speaking of any other righteousness to a dying man? And all are dying men. Let those who will, cry out of man's natural innocence, the dignity of the race, the purity of philosophers, the loveliness of untutored savages, the power of sacraments, and the infallibility of pontiffs; this is the true believer's immovable resolve, 'I will make mention of your righteousness, of yours only.' May this poor, unworthy tongue, whose glory it shall be to glorify you, be for ever dedicated to you, my Lord.

It was comforting to the psalmist to remember that from his earliest days he had been the Lord's disciple. None are too young to be taught of God, and they who begin early make the most proficient scholars. He had learned to tell what he knew, he was a pupil teacher; he continued still learning and declaring, and did not renounce his first master. This, also, was his comfort, but it is one that those who have been seduced from the school of the gospel, into the various colleges of philosophy and scepticism, will not be able to enjoy. A sacred conservatism is much needed in these days, when men are giving up old lights for new. We mean both to learn and to teach the wonders of redeeming love, till we can discover something nobler or more soul-satisfying; for this reason we hope that our grey heads will be found in the same road as we have trodden, even from our beardless youth.

Meditation: *It is an honourable thing to be in Christ before others; this is honourable when you are young; and then going on in the ways of godliness all your young time, and so in your middle age, and till you come to be old* (Jeremiah Burroughs).

Psalm 71:19-24

Suggested further reading: Colossians 3:12-17

Very sublime, unsearchable, exalted and glorious is the holy character of God, and his way of making men righteous. His plan of righteousness uplifts men from the gates of hell to the mansions of heaven. It is a high-doctrine gospel, gives a high experience, leads to high practice, and ends in high felicity. The exploits of others are mere child's play compared with God's, and are not worthy to be mentioned in the same age. Creation, providence and redemption are all unique, and nothing can compare with them.

Adoration is a fit frame of mind for the believer. When he draws near to God, he enters into a region where everything is surpassingly sublime; miracles of love abound on every hand, and marvels of mingled justice and grace. A traveller among the high Alps often feels overwhelmed with awe, amid their amazing sublimities; much more is this the case when we survey the heights and depths of the mercy and holiness of the Lord. 'O God, who is like you?' However low the Lord may permit us to sink, he will fix a limit to the descent, and in due time will bring us up again. Even when we are laid low in the tomb, the mercy is that we can go no lower, but shall retrace our steps and mount to better lands; and all this, because the Lord is ever mighty to save. A little God would fail us, but not Jehovah the Omnipotent. It is safe to lean on him, since he bears up the pillars both of heaven and earth.

Love so amazing calls for sweetest praise. David would give his best music, both vocal and instrumental, to the best of Masters. His harp should not be silent, nor his voice. The essence of song lies in the holy joy of the singer. Soul-singing is the soul of singing. Till men are redeemed, they are like instruments out of tune; but when once the precious blood has set them at liberty, then are they fitted to magnify the Lord who bought them. Being bought with a price is a more than sufficient reason for dedicating ourselves to the earnest worship of God our Saviour. As in many other psalms, the concluding stanzas speak of that as an accomplished fact, which was only requested in former verses. Faith believes that she has her request, and she has it. She is the substance of things hoped for — a substance so real and tangible that it sets the glad soul a-singing.

Meditation: *Hypocrites praise God with the 'lips' only; but David joins the soul to the lips* (William Nicholson).

Psalm 72:1-7

Suggested further reading: 1 Kings 1:28-37

The right to reign was transmitted by descent from David to Solomon, but not by that means alone: Israel was a theocracy, and the kings were but the viceroys of the greater King; hence the prayer that the new king might be enthroned by divine right, and then endowed with divine wisdom. Our glorious King in Zion has all judgement committed unto him. He rules in the name of God over all lands.

What a consolation to feel that none can suffer wrong in Christ's kingdom: he sits upon the great white throne, unspotted by a single deed of injustice, or even mistake of judgement; reputations are safe enough with him. True wisdom is manifest in all the decisions of Zion's King. We do not always understand his actions, but they are always right. Partiality has too often been shown to rich and great men, but the King of the last and best of monarchies deals out even-handed justice, to the delight of the poor and despised. We have the poor mentioned side by side with the king. The sovereignty of God is a delightful theme to the poor in spirit; they love to see the Lord exalted, and have no quarrel with him for exercising the prerogatives of his crown. It is a fictitious wealth that labours to conceal real poverty, which makes men carp at the reigning Lord, but a deep sense of spiritual need prepares the heart loyally to worship the Redeemer King. On the other hand, the King has a special delight in the humbled hearts of his contrite ones, and exercises all his power and wisdom on their behalf, even as Joseph in Egypt ruled for the welfare of his brethren. In a spiritual sense, peace is given to the heart by the righteousness of Christ; and all the powers and passions of the soul are filled with a holy calm, when the way of salvation, by a divine righteousness, is revealed. Then we go forth with joy, and are led forth with peace; the mountains and the hills break forth before us into singing.

Where Jesus reigns he is known as the true Melchizedek, king both of righteousness and peace. Peace based upon right is sure to be lasting, but no other will be. Many a so-called holy alliance has come to the ground before many moons have filled their horns, because craft formed the league, perjury established it, and oppression was its design; but when Jesus shall proclaim the great Truce of God, he will ordain perpetual peace, and men shall learn war no more. The peace that Jesus brings is not superficial or short-lived; it is abundant in its depth and duration. Let all hearts and voices welcome the King of nations; Jesus the Good, the Great, the Just, the Ever-Blessed.

Meditation: *Poor as God's people usually are, the era will surely arrive when the richest of the rich will count it all joy to lay their treasures at Jesus' feet* (C. H. Spurgeon).

Psalm 72:8-14

Suggested further reading: 1 Corinthians 15:20-28

The rule of Messiah shall be widespread. From Pacific to Atlantic and from Atlantic to Pacific, he shall be Lord, and the oceans that surround each pole shall be beneath his sway. All other power shall be subordinate to his; no rival or antagonist shall he know. Jesus shall be Ruler of all mankind. As Solomon's realm embraced all the land of promise, and left no unconquered margin, so shall the Son of David rule all lands given him in the better covenant, and leave no nation to pine beneath the tyranny of the prince of darkness. We are encouraged by such a passage as this to look for the Saviour's universal reign; whether before or after his personal advent we leave for the discussion of others. In this psalm, at least, we see a personal monarch, and he is the central figure, the focus of all the glory; we do not see his servant, but himself possessing the dominion and dispensing the government. Personal pronouns referring to our great King are constantly occurring in this psalm; he has dominion, kings fall down before him; and serve him; for he delivers; he spares, he saves, he lives, and daily is he praised.

Foreign princes from inland regions shall acknowledge the all-embracing monarchy of the King of kings; they shall be prompt to pay their reverential tribute. Religious offerings shall they bring, for their King is their God. Observe that true religion leads to generous giving; we are not taxed in Christ's dominions, but we are delighted to offer freely to him. They shall pay their reverence personally, however mighty they may be. No matter how high their state, how ancient their dynasty, or far-off their realms, they shall willingly accept him as their imperial Lord.

Here is an excellent reason for man's submission to the Lord Christ; it is not because they dread his overwhelming power, but because they are won over by his just and condescending rule. Who would not fear so good a Prince, who makes the needy his peculiar care, and pledges himself to be their deliverer in times of need? The proverb says, 'God helps those that help themselves'; but it is even more true that Jesus helps those who cannot help themselves, nor find help in others. All helpless ones are under the special care of Zion's compassionate King; let them hasten to put themselves in fellowship with him. His is the dominion of souls, a spiritual and not a worldly empire; and the needy, that is to say, the consciously unworthy and weak, shall find that he will give them his salvation. Jesus calls not the righteous, but sinners, to repentance. We ought to be anxious to be among these needy ones whom the Great King so highly favours.

Meditation: *So ardent is Christ's love for his own, that he suffers not one of them to perish, but leads them to full salvation and, opposing himself to both devils and tyrants who seek to destroy their souls, he constrains their fury and confounds their rage* (Mollerus).

Psalm 72:15-20

Suggested further reading: 1 Chronicles 29:10-15

O King, live for ever! He was slain, but is risen and ever lives. These are coronation gifts of the richest kind, cheerfully presented at his throne. How gladly would we give him all that we have and are, and count the tribute far too small! We may rejoice that Christ's cause will not stand still for want of funds; the silver and gold are his, and if they are not to be found at home, far-off lands shall hasten to make up the deficit. Would to God we had more faith and more generosity. May all blessings be upon his head; all his people desire that his cause may prosper, therefore they cry hourly, 'Your kingdom come.' We need not fear for the cause of truth in the land; it is in good hands, where the pleasure of the Lord is sure to prosper. 'Fear not, little flock, it is your Father's good pleasure to give you the kingdom.' When shall these words, which open up such a vista of delight, be fulfilled in the midst of the earth?

In its saving power, as the rallying point of believers, and as renowned and glorified, his name shall remain for ever the same. While time is measured out by days, Jesus shall be glorious among men. There shall be cause for all this honour, for he shall really and truly be a benefactor to the race. He himself shall be earth's greatest blessing; when men wish to bless others they shall bless in his name. The grateful nations shall echo his benedictions, and wish him happy who has made them happy. Not only shall some glorify the Lord, but all; no land shall remain in heathenism; all nations shall delight to do him honour.

As Quesnel well observes, the final verses explain themselves. They call rather for profound gratitude, and emotion of heart, than for an exercise of the understanding; they are more to be used for adoration than for exposition. It is, and ever will be, the acme of our desires, and the climax of our prayers, to behold Jesus exalted King of kings and Lord of lords. He has done great wonders such as none can match, leaving all others so far behind that he remains the sole and only wonder-worker; but equal marvels yet remain, for which we look with joyful expectation. He is the Blessed God, and his name shall be blessed; his name is glorious, and that glory shall fill the whole earth. For so bright a consummation our heart yearns daily, and we cry 'Amen, and Amen.'

Meditation: *It is sometimes inadvertently said that the Old Testament is narrow and exclusive, while the New Testament is broad and catholic in its spirit. This is a mistake. The Old and New Testaments are of one mind on this matter. Many are called, and few chosen. This is the common doctrine of the New as well as of the Old. They are both equally catholic in proclaiming the gospel to all* (James G. Murphy).

Psalm 73:2-14

Suggested further reading: Job 21:4-16

Here begins the narrative of a great soul-battle, a spiritual marathon, a hard and well-fought field, in which the half-defeated became in the end wholly victorious. Errors of heart and head soon affect the conduct. There is an intimate connection between the heart and the feet. Asaph could barely stand, his uprightness was going, his knees were bowing like a falling wall. When men doubt the righteousness of God, their own integrity begins to waver. Asaph could make no progress in the good road, his feet ran away from under him like those of a man on a sheet of ice. He was weakened for all practical action, and in great danger of actual sin, and so of a disgraceful fall. How ought we to watch the inner man, since it has so forcible an effect upon the outward character. The confession in this case is, as it should be, very plain and explicit.

It is a pitiful thing that an heir of heaven should have to confess 'I was envious', but worse still that he should have to put it, 'I was envious at the boastful.' Yet this acknowledgement is, we fear, due from most of us. Look! See! Consider! Here is the standing enigma! The crux of providence! The stumbling-block of faith! Here are the unjust rewarded and indulged, and not just for a day or an hour, but in perpetuity. From their youth onwards, these men, who deserve perdition, revel in prosperity. They deserve to be hung in chains, and chains are hung about their necks; they are worthy to be chased from the world, and yet the world becomes all their own. Poor purblind sense cries, 'Behold this!' Wonder, and be amazed, and make this square with providential justice, if you can. Both wealth and health are their dowry. No bad debts and bankruptcies weigh them down, but robbery and usury pile up their substance. Money runs to money, gold pieces fly in flocks; the rich grow richer, the proud grow prouder. Lord, how is this? Your poor servants, who become yet poorer, and groan under their burdens, are made to wonder at your mysterious ways.

Here is the case stated in the plainest manner, and many a Christian will recognize his own experience. Such knots have we also sought to untie, and have sadly worn our fingers and broken our teeth. Our wisdom has been dearly bought, but we have bought it; and, from now on, we cease to fret because of evildoers, for the Lord has showed us what their end will be.

Meditation: *Prosperity, it seems, is a dangerous weapon and none but the innocent should dare to use it. The psalmist himself, before he thought upon this, began to envy the prosperity of wicked men* (William Crouch).

Psalm 73:15-24

Suggested further reading: Job 21:17-26

It is not always wise to speak one's thoughts; if they remain within, they will only injure ourselves; but once uttered, their mischief may be great. From such a man as the psalmist, the utterance that his discontent suggested would have been a heavy blow and deep discouragement to the whole brotherhood. He, though a saint of God, had acted as if he had been one of the fools whom God abhors. Had he not even envied them? And what is that but to aspire to be like them? The wisest of men have enough folly in them to ruin them unless grace prevents. It was but an evidence of his true wisdom that he was so deeply conscious of his own folly. We see how bitterly good men bewail mental wanderings; they make no excuses for themselves, but set their sins in the pillory, and cast the vilest reproaches upon them. Oh, for grace to detest the very appearance of evil!

His mind entered the eternity where God dwells as in a holy place, he left the things of sense for the things invisible, his heart gazed within the veil, he stood where the thrice holy God stands. Thus he shifted his point of view, and apparent disorder resolved itself into harmony. He had seen too little to be able to judge; a wider view changed his judgement; he saw with his mind's enlightened eye the future of the wicked, and his soul was no longer in debate over the happiness of their condition. No envy gnaws now at his heart, but a holy horror both of their impending doom, and of their present guilt, fills his soul. He recoils from being dealt with in the same manner as the proud sinners, whom just now he regarded with admiration.

The psalmist's sorrow had culminated, not in the fact that the ungodly prospered, but that God had arranged it so. Had it happened by mere chance, he would have wondered, but could not have complained; but how the arranger of all things could so dispense his temporal favours was the vexatious question! Here, to meet the case, he sees that the divine hand purposely placed these men in prosperous and eminent circumstances, not with the intent to bless them but the very reverse. Their position was dangerous, and, therefore, God did not set his friends there but only his foes. He chose, in infinite love, a rougher but safer standing for his own beloved. They were but elevated by judicial arrangement for the fuller execution of their doom. Eternal punishment will be all the more terrible in contrast with the former prosperity of those who are ripening for it. Taken as a whole, the case of the ungodly is horrible throughout; and their worldly joy, instead of diminishing the horror, actually renders the effect more awful, even as the vivid lightning amid the storm does not brighten but intensify the thick darkness which lowers around.

Meditation: *He does not give up his faith, though he confesses his folly. Sin may distress us, and yet we may be in communion with God. It is sin beloved and delighted in which separates us from the Lord* (C. H. Spurgeon).

Psalm 73:1, 25-28

Suggested further reading: 2 Corinthians 4:7-15

'Truly God is good to Israel.' He is only good, nothing else but good to his own covenanted ones. He cannot act unjustly or unkindly to them; his goodness to them is beyond dispute, and without mixture. These are the true Israel, not the ceremonially clean but the actually clean: those who are clean in the inward parts, pure in the vital mainspring of action. To such he is, and must be, goodness itself. The writer does not doubt this, but lays it down as his firm conviction. Whatever may or may not be the truth about mysterious and inscrutable things, there are certainties somewhere; experience has placed some tangible facts within our grasp. Let us, then, cling to these, and they will prevent our being carried away by those hurricanes of infidelity which still come from the wilderness, and, like whirlwinds, smite the four corners of our house and threaten to overthrow it.

'Whom have I in heaven but you?' Thus, then, Asaph turns away from the glitter that fascinated him to the true gold that was his real treasure. He felt that his God was better to him than all the wealth, health, honour and peace which he had so much envied in the worldling. Indeed, he was not only better than all on earth, but also more excellent than all in heaven. He bade all other things depart, that he might be filled with his God. His God would not fail him, either as a protection or a joy. His heart would be kept up by divine love, and filled eternally with divine glory.

There is nothing desirable save God; let us, then, desire only him. All other things must pass away; let our hearts abide in him, who alone abides for ever.

'It is good for me to draw near to God.' Had he done so at first he would not have been immersed in such affliction; when he did so he escaped from his dilemma, and if he continued to do so he would not fall into the same evil again. The greater our nearness to God, the less we are affected by the attractions and distractions of earth. Access into the most holy place is a great privilege, and a cure for a multitude of ills. Faith is wisdom; it is the key of enigmas, the clue of mazes, and the pole star of pathless seas. Trust and you will know. He who believes shall understand, and so be able to teach. Asaph hesitated to utter his evil surmising, but he has no aversion to publish abroad a good matter. God's ways are the more admired the more they are known. He who is ready to believe the goodness of God shall always see fresh goodness to believe in, and he who is willing to declare the works of God shall never be silent for lack of wonders to declare.

Meditation: *How small is the number of those who keep their affections fixed on God alone!* (John Calvin).

Psalm 74:1-8

Suggested further reading: 2 Kings 18:13-25

Sin is usually at the bottom of all the hidings of the Lord's face; let us ask the Lord to reveal its special form to us, that we may repent of it, overcome it, and henceforth forsake it. When a church is in a forsaken condition it must not sit still in apathy, but turn to the hand which smites it, and humbly enquire the reason why.

The ruin made had long been an eyesore to the suppliant, and there seemed no hope of restoration. Havoc lorded it not just for a day or a year, but with perpetual power. Would Jehovah sit still and see his own land made a wilderness, his own palace a desolation? Until he should arise, and draw near, the desolation would remain; only his presence could cure the evil, therefore he is entreated to hasten with uplifted feet for the deliverance of his people. Every stone in the ruined temple appealed to the Lord; on all sides were the marks of impious spoilers, the holiest places bore evidence of their malicious wickedness. Would the Lord permit this for ever? Would he not hasten to overthrow the foe who defied him to his face, and profaned the throne of his glory? Faith finds pleas in the worst circumstances, she uses even the fallen stones of her desolate palaces, and assails the gates of heaven with them, casting them forth with the great engine of prayer. Superstition, unbelief and carnal wisdom have endeavoured to usurp the place of Christ crucified, to the grief of the church of God. The enemies without do us small damage, but those within the church cause her serious harm; by supplanting the truth and placing error in its stead, they deceive the people, and lead multitudes to destruction. As a Jew felt holy horror when he saw an idolatrous emblem set up in the holy place, even so do we when in a Protestant church we see the fooleries of Rome, and when from pulpits once occupied by men of God, we hear philosophy and vain deceit.

To this day the enmity of the human heart is quite as great as ever; and, if providence did not restrain, the saints would still be as fuel for the flames. They made a heap of the temple, and left not one stone upon another. If the powers of darkness could have their way, a like fate would befall the church of Christ. Defilement to the church is destruction; her foes would defile her till nothing of her purity, and consequently of her real self, remained. Yet, even if they could wreak their will upon the cause of Christ, they are not able to destroy it; it would survive their blows and fires. The Lord would hold them still like dogs in a leash, and in the end frustrate all their designs.

Meditation: *Though the people of God may not murmur against his proceedings, yet they may humbly expostulate with him about the cause* (Joseph Alleine).

Psalm 74:9-17

Suggested further reading: Ezekiel 34:1-10

Alas, poor Israel! No Urim and Thummim blazed on the High Priest's bosom, and no Shekinah shone from between the cherubim. The smoke of sacrifice and cloud of incense arose from the holy hill no more; solemn feasts were suspended, and even circumcision, the covenant sign, was forbidden by the tyrant. We, too, as believers, know what it is to lose our evidence and grope in darkness; and too often do our churches also miss the tokens of the Redeemer's presence, and their lamps remain untrimmed. Prophecy was suspended. No inspiring psalm or consoling promise fell from bard or seer. It does not bode well with the people of God when the voice of the preacher of the gospel fails, and a famine of the word of life falls on the people. God-sent ministers are as needful to the saints as their daily bread, and it is a great sorrow when a congregation is destitute of a faithful pastor. It is to be feared that with all the ministers now existing, there is yet a dearth of men whose hearts and tongues are touched with the celestial fire. Contempt of the word is very common, and may well provoke the Lord to withdraw it from us; may his long-suffering endure the strain, and his mercy afford us still the word of life.

Israel in holy loyalty acknowledges her King, and claims to have been his possession from of old, and for that reason she derives a plea for defence and deliverance. If the Lord is indeed the sole monarch of our bosoms, he will in his love put forth his strength on our behalf. If from eternity he has claimed us as his own, he will preserve us from the insulting foe. Jordan was divided by Jehovah's power; the Lord is able to repeat his miracles: what he did with a sea, he can do with a river; lesser difficulties shall be removed as well as greater ones. Observe the repetition of the pronoun 'you'; the song is all for God and the prayer is wholly directed to him. He argues that he who wrought such wonders would be pleased to do the same now that an emergency had arisen.

Land and sea receive their boundaries from you. Continents and islands are mapped by your hand. The argument of our text is that he who bounds the sea can restrain his foes; and he who guards the borders of the dry land can also protect his chosen. Return to us, then, good Lord, the bright summer days of joy. We know that all our changes come from you; we have already felt the rigours of your winter, grant us now the genial glow of your summer smile. The God of nature is the God of grace; and we may argue from the revolving seasons that sorrow is not meant to rule the year, the flowers of hope will blossom, and ruddy fruits of joy will ripen yet.

Meditation: *I am more than ever convinced that all the plans of God's providence, though they may appear extraordinary to my weak reason, are replete with wisdom and goodness* (Christopher Christian Sturm).

Psalm 74:18-23

Suggested further reading: 2 Kings 19:1-7

This is forcible pleading indeed, and reminds us of Moses and Hezekiah in their intercessions, 'What will you do to your great name? ... It may be that the Lord your God will hear the words of Rabshakeh, who has reproached the living God.' Jehovah is a jealous God, and will surely glorify his own name; here our hope finds a foothold. The meanness of the enemy is here pleaded. Sinners are fools. Shall fools be allowed to insult the Lord and oppress his people; shall the abjects curse the Lord and defy him to his face? When error grows too bold its day is near, and its fall certain. Arrogance foreshadows ripeness of evil, and the next step is rottenness. Instead of being alarmed when bad men grow worse and more audacious, we may reasonably take heart, for the hour of their judgement is evidently near.

The covenant is the master-key — heaven's gate must open to this. God is not a man that he should lie; he will not break his covenant, nor alter what has gone forth out of his lips. The Lord had promised to bless the seed of Abraham, and make them a blessing; here they plead that ancient word, even as we also may plead the covenant made with the Lord Jesus for all believers. What a grand word it is! Reader, do you know how to cry, 'Have respect to your covenant'? It is not the way of the Lord to allow any of those who trust in him to be put to shame; for his word is, 'He shall call upon me, and I will deliver him, and he shall glorify me.' The Lord is begged to remember that he is himself reproached, and by a mere man at that — even a fool; and he is also reminded that these foul reproaches are incessant, and repeated with every revolving day. It is bravely done when faith can pluck pleas out of the dragon's mouth, and out of the blasphemies of fools find arguments with God. All the world is in a measure dark, and hence everywhere there are cruel enemies of the Lord's people; but in some places a sevenfold night of superstition and unbelief has settled down, and there rage against the saints reaches to madness. Has not the Lord declared that the whole earth shall be filled with his glory? How can this be if he always permits cruelty to riot in dark places? Surely, he must arise, and end the days of wrong, the era of oppression. This is a most telling missionary prayer.

Meditation: *To hope against hope is the most blessed kind of hope* (William S. Plumer).

Psalm 75:1-5

Suggested further reading: 1 Samuel 2:1-5

Never let us neglect thanksgiving, or we may fear that another time our prayers will remain unanswered. As the smiling flowers gratefully reflect in their lovely colours the various constituents of the solar ray, so should gratitude spring up in our hearts after the smiles of God's providence. We should praise God again and again. Stinted gratitude is ingratitude. For infinite goodness there should be measureless thanks. Faith promises redoubled praise for greatly needed and signal deliverance. God is at hand to answer and do wonders — adore we then the present Deity. We do not sing of a hidden God, who sleeps and leaves the church to her fate, but of one who ever in our darkest days is most near, a very present help in trouble. Glory to the Lord, whose perpetual deeds of grace and majesty are the sure tokens of his being with us always, even to the end of the world.

God sends no delegated judge, but sits upon the throne himself. When anarchy is abroad, and tyrants are in power, everything is unloosed, dissolution threatens all things, the solid mountains of government melt as wax; but even then the Lord upholds and sustains the right. Hence, there is no real cause for fear. While the pillars stand, and stand they must for God upholds them, the house will brave out the storm. In the day of the Lord's appearing a general melting will take place, but in that day our covenant God will be the sure support of our confidence.

The Lord bids the boasters not to boast, and commands the mad oppressors to stay their folly. How calm is he, how quiet are his words, yet how divine the rebuke. If the wicked were not insane, they would even now hear in their consciences the still small voice bidding them cease from evil, and forbear their pride. The horn was the emblem of boastful power; only the foolish, like wild and savage beasts, will lift it high; but they assail heaven itself with it, as if they would gore the Almighty himself. In dignified majesty he rebukes the inane glories of the wicked, who exalt themselves beyond measure in the day of their fancied power. A word from God soon abases the lofty. Would to God that all proud men would obey the word given them here; for, if they do not, he will take effectual means to secure obedience, and then such woe will come upon them as will break their horns and roll their glory in the mire for ever. Impudence before God is madness. The outstretched neck of insolent pride is sure to provoke his axe. Those who carry their heads high shall find that they will be lifted yet higher, as Haman was upon the gallows that he had prepared for the righteous man. Silence, silly boaster! Silence or God will answer you.

Meditation: *Is not he a fool who lays a snare for himself?* (Thomas Watson).

Psalm 75:6-10

Suggested further reading: 1 Samuel 2:6-10

There is a God, and a providence, and things do not happen by chance. Though deliverance is hopeless from all points of the compass, yet God can work it for his people; and though judgement does not come either from the rising or the setting of the sun, or from the wilderness of mountains, yet come it will, for the Lord reigns. Men forget that all things are ordained in heaven; they see but the human force, and the carnal passion, but the unseen Lord is more real than these by far. He is at work behind and within the cloud. The foolish dream that he is not, but he is near even now, and on the way to bring in his hand that cup of spiced wine of vengeance, one draught of which shall stagger all his foes.

Even now he is actually judging. His seat is not vacant; his authority is not abdicated; the Lord reigns evermore. Empires rise and fall at his bidding. A dungeon here, and there a throne, his will assigns. Assyria yields to Babylon, and Babylon to the Medes. Kings are but puppets in his hand; they serve his purpose when they rise and when they fall. God only is; all power belongs to him; all else is shadow, coming and going, unsubstantial, misty, dreamlike.

The punishment of the wicked is prepared; God himself holds it in readiness. He has collected and concocted most dreadful woes, and he holds them in the chalice of his wrath. The retribution is terrible; it is blood for blood, foaming vengeance for foaming malice. The very colour of divine wrath is terrible. What must the taste be? Ten thousand woes are burning in the depths of that fiery cup, which is filled to the brim with indignation. The full cup must be quaffed, the wicked cannot refuse the terrible draught, for God himself pours it out for them and into them. Vain are their cries and entreaties. They could once defy him, but that hour is over, and the time to requite them is fully come. Wrath must proceed even to the bitter end. They must drink on and on for ever, even to the bottom where lies the sediment of deep damnation: this they must suck up, and still must they drain the cup. Oh, the anguish and the heartbreak of the day of wrath! Mark well, it is for all the wicked; all hell for all the ungodly; the dregs for the dregs; bitters for the bitter; wrath for the heirs of wrath. Righteousness is conspicuous, but, over all, terror spreads a tenfold night, cheerless, without a star. Oh, happy are they who drink the cup of godly sorrow, and the cup of salvation! Though these are now despised, then will they be envied by the very men who trod them under foot.

Meditation: *When God's people have drunk the red wine in the cup, the wicked must drink the dregs: the cup passes from place to place till all be drank off* (William Greenhill).

Psalm 76:1-6

Suggested further reading: Exodus 15:1-10

To be known, in the Lord's case, is to be honoured: those
who know his name admire its greatness. Although Judah
and Israel were unhappily divided politically, yet the godly
of both nations were agreed concerning Jehovah their God;
and truly whatever schisms may mar the visible church,
the saints always 'appear as one' in magnifying the Lord
their God. The world knows him not and therefore blas-
phemes him, but his church is full of ardour to proclaim
his fame unto the ends of the earth.

The church of God is the place where the Lord abides,
and he is to her the Lord and giver of peace. It is the glory
of the church that the Redeemer inhabits her by his Holy
Spirit. Vain are the assaults of the enemy, for they do not
attack us alone, but the Lord himself. Immanuel, God with
us, finds a home among his people. Who then shall do us
harm? Without leaving his tranquil abode, he sent forth his
word and snapped the arrows of his enemies before they
could shoot them. Every weapon, offensive and defensive,
the Lord dashed in pieces; death-bearing bolts and life-
preserving armour alike were of no avail when the Breaker
sent forth his word of power. In the spiritual conflicts of
this and every age, the same will be seen; no weapon that
is formed against the church shall prosper, and every tongue
that rises against her in judgement she shall condemn.

Jehovah is to be extolled far more than all the invading
powers that sought to oppress his people, though for power

and greatness they were comparable to mountains. What are the honours of war but brags of murder? What is the fame of conquerors but the reek of manslaughter? But the Lord is glorious in holiness, and his terrible deeds are done in justice for the defence of the weak and the deliverance of the enslaved. Mere power may be glorious, but it is not excellent: when we behold the mighty acts of the Lord, we see a perfect blending of the two qualities. The Israelites always had a special fear of horses and chariots; and, therefore, the sudden stillness of the entire force of the enemy in this department is made the theme of special rejoicing. The horses were stretched on the ground, and the chariots stood still, as if the whole camp had fallen asleep. Thus can the Lord send a judicial sleep over the enemies of the church, a premonition of the second death. Moreover, he can do this when they are in the zenith of power, and, as they imagine, in the very act of blotting out the remembrance of his people. The world's Rabshakehs can write terrible letters, but the Lord does not answer with pen and ink, but with rebukes, which bear death in every syllable.

Meditation: *The whole course of affairs in the world is steered by providence in reference to the good of Salem* (John Owen).

Psalm 76:7-12

Suggested further reading: Exodus 15:11-21

The fear of man is a snare, but the fear of God is a great virtue, and has great power for good over the human mind. God is to be feared profoundly, continually, and alone. Let all worship be to him only. The angels fell when their rebellion provoked his justice; Adam lost his place in paradise in the same manner; Pharaoh and other proud monarchs passed away at his frown; neither is there in earth or hell any who can abide the terror of his wrath. How blest are they who are sheltered in the atonement of Jesus, and hence have no cause to fear the righteous anger of the Judge of all the earth.

Man will not hear God's voice if he can help it, but God takes care to cause it to be heard. How readily can Jehovah command an audience! It may be that in the latter days he will, by some such miracles of power in the realms of grace, constrain all earth's inhabitants to attend to the gospel, and submit to the reign of his all-glorious Son. So be it, good Lord. Men were hushed when he ascended the judgement-seat and actively carried out the decrees of justice. When God is still, the people are in tumult; when he arises they are still as a stone. The Ruler of men has a special eye towards the poor and despised; he makes it his first point to right all their wrongs. They have little enough now, but their avenger is strong and he will surely save them. He who saves his people is the same God who overthrew their enemies; he is as omnipotent to save as to destroy. Glory to his name.

Man with his breath of threatening is but blowing the trumpet of the Lord's eternal fame. Furious winds often drive vessels more swiftly into port. The devil blows the fire and melts the iron, and then the Lord fashions it for his own purposes. Let men and devils rage as they may, they cannot do otherwise than subserve the divine purposes. Malice is tethered and cannot break its bounds. The fire that cannot be utilized shall be damped. Even the most rampant evil is under the control of the Lord, and will in the end be overruled for his praise. Let surrounding nations submit to the only living God, let his own people present their offerings with readiness, and let his priests and Levites be the first with the sacred sacrifice. He who deserves to be praised as our God should not have mere verbal homage, but substantial tribute. Dread Sovereign, behold, I give myself to you.

Meditation: *God turns the wrath of man to the praise of his adorable sovereignty* (Ebenezer Erskine).

Psalm 77:1-9

Suggested further reading: Romans 8:12-21

This psalm has much sadness in it, but we may be sure it
will end well, for it begins with prayer, and prayer never
has an ill outcome. Asaph did not run to man but to the
Lord, and he went to him, not with studied, stately, stilted
words, but with a cry, the natural, unaffected, unfeigned
expression of pain. He used his voice also, for though vocal
utterance is not necessary to the life of prayer, it often seems
forced upon us by the energy of our desires. Sometimes the
soul feels compelled to use the voice, for thus it finds a
freer vent for its agony. It is a comfort to hear the alarm-bell
ringing when the house is invaded by thieves.

He who is the well-spring of delight to faith became an
object of dread to the psalmist's distracted heart. The justice, holiness, power and truth of God all have a dark side,
and indeed all the attributes may be made to look black to
us if our eye is evil; even the brightness of divine love blinds
us, and fills us with a horrible suspicion that we have neither part nor lot in it. He is wretched indeed whose memories of the Ever-Blessed prove distressing to him; yet the
best of men know the depth of this abyss. Great grief is
mute. Deep streams do not brawl among the pebbles like
the shallow brooklets that live on passing showers. Words
fail the man whose heart fails him. He had cried to God but
he could not speak to man. What a mercy it is that if we can
do the first, we need not despair though the second should
be quite out of our power. Sleepless and speechless Asaph

was reduced to great extremities, and yet he rallied, and even so shall we.

At other times his spirit had a song for the darkest hour, but now he could only recall the strain as a departed memory. Where is the harp that once thrilled sympathetically to the touch of these joyful fingers? He did not cease from introspection, for he was resolved to find the bottom of his sorrow, and trace it to its fountain-head. He made sure work of it by talking not with his mind only, but his inmost heart; it was heart work with him. He was no idler, no melancholy trifler; he was up and at it, resolutely resolved that he would not tamely die of despair, but would fight for his hope to the last moment of life. He ransacked his experience, his memory, his intellect, his whole nature, his entire self, either to find comfort or to discover the reason why it was denied him. That man who has enough force of soul remaining to struggle in this fashion will not die by the hand of the enemy.

Meditation: *Words are but the body, the garment, the outside of prayer; sighs are nearer the heart work. Babes have no prayer for the breast, but weeping: the mother can read hunger in weeping* (Samuel Rutherford).

Psalm 77:10-15

Suggested further reading: Romans 8:22-30

The psalmist has won the day, he talks reasonably now, and surveys the field with a cooler mind. He confesses that unbelief is an infirmity, a weakness, a folly, a sin. He may also be understood to mean: 'This is my appointed sorrow', I will bear it without complaint. When we perceive that our affliction is meted out by the Lord, and is the ordained portion of our cup, we become reconciled to it, and no longer rebel against the inevitable. Why should we not be content if it is the Lord's will? What he arranges is not for us to quibble over.

'Fly back, my soul, away from present turmoils, to the grandeurs of history, the sublime deeds of Jehovah, the Lord of Hosts; for he is the same and is ready even now to defend his servants as in the days of yore.' Whatever else may glide into oblivion, the marvellous works of the Lord in days of old must not be allowed to be forgotten. Memory is a fit handmaid for faith. When faith has its seven years of famine, memory like Joseph in Egypt opens her granaries. It is well that the overflow of the mouth should indicate the good matter that fills the heart. Meditation makes rich talking; it is to be lamented that so much of the conversation of professors is utterly barren, because they take no time for contemplation. A meditative man should be a talker, otherwise he is a mental miser, a mill which grinds corn only for the miller. The subject of our meditation should be choice, and then our talk will be edifying; if we meditate on folly and affect to speak wisdom, our double-mindedness will soon be known to all men. Holy talk following upon meditation has a consoling power in it for ourselves as well as for those who listen, hence its value in the connection in which we find it in this passage.

In the holy place we understand our God, and rest assured that all his ways are just and right. When we cannot trace his way, because it is 'in the sea', it is a rich consolation that we can trust it, for it is in holiness. We must have fellowship with holiness if we would understand the ways of God to man. He who would be wise must worship. The pure in heart shall see God, and pure worship is the way to the philosophy of providence. In him the good and the great are blended, he surpasses in both. None can for a moment be compared with the mighty one of Israel. Who will not be strong in faith when there is so strong an arm to lean upon? Shall our trust be doubtful when his power is beyond all question?

Meditation: *He who brought up his people from the house of bondage will continue to redeem and deliver till we come into the promised rest* (C. H. Spurgeon).

Psalm 77:16-20

Suggested further reading: Habakkuk 3:8-15

As if conscious of its Maker's presence, the sea was ready to flee from before his face. The conception is highly poetical: the psalmist has the scene before his mind's eye, and describes it gloriously. The water saw its God, but man refuses to discern him; it was afraid, but proud sinners are rebellious and fear not the Lord. To their heart the floods were made afraid. Quiet caves of the sea, far down in the abyss, were moved with terror; and the lowest channels were left bare, as the water rushed away from its place, in terror of the God of Israel.

Obedient to the Lord, the lower region of the atmosphere yielded its aid to overthrow the Egyptian host. The cloudy chariots of heaven hurried forward to discharge their floods. From the loftier aerial regions thundered the dread artillery of the Lord of Hosts. Peal on peal the skies sounded over the heads of the routed enemies, confusing their minds and adding to their horror. Lightning flew like bolts from the bow of God. Swiftly, hither and thither, went the red tongues of flame, on helm and shield they gleamed; soon with blue bale-fires revealing the innermost caverns of the hungry sea which waited to swallow up the pride of Egypt. Behold, how all the creatures wait upon their God, and show themselves strong to overthrow his enemies. Rushing on with terrific swiftness and bearing all before it, the storm was as a chariot driven furiously, and a voice was heard (even your voice, O Lord!) out of the fiery car, even as when a mighty man in battle urges forward his charger, and shouts to it aloud. All heaven resounded with the voice of the Lord. The entire globe shone in the blaze of Jehovah's lightning. No need for other light amid the battle of that terrible night, every wave gleamed in the fire-flashes, and the shore was lit up with the blaze. How pale were men's faces in that hour, when all around the fire leaped from sea to shore, from crag to hill, from mountain to star till the whole universe was illuminated in honour of Jehovah's triumph. How dreadful are you, O God, when you come forth in your majesty to humble your arrogant adversaries.

The final verse is a sudden transition from tempest to peace, from wrath to love. Quietly as a flock Israel was guided on, by human agency which veiled the excessive glory of the divine presence. The smiter of Egypt was the shepherd of Israel. He drove his foes before him, but went before his people. Heaven and earth fought on his side against the sons of Ham, but they were equally subservient to the interests of the sons of Jacob. Therefore, with devout joy and full of consolation, we close this psalm, the song of one who forgot how to speak and yet learned to sing far more sweetly than his fellows.

Meditation: *There are seasons when even the holiest faith cannot bear to listen to words of reasoning; though it can still find a support whereon to rest, in the simple contemplation, in all their native grandeur, of the deeds that God has wrought* (Joseph Francis Thrupp).

Psalm 78:1-8

Suggested further reading: Deuteronomy 6:1-9

The inspired bard calls on his countrymen to give heed to his patriotic teaching. We naturally expect God's chosen nation to be first in hearkening to his voice. When God gives his truth a tongue, and sends forth his messengers who were trained to declare his word with power, it is the least we can do to give them our ears and the earnest obedience of our hearts. Shall God speak, and his children refuse to hear? His teaching has the force of law, let us yield both ear and heart to it.

Analogies are not only to be imagined, but are also intended by God to be traced between the story of Israel and the lives of believers. Israel was ordained to be a type; the tribes and their marching are living allegories traced by the hand of an all-wise providence. Unspiritual persons may sneer about fancies and mysticism, but Paul spoke well when he said 'which things are symbolic', and Asaph in the present case spoke to the point when he called his narrative 'a parable'. The mind of the poet-prophet was so full of ancient lore that he poured it forth in a copious stream of song, while beneath the gushing flood lay pearls and gems of spiritual truth, capable of enriching those who could dive into the depths and bring them up. The letter of this song is precious, but the inner sense is beyond any price. Whereas the first verse called for attention, the second justifies the demand by hinting that the outer sense conceals an inner and hidden meaning, which only the thoughtful will be able to perceive.

Tradition was of the utmost service to the people of God in olden times, before the more sure word of prophecy had become complete and generally accessible. The receipt of truth from the lips of others laid the instructed believer under solemn obligation to pass on the truth to the next generation. Truth, endeared to us by its fond associations with godly parents and venerable friends, deserves of us our best exertions to preserve and propagate it. Our fathers told us, we heard them, and we know personally what they taught; it remains for us in our turn to hand it on. Blessed be God, we now have the less mutable testimony of written revelation, but this by no means lessens our obligation to instruct our children in divine truth by word of mouth: rather, with such a gracious help, we ought to teach them far more fully the things of God. The testimony for the true God was to be transmitted from generation to generation by the careful instruction of succeeding families. Reader, if you are a parent, have you conscientiously discharged this duty?

Meditation: *It is no small mercy that your children are born in the days of the gospel where they may be instructed in Christianity* (George Swinnock).

Psalm 78:9-25

Suggested further reading: Numbers 11:1-9

Well equipped and furnished with the best weapons of the times, the leading tribe failed in faith and courage and retreated before the foe. There were several particular instances of this, but probably the psalmist refers to the general failure of Ephraim to lead the tribes to the conquest of Canaan. How often have we also, though supplied with every gracious weapon, failed to wage successful war against our sins, we have marched onward gallantly enough till the testing hour has come, and then 'in the day of battle' we have proved false to good resolutions and holy obligations. How altogether vain is unregenerate man! Array him in the best that nature and grace can supply, he still remains a helpless coward in the holy war, so long as he lacks a loyal faith in his God.

Vows and promises were broken, idols were set up, and the living God was forsaken. They were brought out of Egypt in order to be a people separated unto the Lord, but they fell into the sins of other nations, and did not maintain a pure testimony for the one only true God. They gave way to fornication, and idolatry, and other violations of the Decalogue, and were often in a state of rebellion against the benign theocracy under which they lived. They had pledged themselves at Sinai to keep the law, and then they wilfully disobeyed it, and so became covenant-breakers. Although they were in a position of obvious dependence upon God for everything, being in a desert where the soil could yield them no support, yet they were graceless enough to provoke their benefactor. At one time they provoked his jealousy by their hankering after false gods, soon they excited his wrath by their challenges of his power, their slanders against his love, their rebellions against his will. He was all bounty of love, and they were all needlessly disobedient. They were favoured above all nations, and yet none were more ill-favoured. For them the heavens dropped manna, and they returned murmurs; the rocks gave them rivers, and they replied with floods of wickedness. As in a mirror, we see ourselves here. Israel in the wilderness acted out, as in a drama, all the story of man's conduct towards his God.

'They believed not in God.' This is the master sin, the crying sin. God is ready to save, combining power with willingness, but rebellious man will not trust his Saviour, and therefore is condemned already. In the text it appears as if all Israel's other sins were as nothing compared with this; this is the peculiar spot which the Lord points at, the special provocation which angered him. Let every unbeliever learn to tremble more from this unbelief than at anything else. If he is not a fornicator, or thief, or liar, let him reflect that it is quite enough to condemn him that he does not trust in God's salvation.

Meditation: *Their sin was to doubt that God could or would support them in the wilderness, or allow those who followed his leadings to lack any good thing* (Brownlow North).

Psalm 78:26-41

Suggested further reading: Numbers 11:25-35

Winds sleep till God arouses them, and then, like Samuel, each one answers, 'Here am I, for you called me.' If we ourselves were half as obedient as the winds, we should be far superior to what we now are.

Apart from faith life is vanity. To wander up and down in the wilderness was a vain thing indeed, when unbelief had shut them out of the promised land. It was fitting that those who would not live to answer the divine purpose by believing and obeying their God should be made to live to no purpose, and to die before their time, unsatisfied, unblest. Those who wasted their days in sin had little cause to wonder when the Lord cut short their lives, and swore that they should never enter the rest which they had despised. Weary marches were their trouble, and to come to no resting-place was their vanity. Innumerable graves were left all along the track of Israel, and if any ask, 'Who slew all these?' the answer must be, 'They could not enter in because of unbelief.' Doubtless much of the vexation and failure of many lives results from their being sapped by unbelief, and honeycombed by evil passions. None live so fruitlessly and so wretchedly as those who allow sense and sight to override faith, and their reason and appetite to domineer over their fear of God. Our days go fast enough according to the ordinary lapse of time, but the Lord can make them rust away at a more bitter rate, till we feel as if sorrow actually ate out the heart of our life, and like a canker

devoured our existence. Such was the punishment of rebellious Israel; the Lord grant it may not be ours.

They rebelled enough times; they were as constant in
provocation as he was in his patience. In our own case,
who can count his errors? In what book could all our per-
verse rebellions be recorded? The wilderness was a place
of manifest dependence, where the tribes were helpless
without divine supplies, yet they wounded the hand that
fed them while it was in the act of feeding them. Is there no
likeness between us and them? Does it bring no tears into
our eyes, while, as in a glass, we see our own selves? Their
provocations had an effect; God was not insensible to them,
he is said to have been grieved. His holiness could not find
pleasure in their sin, his justice in their unjust treatment,
or his truth in their falsehood. What must it be to grieve
the Lord of love! Yet we also have vexed the Holy Spirit,
and he would have withdrawn himself from us long ago,
were it not that he is God and not man. We are in the desert
where we need our God; let us not make it a wilderness of
sin by grieving him.

Meditation: *The sinner's feast is no sooner served in but
divine justice is preparing to send up a reckoning after it,
and the fearful expectation of this cannot but spoil the taste
of the other* (William Gurnall).

Psalm 78:42-53

Suggested further reading: Exodus 7:1-7

Such displays of divine power as those that smote Egypt with astonishment must have needed some more than usual effort to blot from the tablets of memory. Strange is the faculty of memory in its oblivion as well as its records. Sin perverts man's powers, makes them forceful only in wrong directions, and practically dead for righteous ends.

The plagues were ensigns of Jehovah's presence and proofs of his hatred of idols; these instructive acts of power were carried out in the open view of all, as signals are set up to be observed by those far and near. In the whole land miracles were worked, not in cities alone, but also in the broad territory, in the most select and ancient regions of the proud nation. The Israelites ought not to have forgotten this, for they were the favoured people for whom these memorable deeds were wrought.

The contrast is striking, and ought never to have been forgotten by the people. The wolves were slain in heaps, the sheep were carefully gathered, and triumphantly delivered. The tables were turned, and the poor serfs became the honoured people, while their oppressors were humbled before them. Israel went out in a compact body like a flock; they were defenceless in themselves as sheep, but they were safe under their Great Shepherd; they left Egypt as easily as a flock leaves one pasture for another. Knowing nothing of the way by their own understanding or experience, they were, nevertheless, rightly directed, for the all-wise God knew every spot of the wilderness. To the sea, through the sea, and from the sea, the Lord led his chosen, while their former taskmasters were too cowed in spirit, and broken in power, to dare to molest them. After the first little alarm, natural enough when they found themselves pursued by their old taskmasters, they plucked up courage and ventured boldly into the sea, and afterwards into the desert where no man dwelt. The Egyptians were gone, gone for ever, never to disturb the fugitives again. That tremendous blow effectually defended the tribes for forty years from any further attempt to drive them back. Egypt found the stone too heavy and was glad to let it alone. Let the Lord be praised who thus effectually freed his elect nation.

What a grand narrative we have been considering! Well might the mightiest master of sacred song select 'Israel in Egypt' as a choice theme for his genius; and well may every believing mind linger over every item of the amazing transaction. The marvel is that the favoured nation should live as if unmindful of it all, and yet such is human nature. Alas, poor man! Rather, alas, base heart!

Meditation: *God, in punishing the Egyptians so severely, did nothing but what was just and equitable, when weighed in the balance of right* (A. R. Fausset).

Psalm 78:54-66

Suggested further reading: Judges 2:7-15

The Lord conducted them to the frontier of the Holy Land, where he intended the tabernacle to become the permanent symbol of his abode among his people. He did not leave them halfway upon their journey to their heritage; his power and wisdom preserved the nation till the palm trees of Jericho were within sight on the other side of the river. Nor did he leave them then, but still conducted them till they were in the region round about Zion, which was to be the central seat of his worship. This the Lord had purchased in type of old by the sacrifice of Isaac, fit symbol of the greater sacrifice which was to be presented there in due season: that mountain was also redeemed by power, when the Lord's right hand enabled his valiant men to smite the Jebusites, and take the sacred hill from the insulting Canaanites. Thus shall the elect of God enjoy the sure protection of the Lord of hosts, even to the border land of death, and through the river, up to the hill of the Lord in glory. The purchased people shall safely reach the purchased inheritance.

Not only were armies routed, but whole peoples displaced. The iniquity of the Canaanites was full; their vices made them rot above ground; therefore, the land ate up its inhabitants, the hornets vexed them, the pestilence destroyed them, and the sword of the tribes completed the execution to which the justice of long-provoked heaven had at length appointed them. The Lord was the true conqueror of Canaan. He cast out the nations as men cast out filth from their habitations; he uprooted them as noxious weeds are completely destroyed by the farmer.

Yet a change of condition had not altered their manners. They left their nomadic habits, but not their tendencies to wander from their God. Though every divine promise had been fulfilled to the letter, and the land flowing with milk and honey was actually their own, yet they tried the Lord again with unbelief, and provoked him with other sins. He is not only high and glorious, but also most high, indeed the Most High, the only being who deserves to be so highly held in honour. Yet, instead of honouring him, Israel grieved him with rebellion. They were true to nothing but hereditary treachery: steadfast in nothing but in falsehood. They knew his truth and forgot it, his will and disobeyed it, his grace and perverted it to an occasion for greater transgression. Reader, do you need a mirror? See here is one that suits the present expositor well; does it not also reflect your image?

Meditation: *Not to be settled in the faith is provoking to God* (Thomas Watson).

Psalm 78:67-72

Suggested further reading: Samuel 16:6-13

God had honoured Ephraim, for to that tribe belonged
Joshua the great conqueror, and Gideon the great judge,
and within its borders was Shiloh, the place of the ark and
the sanctuary; but now the Lord would change all this and
set up other rulers. He would no longer leave matters to the
leadership of Ephraim, since that tribe had been tried and
found wanting. Sin had been found in them, folly and in-
stability, and therefore they were set aside as unfit to lead.

To give the nation another trial Judah was elected to
supremacy. This was according to Jacob's dying prophecy.
Our Lord sprang out of Judah and he it is whom his brethren shall praise. The tabernacle and ark were removed to
Zion during the reign of David; no honour was left to the
wayward Ephraimites.

'He also chose David his servant.' It was an election of a
sovereignly gracious kind, and it operated practically by
making the chosen man a willing servant of the Lord. He
was not chosen because he was a servant, but in order that
he might be so. David always esteemed it to be a high honour that he was both elect of God, and a servant of God. He
was upright before God, and never swerved in heart from
the obedient worship of Jehovah. Whatever faults he had,
he was unfeignedly sincere in his allegiance to Israel's
superior king; he shepherded for God with honest heart.
He was a sagacious ruler, and the psalmist magnifies the
Lord for having appointed him. Under David, the Jewish

kingdom first rose to an honourable position among the nations, and exercised an influence over its neighbours. In closing the psalm, which has described the varying conditions of the chosen nation, we are glad to end so peacefully, with all noise of tumult or of sinful rites hushed into silence. After a long voyage over a stormy sea, the ark of the Jewish state rested on its Ararat, beneath a wise and gentle reign, no more to be wafted hither and thither by floods and gales. The psalmist had intended all along to make this his last stanza, and we too may be content to finish all our songs of love with the reign of the Lord's anointed. Only we may eagerly enquire, when will it come? When shall we end these desert roamings, these rebellions, and chastisings, and enter into the rest of a settled kingdom, with the Lord Jesus reigning as 'the Prince of the house of David'?

Thus have we ended this lengthy parable. May we in our life-parable have less of sin, and as much of grace as is displayed in Israel's history, and may we close it under the safe guidance of 'that great Shepherd of the sheep'. AMEN.

Meditation: *Close to Zion the Father of the faithful offered up his only son, and there in future days the great gatherings of his chosen seed would be, and therefore Zion is said to be lovely unto God* (C. H. Spurgeon).

Psalm 79:1-4

Suggested further reading: Lamentations 1:1-11

'O God, the nations have come into your inheritance.' It is
the cry of amazement at sacrilegious intrusion, as if the
poet were struck with horror. The stranger pollutes your
hallowed courts with his tread. All Canaan is your land,
but your foes have ravaged it. Into the inmost sanctuary
they have profanely forced their way, and there behaved
arrogantly. Thus, the holy land, the holy house, and the
holy city, were all polluted by the uncircumcised. It is an
awful thing when wicked men are found in the church and
numbered with her ministry. Then are the tares sown with
the wheat, and the poisoned gourds cast into the pot. Jerusalem, the beloved city, the joy of the nation, the abode of
her God, was totally wrecked. Alas, alas for Israel! It is sad
to see the foe in our own house, but worse to meet him in
the house of God: they strike hardest who smite at our religion. The psalmist piles up the agony; he was a suppliant,
and he knew how to bring out the strong points of his argument. We ought to order our case before the Lord with as
much care as if our success depended on our pleading. Men
in earthly courts use all their powers to obtain their ends,
and so also should we state our case with earnestness, and
bring forward our strong arguments.

The invaders slew men as if their blood was of no more
value than so much water; they caused it to flow as lav-
ishly as when the floods deluge the plains. The city of holy
peace became a field of blood. The enemy did not care to

bury the dead, and there was not a sufficient number of Israel left alive to perform the funeral rites; therefore the precious relics of the departed were left to be devoured by vultures and torn by wolves. Beasts on which man could not feed fed on him. The flesh of creation's Lord became meat for carrion crows and hungry dogs. The calamities of war are dire, yet they have happened to God's saints and servants. This might well move the heart of the poet, and he did well to appeal to the heart of God by reciting the grievous evil. Such might have been the lamentation of an early Christian as he thought of the amphitheatre and all its deeds of blood. Note how the plea is made to turn upon God's property in the temple and the people: we read 'your inheritance', 'your temple, your servants', and 'your saints'. Surely the Lord will defend his own, and will not allow rampant adversaries to despoil them.

Meditation: *If God's professing people degenerate from what they and their fathers were, they must expect to be told of it; and it is well if a just reproach will help to bring us to a true repentance* (Matthew Henry).

Psalm 79:5-13

Suggested further reading: Hosea 8:7-14

There was great cause for the Lord to be jealous, since idols had been set up, and Israel had moved away from his worship, but the psalmist begs the Lord not to consume his people utterly as with fire, but to abate their woes. Sometimes providence appears to deal much more severely with the righteous than with the wicked, and the sixth verse is a bold appeal founded upon such an appearance. It in effect says, 'Lord, if you must empty out the vials of your wrath, begin with those who have no measure of regard for you, but are openly up in arms against you; and be pleased to spare your people, who are yours notwithstanding all their sins.'

In the eyes of the heathen, God's glory was tarnished by the defeat of his people and the profanation of his temple; therefore, his distressed servants implore his aid, that his great name may no more be the scorn of blaspheming enemies. Sin — the root of the evil — is seen and confessed; pardon of sin is sought as well as removal of chastisement, and both are asked not as matters of right, but as gifts of grace. God's name is a second time brought into the pleading. Believers will find it their wisdom to use this noble plea very frequently: it is the great gun of the battle, the mightiest weapon in the armoury of prayer. Faith grows while it prays. The appeal to the Lord's tender mercy is here supplemented by another addressed to the divine power, and the petitioner rises from a request for those who

are brought low, to a prayer for those who are on the verge
of death, set apart as victims for the slaughter. How consoling it is to despondent believers to reflect that God can
preserve even those who bear the sentence of death in themselves. Men and devils may consign us to perdition, while
sickness drags us to the grave, and sorrow sinks us in the
dust; but, there is one who can keep our soul alive, and
bring it up again from the depths of despair. A lamb shall
live between the lion's jaws if the Lord wills it.

The gratitude of the church is lasting as well as deep.
On her tablets are memorials of great deliverance, and, as
long as she shall exist, her sons will rehearse them with
delight. We have a history that will survive all other records,
and it is bright in every line with the glory of the Lord.
God's glory springs from the direst calamities, and the dark
days of his people become the prelude to unusual displays
of the Lord's love and power.

Meditation: *The good which God does to his church, be it
temporal or spiritual, is for his own sake* (William Greenhill).

Psalm 80:1-7

Suggested further reading: Lamentations 5:1-9

We may be quite sure that he who deigns to be a shepherd to his people will not turn a deaf ear to their complaints. The Lord had of old in the wilderness led, guided, shepherded all the tribes; and, therefore, the appeal is made to him. The Lord's doings in the past are strong grounds for appeal and expectation as to the present and the future.

It is wise to mention the names of the Lord's people in prayer, for they are precious to him. Jesus bears the names of his people on his breastplate. Just as the mention of the names of his children has power with a father, so it is with the Lord. The three names were near of kin; Ephraim and Manasseh represent Joseph, and it was fitting that Benjamin, the other son of the beloved Rachel, should be mentioned in the same breath: these three tribes were wont to march together in the wilderness, following immediately behind the ark. The prayer is that the God of Israel would be mighty on behalf of his people, chasing away their foes, and saving his people. Oh, that in these days the Lord may be pleased to remember every part of his church, and make all her tribes see his salvation! We would not mention our own denomination only, but lift up a prayer for all the sections of the one church.

When the Lord turns his people he will soon turn their condition. It needs the Lord himself to do this, for conversion is as divine a work as creation; and those who have been once turned unto God, if they at any time backslide, as much need the Lord to turn them again as to turn them at the first. All that is wanted for salvation is the Lord's favour. No matter how fierce the foe, or dire the captivity, the shining face of God ensures both victory and liberty. This verse is a very useful prayer. Since we too often turn aside, let us often with our lips and heart cry, 'Turn us again, O God, and cause your face to shine, and we shall be saved.' Prayer would seek to enter the holy place but God's wrath battles with it, and prevents its entrance. That he should be angry with us when sinning seems natural enough, but that he should be angry even with our prayers is a bitter grief. 'Restore us, O God of hosts.' The prayer rises in the form of its address to God. He is here the God of Hosts. The more we approach the Lord in prayer and contemplation the higher will our ideas of him become.

Meditation: *It is the part of the shepherd to give ear to the bleatings and cries of the sheep, to call them to mind, that he may readily run to their help* (Venema).

Psalm 80:8-19

Suggested further reading: Isaiah 5:1-7

Glorious was the right hand of the Lord when with power and great wonders he removed his pleasant plant in the teeth of those who sought its destruction. Seven nations were removed to make space for the vine of the Lord; the old trees, which had long engrossed the soil, were torn up root and branch; oaks of Bashan and palm trees of Jericho were displaced for the chosen vine. It was securely placed in its appointed position with divine prudence and wisdom. Small in appearance, very dependent, exceedingly weak, and apt to trail on the ground, yet the vine of Israel was chosen of the Lord, because he knew that by incessant care, and abounding skill, he could make of it a fine fruit-bearing plant. The nation itself was so great that even its tribes were powerful and worthy to take rank among the mighty. It is a noble picture of the prosperity of the Israelites in their best days. In Solomon's time the little land of Israel occupied a high place among the nations. There have been times when the church of God also has been eminently conspicuous, and her power has been felt far and near. Those were brave days for Israel, and would have continued, had not sin cut them short. When the church pleases the Lord, her influence becomes immense, far beyond the proportion that her numbers or her power would lead us to expect. But, alas! when the Lord leaves her she becomes as worthless, useless, and despised as an untended vine, which is of all plants the most valueless.

An unprotected vine is exposed to every form of injury: none regard it, all prey upon it: such was Israel when given over to her enemies. Her cruel neighbours have a pluck at her, and marauding bands, like roaming beasts, needs must pick at her. With God no enemy can harm us, without him none are so weak as to be unable to do us damage. God's rebuke was to Israel what fire and axe would be to a vine. His favour is life, and his wrath is as messengers of death. One angry glance from Jehovah's eye is sufficient to lay all the vineyards of Ephraim desolate. O Lord, look not thus upon our churches. Rebuke us, but not in anger.

'Restore us, O Lord God of hosts.' Here we have another advance in the title and the incommunicable name of Jehovah, the I am is introduced. Faith's day grows brighter as the hours roll on; and her prayers grow more full and mighty. No extremity is too great for the power of God. He is able to save at the last point, and that too by simply turning his smiling face upon his afflicted. Men can do little with their arm, but God can do all things with a glance. Oh, to live for ever in the light of Jehovah's countenance.

Meditation: *During distress God comes: and when he comes it is no more distress* (Gaelic Proverb).

Psalm 81:1-7

Suggested further reading: Numbers 10:1-10

The Lord was the strength of his people in delivering them out of Egypt with a high hand, and also in sustaining them in the wilderness, placing them in Canaan, preserving them from their foes, and giving them victory. To whom do men give honour but to those upon whom they rely, therefore let us sing aloud unto our God, who is our strength and our song.

Obedience is to direct our worship, not whim and sentiment: God's appointment gives a solemnity to rites and times which no ceremonial pomp or hierarchical ordinance could confer. The Jews not only observed the ordained month, but that part of the month that had been divinely set apart. The Lord's people of old welcomed the times appointed for worship; let us feel the same exultation, and never speak of the Sabbath as though it could be other than 'a delight' and 'honourable'. Those who plead this passage as authority for their man-appointed feasts and fasts must be moonstruck. We will keep such feasts as the Lord appoints, but not those which Rome or Canterbury may ordain.

Israel was the drudge and slave of Egypt, but God gave him liberty. It was by God alone that the nation was set free. Other peoples owe their liberties to their own efforts and courage, but Israel received its Magna Carta as a free gift of divine power. The Lord may truly say of every one of his freed men, 'I removed his shoulder from the burden.' How typical all this is of the believer's deliverance from legal bondage, when, through faith, the burden of sin glides into the Saviour's sepulchre, and the servile labours of self-righteousness come to an end for ever.

God heard his people's cries in Egypt, and at the Red Sea: this ought to have bound them to him. Since God does not forsake us in our need, we ought never to forsake him at any time. When our hearts wander from God, our answered prayers cry 'shame' upon us. Out of the cloud the Lord sent forth tempest upon the foes of his chosen. That cloud was his secret pavilion, within it he hung up his weapons of war, his javelins of lightning, his trumpet of thunder; he came out from that pavilion and overthrew the foe that his own elect might be secure. The story of Israel is only our own history in another shape. God has heard us, delivered us, liberated us, and too often our unbelief causes the wretched return of mistrust, murmuring and rebellion. Great is our sin; great is the mercy of our God: let us reflect upon both, and pause a while.

Meditation: *To 'answer in the secret place of thunder' refers us to the pillar of cloud and fire, the habitation of the awful Majesty of God, from which God glanced with angry eyes upon the Egyptians, filled them with consternation and overthrew them* (Venema).

Psalm 81:8-16

Suggested further reading: Joshua 24:14-24

How low have they fallen who will not hearken unto God himself! We are not fond of being upbraided, we would rather avoid sharp and cutting truths; and, though the Lord himself rebuke us, we fly from his gentle reproofs.

No alien god is to be tolerated in Israel's tents. Where false gods are, their worship is sure to follow. Man is so desperate an idolater that the image is always a strong temptation: while the nests are there the birds will be eager to return. No other god had done anything for the Jews, and therefore they had no reason for paying homage to any other. The same argument will apply to us. We owe all to the God and Father of our Lord Jesus Christ: the world, the flesh, the devil, none of these have been of any service to us; they are aliens, foreigners, enemies, and it is not for us to bow down before them. 'Little children keep yourselves from idols,' is our Lord's voice to us, and by the power of his Spirit we would cast out every false god from our hearts.

Sin strips a man of his armour, and leaves him naked to his enemies. Our doubts and fears would have been slain long ago if we had been more faithful to our God. Ten thousand evils that afflict us now would have been driven far from us if we had been more jealous of holiness in our walk and conversation. We ought to consider not only what sin takes from our present stock, but what it prevents our gaining: reflection will soon show us that sin always costs us dear. If we depart from God, our inward corruption is sure to cause a rebellion. Satan will assail us, the world will worry us, doubts will annoy us; and all through our own fault. Solomon's departure from God raised up enemies against him, and it will be so with us, but if our ways please the Lord he will make even our enemies to be at peace with us.

The Lord can do great things for an obedient people. When his people walk in the light of his countenance, and maintain unsullied holiness, the joy and consolation that he yields them are beyond conception. To them the joys of heaven have begun even upon earth. They can sing in the ways of the Lord. The spring of the eternal summer has commenced for them; they are already blest, and they look for brighter things. This shows us by contrast how sad a thing it is for a child of God to sell himself into captivity to sin, and bring his soul into a state of famine by following after another god.

Meditation: *O Lord, for ever bind us to yourself alone, and keep us faithful to the end* (C. H. Spurgeon).

Psalm 82

Suggested further reading: Isaiah 66:18-24

'God stands in the congregation of the mighty.' He is the watcher, who, from his own point of view, sees all that is done by the great ones of the earth. When they sit in state he stands over them, ready to deal with them if they pervert judgement. Judges shall be judged, and to justices justice shall be meted out. He lends them his name, and this is their authority for acting as judges, but they must take care that they do not misuse the power entrusted to them, for the Judge of judges is in session among them.

It is indirectly stated that the magistrates had been unjust and corrupt. They not only excused the wicked, but even decided in their favour against the righteous. It is a wretched plight for a nation to be in when its justices know no justice, and its judges are devoid of judgement. Neither to know his duty nor to wish to know it is rather the mark of an incorrigible criminal than of a magistrate, yet such a stigma was justly set upon the rulers of Israel. When the dispensers of law have dispensed with justice, settlements are unsettled, society is unhinged, the whole fabric of the nation is shaken. When injustice is committed in due course of law the world is indeed out of course. There must be some government among men, and as angels are not sent to dispense it, God allows men to rule over men, and endorses their office, at least until the prostitution of it becomes an insult to his own prerogatives. Magistrates would have no right to condemn the guilty if God had not sanctioned the establishment of government, the administration of law, and the execution of sentences. Here the Spirit speaks most honourably of these offices, even when it censures the officers; and thereby teaches us to render honour to whom honour is due, honour to the office even if we award censure to the office-bearer.

'Arise, O God, judge the earth.' Come, Judge of all mankind, put the bad judges to your bar and end their corruption and baseness. Here is the world's true hope of rescue from the fangs of tyranny. The time will come when all races of men shall own their God, and accept him as their king. There is one who is 'King by right divine', and he is even now on his way. The last days shall see him enthroned, and all unrighteous potentates broken like potters' vessels by his potent sceptre. The second advent is still earth's brightest hope. Come quickly, even so, come, Lord Jesus.

Meditation: *The state is an ordinance of God, having, like the family, its foundation in the very constitution of human nature* (William Binnie).

Psalm 83:1-4

Suggested further reading: Psalm 2

Here the appeal is to EL, the Mighty One. He is entreated to
act and speak, because his nation suffers and is in great
jeopardy. 'Man is clamorous, be not speechless. He rails
and reviles, will you not reply? One word of yours can deliver your people; therefore, O Lord, break your quiet and
let your voice be heard.' Now the psalmist looks entirely to
God; he asks not for 'a leader bold and brave', or for any
form of human force, but casts his burden upon the Lord,
being well assured that his eternal power and Godhead
could meet every difficult situation.

The enemies of Israel were also God's enemies, and are
here described as such by adding intensity to the argument
of the intercession. Confident of conquest, they carry themselves proudly and exalt themselves as if their anticipated
victories were already obtained. They are by no means sparing of their words, they are like a hungry pack of dogs, all
giving voice at once. So sure are they of devouring your
people that they already shout over the feast. The adversaries of the church are usually a noisy and a boastful crew.
Their pride is a brass that always sounds, a cymbal which
is ever tinkling.

Whatever we may do, our enemies use their wits and
lay their heads together; in united conclave they hold dis-
cussions on the demands and plans of the campaign, using
much treachery and serpentine cunning in arranging their
schemes. Malice is cold-blooded enough to plot with

deliberation; and pride, though it is never wise, is often allied with craft. Hidden away from all harm are the Lord's chosen. Their enemies do not think so, but hope to smite them; they might as well attempt to destroy the angels before the throne of God.

'They have said, "Come, and let us cut them off from being a nation."' Easier said than done. Yet it shows how thoroughgoing are the foes of the church. Their policy was one of extermination. They laid the axe at the root of the matter. Rome has always loved this method of warfare, and hence she has gloated over the massacre of Bartholomew, and the murders of the Inquisition. They would blot them out of history as well as out of existence. Evil is intolerant of good. Even if Israel let Edom alone, still Edom cannot be quiet, but seeks like its ancestor to kill the chosen of the Lord. Men would be glad to cast the church out of the world because it rebukes them, and is thus a standing menace to their sinful peace.

Meditation: *Is the Lord silent? Then do not be silent yourself; but cry unto him till he breaks the silence* (Starke, in Lange's Bibelwerk).

Psalm 83:5-8

Suggested further reading: 2 Chronicles 20:1-13

The Lord's enemies are hearty and unanimous in their designs. They seem to have but one heart, and a fierce one at
that, against the chosen people and their God. They aim at
the Lord himself through the sides of his saints. They make
a covenant, and ratify it with blood, resolutely banding
themselves together to war with the mighty God.

Esau despised the birthright, and his descendants despise those who possess it. Leaving their rock-built mansions for the tents of war, the Edomites invaded the land of
Israel. A persecuting spirit ran in the blood of the
Ishmaelites. They perpetuated the old grudge between the
child of the bondwoman and the son of the freewoman.
Born of incest, but yet a near kinsman, the feud of Moab
against Israel was very bitter. Little could righteous Lot have
dreamed that his unhallowed seed would be such unrelenting enemies of his Uncle Abraham's posterity. The
Hagarites were perhaps descendants of Hagar by a second
husband. Whoever they may have been, they cast their
power into the wrong scale, and with all their might sought
the ruin of Israel. Children of Hagar, and all others who
dwell around Mount Sinai, which is in Arabia, are descendants of those that engender bondage, and hence they hate
the descendants of those awarded the promise.

Gebal was probably a near neighbour of Edom. Ammon
and Amalek, two other hereditary foes of Israel, were fierce
and remorseless as ravening wolves. In the roll of infamy

let these names remain detestably immortalized. How thick they stand! Their name is legion, for they are many. Alas, poor Israel, how are you to stand against such a bloody league? Nor is this all. Here comes another tribe of ancient foemen, the Philistines, who once blinded Samson, and captured the ark of the Lord; and here are old allies become new enemies, the builders of the temple conspiring to pull it down, even 'the inhabitants of Tyre'. The latter were mercenaries who did not care at whose bidding they drew sword, so long as they carved something for their own advantage. True religion has had its quarrel with merchants and craftsmen, and because it has interfered with their gains, they have conspired against it.

Assyria was then a rising power, anxious for growth, and it thus early distinguished itself for evil. What a motley group they were; a league against Israel is always attractive, and gathers whole nations within its bonds. Herod and Pilate are friends, if Jesus is to be crucified. Romanism and ritualism make common cause against the gospel. All these have come to the aid of Moab and Ammon, the two nations that were among the fiercest in the conspiracy. There were ten to one against Israel, and yet she overcame all her enemies. Her name is not blotted out; but many, no, most of her adversaries are now a name only, their power and their excellence are alike gone.

Meditation: *Though there may fall out a private grudge between those who are wicked, yet they will all agree and unite against the saints* (Thomas Watson).

Psalm 83:9-12

Suggested further reading: Judges 7:19-25

Faith delights to light upon precedents, and quote them before the Lord; in the present instance, Asaph found a very appropriate one, for the nations in both cases were very much the same, and the plight of the Israelites very similar. Yet Midian perished, and the psalmist trusted that Israel's present foes would meet with a similar overthrow from the hand of the Lord. The hosts were swept away by the suddenly swollen torrent, and utterly perished, which was a second instance of divine vengeance upon confederated enemies of Israel. When God wills it, a brook can be as deadly as a sea. Kishon was as terrible to Jabin as the Red Sea was to Pharaoh. How easily can the Lord smite the enemies of his people! God of Gideon and of Barak, will you not again avenge your heritage of their bloodthirsty foes?

War is cruel, but in this case its vengeance was most just — those who would not give Israel a place above ground are themselves denied a hiding-place under the ground. They counted God's people to be as dung, and they became dung themselves. Asaph would have the same fate befall other enemies of Israel; and his prayer was a prophecy, for so it happened to them. They boastfully compare themselves to ravens and wolves; let them receive the fate that is due to such wild beasts. Zebah and Zalmunna were captured and slain by Gideon, despite their claim to have been anointed to the kingdom. Zebah became a sacrifice, and Zalmunna was sent to those shadowy images from which his name is derived. The psalmist, seeing these four culprits hanging in history upon a lofty gallows, earnestly asks that others of a similar character may, for truth and righteousness' sake, share their fate: 'Smite the great ones as well as the common ruck. Suffer not the ringleaders to escape. As Oreb fell at the rock and Zeeb at the winepress, so mete out vengeance to Zion's foes wherever you may overtake them.'

Viewing the temple, and also the dwellings of the tribes, as all belonging to God, these greedy plunderers determined to push out the inhabitants, slay them, and become themselves landlords and tenants of it all. These were bold words and dark designs, but God could bring them all to nothing. It is in vain for men to say, 'Let us take', if God does not give. He who robs God's house will find that he has a property reeking with a curse; it will plague him and his seed for ever. 'Will a man rob God?' Let him try it, and he will find it hot and heavy work.

Meditation: 'They became as refuse on the earth.' The land was enriched or made fertile by their flesh, their blood, and their bones (Albert Barnes).

Psalm 83:13-18

Suggested further reading: Judges 4:15-24

The Lord will follow up his enemies, alarm them, and chase them till they suffer a hopeless rout. He did this, according to the prayer of the present psalm, for his servant Jehoshaphat; and in like manner he will come to the rescue of any or all of his chosen. Long years have strewn the ground with deep deposits of leaves; being dried in the sun, these are very apt to catch fire, and when they do so the burning is terrific. The underwood and the ferns blaze, the bushes crackle, the great trees kindle and to their very tops are wrapped in fire, while the ground is all red as a furnace. In this way, O Lord, mete out destruction to your foes, and bring all of them to an end. Up the hillsides the hanging woods glow like a great sacrifice, and the forests on the mountain's crown smoke towards heaven. Even thus, O Lord, conspicuously and terribly overthrow the enemies of your people Israel.

Shame has often weaned men from their idols, and set them upon seeking the Lord. If this was not the happy outcome in the present instance with the Lord's enemies, yet it would be so with his people who were so prone to err. They would be humbled by his mercy and ashamed of themselves because of his grace; and then they would return with sincerity to the earnest worship of Jehovah their God, who had delivered them. Where no favourable result followed, and the men remained as fierce and obstinate as ever, justice was invoked to carry out the capital sentence.

What else could be done with them? It was better that they perished than Israel be rooted up. What a terrible doom it will be to the enemies of God to be 'confounded and troubled for ever' — to see all their schemes and hopes defeated, and their bodies and souls full of anguish without end: from such a shameful perishing may our souls be delivered.

Hearing of the Lord's marvellous deeds in defeating such a numerous confederacy, the very heathen would be compelled to acknowledge the greatness of Jehovah. He who is self-existent is infinitely above all creatures, all the earth is but his footstool. The godless race of man disregards this, and yet at times the wonderful works of the Lord compel the most unwilling to adore his majesty.

Thus has this soul-stirring lyric risen from the words of complaint to those of adoration; let us in our worship always seek to do the same. National trouble called out the nation's poet laureate, and how well he discoursed immediately of her sorrows, and prayers, and hopes. Sacred literature thus owes much to sorrow and distress. How enriching is the hand of adversity!

Meditation: *The name of Jesus is now far more mighty in the world than was the name Jehovah in earlier ages* (The Dictionary of Illustrations, 1872).

Psalm 84:1-4

Suggested further reading: Acts 2:40-47

The psalmist does not tell us how lovely the Lord's tabernacle was, because he could not. His expressions show us
that his feelings were inexpressible. Lovely to the memory,
to the mind, to the heart, to the eye, to the whole soul, are
the assemblies of the saints. Earth contains no sight so refreshing to us as the gathering of believers for worship.
Those who see nothing amiable in the services of the Lord's
house are sorry saints. The tabernacle was all and altogether
lovely to David. Outer court, or inner court, he loved every
portion of it. Every cord and curtain was dear to him. Even
when at a distance, he rejoiced to remember the sacred
tent where Jehovah revealed himself, and he cried out with
exultation while he pictured in fond imagination its sacred
services, and solemn rites, as he had seen them in bygone
times.

The desire was deep and insatiable — the very soul of
the man was yearning for his God. He had a holy lovesick-
ness upon him, and was wasted with an inward consump-
tion because he was debarred the worship of the Lord in
the appointed place. To stand once again in those areas
which were dedicated to holy adoration was the soul-
longing of the psalmist. True subjects love the courts of
their king. It was God himself that he pined for, the only
living and true God. His whole nature entered into his longing. Even the clay-cold flesh grew warm through the intense action of his fervent spirit. Seldom, indeed, does the

flesh incline in the right direction, but in the matter of Sabbath services our weary body sometimes comes to the assistance of our longing heart, for it desires the physical rest as much as the soul desires the spiritual repose. The psalmist declared that he could not remain silent in his desires, but began to cry out for God and his house; he wept, he sighed, he pleaded for the privilege. Some need to be whipped to church, while here is David crying for it. He needed no clatter of bells from the belfry to ring him in, he carried his bell in his own bosom: holy appetite is a better call to worship than a full chime.

To come and go is refreshing, but to abide in the place of prayer must be heaven below. To be the guests of God, enjoying the hospitalities of hearer, set apart for holy work, screened from a noisy world, and familiar with sacred things — why, this is surely the choicest heritage a son of man can possess. Communion is the mother of adoration. Those who wander far from the Lord fail to praise him, but those who dwell in him are always magnifying him.

Meditation: *To the pious there is no need of vast or sumptuous temples to the end that they should love the house of God* (Musculus).

Psalm 84:5-8

Suggested further reading: Philippians 3:12-21

Having spoken of the blessedness of those who reside in the house of God, he now speaks of those who are favoured to visit it at appointed seasons, going on a pilgrimage with their devout brethren. He is not, however, indiscriminate in his eulogy, but speaks only of those who heartily attend to the sacred festivals. The blessedness of sacred worship belongs not to half-hearted, listless worshippers, but to those who throw all their energies into it. Neither prayer, nor praise, nor the hearing of the word will be pleasant or profitable to persons who have left their hearts behind them. A company of pilgrims who had left their hearts at home would be no better than a caravan of carcasses, quite unfit to blend with living saints in adoring the living God. Those who love the ways of God are blessed. When we have God's ways in our hearts, and our heart in his ways, we are what and where we should be, and hence we shall enjoy divine approval.

God gives to his people the supplies they need while traversing the roads that he points out for them. Where there were no natural supplies from below, the pilgrims found an abundant compensation in waters from above, and so also shall all the worshipping host of God's elect. Ways, which otherwise would have been deserted from want of accommodation, were made into highways abundantly furnished for the travellers' wants, because the great annual pilgrimages led in that direction. Even so, Christian converse and the joy of united worship make many duties easy and delightful which would otherwise have been difficult and painful. So far from being wearied they gather strength as they proceed. Each individual becomes happier, each company becomes more numerous, each holy song more sweet and full. We grow as we advance if heaven is our goal. If we spend our strength in God's ways we shall find it will increase. Not merely to be in the assembly, but to appear before God was the object of each devout Israelite. Would to God it were the sincere desire of all who in these days mingle in our religious gatherings! Unless we realize the presence of God we have done nothing; the mere gathering together is worth nothing. The repetition of the request for an answer to his prayer denotes his eagerness for a blessing. What a mercy it is that if we cannot gather with the saints, we can still speak to their Master!

Meditation: *There are two distinct thoughts of great practical value to the Christian in this short prayer. There is the sense of divine majesty, and the consciousness of divine relationship. As 'Lord of hosts', he is almighty in power; as the 'God of Jacob', he is infinite in mercy and goodness to his people* (Things New and Old).

Psalm 84:9-12

Suggested further reading: Isaiah 60:15-22

Our best prayers when we are in the best place are for our glorious King, and for the enjoyment of his Father's smile.

Under the most favourable circumstances in which earth's pleasures can be enjoyed, they are not comparable by so much as one in a thousand to the delights of the service of God. To feel his love, to rejoice in the person of the anointed Saviour, to survey the promises and feel the power of the Holy Ghost in applying precious truth to the soul, is a joy which worldlings cannot understand, but which true believers are ravished with. Even a glimpse at the love of God is better than ages spent in the pleasures of sense. The lowest station in connection with the Lord's house is better than the highest position among the godless. Only to wait at his threshold and peep within, so as to see Jesus, is bliss. To bear burdens and open doors for the Lord has more honour than to reign among the wicked. Every man has his choice, and this is ours. God's worst is better than the devil's best. God's doorstep is a happier rest than downy couches within the pavilions of royal sinners, though we might lie there for a lifetime of luxury. Note how he calls the tabernacle the house of my God; there's where the sweetness lies: if Jehovah is our God, his house, his altars, his doorstep, all become precious to us. We know by experience that where Jesus is within, the outside of the house is better than the noblest chambers where the Son of God is not to be found. Grace makes us walk uprightly and this secures every covenant blessing to us. What a wide promise! Some apparent good may be withheld, but no real good, no, not any. God has all good, there is no good apart from him, and there is no good which he either needs to keep back or will on any account refuse us, if we are but ready to receive it. This is true, not of a favoured few but of all the saints for evermore.

'O Lord of hosts, blessed is the man that trusts in you.' Here is the key of the psalm. The worship is that of faith, and the blessedness is peculiar to believers. No formal worshipper can enter into this secret. A man must know the Lord by the life of real faith, or he can have no true rejoicing in the Lord's worship, his house, his Son, or his ways. Dear reader, how does it fare with your soul?

Meditation: *A sign of God's children is to delight to be much in God's presence. Children are to be in the presence of their father; where the King is, there is the court; where the presence of God is, there is heaven* (Thomas Watson).

Psalm 85:1-7

Suggested further reading: Judges 2:11-23

The self-existent, all-sufficient JEHOVAH is addressed: by that name he revealed himself to Moses when his people were in bondage, by that name he is here pleaded with. It is wise to dwell upon that view of the divine character that arouses the sweetest memories of his love. Sweeter still is that dear name of 'Our Father', with which Christians have learned to commence their prayers.

'You have covered all their sin.' All of it, every spot, and wrinkle, the veil of love has covered all. Sin has been divinely put out of sight. Hiding it beneath the propitiatory, covering it with the sea of the atonement, blotting it out, making it cease to be, the Lord has put it so completely away that even his omniscient eye sees it no more. What a miracle is this! To cover up the sun would be easy work compared with the covering up of sin. Not without a covering atonement is sin removed, but by means of the great sacrifice of our Lord Jesus, it is most effectually put away by one act, for ever. What a covering does his blood afford! Having removed the sin, the anger is removed also. How often did the long-suffering of God take away from Israel the punishments that had been justly laid upon them! How often also has the Lord's chastising hand been removed from us when our waywardness called for heavier strokes! Even when judgements had been most severe, the Lord had in mercy stayed his hand. In mid-volley he had restrained his thunder. When ready to destroy, he had averted his face

from his purpose of judgement and allowed mercy to interpose. The book of Judges is full of illustrations of this, and
the psalmist does well to quote them while he intercedes.

If the erring tribes could be rendered penitent, all would
be well. It is not that God needs turning from his anger so
much as we need turning from our sin; here is where the
whole matter is hinged. Our trials frequently arise out of
our sins, they will not go till the sins go. We need to be
turned from our sins, but only God can turn us. God the
Saviour must put his hand to the work; it is indeed a main
part of our salvation. Conversion is the dawn of salvation.
To turn a heart to God is as difficult as to make the world
revolve upon its axis. Yet when a man learns to pray for
conversion there is hope for him; he who turns to prayer is
beginning to turn from sin. It is a very blessed sight to see
a whole people turn to their God; may the Lord send forth
his converting grace on our land.

Meditation: *When God changes the cheer of his people, their
joy should not be in the gift, but in the Giver* (David Dickson).

Psalm 85:8-13

Suggested further reading: John 14:1-11

When we believe that God hears us, it is only natural that we should be eager to hear him. The word that can speak peace to troubled spirits can only come from him. The voices of men are feeble in such a case, a bandage far too narrow for the sore; but God's voice is power, he speaks and it is done, and hence when we hear him our distress is ended. Happy is the suppliant who has grace to lie patiently at the Lord's door, and wait until his love shall act according to its old custom and chase all sorrow far away.

Faith knows that a saving God is always near at hand, but only to those who fear the Lord, and worship him with holy awe. This truth is conspicuously illustrated in the gospel age. If to seeking sinners salvation is nigh, it is assuredly very nigh to those who have once enjoyed it, and have lost its present enjoyment by their folly; they have but to turn unto the Lord and they shall enjoy it again. We do not have to go about by a long round of personal mortifications or spiritual preparations, we may come to the Lord, through Jesus Christ, just as we did at the first, and he will again receive us into his loving embrace.

The person of our adorable Lord Jesus Christ explains these verses most sweetly. In him, the attributes of God unite in glad unanimity in the salvation of guilty men, they meet and embrace in such a manner as otherwise would be inconceivable either to our just fears or to our enlightened hopes. God is as true as if he had fulfilled every letter of his

threatenings, as righteous as if he had never spoken peace
to a sinner's conscience; his love in undiminished splendour shines forth, but none of his other ever-blessed characteristics is eclipsed by it. In him truth is found in our
humanity, and his deity brings divine righteousness among
us. Even now his Spirit's work creates a hallowed harmony
between his church below and the sovereign righteousness
above; and, in the latter day, earth shall be universally
adorned with every precious virtue, and heaven shall hold
intimate communion with it. There is a world of meaning
in these verses, only needing meditation to draw it out.
Reader, 'the well is deep', but if you have the Spirit, it cannot
be said that you have nothing to draw with.

God's march of right will leave a track in which his
people will joyfully follow. He who smote in justice will
also bless in justice, and in both will make his righteousness manifest, so as to affect the hearts and lives of all his
people. Such are the blessings of our Lord's first advent,
and the result of his Second Coming shall be even more
conspicuous. Even so, come Lord Jesus. Amen.

Meditation: *There is truth as well in the promise of mercy as
in the threat of justice* (Lancelot Andrewes).

Psalm 86:1-7

Suggested further reading: Luke 11:5-13

When our prayers are lowly by reason of our humility, or feeble by reason of our sickness, or without wing by reason of our despondency, the Lord will bow down to them, the infinitely exalted Jehovah will respect them. Faith, when she has the loftiest name of God on her tongue, and calls him Jehovah, yet dares to ask from him the most tender and condescending acts of love. Great as he is, he loves his children to be bold with him. Our distress is a forcible reason for our being heard by the Lord God, merciful, and gracious, for misery is ever the master argument with mercy.

The best of men need mercy, and appeal to mercy, indeed to nothing else but mercy: they need it for themselves, and crave it eagerly of their God as a personal requisite. Is there not a promise that importunity shall prevail? May we not, then, plead our importunity as an argument with God? He, who prays every day, and all the day, as the word may mean, may rest assured that the Lord will hear him in the day of his need. If we cried sometimes to man, or other false confidences, we might expect to be referred to them in the hour of our calamity, but if in all previous times we have looked to the Lord alone, we may be sure that he will not desert us now. See how David pleaded, first that he was poor and needy, next that he was the Lord's set-apart one, then that he was God's servant and had learned to trust in the Lord, and lastly that he had been taught to pray daily. Surely these are such holy pleadings as any tried believer may employ when wrestling with a prayer-hearing God, and with such weapons the most trembling suppliant may hope to win the day.

Here was the great reason why the psalmist looked to the Lord alone for his joy, because every joy-creating attribute is to be found in perfection in Jehovah alone. Some men who would be considered good are so self-exaltingly indignant at the injuries done them by others that they cannot forgive. But we may rest assured that the better a being is, the more willing he is to forgive, and the best and highest of all is ever ready to blot out the transgressions of his creatures. God does not dispense his mercy from a slender store, which perhaps may be so impoverished as to give out altogether; but he pours forth the infinite riches of his mercy out of a cornucopia. His goodness flows forth in abounding streams towards those who pray and in adoring worship honour his name.

Meditation: *David believed the Lord to be a living and potent God, and indeed to be 'God alone', and it was on that account that he resolved in every hour of trouble to call upon him* (C. H. Spurgeon).

Psalm 86:8-13

Suggested further reading: 1 Samuel 5:1-12

It is a grand thing when greatness and goodness are united; it is only in the Divine Being that either of them exists absolutely, and essentially. How happy it is for us that they both exist in the Lord to an equal degree! To be great and not good might lead to tyranny in the King; and for him to be good and not great might involve countless calamities upon his subjects from foreign foes, so that either alternative would be terrible. Put the two together, and we have a monarch in whom the nation may rest and rejoice. Being good, he is said to be ready to forgive; being great, he works wonders: we may blend the two, for there is no wonder so wonderful as the pardon of our transgressions. All that God does or makes has wonder in it; he breathes, and the wind is mystery; he speaks, and the thunder astounds us; even the commonest daisy is a marvel, and a pebble enshrines wisdom. Only to fools is anything that God has made uninteresting: the world is a world of wonders.

'You are God alone'. Alone were you, God, before your creatures were; you are still alone in godhead now that you have given life to throngs of beings; alone for ever shall you be, for none can ever rival you. True religion makes no compromises, it does not admit Baal or Dagon to be a god; it is exclusive and monopolizing, claiming for Jehovah nothing less than all. The vaunted liberality of certain professors of modern thought is not to be cultivated by believers in the truth. 'Philosophic breadth' aims at building a pantheon, and piles a pandemonium; it is not for us to be helpers in such an evil work. Benevolently intolerant, we would, for the good of mankind, as well as for the glory of God, undeceive mankind as to the value of their compromises — they are mere treason to truth. Our God is not to be worshipped as one among many good and true beings, but as God alone; and his gospel is not to be preached as one of several saving systems, but as the one sole way of salvation. Lies can face each other beneath one common dome; but in the temple of truth the worship is one and indivisible.

From the direst death and the deepest dishonour David had been kept by God, for his enemies would have done more than send him to hell had they been able. His sense of sin also made him feel as if the most overwhelming destruction would have been his portion had not grace prevented, therefore he speaks of deliverance from the 'depths of Sheol'. The psalmist claims to sing among the loudest, because his debt to divine mercy is among the greatest.

Meditation: God is able as well as willing to help, and every being on the face of the earth who receives help receives it from the hand of him who is the only God, and who shall one day be recognized as the only God (J. J. S. Perowne).

Psalm 86:14-17

Suggested further reading: Luke 18:1-14

None hate good men so fiercely as do the high-minded and domineering. Those who do not fear God are not afraid to commit violent and cruel acts. An atheist is a misanthrope. Irreligion is akin to inhumanity.

We get away from the bullying and blustering of proud but puny men to the glory and goodness of the Lord. We turn from the boisterous foam of chafing waves to the sea of glass mingled with fire, calm and serene. 'You, O Lord, are a God full of compassion, and gracious, long-suffering, and abundant in mercy and truth.' This is a truly glorious doxology, in which there is not one redundant word. Here is compassion for the weak and sorrowing, grace for the undeserving, long-suffering for the provoking, mercy for the guilty, and truth for the tried. God's love assumes many forms, and is lovely in them all. Into whatsoever state we may be cast, there is a peculiar hue in the light of love that will harmonize with our condition; love is one and yet sevenfold, its white ray contains the chromatic scale. Are we sorrowful? We find the Lord full of compassion. Are we contending with temptation? His grace comes to our aid. Do we err? He is patient with us. Have we sinned? He is plenteous in mercy. Are we resting on his promise? He will fulfil it with abundant truth.

One turn of God's face will turn all our darkness into day. 'Have mercy on me,' that is all he asks, for he is lowly in heart; that is all he wants, for mercy answers all a sinner's needs. When the Lord gives us his own strength we are sufficient for all emergencies, and have no cause to fear any adversaries. As the sons of slaves were their master's property by their birth, so he gloried in being the son of a woman who herself belonged to the Lord. What others might think a degrading illustration he uses with delight, to show how intensely he loved the Lord's service; and also as a reason why the Lord should interpose to rescue him, seeing that he was no newly-purchased servant, but had been in the house from his very birth.

God does nothing by halves, those whom he helps he also consoles, and so makes them not merely safe but joyful. This makes the foes of the righteous exceedingly displeased, but it brings to the Lord double honour. Lord, deal in this way with us evermore, so we will glorify you, world without end. Amen.

Meditation: *Is it not a bold request to say, Lord, will you give me all your strength to help me? A very bold request indeed; but his mercy moves him to grant it* (Thomas Goodwin).

Psalm 87:1-3

Suggested further reading: Isaiah 60:1-9

The foundation of the church, which is the mystical Jerusalem, is laid in the eternal, immutable and invincible decrees of Jehovah. He wills that the church shall be, he settles all arrangements for her calling, salvation, maintenance and perfection and all his attributes like the mountains round about Jerusalem lend their strength for her support. What a theme for meditation is the founding of the church of God in the ancient covenant engagements of eternity! Rome stands on her seven hills and has never lacked a poet's tongue to sing her glories, but more glorious by far are you, O Zion, among the eternal mountains of God: while pen can write or mouth can speak, your praises shall never lie buried in inglorious silence.

The love of God is greatest to his own elect nation, descended from his servant Jacob, yet the central seat of his worship is dearer still. No other supposable comparison could have so fully displayed the favour that Jehovah bore to Jerusalem — he loves Jacob best and Zion better than the best. God delights in the prayers and praises of Christian families and individuals, but he has a special eye to the assemblies of the faithful, and he has a special delight in their devotions in their church capacity. The great festivals, when the crowds surrounded the temple gates, were fair in the Lord's eyes, and just the same are the general assembly and church of the first-born, whose names are written in heaven. This should lead each separate believer to identify himself with the church of God; where the Lord reveals his love the most, there should each believer most delight to be found. Our own dwellings are very dear to us, but we must not prefer them to the assemblies of the saints; we must say of the church: 'Here, my best friends, my kindred, dwell. Here God, my Saviour, reigns.'

Jerusalem's history, which is the story of the nation of which she is the capital, is full of glorious incidents, and her use and end as the abode of the true God, and of his worship, was pre-eminently glorious. Glorious things were foretold of her, and she was the symbol of the most glorious things of all. This is even more true of the church: she is founded in grace, but her pinnacles glow with glory. Men may glory in her without being braggarts; she has a lustre about her brow which none can rival. Whatever glorious things the saints may say of the church in their eulogies, they cannot exceed what prophets have foretold, what angels have sung, or what God himself has declared. Happy are the tongues which learn to occupy themselves with so excellent a subject; may they be found around our firesides, in our market-places, and in all the spots where men most congregate.

Meditation: *Some absent themselves from public worship, under pretence that they can serve the Lord at home as well in private. How do men of this conceit run counter to the Lord? He prefers the gates of Zion, not only before one or some, but also before all the dwellings of Jacob; and they prefer one such dwelling before the gates of Zion* (David Clarkson).

Psalm 87:4-7

Suggested further reading: Isaiah 4:2-6

Not as nations only, but one by one, as individuals, the citizens of the New Jerusalem shall be counted, and their names publicly declared. Man by man will the Lord reckon them, for they are each one precious in his sight; the individual shall not be lost in the mass, but each one shall be of high account. What a patent of nobility is it, for a man to have it certified that he was born in Zion; the twice born are a royal priesthood, the true aristocracy, the imperial race of men. The original, by using the noblest word for man, intimates that many remarkable men will be born in the church, and indeed every man who is renewed in the image of Christ is an eminent personage, while there are some who, even to the dim eyes of the world, shine forth with a lustre of character which cannot but be admitted to be unusual and admirable. The church has illustrious names of prophets, apostles, martyrs, confessors, reformers, missionaries and the like, which bear comparison with the grandest names honoured by the world, no, in many respects far excel them. Zion has no reason to be ashamed of her sons, nor her sons of her.

When the numbers of the faithful are increased by the new birth, the Lord proves himself to be the upbuilder of the church. The Lord alone deserves to wear the title of Defender of the Faith; he is the sole and sufficient Patron and Protector of the true church. There is no fear for the Lord's heritage, his own arm is sufficient to maintain his rights. The Highest is higher than all those who are against us, and the good old cause shall triumph over all. Churches have not such all-sufficiency within them that we can afford to look to them for all, but the Lord who founded the church is the eternal source of all our supplies, and looking to him we shall never flag or fail. How truly does all our experience lead us to look to the Lord by faith, and say, 'All my springs are in you.' The springs of my faith and all my graces; the springs of my life and all my pleasures; the springs of my activity and all its right doings; the springs of my hope, and all its heavenly anticipations, all lie in you, my Lord. Without your Spirit I should be as a dry well, a mocking cistern, destitute of power to bless myself or others. O Lord, I am assured that I belong to the regenerate whose life is in you, for I feel that I cannot live without you; therefore, with all your joyful people will I sing your praises.

Meditation: *Whatever conduit pipe be used, Christ is the fountain and foundation of every drop of comfort; Christ is the God of all true consolation* (Ralph Robinson).

Psalm 88:1-9

Suggested further reading: 2 Corinthians 4:16 - 5:8

Assuredly, if ever there was a song of sorrow and a psalm of sadness, this is one. Whoever wrote the psalm must have been a man of deep experience, who had done business on the great waters of soul trouble.

'O Lord, God of my salvation.' This is a hopeful title by which to address the Lord, and it has about it the only ray of comfortable light that shines throughout the psalm. The writer has salvation, he is sure of that, and God is the sole author of it. While a man can see God as his Saviour, it is not altogether midnight with him. It is one of the characteristics of true faith that she turns to Jehovah, the saving God, when all other confidences have proved liars to her. His distress had not blown out the sparks of his prayer, but quickened them into a greater ardency, till they burned perpetually like a furnace at full blast. Prayers must be directed to heaven with earnest care. So thought Heman — his cries were all meant for the heart of his God. He had no eye to onlookers as Pharisees have, but all his prayers were before his God.

He felt as if he must die, indeed he thought himself half-dead already. All his life was going, his spiritual life declined, his mental life decayed, his bodily life flickered; he was nearer dead than alive. Are good men ever permitted to suffer in this way? Indeed they are; and some of them are even subject to bondage all their lifetime. Heman sighed out his soul in loneliest sorrow, feeling as if even God himself had quite forgotten him. How low the spirits of good and brave men will sometimes sink. Under the influence of certain disorders everything will wear a sombre aspect, and the heart will dive into the profoundest deeps of misery. It is all very well for those who are in robust health and full of spirit to blame those whose lives are overshadowed with the pale cast of melancholy, but the evil is as real as a gaping wound, and all the more hard to bear because it lies so much in the region of the soul that to the inexperienced it appears to be a mere matter of fancy and diseased imagination. Reader, never ridicule the apprehensive and fearful depressed, their pain is real. Poor Heman felt as if God himself had put him away, smitten him and laid him among the corpses of those executed by divine justice. He mourned that the hand of the Lord had gone out against him, and that he was divided from the great Author of his life. This is the essence of wormwood. Man's blows are trifles, but God's smitings are terrible to a gracious heart. To feel utterly forsaken of the Lord and cast away as though hopelessly corrupt is the very climax of heart-desolation.

Meditation: *Weeping must not hinder praying; we must sow in tears* (Matthew Henry).

Psalm 88:10-18

Suggested further reading: 2 Corinthians 12:1-10

If the Lord allowed his servant to die before the divine promise was fulfilled, it would be quite impossible for his faithfulness to be proclaimed. The poet is dealing with this life
only, and looking at the matter from the point of view afforded by time and the present race of men. If a believer
was deserted and permitted to die in despair, there could
come no voice from his grave to inform mankind that the
Lord had rectified his wrongs and relieved him of his trials;
no songs would leap up from the cold earth to hymn the
truth and goodness of the Lord; but as far as men are concerned, a voice which loved to magnify the grace of God
would be silenced, and a loving witness for the Lord
removed from the sphere of testimony.

His affliction had lasted so long that he could hardly
remember when it commenced; it seemed to him as if he
had been at death's door ever since he was a child. This
was no doubt an exaggeration of a depressed spirit, and yet
perhaps Heman may have been born under the cypress,
and have been afflicted with some chronic disease or bodily
infirmity all his days. There are holy men and women whose
lives are a long apprenticeship to patience, and these deserve both our sympathy and our reverence — our reverence we have ventured to say, for since the Saviour became
the acquaintance of grief, sorrow has become honourable
in believers' eyes. A lifelong sickness may by divine grace

prove to be a lifelong blessing. Better suffer from childhood to old age than be let alone to find pleasure in sin.

Long use had not blunted the edge of sorrow, God's terrors had not lost their terror; rather had they become more overwhelming and had driven the man to despair. He was unable to collect his thoughts, he was so tossed about that he could not judge and weigh his own condition in a calm and rational manner. How similar to madness soul-depression sometimes may be, it is not our province to decide; but we speak what we do know when we say that a featherweight might be sufficient to turn the scale at times. Thank God, O tempted ones, who still retain your reason! Thank him that the devil himself cannot add that feather while the Lord stands by to adjust all things.

Such is the permeating and pervading power of spiritual distress, there is no shutting it out; it soaks into the soul like the dew into Gideon's fleece; it sucks the spirit down as the quicksand swallows the ship; it overwhelms it as the deluge submerged the green earth. Grief hemmed him in. He was like the deer in the hunt, when the dogs are all around and at his throat. Poor soul! and yet he was a man greatly beloved of heaven!

Meditation: *There is something associated with the Christian's present darkness of spirit that distinguishes it from the hypocrite's horror; and that is the lively working of grace* (William Gurnall).

Psalm 89:1-4

Suggested further reading: 1 Kings 8:12-21

Because God is, and ever will be, faithful, we have a theme for song which will not be out of date for future generations; it will never be worn out, never be disproved, never be unnecessary, never be an idle subject, valueless to mankind. It will also be always desirable to make it known, for men are too apt to forget it, or to doubt it, when hard times press upon them. We cannot multiply too many times, testimonies to the Lord's faithful mercy — if our own generation should not need them, others will. Sceptics are so ready to repeat old doubts and invent new ones that believers should be equally prompt to bring forth evidences both old and new.

The covenant was the ground of the psalmist's confidence in God's mercy and truth, for he knew that the Lord had made a covenant of grace with David and his seed, and confirmed it by an oath. David's house must be royal: as long as there was a sepulchre in Judah, David's seed must be the only rightful dynasty. The great 'King of the Jews' died with that title above his head in the three current languages of the then known world, and at this day he is owned as king by men of every tongue. The oath sworn to David has not been broken, though the temporal crown is no longer worn, for in the covenant itself his kingdom was spoken of as enduring for ever. In Christ Jesus there is a covenant established with all the Lord's 'chosen', and they are by grace led to be the Lord's 'servants', and then are ordained kings and priests by Christ Jesus.

David must always have a seed, and truly in Jesus this is fulfilled beyond his hopes. The Son of David is the great progenitor, the second Adam, the everlasting Father, he sees his seed, and in them beholds the travail of his soul. David's dynasty never decays, but, on the contrary, is evermore consolidated by the great Architect of heaven and earth. Jesus is a king as well as a progenitor, and his throne is ever being built up — his kingdom comes — his power extends.

Thus runs the covenant; and when the church declines, it is ours to plead it before the ever-faithful God, as the psalmist does in the latter verses of this sacred song. Christ must reign, but why is his name blasphemed and his gospel so despised? The more gracious Christians are, the more they will be moved to jealousy by the sad estate of the Redeemer's cause, and the more they will argue the case with the great Covenant-maker, crying day and night before him, 'Your kingdom come.'

Meditation: *We must ponder here with pious wonder how God has deigned to enter into a covenant with man, the immortal with the mortal, the most powerful with the weakest, the most just with the most unjust, the richest with the poorest, the most blessed with the most wretched* (Musculus).

Psalm 89:5-14

Suggested further reading: 1 Kings 8:22-30

Looking down upon what God had done, and was about to do, in connection with his covenant of grace, all heaven would be filled with adoring wonder. The sun and moon, which had been made tokens of the covenant, would praise God for such an extraordinary display of mercy, and the angels and redeemed spirits would sing 'a new song'.

The holiest tremble in the presence of the thrice Holy One; their familiarity is seasoned with the profoundest awe. Perfect love casts out the fear that torments, and works instead of that other fear that is akin to joy unutterable. How reverent should our worship be! Where angels veil their faces, men should surely bow in lowliest fashion. Sin is akin to presumptuous boldness, but holiness is sister to holy fear. Irreverence is rebellion. Thoughts of the covenant of grace tend to create a deeper awe of God, they draw us closer to him, and the more his glories are seen by us in that nearer access, the more humbly we prostrate ourselves before his Majesty.

All things alike belong to God — rebellious earth as well as adoring heaven. Let us not despair of the kingdom of truth; the Lord has not abdicated the throne of earth or handed it over to the sway of Satan. The habitable and cultivated earth, with all its produce, acknowledges the Lord as its creator and sustainer, builder and upholder. The power of God so impressed the psalmist that in many ways he repeated the same thought: and indeed the truth of God's omnipotence is so full of refreshment to gracious hearts that it cannot be dwelt upon too much, especially when viewed in connection with his mercy and truth. 'Righteousness and justice' are the basis of the divine government, the sphere within which his sovereignty moves. God as a sovereign is never unjust or unwise. He is too holy to be unrighteous, too wise to be mistaken; this is constant matter for joy to the upright in heart. 'Mercy and truth' are the harbingers and heralds of the Lord. He calls these to the front to deal with guilty and changeful man; he makes them, in the person of the Lord Jesus, to be his ambassadors, and so poor, guilty man is enabled to endure the presence of his righteous Lord. If mercy had not paved the way, the coming of God to any man must have been swift destruction.

Thus has the poet sung the glories of the covenant God. It was fitting that before he poured forth his lament he should record his praise, lest his sorrow should seem to have withered his faith. Before we argue our case before the Lord, it is most becoming to acknowledge that we know him to be supremely great and good, whatever may be the appearance of his providence. This is a course that will be taken by every wise man who desires to have an answer of peace in the day of trouble.

Meditation: *The worship of God is to be performed with great fear and reverence* (John Flavel).

Psalm 89:15-18

Suggested further reading: 1 Kings 8:54-61

He is a blessed God of whom the psalmist has been singing, and therefore they are a blessed people who partake of
his bounty, and know how to exult in his favour. Praise is a
peculiarly joyful sound, and blessed are those who are
familiar with its strains. The covenant promises also have
a precious sound beyond measure, and those who understand their meaning and recognize their own personal
interest in them are highly favoured. Only a covenant God
could look with favour upon men, and those who have
known him in that relationship learn to rejoice in him, indeed, to walk with him in fellowship, and to continue in
communion with him we give God our ear and hear the
joyful sound. He will show us his face and make us glad.
While the sun shines, men walk without stumbling on their
feet, and when the Lord smiles on us we live without grief
to our souls.

To the soul which, in Christ Jesus, has entered into covenant with God, every attribute is a fountain of delight.
There is no hour in the day, and no day in our life, in which
we may not rejoice in the name, person and character of
the Lord. We need no other reason for rejoicing. As philosophers could make merry without music, so we can
rejoice without carnal comforts; the Lord All-Sufficient is
an all-sufficient source of joy. By the Lord's righteous dealings the saints are uplifted in due time, however great may
have been the oppression and the depression from which

they may have suffered. In the righteousness which the covenant supplies, which is entirely of the Lord, believers are set on high, in a secure and blessed position, so that they are full of sacred happiness. If God were unjust, or if he regarded us as being without righteousness, we must be filled with misery; but as neither of these things is so, we are exalted indeed, and would extol the name of the Lord.

Surely in the Lord Jehovah we have both righteousness and strength. He is our beauty and glory when we are strong in him, as well as our comfort and sustenance when we tremble because of conscious weakness in ourselves. The title 'the Holy One of Israel' is peculiarly delightful to the renewed heart. God is one; we worship none beside. He is holiness itself, the only being who can be called 'the Holy One', and in his perfection of character we see the most excellent reason for our faith. He who is holy cannot break his promises, or act unjustly concerning his oath and covenant. Moreover, he is the Holy One of Israel, being specially the God of his own elect, ours by peculiar ties, ours for ever and ever. Who among the saints will not rejoice in the God of election? Are they not indeed a people greatly blessed who can call this God their God, for ever and ever?

Meditation: *Next to the love of God's heart, believers value the smiles of his face* (Augustus Toplady).

Psalm 89:19-23

Suggested further reading: Hebrews 1:1-12

The psalmist returns to a consideration of the covenant
made with David. The holy one meant here may be either
David or Nathan the prophet, but most probably the latter,
for it was to him that the word of the Lord came by night.
God condescends to employ his gracious ministers to be
the means of communication between himself and his favoured ones — even to King David the covenant was
revealed by Nathan the prophet; thus the Lord bestows
honour upon his ministers. The Lord had made David a
mighty man of valour, and now he covenants to make him
the helper and defender of the Jewish state. In a far fuller
sense the Lord Jesus is essentially and immeasurably
mighty, and on him the salvation of his people rests by
divine appointment, while his success is secured by the
engagement of divine strength with him. Let us lay our faith
where God has laid our help. David was God's elect, elect
out of the people, as one of themselves, and elect to the
highest position in the state. His extraction, election and
exaltation, eminently foreshadowed the Lord Jesus, who is
the man of the people, the chosen of God, and the king of
his church. Whom God exalts let us exalt. Woe unto those
who despise him, they are guilty of contempt of court before
the Lord of Hosts, as well as of rejecting the Son of God.

David was discovered by the Lord among the sheepfolds
and recognized as a man of gracious spirit, full of faith and
courage, and therefore fit to be leader in Israel. The hand

of Samuel anointed David to be king long before he ascended the throne. This must also be expounded of the
Prince Emanuel; he became the servant of the Lord for our
sakes, the Father having found for us in his person a mighty
deliverer. Therefore the Spirit rested upon him without
measure, to qualify him for all the offices of love to which
he was set apart. We do not have a self-appointed and un-
qualified Saviour, but one sent of God and divinely endowed
for his work. Our Saviour Jesus is also the Lord's Christ, or
anointed. The oil with which he is anointed is God's own
oil, and holy oil; he is divinely endowed with the Spirit of
holiness. The almighty strength of God abides permanently
with Jesus in his work as Redeemer and ruler of his
people. The fulness of divine power shall attend him.
This covenant promise ought to be urged in prayer before
the Lord, for the great lack of the church at this time is
power. We have everything except the divine energy, and
we must never rest content until we see it in full operation among us.

Meditation: *Jesus must be among us, and then there will
be no lack of force in any of our church agencies* (C. H.
Spurgeon).

Psalm 89:24-29

Suggested further reading: Ephesians 1:15-23

'Faithfulness and mercy' were the two attributes of which the psalmist began to sing in the first verse of the psalm, doubtless because he saw them to be most prominent in the covenant which he was about to plead with God. To David and his seed, God was gracious and faithful, though through their sin the literal kingdom lost all its glory and the dynasty became obscure. Yet the line remained unbroken and more than all its former glory was restored by the enthroning of the one who is Prince of the kings of the earth, with whom the Lord's mercy and faithfulness remain for ever. All who are in Jesus should rejoice, for they shall prove in their own experience the faithful mercy of the Lord. The Lord Jesus gloriously lifts up his head, raised to the highest place of honour by the mandate of the Father. In their dignity David and Solomon were but faint types of the Lord Jesus, who is far above all principalities and powers.

David's seed would be a praying race, and so in the main were they, and when they were not, they suffered the consequences for it. The Lord Jesus was pre-eminent in prayer, and his favourite mode of address was 'Father'. Never was there a son more filial in his cries than 'the Firstborn among many brethren'. 'My God': so our Lord called his Father when upon the cross. It was to his Father that he turned for help when in sore anguish in Gethsemane, and to him he committed his spirit on the particular occasion of his death.

True sons should imitate him in this filial crying. This is the common language of the elect family: adoption, reverence, trust, must all speak in their turns, and will do if we are heirs according to promise. To say to God, 'You are my father' is more than learning and talent can teach us; the new birth is essential to this. Reader, have you the nature of a child and the spirit of one who can cry, 'Abba, Father'?

With Jesus the covenant is ratified both by blood of sacrifice and by oath of God; it cannot be cancelled or altered, but is an eternal truth, resting upon the truthfulness of one who cannot lie. What exultation fills our hearts as we see that the covenant of grace is sure to all the seed because it stands fast with him with whom we are indissolubly united. David's seed lives on in the person of the Lord Jesus, and the seed of Jesus in the persons of believers. Saints are a race that neither death nor hell can kill. As long as God lives, his people must live. Jesus reigns on, and will reign till the skies shall fall; indeed, and when the heavens shall pass away with a great noise, and the elements shall melt with fervent heat, his throne shall stand. What a blessed covenant is this!

Meditation: *God had one Son without sin, but he never had a son who lived without prayer* (C. H. Spurgeon).

Psalm 89:30-37

Suggested further reading: Titus 1:1-4

It was possible that David's posterity might wander from the Lord; indeed they did so, but what then? Was the mercy of God to pass away from David's seed? Far from it! So, too, the seed of the Son of David are apt to divert, but are they therefore cast away? Not a single word gives liberty for such an idea, but the very reverse.

The dreadful 'if' is suggested, and the sad case is stated in other forms. But if it should be so, what then? Death and rejection? Ah, no! Blessed be God, no! If their sin is negative or positive, if it is forsaking or profanation, if either judgements or commandments or both are violated, yet there is not a word as to final destruction, but the very opposite. 'I will visit their transgression with the rod', not with the sword, not with death and destruction; but still with a smarting, tingling, painful rod. Saints must smart if they sin, God will see to that. He hates sin too much not to visit it, and he loves his saints too well not to chasten them. God never plays with his rod, he lays it well home to his children, he 'visits' them with it in their houses, bodies and hearts, and lets them know that he is grieved with their ways. The rod is a covenant blessing, and is meant to be used. As sin is so frequent, the rod never rests for long together; in God's family the rod is not spared, or the children would be spoiled. If the covenant could be made void by our sins it would have been void long before this; and if renewed its tenure would not be worth an hour's purchase if it had remained dependent upon us. God may leave his people, and they may suffer much and fall very low because of it, but he never can remove his love from them utterly and altogether; for that would be to cast a reflection upon his own truth, and this he will never allow. Man fails in all points but God in none. To be faithful is one of the eternal characteristics of God, in which he always places a great part of his glory: his truth is one of his peculiar treasures and crown jewels, and he will never endure it to be tarnished to any degree. This passage sweetly assures us that the heirs of glory shall not be utterly cast off. Let those who choose to do so deny the safety of the saints, but we have not learned this of Christ. We believe in the gospel rod, but not in the penal swats for the adopted sons.

Meditation: *Mercy may seem to depart from the Lord's chosen, but it shall never altogether do so* (C. H. Spurgeon).

Psalm 89:38-45

Suggested further reading: Lamentations 5:10-22

The Lord had promised not to cast off the seed of David, and yet it looked as if he had done so, and in the most angry manner, as if he loathed the person of the king. God's actions may appear to us to be the reverse of his promises, and then our best course is to come before him in prayer and put the matter before him just as it strikes our apprehension. We are allowed to do this, for this holy and inspired man did so unrebuked, but we must do it humbly and in faith.

Israel's king was no longer sheltered from the slanderous assaults of contemptuous tongues; the awe which should guard the royal name had ceased to separate him from his fellows. The 'divinity which hedges a king' had departed. Hitherto, the royal family had been like a vine within an enclosure, but the wall was now laid low, and the vine was unprotected. It is sorrowfully true that in many places the enclosures of the church have been destroyed, the line of demarcation between the church and the world has almost vanished, and godless men fill the sacred offices. Alas, O Lord God, shall it always be so? Shall your true vine be deserted by you, O great Husbandman? Set up the boundaries again, and keep your church as a vineyard reserved for yourself. The forts of the land were in the possession of the enemy and were dismantled, the defences of the kingdom were overthrown. This is how precious truths, which were the bulwarks of the church, have been assailed by heresy, and the citadels of sound doctrine have been abandoned to the foe. O God, how can you suffer this? As the God of truth, will you not arise and tread down falsehood?

He has lost his power to govern at home or to conquer abroad. This happened to kings of David's line, and, more grievous to relate, it is happening in these days to the visible kingdom of the Lord Jesus. Where are the glories of Pentecost? Where is the majesty of the Reformation? Where does his kingdom come among the sons of men? Woe unto us, for the glory has departed, and the gospel throne of Jesus is hidden from our eyes! In this our day we have to bemoan the lack of rigour in religion — the heroic days of Christianity are over, her raven locks are sprinkled with untimely grey. Is this according to the covenant? Can this be as the Lord has promised? Let us plead with the righteous Judge of all the earth, and beseech him to fulfil his word in which he has promised that those who wait upon him will renew their strength.

Meditation: *It is sad for the church when those that should stand up for it cannot stand* (Matthew Henry).

Psalm 89:46-52

Suggested further reading: Ezekiel 34:17-24

The appeal is to Jehovah, and the argument is the length of the affliction endured. Chastisement with a rod is not a lengthened matter, therefore he appeals to God to cut short the time of tribulation. 'Will your wrath burn like fire?' Shall it go on and on evermore till it utterly consumes its object? Be pleased to set a bound! How far will you go? Will you burn up the throne that you have sworn to perpetuate? Even to this extent we would entreat the Lord to remember the cause of Christ in these days. Can he be so angry with his church as to leave her much longer? How far will he allow things to go? Shall truth die out, and saints exist no more? How long will he leave matters to take their course? Surely he must interpose soon, for, if he does not, true religion will be utterly consumed, as it were, with fire.

If the Lord does not shine upon his work we live for nothing — we no longer count it life if his cause does not prosper. We live if the King lives, but not otherwise. Everything is vanity if religion is vanity. If the kingdom of heaven should fail, everything is a failure. Creation is a blot, providence an error, and our own existence a hell, if the faithfulness of God can fail and his covenant of grace can be dissolved. If the gospel system can be disproved, nothing remains for us, or any other of the sons of men, that makes life worth living.

We may remind the Lord of his first deeds of love, his former love to his church, his former favour to ourselves.

Then we may plead his oath, and beg him to remember that he has sworn to bless his chosen; and we may wrestle hard also, by urging upon him his own character, and laying hold upon his inviolable truth. When things look black we may bring forth our strong reasons, and debate the case with our condescending God, who has himself said, 'Come now, and let us reason together.'

David ends where he began; he has sailed round the world and reached port again. Let us bless God before we pray, while we pray, and when we have done praying, for he always deserves it from us. If we cannot understand him, we will not distrust him. When his ways are beyond our judgement we will not be so foolish as to judge; yet we shall do so if we consider his dealings to be unkind or unfaithful. He is, he must be, he shall be, for ever, our blessed God.

Meditation: *The reproach of religion and of the godly lies near, and should lie near, the heart of every lively member of the church* (David Dickson).

Psalm 90:1-6

Suggested further reading: Deuteronomy 32:1-14

To the saints the Lord Jehovah, the self-existent God, stands instead of mansion and roof; he shelters, comforts, protects, preserves and cherishes all his own. We do not dwell in the tabernacle or the temple, but in God himself, and we have always done so since there was a church in the world. Kings' palaces have vanished beneath the crumbling hand of time — they have been burned with fire and buried beneath mountains of ruins, but the imperial race of heaven has never lost its regal habitation. Where our fathers dwelt, a hundred generations since, there we dwell still. The Holy Ghost has said of New Testament saints, 'He that keeps his commandments dwells in God and God in him!' It was a divine mouth that said, 'Abide in me,' and then added, 'he that abides in me and I in him brings forth much fruit.' It is most sweet to speak with the Lord as Moses did, saying, 'Lord, you have been our dwelling place', and it is wise to draw reasons for expecting present and future mercies from the Lord's eternal condescension.

God was, when nothing else was. In this Eternal One there is a safe abode for the successive generations of men. If God himself were of yesterday, he would not be a suitable refuge for mortal men; if he could change and cease to be God he would be but an uncertain dwelling-place for his people. The eternal existence of God is mentioned here to make known, by contrast, the brevity of human life. The frailty of man is forcibly set forth; God creates him out of the dust and, at the word of his Creator, back to dust he goes. God resolves and man dissolves. A word created and a word destroys. Observe how the action of God is recognized: man is not said to die because of the decree of fate, or the action of inevitable law, but the Lord is made the agent of all, his hand turns and his voice speaks. Without these we should not die; no power on earth or hell could kill us. As when a torrent rushes down the river bed and bears all before it, so the Lord bears away the succeeding generations of men by death. As the hurricane sweeps the clouds from the sky, so time removes the children of men. Before God men must appear as unreal as the dreams of the night, the phantoms of sleep. Not only are our plans and devices like a sleep, but so are we, ourselves. 'We are such stuff as dreams are made of.' As grass is green in the morning and hay at night, so men are changed from health to corruption in a few hours. We are not cedars, or oaks, but only poor grass, which is vigorous in the spring, but does not last a summer through. What is there upon earth more frail than us!

Meditation: *The everlastingness of which Moses speaks is to be referred not only to the essence of God, but also to his providence, by which he governs the world. He intends not merely that he is, but that he is God* (John Calvin).

Psalm 90:7-11

Suggested further reading: Deuteronomy 32:15-27

It must have been a very mournful sight to Moses to see the whole nation melt away during the forty years of their pilgrimage, till none remained of all that came out of Egypt. As God's favour is life, so his anger is death; grass might as well grow in an oven as men flourish when the Lord is angry with them. A sense of divine anger confounded them, so that they lived as men who knew that they were doomed. This is true of us in a measure, but not altogether, for now that immortality and life are brought to light by the gospel, death has changed its aspect, and, to believers in Jesus, it is no more a judicial execution. Anger and wrath are the sting of death, and believers have no share in these. Love and mercy now conduct us to glory by the way of the tomb. It is not seemly to read these words at a Christian's funeral without words of explanation, without a distinct endeavour to show how little they belong to believers in Jesus, and how far we are privileged beyond those with whom he was not well pleased, 'whose bodies fell in the wilderness'. When, however, a soul is under conviction of sin, the language of this psalm is highly appropriate to his situation, and will naturally suggest itself to the distracted mind. No fire consumes like God's anger, and no anguish so troubles the heart as his wrath.

There are no secrets before God; he unearths man's hidden things, and exposes them to the light. Sunlight can never be compared with the light of he who made the sun,

of whom it is written, 'God is light, and in him is no darkness at all.' If by his countenance is here meant his love
and favour, it is not possible for the heinousness of sin to
be more clearly manifested than when it is seen to involve
ingratitude to one so infinitely good and kind. Rebellion in
the light of justice is black, but in the light of love it is
devilish. How can we grieve so good a God? The children
of Israel had been brought out of Egypt with a high hand,
fed in the wilderness with a liberal hand, and guided with
a tender hand; and their sins were peculiarly atrocious.
We, too, having been redeemed by the blood of Jesus, and
saved by abounding grace, will be truly guilty if we forsake
the Lord. What manner of persons ought we to be? How
ought we to pray for cleansing from secret faults?

Who is able to stand against this justly angry God? Who
will dare to tempt the edge of his sword? Let us submit
ourselves as dying sinners to this eternal God, who can,
even at this moment, command us to the dust, and from
there to hell.

Meditation: *Recollect that the God, in whose presence you
are, is the Being who forbids sin, the Being of whose eternal
law sin is the transgression, and against whom every sin is
committed* (Edward Payson).

Psalm 90:12-17

Suggested further reading: Deuteronomy 32:29-36

We are more anxious to count the stars than our days, and yet the latter is by far more practical. Men are led by reflections upon the brevity of time to give their earnest attention to eternal things. They become humble as they look into the grave that is so soon to be their bed, their passions cool in the presence of mortality, and they yield themselves up to the dictates of unerring wisdom. But this is only the case when the Lord himself is the teacher; he alone can teach to real and lasting profit.

Israel had rebelled, but they had not utterly forsaken the Lord; they acknowledged their obligations to obey his will, and pleaded them as a reason for pity. Will not a man spare his own servants? Though God smote Israel, yet they were his people, and he had never disowned them, therefore is he entreated to deal favourably with them. If they might not see the promised land, still he is begged to cheer them on the road with his mercy, and to turn his frown into a smile. The prayer is like others which came from the meek lawgiver when he boldly pleaded with God for the nation; it is Moses-like. He here speaks with the Lord as a man speaks with his friend. Moses asks for conspicuous displays of divine power and providence, that they might cheer all the people. They could find no solace in their own faulty works, but in the work of God they would find comfort.

The daily object of our petitions should be sanctification. Let what we do be done in truth, and last when we are in the grave; may the work of the present generation minister permanently to the building up of the nation. Good men are anxious not to work in vain. They know that without the Lord they can do nothing, and therefore they cry to him for help in the work, for acceptance of their efforts, and for the establishment of their designs. The church as a whole earnestly desires that the hand of the Lord may so work with the hand of his people, that a substantial, indeed, an eternal edifice to the praise and glory of God may be the result. We come and go, but the Lord's work abides. We are content to die, so long as Jesus lives and his kingdom grows. Since the Lord abides for ever the same, we trust our work in his hands, and feel that since it is far more his work than ours he will secure it immortality. When we have withered like grass, our holy service, like gold, silver and precious stones, will survive the fire.

Meditation: *We can number other men's days and years, and utterly forget our own, therefore this is the true wisdom of mortal men, to number their own days* (Thomas Tymme).

Psalm 91:1-4

Suggested further reading: Isaiah 25:1-5

The omnipotent Lord will shield all those who dwell with him, they shall remain under his care as guests under the protection of their host. In the most holy place the wings of the cherubim were the most conspicuous objects, and they probably suggested to the psalmist the expression employed here. Those who commune with God are safe with him; no evil can reach them, for the outstretched wings of his power and love cover them from all harm. This protection is constant — they 'abide' under it, and it is all-sufficient, for it is the shadow of 'the Almighty', whose omnipotence will surely screen them from all attack. No shelter can be imagined at all comparable to the protection of Jehovah's own shadow. The Almighty himself is where his shadow is, and hence those who dwell in his secret place are shielded by him. Communion with God is safety. The more closely we cling to our Almighty Father the more confident may we be. He who dwells in an impregnable fortress naturally trusts in it. Shall not he who dwells in God feel well at ease, and repose his soul in safety? Oh, that we more fully carried out the psalmist's resolve! We have trusted in God, let us trust him still. He has never failed us, why then should we suspect him? To trust in man is natural to fallen nature, to trust in God should be as natural to regenerated nature. Where there is every reason and warrant for faith, we ought to place our confidence without hesitancy or wavering. Dear reader, pray for grace to say, 'In him will I trust.'

Assuredly no subtle plot shall succeed against one who has the eyes of God watching for his defence. We are foolish and weak as poor little birds, and are very apt to be lured to our destruction by cunning foes; but if we dwell near to God, he will see to it that the most skilful deceiver shall not entrap us. He who is a Spirit can protect us from evil spirits, he who is mysterious can rescue us from mysterious dangers, and he who is immortal can redeem us from mortal sickness. There is a deadly pestilence of error: we are safe from that if we dwell in communion with the God of truth. There is a fatal pestilence of sin: we shall not be infected by it if we abide with the thrice Holy One. There is also a pestilence of disease, and even from that calamity our faith shall win immunity if it is of that high order which abides in God, walks on in calm serenity, and ventures all things for duty's sake. Faith, by cheering the heart, keeps it free from the fear that, in times of pestilence, kills more than the plague itself.

Meditation: *It is making God our habitation upon which our safety lies; and this is the way to make God a habitation, to pitch and cast ourselves by faith upon his power and providence* (Jeremiah Dyke).

Psalm 91:5-10

Suggested further reading: Job 5:17-27

Such frail creatures are we that both by night and by day we are in danger, and so sinful are we that in either season we may be readily carried away by fear. The promise before us secures the favourite of heaven both from danger and from the fear of it. Night is the congenial hour of horrors, when alarms walk abroad like beasts of prey, or ghouls from among the tombs. Our fears turn the sweet season of repose into one of dread, and though angels are abroad and fill our chambers, we dream of demons and dire visitants from hell. Blessed is that communion with God that renders us impervious to midnight frights, and horrors born of darkness! Not to be afraid is, in itself, an unspeakable blessing, since for every suffering which we endure from real injury we are tormented by a thousand griefs that arise from fear only. The shadow of the Almighty removes all gloom from the shadow of night: once covered by the divine wing, we do not care what winged terrors may fly abroad in the earth.

In these verses the psalmist assures the man who dwells in God that he shall be secure. Though faith claims no merit of its own, yet the Lord rewards it wherever he sees it. He who makes God his refuge shall find him a refuge; he who dwells in God shall find his dwelling protected. We must make the Lord our habitation by choosing him for our trust and rest, and then we shall receive immunity from harm; no evil shall touch us personally, and no stroke of judgement shall assail our household. The 'dwelling' intended here by the original was only a tent, yet the frail covering would prove to be a sufficient shelter from all sorts of harm. It matters little whether our abode is a beggar's hut or a monarch's palace if the soul has made the Most High its habitation. Get into God and you dwell in all good, and ill is banished far away. It is not because we are perfect or highly esteemed among men that we can hope for shelter in the day of evil, but because our refuge is the eternal God, and our faith has learned to hide beneath his sheltering wing. It is impossible that any ill should happen to the man who is beloved of the Lord; the most crushing calamities can only shorten his journey and hasten him to his reward. Ill to him is no ill, but only good in a mysterious form. Losses enrich him, sickness is his medicine, reproach is his honour, and death is his gain. No evil in the strict sense of the word can happen to him, for everything is overruled for good. Happy is he who is in such a situation. He is secure where others are in peril, he lives where others die.

Meditation: *God does not say no afflictions shall befall us, but no evil* (Thomas Watson).

Psalm 91:11-16

Suggested further reading: Isaiah 63:7-14

When men have a charge they become doubly careful, and therefore the angels are represented as bidden by God himself to see to it that the elect are secured. It is down in the marching orders of the hosts of heaven that they take special note of the people who dwell in God. It is not to be wondered at that the servants are ordered to take care of the comfort of their Master's guests; and we may be quite sure that when they are specially charged by the Lord himself they will carefully discharge the duty imposed upon them. The limit of this protection 'in all your ways' is yet no limit to the heart that is right with God. It is not the way of the believer to go out of his way. He keeps in the way, and then the angels keep him. The protection promised here is exceedingly broad as to place, for it refers to all our ways, and what more do we wish for? How angels keep us in this way, we cannot tell. Whether they repel demons, counteract spiritual plots, or even ward off the subtler physical forces of disease, we do not know. Perhaps one day we shall stand amazed at the multiple services of the unseen bands to us.

The Lord speaks of his own chosen one. Not because he deserves to be kept like this, but because with all his imperfections he does love his God. Therefore not only the angels of God, but also the God of angels himself will come to his rescue at all perilous times, and will effectually deliver him. When the heart is enamoured of the Lord, all taken up with him, and intensely attached to him, the Lord will recognize the sacred flame, and preserve the man who bears it in his bosom. It is love — love set upon God — which is the distinguishing mark of those whom the Lord secures from ill. None abide in intimate fellowship with God unless they possess a warm affection towards God, and an intelligent trust in him. These grits of grace are precious in Jehovah's eyes, and wherever he sees them he smiles upon them. How elevated is the standing that the Lord gives to the believer! We ought to covet it most earnestly. If we climb on high it may be dangerous, but if God sets us there it is glorious.

Heirs of heaven are conscious of a special divine presence in times of severe trial. God is always near in sympathy and in power to help his tried ones. Believers are not delivered or preserved in a way that lowers them, and makes them feel themselves degraded; far from it, the Lord's salvation bestows honour upon those it delivers. God first gives us conquering grace, and then rewards us for it.

Meditation: *There is a great deal of safety in the knowledge of God, in his attributes, and in his Christ* (Jeremiah Dyke).

Psalm 92:1-4

Suggested further reading: Hebrews 4:1-10

When duty and pleasure combine, who will be backward? To give thanks to God is but a small return for the great benefits with which he daily loads us; yet as he by his Spirit calls it a good thing, we must not despise it, or neglect it. We thank men when they oblige us; how much more ought we to bless the Lord when he benefits us. Devout praise is always good: it is never out of season, never superfluous, but it is especially suitable to the Sabbath. A Sabbath without thanksgiving is a Sabbath profaned.

The day should begin with praise; no hour is too early for holy song. Loving-kindness is a most appropriate theme for those dewy hours when morn is sowing all the earth with orient pearl. We should magnify the Lord eagerly and promptly; we leave unpleasant tasks as long as we can, but our hearts are so engrossed with the adoration of God that we would rise in good time to attend to it. There is a peculiar freshness and charm about early morning praises; the day is loveliest when it first opens its eyelids, and God himself then seems to distribute the day's manna, which tastes most sweetly if gathered before the sun is hot. It seems most fitting that if our hearts and harps have been silent through the shades of night, we should be eager to take our place again among the chosen choir who ceaselessly hymn the Eternal One. No hour is too late for praise; the end of the day must not be the end of gratitude. When nature seems to adore its Maker in silent contemplation, it hardly befits the children of God to refrain their thanksgiving. Evening is the time for retrospect, memory is busy with the experience of the day, hence the appropriate theme for song is the divine 'faithfulness', of which another day has furnished fresh evidences.

It was natural for the psalmist to sing, because he was glad, and to sing unto the Lord, because his gladness was caused by a contemplation of the divine work. If we consider either creation or providence, we shall find overflowing reasons for joy; but when we come to review the work of redemption, gladness knows no bounds, but feels that she must praise the Lord with all her might. There are times when in the contemplation of redeeming love we feel that if we did not sing we must die; silence would be as horrible to us as if we were gagged by inquisitors, or stifled by murderers. In the first sentence of the fourth verse he expresses the unity of God's 'work', and in the second the variety of his 'works'; in both, there is reason for gladness and triumph. When God reveals his work to a man, and performs a work in his soul, he makes his heart glad most effectually, and then the natural consequence is continual praise.

Meditation: *Giving of thanks is more noble and perfect in itself than petition; because in petition often our own good is eyed and regarded, but in giving of thanks only God's honour* (William Ames).

Psalm 92:5-9

Suggested further reading: Daniel 4:28-37

The Lord's plans are as marvellous as his acts; his designs are as profound as his doings are vast. Creation is immeasurable, and the wisdom displayed in it unsearchable. Some men think but cannot work, and others are mere drudges working without thought: in the Eternal the conception and the execution go together. Providence is inexhaustible, and the divine decrees that originate it are inscrutable. Redemption is grand beyond conception, and the thoughts of love that planned it are infinite. Man is superficial, God is inscrutable; man is shallow, God is deep. Dive as we may we shall never fathom the mysterious plan, or exhaust the boundless wisdom of the all-comprehending mind of the Lord. We stand by the fathomless sea of divine wisdom, and exclaim with holy awe, 'O the depth!'

The effect of the psalm is heightened by contrast; the shadows are thrown in to bring out the lights more prominently. What a stoop from the saint to the brute, from the worshipper to the boor, from the psalmist to the fool! Yet, alas, the character described here is no uncommon one. The boorish or boarish man, for this is almost the same Hebrew word, sees nothing in nature; and if it is pointed out to him, his foolish mind will not comprehend it. He may be a philosopher, and yet be such a brutish being that he will not acknowledge the existence of a Maker for the ten thousand matchless creations around him, which wear, even upon their surface, the evidences of profound design.

Boast as it will, the unbelieving heart does not know; and with all its parade of intellect, it does not understand. A man must either be a saint or a brute; he has no other choice. He must be as the adoring seraph, or the ungrateful swine. So far from paying respect to great thinkers who will not acknowledge the glory or the being of God, we ought to regard them as comparable to the beasts which perish, only vastly lower than mere brutes, because their degrading condition is of their own choosing. O God, how sorrowful it is that men whom you have so largely gifted, and made in your own image, should so brutalize themselves that they will neither see nor understand what you have made so clear. An eccentric writer might well say, 'God made man a little lower than the angels at first, and he has been trying to get lower ever since.'

Verse eight is the middle verse of the psalm, and the great fact that this Sabbath song is meant to illustrate. God is at one and the same time the highest and most enduring of all beings. Others rise to fall, but he is the Most High to eternity. Glory to his name! How great a God we worship! Who would not fear you, O High Eternal One! The ungodly are destroyed for ever, and God is most high for ever; evil is cast down, and the Holy One reigns supreme eternally.

Meditation: *It is observable that the name JEHOVAH occurs in the psalm seven times — the sabbatical number (1, 4, 5, 8, 9, 13, 15)* (C. Wordsworth).

Psalm 92:10-15

Suggested further reading: Jeremiah 17:5-14

The believer rejoices that he shall not be allowed to perish, but shall be strengthened and enabled to triumph over his enemies, by divine aid. Faith takes delight in foreseeing the mercy of the Lord, and sings of what he will do as well as of what he has done.

In the courtyards of Oriental houses trees were planted, and being thoroughly screened, they would be likely to bring forth their fruit to perfection in trying seasons. Even so, those who by grace are brought into communion with the Lord shall be likened to trees planted in the Lord's house, and shall find it good to their souls. No heart has so much joy as that which abides in the Lord Jesus. Fellowship with the stem gives rise to fertility in the branches. If a man abides in Christ he brings forth much fruit. Those professors who are rooted to the world do not flourish; those who send forth their roots into the marshes of frivolous pleasure cannot be in a vigorous condition; but those who dwell in habitual fellowship with God shall become men of full growth, rich in grace, happy in experience, mighty in influence, honoured and honourable. Much depends upon the soil in which a tree is planted. In our case, everything depends upon our abiding in the Lord Jesus, and deriving all our supplies from him. If we are ever to really grow in the courts of the Lord's house we must be planted there, for no tree grows in God's garden self-sown. Once planted of the Lord, we shall never be rooted up, but in his courts we shall take root downward, and bring forth fruit upward to his glory for ever. Nature decays but grace thrives. Fruit, as far as nature is concerned, belongs to days of vigour; but in the garden of grace, when plants are weak in themselves, they become strong in the Lord, and abound in fruit acceptable with God. Happy are they who can sing this Sabbath psalm, enjoying the rest that breathes through every verse of it. No fear for the future can distress them, for their evil days, when the strong man fails, are the subject of a gracious promise, and therefore they await them with quiet expectancy.

For shelter, for defence, for indwelling, for foundation, God is our rock; up to now he has been to us all that he said he would be, and we may be doubly sure that he will remain the same even to the end. He has tried us, but he has never allowed us to be tempted above what we are able to bear: he has delayed our reward, but he has never been unrighteous to forget our work of faith and labour of love. He is a friend without fault, a helper without fail. Whatever he may do with us, he is always in the right; his dispensations have no flaw in them; no, not the most minute. He is altogether true and righteous.

Meditation: *The fulness of Christ is manifested by the fruitfulness of a Christian* (Ralph Robinson).

Psalm 93

Suggested further reading: Revelation 11:15-19

Whatever opposition may arise, the Lord's throne is unmoved; he has reigned, does reign, and will reign for ever
and ever. Whatever turmoil and rebellion there may be
beneath the clouds, the eternal King sits above all in
supreme serenity; and everywhere he is really Master, let
his foes rage as they may. All things are ordered according
to his eternal purposes, and his will is done. His is not the
semblance but the reality of sovereignty. In nature, providence and salvation, the Lord is infinite in majesty. Happy
are the people among whom the Lord appears in all the
glory of his grace, conquering their enemies, and subduing
all things unto himself; then indeed is he seen to be clothed
with majesty. The Lord himself is eternal. Let the believer
rejoice that the government under which he dwells has an
immortal ruler at its head, has existed from all eternity and
will flourish when all created things will have passed away
for ever. The rebellions of mortals are vain; the kingdom of
God is not shaken.

As in providence the throne of God is fixed beyond all
risk, so in revelation his truth is beyond all question. Other
teachings are uncertain, but the revelations of heaven are
infallible. As the rocks remain unmoved amid the tumult
of the sea, so does divine truth resist all the currents of
man's opinion and the storms of human controversy; they
are not only sure, but 'very sure'. Glory be to God, we have
not been deluded by a cunningly devised fable: our faith is

grounded upon the eternal truth of the Most High. Truth does not change in its doctrines, which are very sure, nor holiness in its precepts, which are incorruptible. The teaching and the character of God are both unaltered. God has not admitted evil to dwell with him, he will not tolerate it in his house, he is eternally its enemy, and is for ever the sworn friend of holiness. The church must remain unchanged, and for ever be holiness unto the Lord; indeed, her King will keep her undefiled by the intruder's foot. The church of Jesus Christ is sacred unto the Lord, and so shall she be kept evermore. 'The Lord reigns' is the first word and the main doctrine of the psalm, and holiness is the final result: a due esteem for the great King will lead us to adopt behaviour becoming his royal presence. Divine sovereignty both confirms the promises as sure testimonies, and enforces the precepts as seemly and becoming in the presence of so great a Lord.

Meditation: *There is no truth more precious to the heart of the Christian than that 'the Lord reigns'. The conviction of this must carry us far above all cares and fears. A personal God, a living God, a reigning God — alike in the armies of heaven and among the inhabitants of the earth — and this God the Father of our Lord and Saviour Jesus Christ — such are the steps by which we reach a height, where, far removed from the turmoil of men, we gain a comprehensive and clear view of earth and its concerns* (Alfred Edersheim).

Psalm 94:1-7

Suggested further reading: 2 Thessalonians 1:1-12

If the execution of justice is a right thing — and who can deny the fact? — then it must be a very proper thing to desire it; not out of private revenge, in which case a man would hardly dare to appeal to God, but out of sympathy with right, and pity for those who are made to suffer wrongfully. Who can see a nation enslaved, or even an individual downtrodden, without crying to the Lord to arise and vindicate the righteous cause? Here the toleration of injustice is attributed to the Lord's being hidden, and it is implied that the bare sight of him will be enough to alarm the tyrants into ceasing their oppressions. God has but to show himself, and the good cause wins the day. He comes, he sees, he conquers! Truly in these evil days we need a manifest display of his power, for the ancient enemies of God and man are again struggling for the mastery, and if they gain it, woe unto the saints of God.

Are slavery, robbery and tyranny never to cease? Since there is certainly a just God in heaven, armed with almighty power, surely sooner or later there must be an end to the ascendancy of evil; innocence must one day find a defender. This 'how long?' of the text is the bitter lament of all the righteous in all ages, and expresses wonder caused by that great enigma of providence, the existence and predominance of evil. The sound 'how long?' is very akin to howling, as if it were one of the saddest of all the utterances in which misery bemoans itself. Many a time has this bitter complaint been heard in the dungeons of the Inquisition, at the whipping-posts of slavery, and in the prisons of oppression. In due time God will publish his reply, but the full end is not yet.

When men believe that the eyes of God are dim, there is no reason to wonder that they give full licence to their brutal passions. The persons mentioned above not only cherished an infidel unbelief, but dared to avow it, uttering the monstrous doctrine that God is too far away to take notice of the actions of men. If God has actually become his people's God, and proved his care for them by a thousand acts of grace, how dare the ungodly assert that he will not notice the wrongs done to them? There is no limit to the proud man's profanity, reason itself cannot restrain him; he has broken through the bounds of common sense. 'Touch not my anointed, and do my prophets no harm'; and yet these brutish ones profess to believe that he neither sees nor regards the injuries wrought upon the elect people! Surely in such unbelievers is fulfilled the saying of the wise, that those whom the Lord means to destroy he leaves to the madness of their corrupt hearts.

Meditation: *That the self-existent and eternal God should not see, is a palpable absurdity; and scarcely less so, that the God of Israel should suffer his own people to be slaughtered without even observing it. The last verb means to mark, note, notice* (J. A. Alexander).

Psalm 94:8-15

Suggested further reading: 1 Corinthians 3:10-23

God made you hear, can he not himself hear? Unanswerable question! It overwhelms the sceptic and covers him
with confusion. He gives us vision; is it conceivable that
he has no sight himself? With skilful hand he fashioned
the optic nerve, and the eyeball, and all its curious mech-
anism, and it surpasses all conception that he can himself
be unable to observe the doings of his creatures. If there is
a God, he must be a personal intelligent being, and no limit
can be set to his knowledge.

   Whether men admit or deny that God knows, one thing
is declared here, namely, that 'The Lord knows the thoughts
of man, that they are futile.' Not their words alone are heard,
and their works seen, but he reads the secret motions of
their minds, for men themselves are not hard for him to
discern, before his glance they themselves are but vanity.
In the Lord's esteem it is no great matter to know the
thoughts of such transparent pieces of vanity as mankind
are, he sums them up in a moment as poor vain things.
Poor man! And yet such a creature as this boasts, plays at
monarch, tyrannizes over his fellow worms, and defies his
God! Madness is mingled with human vanity, like smoke
with the fog, to make it fouler but not more substantial than
it would have been alone. How foolish are those who think
that God does not know their actions, when the truth is
that their vain thoughts are all perceived by him! How
absurd to make nothing of God when in fact we ourselves
are as nothing in his sight!

The psalmist's mind is growing quiet. He no longer complains to God or argues with men, but tunes his harp to softer melodies, for his faith perceives that with the most afflicted believer all is well. Though he may not feel blessed while smarting under the rod of chastisement, yet blessed he is; he is precious in God's sight, or the Lord would not take the trouble to correct him, and he will be truly happy as a result of his correction. The book and the rod, the law and the chastening, go together, and are made doubly useful by being found in connection. Affliction without the word is a furnace for the metal, but there is no flux to aid the purifying; the Word of God supplies that need, and makes the fiery trial effectual. After all, the blessing of God belongs rather more to those who suffer under the divine hand than to those who make others suffer. It is better by far to lie and cry out as a man under the hand of our heavenly Father, than to roar and rave as a brute, and to bring down upon oneself a death blow from the destroyer of evil.

Meditation: *The chastening hand and instructive book are sanctified to us, so that we learn to rest in the Lord* (C. H. Spurgeon).

Psalm 94:16-23

Suggested further reading: Joshua 7:10-26

Notwithstanding the psalmist's persuasion that all would be well eventually, he could not at the time perceive any one who would stand side by side with him in opposing evil; no champion of the right was forthcoming, the faithful failed from among men. This also is a bitter trial, and a sore evil under the sun; yet it has its purpose, for it drives the heart still more completely to the Lord, compelling it to rest alone in him. If we could find friends elsewhere, it may be that our God would not be so dear to us; but when, after calling upon heaven and earth to help, we meet with no succour but that which comes from the eternal arm, we are led to prize our God, and rest upon him with undivided trust. Never is the soul safer or more at rest than when, all other helpers failing, she leans upon the Lord alone.

God enters into no alliance with unjust authority, he gives no sanction to unrighteous legislation. Nothing can last for ever but impartial right. No injustice can be permanent, for God will not set his seal upon it, nor have any fellowship with it, and therefore down it must come, and happy shall be the day that sees it fall. Let the wicked gather as they may, the psalmist is not afraid, but sweetly sings. Jehovah's love is firm as a rock and there we take ourselves for shelter. In him, even in him alone, we find safety, let the world rage as it may; we do not ask aid from man, but are content to flee into the bosom of omnipotence. The natural result of oppression is the destruction of the despot; his own iniquities crush him before long. Providence arranges retaliations as remarkable as they are just. High crimes in the end bring on heavy judgements, to sweep away evil men from off the face of the earth; indeed, God himself interposes in a special manner, and cuts short the career of tyrants while they are in the very midst of their crimes. Wicked men are often caught red-handed by the pursuits of divine justice, with the evidences of their guilt upon them. While the stolen bread is in their mouths wrath slays them, while the ill-gotten wedge of gold is yet in their tent judgement overtakes them. God himself conspicuously visits them, and reveals his own power in their overthrow. Here, then, the matter ends; faith reads the present in the light of the future, and ends her song without a trembling note.

Meditation: *It is an ill work wicked ones are about, they make fetters for their own feet, and build houses to fall upon their own heads; so mischievous is the nature of sin that it damnifies and destroys the parents of it* (William Greenhill).

Psalm 95:1-5

Suggested further reading: Hebrews 13:8-16

Other nations sing unto their gods, let us sing unto Jehovah. We love him, we admire him, we reverence him, let us express our feelings with the choicest sounds, using our noblest faculty for its noblest end. It is well thus to urge others to magnify the Lord, but we must be careful to set a worthy example ourselves, so that we may be able not only to cry 'Come', but also to add 'Let us sing', because we are singing ourselves. It is to be feared that very much, even of religious singing, is not unto the Lord, but unto the ear of the congregation. Above all things in our service of song we must take care that all we offer is with the heart's most sincere and fervent intent directed towards the Lord himself.

God is present everywhere, but there is a peculiar presence of grace and glory into which men should never come without the profoundest reverence. We may make bold to come before the immediate presence of the Lord — for the voice of the Holy Spirit in this psalm invites us, and when we do draw near to him we should remember his great goodness to us and cheerfully confess it. Our worship should have reference to the past as well as to the future; if we do not bless the Lord for what we have already received, how can we reasonably look for more. We are permitted to bring our petitions, and therefore we are in honour bound to bring our thanksgivings. It is not always easy to unite enthusiasm with reverence, and it is a frequent fault to destroy one of these qualities while straining after the other. The perfection of singing is that which unites joy with gravity, exultation with humility, fervency with sobriety. The invitation given in the first verse is thus repeated in the second with the addition of directions, which indicate more fully the intent of the writer. One can imagine David in earnest tones persuading his people to go up with him to the worship of Jehovah with sound of harp and hymn, and holy delight.

No doubt the surrounding nations imagined Jehovah to be a merely local deity, the god of a small nation, and therefore one of the inferior deities; the psalmist utterly repudiates such an idea. Idolaters tolerated many gods and many lords, giving to each a certain measure of respect; the monotheism of the Jews was not content with this concession, it rightly claimed for Jehovah the chief place, and the supreme power. He is great, for he is all in all; he is a great King above all other powers and dignitaries, whether angels or princes, for they owe their existence to him; as for the idol gods, they are not worthy to be mentioned. Here we find some of the reasons for worship, drawn from the being, greatness, and sovereign dominion of the Lord.

Meditation: *God is the Lord of all, as he is the sustainer of all by his power, as well as the Creator of all by his word* (Stephen Charnock).

Psalm 95:6-11

Suggested further reading: Hebrews 3:7-19

The exhortation to worship is renewed and backed with a motive which, to Israel of old, and to Christians now, is especially powerful; for both the Israel after the flesh and the Israel of faith may be described as the people of his pasture, and by both he is called 'our God'. The adoration is to be humble. The joyful noise is to be accompanied with lowliest reverence. We are to worship in such a style that the bowing down shall indicate that we count ourselves to be as nothing in the presence of the all-glorious Lord.

'He is our God.' Here is the master reason for worship. Jehovah has entered into covenant with us, and from all the world beside has chosen us to be his own elect. If others refuse him homage, we at least will render it cheerfully. He is ours, and our God; ours, therefore will we love him; our God, therefore will we worship him. Happy is that man who can sincerely believe that this sentence is true for himself. As he belongs to us, so we belong to him, and we are his as the people whom he daily feeds and protects. We are his, even as sheep belong to the shepherd, and his hand is our rule, our guidance, our government, our succour, our source of supply. Israel was led through the desert, and we are led through this life by 'that great Shepherd of the sheep'. The hand that cleft the sea and brought water from the rock is still with us, working equal wonders. Can we refuse to 'worship and bow down' when we clearly see that 'this God is our God for ever and ever, and will be our guide, even unto death'?

But what is this warning which follows? Alas, it was sorrowfully needed by the Lord's ancient people, and is not one whit the less required by ourselves. The favoured nation grew deaf to their Lord's command, and proved not to be truly his sheep, of whom it is written, 'My sheep hear my voice'. Will this turn out to be our character also? God forbid. 'Today if you will hear his voice.' Dreadful 'if'. Many would not hear; they put off the claims of love, and provoked their God. 'Today', in the hour of grace, in the day of mercy, we are tried as to whether we have an ear for the voice of our Creator. Nothing is said of tomorrow, he presses for immediate attention, for our own sakes he asks instantaneous obedience. Shall we yield it? The Holy Spirit says 'Today'. Will we grieve him by delay? We cannot soften our hearts, but we can harden them, and the consequences will be fatal. Today is too good a day to be profaned by the hardening of our hearts against our own mercies. While mercy reigns, let not obduracy rebel. Reader, this is for you, even if you can say, 'He is our God.'

Meditation: *You cannot repent too soon, because you do not know how soon it may be too late* (Thomas Fuller).

Psalm 96:1-6

Suggested further reading: 1 Chronicles 16:7-22

New joys are filling the hearts of men, for the glad tidings of blessing to all people are proclaimed, therefore let them sing a new song. Angels inaugurated the new age with new songs, and shall we not take up the strain?

Three times the name of the Lord is repeated, and not without meaning. Is it not unto the triune Lord that the enlightened nations will sing? Unitarianism is the religion of units; it is too cold to warm the world to worship; the sacred fire of adoration only burns with vehement flame where the Trinity is believed in and beloved. The blessed Lord is to be blessed in other ways besides singing. His name, his fame, his character, his revealed word and will are to be delighted in, and remembered with perpetual thanksgiving. We may well bless him who so divinely blesses us. At the very mention of his name it is fitting to say, 'Let him be blessed for ever.'

The Lord is no petty deity, presiding, as the heathen imagined their gods to do, over some nation, or one department of nature. Jehovah is great in power and dominion, great in mind and act; nothing mean or narrow can be found in him or his acts, in all things he is infinite. Praise should be proportionate to its object, therefore let it be infinite when rendered unto the Lord. We cannot praise him too much, too often, too zealously, too carefully, too joyfully. He is to be feared, for there is cause to fear. Dread of other gods is mere superstition; awe of the Lord is pure religion.

Holy fear is the beginning of the graces, and yet it is the accompaniment of their highest range. Fear of God is the blush upon the face of holiness enhancing its beauty. The reality of his Godhead is proved by his works, and foremost among these the psalmist mentions that matchless piece of architecture that casts its arch over every man's head, whose lamps are the light of all mankind, whose rains and dew fall upon the fields of every people, and from where the Lord is heard speaking to every creature in voice of thunder. The idol gods have no existence, but our God is the author of all existences; they are mere earthly vanities, while he is not only heavenly, but made the heavens. This is mentioned as a reason for Jehovah's universal praise. Who can be worshipped but he? Since none can rival him, let him alone be adored. Honour and majesty are with him and with him alone. In the presence of Jehovah real glory and sovereignty abide, as constant attendants.

Meditation: *Other news delights us only at first hearing; but the good news of our redemption is sweet from day to day* (John Trapp).

Psalm 96:7-13

Suggested further reading: 1 Chronicles 16:23-36

The first six verses commenced with an exhortation to sing, repeated three times, with the name of the Lord mentioned three times. Here we meet with the expression 'Give to the Lord', similarly used three times. This is after the manner of those poets whose flaming sonnets have best won the ear of the people; they reiterate choice words till they penetrate the soul and fire the heart.

The 'beauty of holiness' is the only beauty that he cares for in our public services, and it is one for which no other can compensate. Beauty of architecture and apparel he does not regard; moral and spiritual beauty is that in which his soul delights. Worship must not be rendered to God in a slovenly, sinful, superficial manner; we must be reverent, sincere, earnest, and pure in heart both in our prayers and praises. Purity is the white linen of the Lord's choristers, righteousness is the comely garment of his priests, holiness is the royal apparel of his servants. There is a sacred trembling which is quite consistent with joy, the heart may even quiver with an awful excess of delight. The sight of the King in his beauty caused no alarm to John in Patmos, and yet it made him fall at his feet as dead. Oh, to behold him and worship him with prostrate awe and sacred fear!

This is the gladdest news that can be carried to the nations: the Lord Jehovah, in the person of his Son, has assumed the throne, and taken up his great power. Tell this out among the nations, and let the nations themselves, being converted, repeat the same with rejoicing. The dominion of Jehovah Jesus is not irksome, his rule is fraught with untold blessings, his yoke is easy, and his burden is light. Above and below let the joy be manifested. Let the angels who have stood in amazement at the wickedness of men, now rejoice over their repentance and restoration to favour, and let men themselves express their pleasure in seeing their true prince set upon his throne. The book of creation has two covers, and on each of these let the glory of the Lord be emblazoned in letters of joy. Let us, ourselves, join in the song. Since the whole universe is to be clothed with smiles, shall we not be glad? As John Howe observes, 'Shall we not partake in this common dutiful joy, and fall into concert with the adoring loyal chorus? Will we cut ourselves off from this gladsome pleasant throng? And that which should put a congenial face and aspect upon the whole world, shall it only leave our faces covered with clouds and a mournful sadness?'

Meditation: *Things in heaven, as well as things on earth, rejoice together in the acknowledged blessing of the Lord of peace* (Arthur Pridham).

Psalm 97:1-6

Suggested further reading: Exodus 19:16-25

This is the watchword of the psalm — the Lord reigns. It is also the essence of the gospel proclamation, and the foundation of the gospel kingdom. Jesus has come, and all power is given unto him in heaven and in earth, therefore men are bidden to yield him their obedient faith. Saints draw comfort from these words, and only rebels cavil at them.

As the Lord revealed himself at Sinai, so must he ever surround his essential Deity when he shows himself to the sons of men, or his excessive glory would destroy them. Every revelation of God must also be an obvelation; there must be a veiling of his infinite splendour if anything is to be seen by finite beings. It is often thus with the Lord in providence; when working out designs of unmingled love he conceals the purpose of his grace that it may be more clearly discovered at the end. 'It is the glory of God to conceal a thing.' Around the history of his church dark clouds of persecution hover, and an awful gloom at times settles down, still the Lord is there; and though for a while men do not see the bright light in the clouds, it bursts forth in due season to confuse the adversaries of the gospel. This passage should teach us the impertinence of attempting to pry into the essence of the Godhead, the vanity of all endeavours to understand the mystery of the Trinity in unity, the arrogance of arraigning the Most High before the bar of human reason, the folly of dictating to the Eternal One the manner in which he should proceed. Wisdom veils her face and adores the mercy that conceals the divine purpose; folly rushes in and perishes, blinded first, and by and by consumed by the blaze of glory.

His dominion is universal, and his power is felt everywhere. Men cannot move the hills, they climb them, with difficulty, they pierce their way through their fastnesses with incredible toil, but it is not so with the Lord. His presence makes a clear pathway, obstacles disappear, a highway is made, not by his hand as though it cost him pain, but by his mere presence, for power goes forth from him with a word or a glance. Oh, for such a presence of the Lord with his church at this hour! It is our one and only need. The mountains of difficulty would flee away with it, and all obstacles would disappear. May it come to pass before long that, by a revival of the old missionary ardour, the glad tidings may yet be carried to every tribe of Adam's race, and once again all flesh may see the glory of Jehovah. It must be so, therefore let us rejoice before the Lord.

Meditation: *Fire is the sign both of grace and wrath. Majesty marches forth in both displays of deity* (C. H. Spurgeon).

Psalm 97:7-12

Suggested further reading: Hebrews 12:18-29

When a man gravely worships what has been engraved by a man's hand, and puts his trust in a mere nothing and nonentity, he is indeed brutish, and when he is converted from such absurdity he may well be ashamed. A man who worships an image is but the image of a man; his senses must have left him. He who boasts of an idol makes an idle boast. All powers are bound to recognize the chief power; since they derive their only rightful authority from the Lord, they should be careful to acknowledge his superiority at all times by the most reverent adoration.

Each individual believer is glad when he sees false systems broken up and idol gods broken down; the judgements of the Lord afford unalloyed delight to those who worship the true God in spirit and in truth. In the first ages of Christianity the believing Israel rejoiced to see Christ's kingdom victorious among the heathen, and even yet, though for a while turning aside, the daughters of Judah will sympathize in the widespread reign of Jehovah their God, through the gospel of his dear Son. There is but one God, there cannot be another, and he is and ever must be over all. Jehovah is not only high over Judea, but over all the earth; nor is he exalted over men only, but over everything that can be called god. The days are coming when all men shall discern this truth, and shall render unto the Lord the glory which is due alone to him.

We cannot love God without hating that which he hates. We are not only to avoid evil, and to refuse to countenance it, but we must be in arms against it, and bear a hearty indignation towards it. The saints are the safe ones: they have been saved and shall be saved. God keeps those who keep his law. Those who love the Lord shall see his love manifested to them in their preservation from their enemies, and as they keep far from evil so shall evil be kept far from them.

To remember that Jehovah is holy is becoming in those who dwell in his courts, to give thanks as a result of that remembrance is the sure index of their fitness to abide in his presence. Referring to the triumphs of the gospel, this text teaches us to rejoice greatly in its purifying effect; it is the death of sin and the life of virtue. An unholy gospel is no gospel. The holiness of the religion of Jesus is its glory, it is that which makes it glad tidings, since while man is left in his sins no bliss can be his portion. Salvation from sin is the priceless gift of our thrice holy God, therefore let us magnify him for ever and ever. He will fill the world with holiness, and so with happiness, therefore let us glory in his holy name, world without end. Amen.

Meditation: *There is no less, but rather more wrath attending the despisers of the gospel, than did attend the giving out of the law* — *Hebrews 12:29* (David Dickson).

Psalm 98:1-3

Suggested further reading: Luke 1:46-56

We had a new song before (Psalm 96) because the Lord was coming, but now we have another new song because he has come, and seen and conquered. Jesus, our King, has lived a marvellous life, died a marvellous death, risen by a marvellous resurrection, and ascended marvellously into heaven. By his divine power he has sent forth the Holy Spirit doing marvellous deeds, and by that sacred energy his disciples have also wrought marvellous things and astonished all the earth. Idols have fallen, superstitions have withered, systems of error have fled, and empires of cruelty have perished. For all this he deserves the highest praise. His acts have proved his deity, Jesus is Lord, and therefore we sing unto him as the LORD. Sin, death and hell fell beneath his solitary prowess, and the idols and the errors of mankind have been overthrown and smitten by his hand alone. The victories of Jesus among men are all the more wonderful because they are accomplished, to all appearance, by most inadequate means. They are due not to physical but to moral power — the energy of goodness, justice, truth; in a word, to the power of his holy arm. His holy influence has been the sole cause of success. Glory be to the Conqueror, let new songs be chanted to his praise.

The Lord is to be praised not only for effecting human salvation, but also for making it known, for man would never have discovered it for himself; no, not so much as one single soul would ever have found out for himself the way of mercy through a Mediator. In every case it is a divine revelation to the mind and heart. In God's own light his light is seen. He must reveal his Son in us, or we shall be unable to discern him. Grace has been given not only to Abraham's seed of the flesh, but also to the elect among all nations; therefore, let the whole church of God sing unto him a new song. It was no small blessing, or little miracle, that throughout all lands the gospel should be published in so short a time, with such singular success and such abiding results. Pentecost deserves a new song as well as the Passion and the resurrection; let our hearts exult as we remember it. Our God, our own far ever-blessed God, has been honoured by those who once bowed down before dumb idols. His salvation has not only been heard of but seen among all people: it has been experienced as well as explained; his Son is the actual Redeemer of a multitude out of all nations.

Meditation: *This psalm is an evident prophecy of Christ's coming to save the world; and what is here foretold by David is, in the Blessed Virgin's song, chanted forth as being accomplished* (Adam Clarke).

Psalm 98:4-9

Suggested further reading: Revelation 1:4-8

As men shout when they welcome a king, so must we. Loud hosannas, full of happiness, must be lifted up. If ever men shout for joy it should be when the Lord comes among them in the proclamation of his gospel reign. John Wesley said to his people, 'Sing lustily, and with a good courage. Beware of singing as if you were half dead or half asleep; but lift up your voice with strength. Be no more afraid of your voice now, nor more ashamed of its being heard, than when you sung the songs of Satan.'

God's worship should be heartily loud. The far-resounding trump and horn well symbolize the power that should be put forth in praise. On coronation days, and when beloved monarchs ride abroad, the people shout and the trumpets sound till the walls ring again. Shall men be more enthusiastic for their earthly princes than for the divine King? Is there no loyalty left among the subjects of the blessed and only Potentate? King Jehovah is his name; and there is none like it. Have we no joyful noise for him? Let but the reigning power of Jesus be felt in the soul and we shall cast aside that chill mutter, drowned by the pealing organ, which is now so commonly the substitute for earnest congregational singing.

The sea is his, let it praise its Maker. Even its thunders will not be too grand for such a theme. Within and upon its bosom it bears a wealth of goodness. Why should it be denied a place in the orchestra of nature? Its deep bass will excellently suit the mystery of the divine glory. The land should be in harmony with the ocean. Its mountains and plains, cities and villages should prolong the voice of jubilee that welcomes the Lord of all. Yet no song is equal to the majesty of the theme when Jehovah, the King, is to be extolled. The rule of Christ is the joy of nature. All things bless his throne, indeed, and its very coming. As the dawn sets the earth weeping for joy at the rising of the sun, till the dewdrops stand in her eyes, so should the approach of Jesus' universal reign make all creation glad. No tyrant and no weakling is he, to oppress the good or to indulge the vain; his law is good, his action right, his government the embodiment of justice. If ever there was a thing to rejoice in upon this poor, travailing earth, it is the coming of such a deliverer, the ascension to the universal throne of such a governor. All hail, Jesus! all hail! Our soul faints with delight at the sound of your approaching chariots, and can only cry, 'Come quickly. Even so, come quickly, Lord Jesus!'

Meditation: *The most ardent attempts men make to celebrate the great work of the world's redemption fall short of the riches of the grace of God* (John Calvin).

Psalm 99:1-3

Suggested further reading: Isaiah 6:1-5

Saints quiver with devout emotion, and sinners quiver with terror when the rule of Jehovah is fully perceived and felt. It is not a light or trifling matter, it is a truth which, above all others, should stir the depths of our nature. In grandeur of sublime glory, yet in nearness of mediatorial condescension, Jehovah revealed himself above the mercy seat, on which stood the likeness of those flaming ones who gaze upon his glory, and for ever cry, 'Holy, Holy, Holy, Lord God of hosts.' The Lord reigning on that throne of grace which is sprinkled with atoning blood, and veiled with the covering wings of mediatorial love, is more wonderful than all other revelations, and fitted to excite emotion among all mankind. Not merely 'the people', but the whole earth should feel a movement of adoring awe when it is known that on the mercy seat God sits as universal monarch. The pomp of heaven surrounds him, and is symbolized by the outstretched wings of waiting cherubs. Let not the earth be less moved to adoration, rather let all her tribes bow before his infinite majesty, indeed, let the solid earth itself acknowledge his presence with reverent tremor.

In times past, the temple's sacred hill was the centre of the worship of the great King, and the place where his grandeur was most clearly beheld. His church is now his favoured palace, where his greatness is displayed, acknowledged and adored. He there unveils his attributes and commands the lowliest homage; the ignorant forget him, the wicked despise him, the atheists oppose him, but among his own chosen he is great beyond comparison. He is great in the esteem of the gracious, great in his acts of mercy, and really great in himself: great in mercy, power, wisdom, justice and glory. The highest are not high to him, yet, blessed be his name, the lowliest are not despised by him. In such a God we rejoice, his greatness and loftiness are exceedingly delightful in our esteem; the more he is honoured and exalted in the hearts of men, the more exultant are his people.

Under the most terrible aspect the Lord is still to be praised. Many profess to admire the milder beams of the sun of righteousness, but burn with rebellion against its more flaming radiance. It ought not to be so: we are bound to praise a terrible God and worship the one who casts the wicked down to hell. The terrible Avenger is to be praised, as well as the loving Redeemer. Against this the sympathy of man's evil heart with sin rebels; it cries out for an effeminate God in whom pity has strangled justice. The well-instructed servants of Jehovah praise him in all the aspects of his character, whether terrible or tender. Grace streaming from the mercy seat can alone work in us this admirable frame of mind. In him is no flaw or fault, excess or deficiency, error or iniquity. He is wholly excellent, and is therefore called holy. O come, let us worship and bow down before him.

Meditation: *This may be called* THE SANCTUS, *or,* THE HOLY, HOLY, HOLY PSALM, *for the word 'holy' is the conclusion and the refrain of its three main divisions* (C. H. Spurgeon).

Psalm 99:4-5

Suggested further reading: Isaiah 61:4-11

God is the king, the mercy seat is his throne, and the sceptre that he sways is holy like himself. His power never exerts itself tyranically; he is a sovereign, and he is absolute in his government, but his might delights in right, his force is used for just purposes only. Men in these days are continually arraigning the Lord's government, and setting up to judge whether he does right or not; but saintly men in the past were of another mind. They were sure that what the Lord did was just, and instead of calling him to account they humbly submitted themselves to his will, rejoicing in the firm persuasion that with his whole omnipotence God was pledged to promote righteousness, and work justice among all his creatures. The Lord our God demolishes every system of injustice, and right alone is made to stand. Justice is not merely established, but executed in God's kingdom; the laws are carried out, the executive is as righteous as the legislative. In this, let all the oppressed, indeed, and all who love that which is right, find great occasion for praise. The annals of most human governments have been written in the tears of the downtrodden, and the curses of the oppressed; the chronicles of the Lord's kingdom are of another sort, truth shines in each line, goodness in every syllable, and justice in every letter. Glory be to the name of the King, whose gentle glory beams from between the cherubic wings.

If no others adore him, let his own people render to him the most ardent worship. Infinite condescension makes him stoop to be called our God, and truth and faithfulness bind him to maintain that covenant relationship; and surely we, to whom by grace he so lovingly gives himself, should exalt him with all our hearts. When he reveals himself in Christ Jesus, as our reconciled God who allows us to approach even to his throne, it is appropriate that we unite earnestness and humility, joy and adoration, and, while we exalt him, prostrate ourselves in the dust before him. Do we need to be excited to worship in this way? How much ought we to blush for such backwardness! It ought to be our daily delight to magnify so good and great a God. Holiness is the harmony of all the virtues. The Lord has not one glorious attribute alone, or in excess, but all glories are in him as a whole; this is the crown of his honour and the honour of his crown. His power is not his choicest jewel, nor his sovereignty, but his holiness. In this all-comprehensive moral excellence he would have his creatures take delight, and when they do so their delight is evidence that their hearts have been renewed, and they themselves have been partakers of his holiness. The gods of the heathen were, according to their own devotees, lustful, cruel and brutish; their only claim to reverence lay in their supposed potency over human destinies. Who would not far rather adore Jehovah, whose character is unsullied purity, unswerving justice, unbending truth, unbounded love, in a word, perfect holiness?

Meditation: *Our King loves righteousness: he will execute perfect justice, tempered with perfect mercy* (The Plain Commentary).

Psalm 99:6-9

Suggested further reading: Numbers 14:11-23

The three holy men mentioned here all stood in his courts, and saw his holiness, each one after his own order. Moses saw the Lord revealing his perfect law in flaming fire, Aaron often watched the sacred fire devour the sin-offering, and Samuel witnessed the judgement of the Lord on Eli's house, because of the error of his way. Each one stood in the gap when the wrath of God broke forth, because his holiness had been insulted; and acting as intercessors, they screened the nation from the great and terrible God, who otherwise would have executed judgement in Jacob in a dreadful manner. Let these men, or men like these, lead us in our worship, and let us approach the Lord at the mercy seat as they did, for he is as accessible to us as to them. They made it their life's business to call upon him in prayer, and by so doing brought down innumerable blessings upon themselves and others. Does not the Lord call us also to come up into the mount with Moses, and to enter the most holy place with Aaron? Do we not hear him call us by our name as he did Samuel? And do we not answer, 'Speak, Lord, for your servant hears'?

In a very special manner our covenant God heard his three servants when they pleaded for the people. He forgave the sinners, but he slew their sins. We believe that the passage refers to the nation that was spared through the intercession of these three holy men, but yet was severely chastened for its transgressions. In answer to the cry of

Moses the tribes lived on, but the then existing generation could not enter Canaan: Aaron's golden calf was broken, though the fire of the Lord did not consume the people; and Israel smarted under the harsh government of Saul, though at Samuel's request its murmurings against the theocratic rule of their fathers' God was not visited with pestilence or famine. So to forgive sin at the same time as to express abhorrence of it is the peculiar glory of God, and is best seen in the atonement of our Lord Jesus. Reader, are you a believer? Then your sin is forgiven you; but as surely as you are a child of God the rod of paternal discipline will be laid upon you if your walk is not close with God. 'You only have I known of all the nations of the earth, therefore I will punish you for your iniquities.'

Meditation: *The psalm is Trinitarian in its whole structure. In each of his sacred persons the Lord is the God of his people; the Father is ours, the Son is ours, and the Holy Spirit is ours: let us exalt him with all our ransomed powers. Oh, for hearts made pure within, so that we may rightly perceive and worthily praise the infinite perfection of the Triune Lord* (C. H. Spurgeon).

Psalm 100

Suggested further reading: Isaiah 40:1-11

Our happy God should be worshipped by a happy people; a cheerful spirit is in keeping with his nature, his acts, and the gratitude which we should cherish for his mercies. In every land Jehovah's goodness is seen, therefore in every land he should be praised. Never will the world be in its proper condition till with one unanimous shout it adores the only God.

The invitation to worship given here is not a melancholy one, as though adoration were a funeral solemnity, but a cheery exhortation, as though we were bidden to a marriage feast. In worship we ought to realize the presence of God, and to approach him by an effort of the mind. This is an act which must to every rightly instructed heart be one of great solemnity, but at the same time it must not be performed in the servility of fear; and therefore we come before him, not with weeping and wailing, but with psalms and hymns. Singing, as it is a joyful, and at the same time a devout, exercise, should be a constant form of approach to God. The measured, harmonious, hearty utterance of praise by a congregation of really devout persons is not merely decorous but delightful, and is a fit anticipation of the worship of heaven, where praise has absorbed prayer, and become the sole mode of adoration.

Only those who practically recognize his Godhead are at all likely to offer acceptable praise. Shall not the creature reverence its Maker? Some men live as if they made themselves; they call themselves 'self-made men', and they adore their supposed creators; but Christians recognize the origin of their being and their well-being, and take no honour to themselves either for being, or for being what they are. Neither in our first or second creation dare we put so much as a finger upon the glory, for it is the sole right and property of the Almighty. Philosophy has laboured hard of late to prove that all things have been developed from atoms, or have, in other words, made themselves. If this theory shall ever find believers, there will certainly remain no reason for accusing the superstitious of credulity, for the amount of credence necessary to accept this dogma of scepticism is a thousandfold greater than that which is required even by an absurd belief in winking Madonnas, and smiling Bambinos. For our part, we find it far easier to believe that the Lord made us than that we were developed by a long chain of natural selections from floating atoms which fashioned themselves.

'The Lord is good.' This sums up his character and contains a mass of reasons for praise. He is good, gracious, kind, bountiful, loving; indeed, God is love. He who does not praise the good is not good himself. Our heart leaps for joy as we bow before one who has never broken his word or changed his purpose.

Meditation: *It is a sign the oil of grace has been poured into the heart 'when the oil of gladness' shines on the countenance. Cheerfulness credits religion* (Thomas Watson).

Psalm 101:1-4

Suggested further reading: 2 Samuel 6:10-19

Everything in God's dealings with us may fittingly become the theme of song, and we have not viewed it aright until we feel we can sing about it. We ought to bless the Lord as much for the judgement with which he chastens our sin, as for the mercy with which he forgives it; there is as much love in the blows of his hand as in the kisses of his mouth. Upon a retrospect of their lives instructed saints scarcely know which to be most grateful for — the comforts which have cheered them, or the afflictions which have purged them.

To be holy is to be wise; a perfect way is a wise way. David's resolve was excellent, but his practice did not fully tally with it. Alas! he was not always wise or perfect, but it was well that it was in his heart. He who does not even resolve to do well is likely to do very ill. Householders, employers, and especially ministers, should pray for both wisdom and holiness, for they will need them both. Piety must begin at home. Our first duties are those within our own abode. Notice that these words are a part of a song, and that there is no music like the harmony of a gracious life, no psalm so sweet as the daily practice of holiness. Reader, how does it fare with your family? Do you sing in the choir and sin in the chamber? Are you a saint abroad and a devil at home? For shame! What we are at home, that we are indeed.

The psalmist is very sweeping in his resolve, he declines the least, the most reputable, the most customary form of evil — no wicked thing: not only shall it not dwell in his heart, but not even before his eyes, for what fascinates the eye is very apt to gain admission into the heart. Hatred of sin is a good sentinel for the door of virtue. It is greatly to be deplored that in after years he did not keep himself clear in this matter in every case, though, in the main he did. How much do we all need divine keeping! We are no more perfect than David, no, we fall far short of him in many things; and, like him, we shall find need to write a psalm of penitence very soon after our psalm of good resolution. Sin, like pitch, is very apt to stick. In the course of our family history crooked things will turn up, for we are all imperfect, and some of those around us are far from being what they should be. It must, therefore, be one great object of our care to disentangle ourselves, to keep clear of transgression, and of all that comes of it: this cannot be done unless the Lord both comes to us, and abides with us evermore.

Meditation: *It is in vain to talk of holiness if we can bring no letters testimonial from our holy walking with our relations* (William Gurnall).

Psalm 101:5-8

Suggested further reading: Romans 13:1-7

David had known so bitterly the miseries caused by slanderers that he intended to deal severely with such vipers when he came into power, not to revenge his own ills, but to prevent others from suffering as he had done. To give one's neighbour a stab in the dark is one of the most atrocious of crimes, and cannot be too heartily reprobated, yet those who are guilty of it often find patronage in high places, and are considered to be men of penetration, trusty ones who have a keen eye, and they take care to keep their lords well informed. Proud men are generally hard, and therefore very unfit for office; persons of high looks provoke enmity and discontent, and the fewer of such people about a court the better for the stability of a throne. It would greatly profit us all if we chose our servants rather by their piety than by their cleverness; he who gets a faithful servant gets a treasure, and he ought to do anything sooner than part with him. Those who are not faithful to God will not be likely to be faithful to men. If we are faithful ourselves, we shall not care to have those about us who cannot speak the truth or fulfil their promises; we shall not be satisfied until all the members of our family are upright in character.

At the very outset of his government he would promptly deal out justice to the worthless, he would leave them no rest, but make them leave their wickedness or feel the lash of the law. The righteous magistrate 'bears not the sword in vain'. To favour sin is to discourage virtue; undue leniency to the bad is unkindness to the good. When our Lord comes in judgement, this will be fulfilled on a large scale; till then he sinks the judge in the Saviour, and bids men leave their sins and find pardon. Under the gospel we also are bidden to suffer long, and to be kind, even to the unthankful and the evil; but the office of the magistrate is of another kind, and he must have a sterner eye to justice than would be proper in private persons. Is he not to be a terror to evil-doers? Jerusalem was to be a holy city, and the psalmist meant to be doubly careful in purging it from ungodly men. Judgement must begin at the house of God. Jesus reserves his scourge of small cords for sinners inside the temple. How pure ought the church to be, and how diligently should all those who hold office in it labour to keep out and chase out men of unclean lives. Honourable offices involve ser-ious responsibilities; to trifle with them will bring our own souls into guilt, and injure beyond calculation the souls of others. Lord, come to us, that we, in our several positions in life, may walk before you with perfect hearts.

Meditation: *The holy vow 'to destroy all the wicked of the land', and to 'cut off all evildoers from the city of the Lord', must begin at our own hearts as his sanctuary, the temple of the Holy Ghost* (Alfred Edersheim).

Psalm 102:1-11

Suggested further reading: Lamentations 3:1-18

Sincere suppliants are not content with praying for praying's sake, they desire really to reach the ear and heart of
the great God. It is a great relief in time of distress to acquaint
others with our trouble, we are eased by their hearing our
lamentations, but it is the sweetest solace of all to have
God himself as a sympathizing listener to our complaint.
That he is such is no dream or fiction, but an assured fact.
It would be the direst of all our woes if we could be indis-
putably convinced that with God there is neither hearing
nor answering. He who could argue us into so dreary a belief would do us no better service than if he had read us
our death-warrants. Better die than be denied the mercy
seat. We may as well immediately become atheists as believe in an unhearing, unfeeling God. We may ask to have
answers to prayer as soon as possible, but we may not complain if the Lord thinks it more wise to delay. We have permission to request and to use importunity, but no right to
dictate or to be petulant. If it is important that the deliverance should arrive at once, we are quite right in making an
early time a point of our entreaty, for God is as willing to
grant us a favour now as tomorrow, and he is not slack
concerning his promise.

This is a telling description of all-saturating, all-
embittering sadness — and this was the portion of one of
the best of men, and for no fault of his own, but because of
his love to the Lord's people. If we, too, are called to mourn,

let us not be amazed by the fiery trial as though some strange thing had happened to us. Both in meat and drink we have sinned; it is not therefore surprising if in both we are made to mourn. A sense of the divine wrath that had been manifested in the overthrow of the chosen nation and their sad captivity led the psalmist into the greatest distress. He felt like a sere leaf caught up by a hurricane and carried right away, or the spray of the sea that is dashed upwards that it may be scattered and dissolved. There are times when through depression of spirit a man feels as if all life were gone from him, and existence had become merely a breathing death. Heartbreak has a marvellously withering influence over our entire system; our flesh at its best is but as grass, and when it is wounded with sharp sorrows, its beauty fades, and it becomes a shrivelled, dried, unseemly thing.

Meditation: *The Lord suffers his babbling children to speak to him in their own form of speech, such as, 'Hear me, hide not your face, incline your ear to me,' and such other like speeches* (David Dickson).

Psalm 102:12-28

Suggested further reading: Nehemiah 1:1-11

The writer's mind is turned away from his personal and relative troubles to the true source of all consolation, namely, the Lord himself, and his gracious purposes towards his own people. The sovereignty of God in all things is an unfailing ground for consolation; he rules and reigns whatever happens, and therefore all is well.

To the church of God no token can be more full of hope than to see its members deeply interested in all that concerns her; no prosperity is likely to rest upon a church when carelessness about ordinances, enterprises and services is manifest; but when even the least and lowest matter connected with the Lord's work is carefully attended to, we may be sure that the set time to favour Zion is come. The poorest church member, the most grievous backslider, the most ignorant convert, should be precious in our sight, because they are forming a part, although possibly a very feeble part, of the new Jerusalem. If we do not care about the prosperity of the church to which we belong, need we wonder if the blessing of the Lord is withheld? Mercy within the church is soon perceived by those without. When a candle is lit in the house, it shines through the window. When Zion rejoices in her God, the heathen begin to reverence his name, for they hear of the wonders of his power, and are impressed by it.

The psalmist intends to say that the rebuilding of Jerusalem would be a fact in history for which the Lord would be praised from age to age. Revivals of religion not only cause great joy to those who are immediately concerned in them, but they also give encouragement and delight to the people of God long after, and are indeed perpetual incentives to adoration throughout the church of God. This teaches us that we ought to have an eye to posterity, and we should especially endeavour to perpetuate the memory of God's love to his church and to his poor people, so that young people, as they grow up, may know that the Lord God of their fathers is good and full of compassion. Early in the psalm the psalmist had looked forward to a future generation, and speaks with confidence that such a race would arise and be preserved and blessed of God. It is full of good cheer to us; we may plead for the Lord's favour to our children, and we may expect that the cause of God and truth will revive in future generations. Let us hope that those who are to succeed us will not be so stubborn, unbelieving and erring as we have been. If the church has been diminished and brought low by the lukewarmness of the present race, let us entreat the Lord to raise up a better order of men, whose zeal and obedience shall win and hold a long prosperity. May our own dear ones be among the better generation who shall continue in the Lord's ways, obedient to the end.

Meditation: *It is worthy of observation that he ascribes the redemption and restoration of the people to the prayers of the faithful* (Mollerus).

Psalm 103:1-10

Suggested further reading: Mark 12:28-34

Soul music is the very soul of music. The psalmist strikes the best keynote when he begins with stirring up his inmost self to magnify the Lord. He soliloquizes, holds self-communion and exhorts himself, as though he felt that dullness would all too soon steal over his faculties, as, indeed, it will over us all, unless we are diligently on the watch. Our very life and essential self should be engrossed with this delightful service, and each one of us should arouse his own heart to its engagement. Let others forbear if they can: 'Bless the Lord, O MY soul.'

David begins his list of blessings received, which he rehearses as themes and arguments for praise. He selects a few of the choicest pearls from the casket of divine love, threads them on the string of memory, and hangs them about the neck of gratitude. Pardoned sin is, in our experience, one of the choicest boons of grace, one of the earliest gifts of mercy — in fact, the needful preparation for enjoying all that follows it. Till iniquity is forgiven, healing, redemption and satisfaction are unknown blessings. Forgiveness is first in the order of our spiritual experiences and in some respects first in value.

Our own personal obligations must not absorb our song; we must also magnify the Lord for his goodness to others. It is a great act of sovereign grace and condescending love when the Lord reveals himself to any people, and they ought to appreciate the distinguished favour shown to them. We, as believers in Jesus, know the Lord's ways of covenant grace, and we have by experience been made to see his acts of mercy towards us. How heartily ought we to praise our divine teacher, the Holy Spirit, who has made these things known to us, for had it not been for him we should have continued in darkness to this day. 'Lord, how is it that you manifest yourself to us and not to the world?' Why have you made us 'of the election who have obtained it' while the rest are blinded?

Observe how prominent is the personality of God in all this gracious teaching: 'He made known'. He did not leave Moses to discover truth for himself, but became his instructor. What should we ever know if he did not make it known? God alone can reveal himself. Those with whom he deals are sinners. However much he favours them they are guilty and need mercy at his hands, nor is he slow to show compassion towards their lost estate, or reluctant by his grace to lift them out of it. Mercy pardons sin, grace bestows favour; in both the Lord abounds. He is God, and not man, or our sins would soon drown his love; yet above the mountains of our sins the floods of his mercy rise.

Meditation: *Forget not any of his benefits* (David Dickson).

Psalm 103:11-22

Suggested further reading: 1 Peter 1:13-25

Boundless in extent towards his chosen is the mercy of the Lord; it is no more to be measured than the height of heaven or the heaven of heavens. Godly fear is one of the first products of the divine life in us, it is the beginning of wisdom, yet it fully ensures to its possessor all the benefits of divine mercy, and is, indeed, here and elsewhere, employed to set forth the whole of true religion. Those who are presuming upon the infinite extent of divine mercy should be led here to consider that although it is wide as the horizon and high as the stars, yet it is only meant for those that fear the Lord; and as for obstinate rebels, they shall have justice without mercy measured out to them.

Sin is removed from us by a miracle of love! What a load to move, and yet it is removed so far that the distance is incalculable. Fly as far as the wing of imagination can bear you, and if you journey through space eastward, you are further from the west at every beat of your wing. If sin is removed so far, then we may be sure that the scent, the trace, the very memory of it must be entirely gone. If this is the distance of its removal, there is no shade of fear of its ever being brought back again; even Satan himself could not achieve such a task. Our sins are gone; Jesus has borne them away. Far as the place of sunrise is removed from yonder west, where the sun sinks when his day's journey is done, so far were our sins carried by our scapegoat so many centuries ago, and now if they are sought after, they shall not be found, indeed, they shall not be, says the Lord. Come, my soul, awaken yourself thoroughly and glorify the Lord for this richest of blessings. Hallelujah! The Lord alone could remove sin at all, and he has done it in a godlike fashion, making a final sweep of all our transgressions.

How vast the contrast between the fading flower and the everlasting God! How wonderful that his mercy should link our frailty with his eternity, and make us everlasting too! From all eternity the Lord viewed his people as objects of mercy, and as such chose them to become partakers of his grace. The doctrine of eternal election is most delightful to those who have light to see it and love with which to accept it. It is a theme for deepest thought and highest joy. Jehovah does not change, he has mercy without end as well as without beginning. Those who fear him will never find that either their sins or their needs have exhausted the great deep of his grace.

Meditation: *The main question is, 'Do we fear him?' If we are lifting up to heaven the eye of filial fear, the gaze of paternal love is never removed from us, and it never will be, world without end* (C. H. Spurgeon).

Psalm 104:1-6

Suggested further reading: Genesis 1:1-8

The psalm gives an interpretation to the many voices of nature, and sings sweetly both of creation and providence. The poem contains a complete cosmos: sea and land, cloud and sunlight, plant and animal, light and darkness, life and death are all proved to be expressive of the presence of the Lord. Traces of the six days of creation are very evident, and though the creation of man, which was the crowning work of the sixth day, is not mentioned, this is accounted for by the fact that man is himself the singer: some have even discerned marks of the divine rest upon the seventh day in verse 31. It is a poet's version of Genesis.

'O Lord my God, you are very great.' This ascription has in it a remarkable blending of the boldness of faith, and the awe of holy fear: for the psalmist calls the infinite Jehovah 'my God', and at the same time, prostrate in amazement at the divine greatness, he cries out in utter astonishment, 'You are very great.' The declaration of Jehovah's greatness given here would have been very much in place at the end of the psalm, for it is a natural inference and deduction from a survey of the universe. Its position at the very commencement of the poem is an indication that the whole psalm was well considered and digested in the mind before it was actually put into words; only on this supposition can we account for the emotion preceding the contemplation. Observe also, that the wonder expressed does not refer to the creation and its greatness, but to Jehovah himself. It is not 'The universe is very great!' but 'You are very great.' Many stay at the creature, and so become idolatrous in spirit; to pass onward to the Creator himself is true wisdom.

The Lord is seen in his works as worthy of honour for his skill, his goodness and his power, and as claiming majesty, for he has fashioned all things in sovereignty, doing as he wills, and asking no man's permission. He must be blind indeed who does not see that nature is the work of a king. These are solemn strokes of God's severer mind, terrible touches of his sterner attributes, broad lines of inscrutable mystery, and deep shadings of overwhelming power. These make creation's picture a problem never to be solved, except by admitting that he who drew it gives no account of his matters, but rules all things according to the good pleasure of his will. His majesty is, however, always so displayed as to reflect honour upon his whole character; he does as he wills, but he wills only that which is thrice holy, like himself. The very robes of the unseen Spirit teach us this, and it is ours to recognize it with humble adoration.

Meditation: It is the joy of the saints that he who is their God is a great God; the grandeur of the prince is the pride and pleasure of all his good subjects (Matthew Henry).

Psalm 104:7-18

Suggested further reading: Genesis 1:9-13

God appoints to the lowliest creature its portion and takes care that it has it. Divine power is as truly and as worthily put forth in the feeding of beasts as in the nurturing of man; watch but a blade of grass with a devout eye and you may see God at work within it. The herb is for man, and he must till the soil or it will not be produced, yet it is God that causes it to grow in the garden, even the same God who made the grass to grow in the open pastures of the wilderness. Man forgets this and talks of his produce, but in actual truth, without God he would plough and sow in vain. The Lord causes each green blade to spring and each ear to ripen: just watch with opened eye and you shall see the Lord walking through the cornfields. Both grass for cattle and corn for man are food brought forth out of the earth, and they are signs that it was God's design that the very dust beneath our feet, which seems better adapted to bury us than to sustain us, should actually be transformed into the staff of life. The more we think of this the more wonderful it will appear. How great is that God who from among the sepulchres finds the support of life, and out of the ground that was cursed brings forth the blessings of corn and wine and oil.

What would our psalmist have said to some of the trees in the Yosemite valley? Truly these are worthy to be called the trees of the Lord, for towering stature and enormous girth. Thus the care of God is seen to be effectual and all sufficient. If trees uncared for by man are yet so full of sap, we may rest assured that the people of God who by faith live upon the Lord alone shall be equally well sustained. Planted by grace, and owing all to our heavenly Father's care, we may defy the hurricane, and laugh at the fear of drought, for none that trust in him shall ever be left unwatered. Has the reader ever walked through a forest of great trees and felt the awe that strikes the heart in nature's sublime cathedral? Then he will remember to have felt that each bird was holy, since it dwelt amid such sacred solitude. Those who cannot see or hear of God except in Gothic edifices, amid the swell of organs, and the voices of a surpliced choir, will not be able to enter into the feeling that makes the simple, unsophisticated soul hear 'the voice of the Lord God walking among the trees'.

Meditation: *If the transitory earth is so full of the good things of God, what will we have when we come to the land of the living?* (Starke, in Lange's Commentary).

Psalm 104:19-30

Suggested further reading: Genesis 1:14-25

The appointed rule of the great lights is now the theme for praise. The moon is mentioned first, because in the Jewish day the night leads the way. By the waxing and waning of the moon the year is divided into months, and weeks, and by this means the exact dates of the holy days are arranged. Thus the lamp of night is made to be of service to man, and in fixing the period of religious assemblies (as it did among the Jews) it enters into connection with his noblest being. Never let us regard the moon's motions as the inevitable result of inanimate impersonal law, but as the appointment of our God.

Night, as well as day, has its voice of praise. It is more soft and hushed, but it is none the less true. The moon lights up a solemn silence of worship among the fir trees, through which the night wind softly breathes its 'songs without words'. Every now and then a sound is heard, which, however simple by day, sounds startling and weird-like among the shadows, as if the presence of the unknown had filled the heart with trembling, and made the influence of the Infinite to be realized. Imagination awakens herself; unbelief finds the silence and the solemnity uncongenial, faith looks up to the skies above her and sees heavenly things all the more clearly in the absence of the sunlight, and adoration bows itself before the Great Invisible! There are spirits that keep the night watches, and the spell of their presence has been felt by many a wanderer in the solitude of nature: God himself is also abroad all night long, and the glory which conceals is often felt to be even greater than that which reveals. Bless the Lord, O my soul!

Works in the heavens above and in the earth beneath, and in the waters under the earth, works which abide the ages, works which come to perfection and pass away in a year, works which with all their beauty do not outlive a day, works within works, and works within these — who can number one of a thousand? God is the great worker, and ordainer of variety. It is ours to study his works, for they are great, and sought by all those that take pleasure in them. They are all his works, wrought by his own power, and they all display his wisdom. It was wise to make them — none could be spared; every link is essential to the chain of nature — wild beasts as much as men, poisons as truly as odoriferous herbs. They are wisely made — each one fits its place, fills it, and is happy in so doing. As a whole, all of creation is a wise achievement, and however it may be chequered with mysteries, and clouded with terrors, it all works together for good, and as one complete harmonious piece of workmanship it answers the great Worker's end.

Meditation: *The kingdom of grace contains as manifold and as great works as that of nature, but the chosen of the Lord alone discern them* (C. H. Spurgeon).

Psalm 104:31-35

Suggested further reading: Genesis 1:26 - 2:3

The poet finds his heart gladdened by beholding the works of the Lord, and he feels that the Creator himself must have felt unspeakable delight in exercising so much wisdom, goodness and power. If it was only for what he has already done, the Lord deserves to be praised without ceasing. His personal being and character ensure that he would be glorious even if all the creatures were dead.

Here and hereafter the psalmist would continue to praise the Lord, for the theme is an endless one, and remains for ever fresh and new. The birds sang God's praises before men were created, but redeemed men will sing his glories when the birds are no more. Jehovah, who ever lives and makes us to live, shall be for ever exalted, and extolled in the songs of redeemed men. Meditation is the soul of religion. It is the tree of life in the midst of the garden of piety, and its fruit is very refreshing to the soul that feeds upon it. And as it is good towards man, so is it towards God. As the fat of the sacrifice was the Lord's portion, so are our best meditations due to the Most High and are most acceptable to him. We ought, therefore, both for our own good and for the Lord's honour, to take much time in meditation, and that meditation should chiefly dwell upon the Lord himself: it should be 'meditation of him'. Failure to do so will result in much communion being lost and much happiness missed. To the meditative mind every thought of God is full of joy. Each one of the divine attributes is a well-spring of delight now that in Christ Jesus we are reconciled to God.

In holy indignation the psalmist would rid the world of beings so base as not to love their gracious Creator, so blind as to rebel against their Benefactor. He does but ask for that which just men look forward to as the end of history; for the day is eminently to be desired when in all God's kingdom there shall not remain a single traitor or rebel. The Christian way of putting it will be to ask that grace may turn sinners into saints, and win the wicked to the ways of truth. 'Bless the Lord, O my soul.' Here is the end of the matter — whatever sinners may do, my soul, stand to your colours, and be true to your calling. Their silence must not silence you, but rather provoke you to redoubled praise to make up for their failures. Nor can you alone accomplish the work; others must come to help. O saints, 'Praise the Lord.' Let your hearts cry HALLELUJAH for that is the word in the Hebrew. Heavenly word! Let it close the psalm: for what more remains to be said or written? HALLELUJAH. 'Praise the Lord.'

Meditation: *The soul which blesses shall be made fat... Reined in by this rein of divine praise, he shall never perish* (Lorinus).

Psalm 105:1-15

Suggested further reading: Genesis 15:7-21

We are now among the long psalms, as at other times we have been among the short ones. These varying lengths of the sacred poems should teach us not to lay down any law either of brevity or prolixity in either prayer or praise. Short petitions and single verses of hymns are often the best for public occasions, but there are seasons when a whole night of wrestling or an entire day of psalm-singing will be none too long. The Spirit is ever free in his operations, and is not to be confined within the rules of conventional propriety. Our last psalm sang the opening chapters of Genesis, and this takes up its closing chapters and conducts us into Exodus and Numbers.

Memory is never better employed than upon the things that God has done. Alas, we are far more ready to recollect foolish and evil things than to retain in our minds the glorious deeds of Jehovah. If we would keep these in remembrance our faith would be stronger, our gratitude warmer, our devotion more fervent, and our love more intense. Here is the basis of all his dealings with his people; he had entered into covenant with them in their father Abraham, and to this covenant he remained faithful. The exhortation to 'remember' receives great force from the fact that God has remembered. If the Lord has his promise in memory, surely we ought not to forget the wonderful manner in which he keeps it. To us it should be matter for deepest joy that never in any instance has the Lord been unmindful of his covenant engagements, nor will he be so world without end. Oh, that we were as mindful of them as he is.

When the victims were divided and the burning lamp passed between the pieces then the Lord made, or ratified, the covenant with the patriarch. This was a solemn deed, performed not without blood, and the cutting in pieces of the sacrifice: it points us to the greater covenant which in Christ Jesus is signed, sealed and ratified, that it may stand fast for ever and ever. Isaac did not see the solemn making of the covenant in vision, but the Lord renewed to him his oath. This was enough for him, and must have established his faith in the Most High. We have the privilege of seeing in our Lord Jesus both the sacrificial seal and the eternal oath of God, which makes every promise of the covenant yes and amen to all the chosen seed.

Meditation: The 105th psalm is a meditation on the covenant as performed on the part of God, the 106th on the covenant as kept by Israel. They both dwell on the predestinating will of God, electing men to holiness and obedience, and the mode in which human sin opposes itself to that will, and yet cannot make it void (The Plain Commentary).

Psalm 105:16-23

Suggested further reading: Genesis 41:37-46

The presence of God remained with his chosen ones while they sojourned in Canaan, and it did not desert them when they were called to go down into Egypt. They did not go there of their own choice, but under divine direction, and hence the Lord prepared their way and prospered them until he saw fit to conduct them again to the land of promise. Joseph was the advance guard and pioneer for the whole clan. His brethren sold him, but God sent him. Where the hand of the wicked is visible God's hand may be invisibly at work, overruling their malice. No one was more of 'a man', or more fit to lead the van than Joseph. An interpreter of dreams was wanted, and his brethren had said of him, 'Look, the dreamer comes.' Were we to send a man on such an errand we should furnish him with money — Joseph goes as a pauper; we should clothe him with authority — Joseph goes as a slave; we should leave him with full liberty — Joseph is a bondman. Yet money would have been of little use when grain was so dear, authority would have been irritating rather than influential with Pharaoh, and freedom might not have thrown Joseph into connection with Pharaoh's captain and his other servants, and so the knowledge of his skill in interpretation might not have reached the monarch's ear. God's way is the way. Our Lord's path to his mediatorial throne ran by the cross of Calvary; our road to glory runs by the rivers of grief.

Pharaoh empowered Joseph to manage the storing of the seven plenteous harvests, and to dispense the provisions in the coming days of scarcity. All the treasures of Egypt were under his lock and key, indeed, the granaries of the world were sealed or opened at his bidding. Thus was he in the best conceivable position for keeping alive the house of Israel with whom the covenant was made. As our Lord was himself secured in Egypt from Herod's enmity, so, ages before, the redeemed race found an equally available shelter in the hour of need. God has always a refuge for his saints, and if the whole earth could not afford them sanctuary, the Lord himself would be their dwelling-place, and take them up to lie in his own bosom. We are always sure to be fed if all the world should starve. It is delightful to think of our greater Joseph ruling the nations for the good of his own household, and it becomes us to abide in quiet confidence in every political disaster, since Jesus is on the throne of providence, King of kings and Lord of lords, and will be so till this age ends.

Meditation: *Joseph was a type of Jesus Christ, who, as God, is possessor of heaven and earth, being the creator of them* (John Gill).

Psalm 105:24-45

Suggested further reading: Exodus 12:31-42

It was God's goodness to Israel that called forth the ill will of the Egyptian court, and so far the Lord caused it. Moreover, he made use of this feeling to lead on to the discomfort of his people, and so to their readiness to leave the land to which they had evidently become greatly attached. Thus far but no further did the Lord turn the hearts of the Egyptians. God cannot in any sense be the author of sin so far as being morally responsible for its existence, but it often happens through the evil which is inherent in human nature that the acts of the Lord arouse the ill feelings of ungodly men. Is the sun to be blamed because while it softens wax it hardens clay? Is the orb of day to be accused of creating the foul exhalations that are drawn by its warmth from the pestilential marsh? The sun causes the reek of the dunghill only in a certain sense; had it been a bed of flowers its beams would have called forth fragrance. The evil is in men, and the honour of turning it to good and useful purposes is with the Lord.

The miracles which were wrought by Moses were the Lord's, not his own; hence they are here called 'his signs', as being the marks of Jehovah's presence and power. The plagues were speaking marvels, which testified more plainly than words to the omnipotence of Jehovah, to his determination to be obeyed, to his anger at the obstinacy of Pharaoh. Never were discourses more plain, pointed, personal or powerful and yet it took ten of them to accomplish the end designed.

The covenant and the one for whose sake it was made are ever on the heart of the Most High. Here is the secret reason for all this grace. He remembered his people because he remembered his covenant. He could not violate that gracious compact for it was sacred to him — 'his holy promise'. A holy God must keep his promise holy. In our case the Lord's eye is upon his beloved Son and his engagements with him on our behalf, and this is the source and well-head of those innumerable favours which enrich us in all our wanderings through this life's wilderness.

The chosen nation was to be the conservator of truth, the exemplar of morality, the pattern of devotion: everything was so ordered as to place them in advantageous circumstances for fulfilling this trust. Theirs was a high calling and a glorious election. It involved great responsibilities, but it was in itself a distinguished blessing, and one for which the nation was bound to give thanks. The music then most justly closed with the jubilant but solemn shout of HALLELUJAH. 'Praise the Lord.' If this history did not make Israel praise God, what would?

Meditation: *'They inherited the labour of the nations.' In like manner the heavenly Canaan is enjoyed by the saints without any of their labours; this inheritance is not of the law, nor of the works of it; it is the gift of God* (John Gill).

Psalm 106:1-12

Suggested further reading: Exodus 15:11-26

Here Israel's history is written with the view of showing human sin, even as the preceding psalm was composed to magnify divine goodness. It is, in fact, a national confession, and includes an acknowledgement of the transgressions of Israel in Egypt, in the wilderness, and in Canaan, with such devout petitions for forgiveness as rendered the psalm suitable for use in all succeeding generations, and especially in times of national captivity. While we are studying this holy psalm, let us all along see ourselves in the Lord's ancient people, and bemoan our own provocations of the Most High, at the same time admiring his infinite patience, and adoring him because of it. May the Holy Spirit sanctify it to the promotion of humility and gratitude.

This song is for the assembled people, and they are all exhorted to join in praise to Jehovah. It is not meet for a few to praise and the rest to be silent; but all should join in. If David was present in churches where quartets and choirs carry on all the singing, he would turn to the congregation and say, 'Praise the Lord.' Those who praise the Lord have an infinite subject, a subject which will not be exhausted throughout eternity by the most enlarged intellects, no, nor by the whole multitude of the redeemed, though no man can number them.

Confession of sin is the most effective way to secure an answer to prayer; God visits with his salvation the soul that acknowledges its need of a Saviour. Men may be said to have sinned with their fathers when they imitate them, when they follow the same objects, and make their own lives to be mere continuations of the follies of their fore-fathers. Moreover, Israel was but one nation in all time, and the confession that follows sets forth the national rather than the personal sin of the Lord's people. They enjoyed national privileges, and therefore they shared in national guilt. The confession is repeated three times, as a token of its sincerity and heartiness. Sins of omission, commission and rebellion we ought to acknowledge under distinct heads, that we may show a due sense of the number and heinousness of our offences. The Lord very jealously guards his own name and honour. It shall never be said of him that he cannot or will not save his people, or that he cannot abate the haughtiness of his defiant foes. This respect to his own honour always leads him to deeds of mercy, and hence we may well rejoice that he is a jealous God.

Meditation: Shall the Lord put forth so much of grace upon a people that were under the law; and not put forth much more of his grace upon those that are under the gospel? (William Bridge).

Psalm 106:13-23

Suggested further reading: Exodus 32:1-14

Prayer may be answered in anger and denied in love. The fact that God gives a man his desire is no proof that he is the object of divine favour, everything depends upon what that desire is. The meat was poison to them when it came without a blessing; whatever it might do in fattening the body, it was poor stuff when it made the soul lean. If we must know scantiness, may God grant it may not be scantiness of soul — yet this is a common attendant upon worldly prosperity! With many a man, when wealth grows, his worldly estate is fatter, but his soul's state is leaner. To gain silver and lose gold is a poor increase; but to win for the body and lose for the soul is far worse. How earnestly might Israel have unprayed her prayers had she known what would come with their answer! The prayers of lust will have to be wept over. We fret and fume till we have our desire, and then we have to fret still more because the attainment of it ends in bitter disappointment.

In the very place where they had solemnly pledged themselves to obey the Lord they broke the second, if not the first, of his commandments, set up the Egyptian symbol of the ox, and bowed before it. The Israelites were foolish indeed when they thought they saw the slightest divine glory in a bull, no, in the mere image of a bull. To believe that the image of a bull could be the image of God must need great credulity. This was sheer madness. After the same fashion the ritualists needed to set up their symbols and multiply them greatly. They seem unable to apprehend spiritual worship; their worship is sensuous to the highest degree, and appeals to eye, ear and nose. Oh, the folly of men, to block up their own way to acceptable worship, and to make the path of spiritual religion, which is hard to our nature, harder still through the stumbling-blocks which they cast into it. We have heard the richness of popish paraphernalia much extolled, but an idolatrous image when made of gold is not one jot the less abominable than it would have been had it been made of dross and dung: the beauty of art cannot conceal the deformity of sin. We are told also of the suggestiveness of their symbols, but what of that, when God forbids the use of them? It is also vain to plead that such worship is hearty. So much the worse! Heartiness in forbidden actions is only an increase of transgression. The psalmist is very contemptuous, and justly so: irreverence towards idols is an indirect reverence to God. False gods, attempts to represent the true God, and indeed, all material things which are worshipped are so much filth upon the face of the earth, whether they be crosses, crucifixes, virgins, wafers, relics, or even the pope himself. We are by far too mealy-mouthed about these infamous abominations: God abhors them, and so should we.

Meditation: *To renounce the glory of spiritual worship for outward pomp and show is the height of folly, and deserves to be treated as such* (C. H. Spurgeon).

Psalm 106:24-39

Suggested further reading: Numbers 25:1-13

They spoke of Egypt, the land of their iron bondage, as though they preferred it to Canaan, the land that flowed with milk and honey. It is an ill sign with a Christian when he begins to think lightly of heaven and heavenly things. It indicates a perverted mind, and it is, moreover, a high offence to the Lord to despise the thing that he esteems so highly that he in infinite love reserves it for his own chosen. To prefer earthly things to heavenly blessings is to prefer Egypt to Canaan, the house of bondage to the land of promise. Unbelief is the root sin. If we do not believe the Lord's word, we shall think lightly of his promised gifts. When pilgrims to the Celestial City begin to doubt the Lord of the way, they soon come to think little of the rest at the journey's end, and this is the surest way to make them bad travellers.

Ritualism led on to the adoration of false gods. If we choose a false way of worship we shall, before long, choose to worship a false god. This abomination of the Moabites was an idol in whose worship women gave up their bodies to the most shameless lust. Think of the people of a holy God coming down to this. Israel joined in the orgies with which the Baalites celebrated their detestable worship, partaking even in their sacrifices as earnest inner-court worshippers, though the gods were but dead idols. Perhaps they assisted in necromantic rites which were intended to open a communication with departed spirits, thus endeavouring to break the seal of God's providence, and burst into the secret chambers which God has shut up. Those who are weary of seeking the living God have often shown a hankering after dark sciences, and have sought after fellowship with demons and spirits. What strong delusions often grip those who cast off the fear of God! This remark is as much needed now as in days gone by.

It was not the wilderness that caused Israel's sins; they were just as disobedient when settled in the land of promise. They found evil company, and delighted in it. Those whom they should have destroyed they made their friends. Having enough faults of their own, they were yet ready to go to school to the filthy Canaanites, and educate themselves still more in the arts of iniquity. It was certain that they could learn no good from men whom the Lord had condemned to utter destruction. Few would wish to go to the condemned cell for learning, yet Israel sat at the feet of accursed Canaan, and rose up proficient in every abomination. This, too, is a grievous but common error among professing believers: they court worldly company and copy worldly fashions, and yet it is their calling to bear witness against these things.

Meditation: *None can tell what evil has come of the folly of worldly conformity* (C. H. Spurgeon).

Psalm 106:40-48

Suggested further reading: Judges 3:1-14

'The wrath of the Lord was kindled against his people, so that he abhorred his own inheritance.' Not that even then he broke his covenant or utterly cast off his offending people, but he felt the deepest indignation, and even looked upon them with abhorrence. How far the divine wrath can burn against those whom he yet loves in his heart it was hard to say, but certainly Israel pushed the experiment to the extreme.

Leniency to Canaan turned out to be cruelty to themselves. They were bowed down by laborious bondage, and made to lie low under tyranny. In their God they had found a kind master, but in those with whom they had perversely sought fellowship they found despots of the most barbarous sort. He who leaves his God leaves happiness for misery. God can make our enemies to be rods in his hands to flog us back to our best Friend. By reading the book of Judges we shall see how truthful this is: again and again their foes were routed, and they were set free again, only to return with rigour to their former evil ways. With deliberation they agreed to transgress anew; self-will was their counsellor, and they followed it to their own destruction. Worse and worse were the evils brought upon them, lower and lower they fell in sin, and consequently in sorrow. In dens and caves of the earth they hid themselves; they were deprived of all warlike weapons, and were utterly despised by their conquerors; they were rather a race of serfs than of free men until the Lord in mercy raised them up again. Could we but fully know the horrors of the wars that desolated Palestine, and the ravages which caused famine and starvation, we should shudder at the sins which were thus rebuked. The sin of idolatry must have been deeply engrained in their nature, or they would not have returned to it with such persistence in the teeth of such penalties; we need not marvel at this, there is a still greater wonder, man prefers sin and hell to heaven and God.

Notwithstanding all these provoking rebellions and detestable enormities the Lord still heard their prayer and pitied them. This is very wonderful, very godlike. One would have thought that the Lord would have shut out their prayer, seeing they had shut their ears against his admonitions; but no, he had a father's heart, and a sight of their sorrows touched his soul, the sound of their cries overcame his heart, and he looked upon them with compassion. His fiercest wrath towards his own people is only a temporary flame, but his love burns on for ever like the light of his own immortality. The covenant is the sure foundation of mercy, and when the whole fabric of outward grace manifested in the saints lies in ruins, this is the fundamental basis of love which is never moved, and upon it the Lord proceeds to build again a new structure of grace.

Meditation: *Covenant mercy is sure as the throne of God* (C. H. Spurgeon).

Psalm 107:1-9

Suggested further reading: Isaiah 43:8-13

Whatever others may think or say, the redeemed have overwhelming reasons for declaring the goodness of the Lord.
Theirs is an extraordinary redemption, and they ought to
render extraordinary praise for it. The Redeemer is so
glorious, the ransom price so immense, and the redemption so complete, that they are under sevenfold obligations
to give thanks unto the Lord, and to exhort others to do so.
Let them not only feel so but also say so; let them both sing
and bid their fellows sing. Some have wandered one way
and some another, they have all left Immanuel's land and
strayed as far as they could, and great are the grace and
power by which they are all collected into one flock by the
Lord Jesus. With one heart and voice let the redeemed praise
the Lord who gathers them into one.

There are many wrong ways, but only one right one,
and into this none can lead us but God himself. When the
Lord is leader the way is sure to be right; we never need
question that. Out from the pathless mazes of the desert he
conducted the lost ones; he found the way, made the way
and enabled them to walk along it, faint and hungry as
they were. The end was worthy of the way, he did not lead
them from one desert to another, but he gave the wander-
ers an abode, the weary ones a place of rest. These favours
are bestowed upon our race, upon children of the family to
which we belong, and therefore we ought to join in the
praise. The children of men are so insignificant, so feeble

and so undeserving, that it is a great wonder that the Lord should do anything for them; but he is not content with doing little works, he puts forth his wisdom, power and love to perform marvels on the behalf of those who seek him. In the life of each one of the redeemed there is a world of wonders, and therefore from each there should resound a world of praises. As to the marvels of grace that the Lord has wrought for his church as a whole there is no estimating them, they are as high above our thoughts as the heavens are high above the earth. When shall the day dawn when the favoured race of man shall be as devoted to the praise of God as they are distinguished by the favour of God?

The Lord sets us longing and then completely satisfies us. That longing leads us into solitude, separation, thirst, faintness and self-despair, and all these conduct us to prayer, faith, divine guidance, satisfying of the soul's thirst, and rest: the good hand of the Lord is to be seen in the whole process and in the divine result.

Meditation: It is walking 'in a solitary way' that makes the path of trial and temptation so painful to God's family (J. C. Philpot).

Psalm 107:10-22

Suggested further reading: Isaiah 45:1-7

God's words are not to be trifled with, and those who venture on such rebellion will bring themselves into bondage. This was the general cause of servitude among the ancient people of God, they were given over to their adversaries because they were not loyal to the Lord. In their wretched plight the rebellious Israelites became more lowly in mind, and thought more tenderly of God and of their offences against him. When a soul finds all its efforts at self-salvation prove abortive, and feels that it is now utterly without strength, then the Lord is at work hiding pride from man and preparing the afflicted one to receive his mercy. The spiritual case which is figuratively described here is desperate, and therefore affords the finer field for divine interposition; some of us remember well how brightly mercy shone in our prison, and what music the fetters made when they fell off from our hands. Nothing but the Lord's love could have delivered us; without it we must have utterly perished.

Verses 17-20 describe a sin-sick soul, foolish but yet aroused to a sense of guilt, it refuses comfort from any and every quarter, and a lethargy of despair utterly paralyses it. To its own understanding nothing remains but utter destruction in many forms: the gates of death stand open before it, and it is, in its own apprehension, hurried in that direction. Then is the soul driven to cry in the bitterness of its grief unto the Lord, and Christ, the eternal Word, comes with healing power in the direst extremity, saving to the uttermost. It is marvellous that men can be restored from sickness and yet refuse to bless the Lord. It would seem impossible that they should forget such great mercy, for we should expect to see both themselves and the friends to whom they are restored uniting in a lifelong act of thanksgiving. Yet when ten are healed it is seldom that more than one returns to give glory to God. Alas, where are the nine? When a spiritual cure is wrought by the great Physician, praise is one of the surest signs of renewed health. A mind rescued from the disease of sin and the weary pains of conviction must and will adore the healing God: yet it would be good if there were a thousand times as much even of this. In such a situation let there be gifts and oblations as well as words. Let the good Physician have his fee of gratitude. Let life become a sacrifice to he who has prolonged it, let the deed of self-denying gratitude be repeated again and again, there must be many cheerful sacrifices to celebrate the marvellous boon. Such things are worth telling, for the personal declaration honours God, relieves ourselves, comforts others, and puts all men in possession of facts concerning the divine goodness which they will not be able to ignore.

Meditation: *We must acknowledge God's goodness to the children of men, as well as to the children of God: to others as well as to ourselves* (Matthew Henry).

Psalm 107:23-32

Suggested further reading: Jonah 1:1-16

Navigation was so little practised among the Israelites that mariners were invested with a high degree of mystery, their craft was looked upon as one of singular daring and peril. Tales of the sea thrilled all hearts with awe, and he who had been to Ophir or to Tarshish and returned alive was looked upon as a man of renown, an ancient mariner to be listened to with reverent attention.

Those who have been on the spiritual deep in one of the great storms that occasionally agitate the soul know what these verses mean. In these spiritual cyclones presumption alternates with despair, indifference with agony! No heart is left for anything, courage is gone, hope is almost dead. Such an experience is as real as the tossing of a literal tempest and far more painful. Some of us have weathered many such an internal hurricane, and have indeed seen the Lord's wondrous works. When God makes peace it is peace indeed, the peace of God which passes all understanding. He can in an instant change the condition of a man's mind, so that it shall seem an absolute miracle to him that he has passed so suddenly from hurricane to calm. Oh, that the Lord would thus work in the reader, should his heart be storm-beaten with outward troubles or inward fears. Lord, say the word and peace will come at once.

By storms and by favourable breezes, through tempest and fair weather, the great Pilot and Ruler of the sea brings mariners to port, and his people to heaven. He must have the glory of the successful voyage of time, and when we are moored in the river of life above we shall take care that his praises are not forgotten. We should have been wrecked long ago if it had not been for his preserving hand, and our only hope of outliving the storms of the future is based upon his wisdom, faithfulness and power. Our heavenly haven shall ring with shouts of grateful joy when once we reach its blessed shore.

Not all believers have the same deep experience; but for wise ends, that they may do business for him, the Lord sends some of his saints to the sea of soul-trouble, and there they see, as others do not, the wonders of divine grace. Sailing over the deeps of inward depravity, the waste waters of poverty, the billows of persecution, and the rough waves of temptation, they need God above all others, and they find him. When a heart has been in great spiritual storms and has at last found peace, there will follow as a duty and a privilege the acknowledgement of the Lord's mercy before his people; and it is well that this should be done in the presence of those who hold office in the church, and who from their riper years are better able to appreciate the testimony.

Meditation: If the sailor can do nothing else than trust in the Lord, so is it with us in the storms of life. Like the mariner, we must use lawful means for our protection; but what are means without the divine blessing? (William S. Plumer).

Psalm 107:33-43

Suggested further reading: 1 Kings 17:1-7

When the Lord deals with rebellious men he can soon deprive them of those blessings of which they feel most assured, their rivers and perennial springs they look upon as certain never to be taken from them, but at a word the Lord can deprive them even of these. In hot climates after long droughts, streams of water utterly fail, and even springs cease to flow, and this also has happened in other parts of the world when great convulsions of the earth's surface have occurred. In providence this physical catastrophe finds its counterpart when business ceases to yield profit and sources of wealth are made to fail; as also when health and strength are taken away, when friendly aids are withdrawn, and comfortable associations are broken up. So, too, in soul matters, the most prosperous ministries may become dry, the most delightful meditations cease to benefit us, and the most fruitful religious exercises grow void of the refreshment of grace which they formerly yielded.

With another turn of his hand he more than restores that which in judgement he took away. He does his work of mercy on a royal scale, for a deep lake is seen where before there was only a sandy waste. It is not by natural laws, working by some innate force, that this wonder is wrought, but by himself. Men work when God works. His blessing encourages the sower, cheers the planter and rewards the labourer. Not only necessaries but luxuries are enjoyed, wine as well as corn, when the heavens are caused to yield the needed rain to fill the watercourses. Divine visitations bring great spiritual riches, foster varied works of faith and labours of love, and cause every good fruit to abound to our comfort and to God's praise. When God sends the blessing it does not supersede, but encourages and develops human exertion. Paul plants, Apollos waters, and God gives the increase. God's blessing is everything.

Those who notice providences shall never be long without a providence to notice. It is wise to observe what the Lord does, for he is wonderful in counsel, has given us eyes to see with, and it is foolish to close them when there is most to observe; but we must observe wisely, otherwise we may soon confuse ourselves and others with hasty reflections upon the dealings of the Lord. The loving-kindness of the Lord is shown in a thousand ways, and if we will but prudently watch, we shall come to a better understanding of it. To understand the delightful attribute of loving-kindness is an attainment as pleasant as it is profitable; those who are proficient scholars in this art will be among the sweetest singers to the glory of Jehovah.

Meditation: *The righteous shall see and admire, and be thankful for the wonders of God's redeeming love, which are recorded in this divine hymn* (William Romaine).

Psalm 108:1-5

Suggested further reading: Romans 15:7-13

It is my glory to be able to speak and not to be a dumb animal, therefore my voice will show forth your praise; it is my glory to know God and not to be a heathen, and therefore my instructed intellect will adore you; it is my glory to be a saint and no longer a rebel, therefore the grace I have received will bless you; it is my glory to be immortal and not a mere brute which perishes, therefore my inmost life will celebrate your majesty. When he says 'I will', he supposes that there might be some temptation to refrain, but this he puts on one side, and with fixed heart prepares himself for the joyful engagement. He who sings with a fixed heart is likely to sing on, and all the while to sing well.

Whoever may come to hear me, devout or profane, believer or heathen, civilized or barbarian, I shall not cease my music. David seemed inspired to foresee that his psalms would be sung in every land, from Greenland's icy mountains to India's coral strand. His heart was large, he would have the whole race of man listen to his joy in God, and lo, he has his desire, for his psalmody is cosmopolitan; no poet is so universally known as he. He had but one theme, he sang Jehovah and none beside, and his work being thus made of gold, silver and precious stones has endured the fiery ordeal of time, and was never more prized than in this day. Happy man, to have thus made his choice to be the Lord's musician, he retains his office as the Poet Laureate of the kingdom of heaven, and shall retain it till the crack of doom. He would carry his religion with him wherever he pushed his conquests, and the vanquished should not hear the praises of David, but the glories of the Lord of Hosts. Would to God that wherever professing Christians travel they would carry the praises of the Lord with them! It is to be feared that some leave their religion when they leave their homes. Nations and peoples would soon know the gospel of Jesus if every Christian traveller were as intensely devout as the psalmist. Alas, it is to be feared that the Lord's name is profaned rather than honoured among the heathen by many who are named by the name of Christ. This is a truly missionary prayer. David had none of the exclusiveness of the modern Jew or the narrow-heartedness of some nominal Christians. For God's sake, that his glory might be revealed everywhere, he longed to see heaven and earth full of divine praise. Amen, so let it be.

Meditation: *The mercy of God was then great above the heavens, when the God-man, Christ Jesus, was raised to the highest heavens, and the truth of our salvation established on the very throne of God* (W. Wilson).

Psalm 108:6-13

Suggested further reading: 1 Chronicles 17:16-27

Now prayer follows upon praise, and from there derives strength of faith and holy boldness. It is frequently best to begin worship with a hymn, and then to bring forth our vials full of odours after the harps have commenced their sweeter sounds.

The Lord had made large promises to David, and these his holiness had guaranteed. The divine attributes were pledged to give the son of Jesse great blessings; there was no fear that the covenant God would run back from his plighted word. If God has spoken we may well be glad: the very fact of a divine revelation is a joy. If the Lord had meant to destroy us he would not have spoken to us as he has done. But what God has spoken is a still further reason for gladness, for he has declared 'the sure mercies of David', and promised to establish his seed upon his throne, and to subdue all his enemies. David greatly rejoiced after the Lord had spoken to him by the mouth of Nathan. He sat before the Lord in a wonder of joy. See 1 Chronicles 17, and note that in the next chapter David began to act vigorously against his enemies, even as he vows to do in this psalm. Home conquests come first. Foes must be dislodged from Israel's territory, and lands properly settled and managed. On the other side of Jordan as well as on this the land must be put in order, and secured against all wandering marauders. Some rejoicing leads to inaction, but not that which is grounded upon a lively faith in the promise of God. See how David prays, as if he had the blessing already, and could share it among his men: this comes of having sung so heartily unto the Lord his helper. See how he resolves to act, like a man whose prayers are only a part of his life, and vital portions of his action.

Faith is neither a coward nor a sluggard, she knows that God is with her, and therefore she does valiantly. She knows that he will tread down her enemies, and therefore she arises to tread them down in his name. Where praise and prayer have preceded the battle, we may expect to see heroic deeds and decisive victories. 'Through God' is our secret support; from that source we draw all our courage, wisdom and strength. The church shall yet arouse herself to praise her God with all her heart, and then with songs and hosannas she will advance to the great battle. Her foes shall be over-thrown and utterly crushed by the power of her God, and the Lord's glory shall be above all the earth. Send it in our time, we beseech you, O Lord.

Meditation: *Because the church is God's beloved, the care of it should be most in our mind, and the love of the preservation of it should draw forth our prayer most in favour of it* (David Dickson).

Psalm 109:1-5

Suggested further reading: Jeremiah 17:14-18

'Do not keep silent, O God' is the cry of a man whose confidence in God is deep, and whose communion with him is very close and bold. Note that he only asks the Lord to speak: a word from God is all a believer needs. If we take care of God's honour he will take care of ours. We may look to him as the guardian of our character if we truly seek his glory. If we live to God's praise, he will in the long run give us praise among men.

Wicked men must say wicked things, and these we have reason to dread; but in addition they utter false and deceitful things, and these are worst of all. There is no knowing what may come out of mouths that are at once lewd and lying. No heart can imagine the misery caused to a good man by slanderous reports but that which is wounded by them: in all Satan's armoury there are no worse weapons than deceitful tongues. To have a reputation, over which we have watched with daily care, suddenly bespattered with the foulest aspersions, is painful beyond description; but when wicked and deceitful men get their mouths fully opened we can hardly expect to escape any more than others. Lying tongues cannot lie still. Bad tongues are not content to vilify bad men, but choose the most gracious of saints to be the objects of their attacks. Here is reason enough for prayer. The heart sinks when assailed with slander, for we do not know what may be said next, what friend may be alienated, what evil may be threatened, or what

misery may be caused to us and others. The air is full of
rumours, and impalpable shadows flit around; the mind is
confused with dread of unseen foes and invisible arrows.

Whichever way he turned they would hedge him in with
falsehood, misrepresentation, accusation and scorn. Whispers, sneers, insinuations, satires and open charges filled
his ear with a perpetual buzz, and all for no reason but
sheer hate. Each word was as full of venom as an egg is full
of meat; they could not speak without showing their teeth.
He had not provoked the quarrel or contributed to it, yet in
a thousand ways they laboured to 'corrode his comfort, and
destroy his case'. All this tended to make the suppliant feel
even more acutely the wrongs that were done to him. This
was a cruel case, and the sensitive mind of the psalmist
writhed under it. He did nothing else but pray. He became
prayer as they became malice. This was his answer to his
enemies: he appealed from men and their injustice to the
Judge of all the earth, who must do right. True bravery alone
can teach a man to leave his traducers unanswered, and
carry the case unto the Lord.

Meditation: *None prove worse enemies than those that have
received the greatest kindnesses, when once they turn unkind*
(Abraham Wright).

Psalm 109:6-20

Suggested further reading: Acts 1:15-20

We saw the harmless and innocent man upon his knees pouring out his lamentation: we are now to observe him rising from the mercy seat, inspired with prophetic energy, and pouring forth upon his foes the forewarnings of their doom. We shall hear him speak like a judge clothed with stern severity, or like the angel of doom robed in vengeance, or as the naked sword of justice when she bares her arm for execution. It is not for himself that he speaks so much as for all the slandered and the downtrodden, of whom he feels himself to be the representative and mouthpiece. He asks for justice, and as his soul is stung with cruel wrongs he asks with solemn deliberation, making no stint in his demands. To pity malice would be malice to mankind; to screen the crafty seekers of human blood would be cruelty to the oppressed. No, love, and truth, and pity lift their wounds to heaven, and implore vengeance on the enemies of the innocent and oppressed; those who render goodness itself a crime, and make innocence a motive for hate, deserve to find no mercy from the great Preserver of men. Vengeance is the prerogative of God, and as it would be a boundless calamity if evil were to go unpunished for ever, so it is an unspeakable blessing that the Lord will recompense the wicked and cruel man, and there are times and seasons when a good man ought to pray for that blessing. When the Judge of all threatens to punish tyrannical cruelty and false-hearted treachery, virtue gives her assent and consent. Amen, so let it be, says every just man in his inmost soul.

The Jews were so used to looking upon these verses as the doom of traitors, of cruel and deceitful mind, that Peter saw at once in the speedy death of Judas a fulfilment of this sentence, and a reason for the appointment of a successor who should take his place of oversight. A bad man does not make an office bad: another may use with benefit that which he perverted to ill uses.

Retaliation, not for private revenge, but as a measure of public justice, is demanded by the psalmist and deserved by the crime. Surely the malicious man cannot complain if he is judged by his own rule, and has his corn measured with his own bushel. Let him have what he loved. They are his own chickens, and they ought to come home to roost. He made the bed, let him lie on it himself. As he brewed, so let him drink. So all men say as a matter of justice, and though the higher law of love overrides all personal anger, yet as against the base characters described here even Christian love would not wish to see the sentence mitigated.

Meditation: *David was a man of gentle mould, and remark-ably free from the spirit of revenge, and therefore we may here conceive him to be speaking as a judge or as a repre-sentative man, in whose person great principles needed to be vindicated and great injuries redressed* (C. H. Spurgeon).

Psalm 109:21-31

Suggested further reading: Psalm 31:9-20

God's mercy is the star to which the Lord's people turn their eye when they are tossed with tempest and not comforted, for the peculiar bounty and goodness of that mercy have a charm for weary hearts. When man has no mercy we shall still find it in God. When man would devour we may look to God to deliver. His name and his mercy are two firm grounds for hope, and happy are those who know how to rest upon them. The Lord always has a tender regard to broken-hearted ones, and this is what the psalmist had become: the undeserved cruelty, the baseness, the slander of his remorseless enemies had pierced him to the soul, and he pleads this sad condition as a reason for speedy help. It is time for a friend to step in when the adversary cuts so deep. The case has become desperate without divine aid; now, therefore, is the Lord's time. The psalmist entreats the divine pity, because he had been brought to this forlorn and feeble condition by the long persecution that his tender heart had endured. Those who use these poisoned arrows are not always aware of the consequences; they scatter firebrands and death and say it is sport.

Laying hold of Jehovah by the appropriating word 'my', he implores his aid both to help him to bear his heavy load and to enable him to rise superior to it. He has described his own weakness, and the strength and fury of his foes, and by these two arguments he urges his appeal with double force. This is a very rich, short and suitable prayer for believers in any situation of peril, difficulty, or sorrow. God will not be absent when his people are on their trial; he will hold a brief for them and stand in court as their advocate, prepared to plead on their behalf. How different is this from the doom of the ungodly who has Satan at his right hand (v. 6). The court only met as a matter of form, the malicious had made up their minds to the verdict, they judged him guilty, for their hate condemned him, indeed, they pronounced sentence of damnation upon the very soul of their victim: but what did it matter? The great King was in court, and their sentence was turned against themselves. Nothing can more sweetly sustain the heart of a slandered believer than the firm conviction that God is near to all who are wronged, and is sure to work out their salvation. O Lord, save us from the severe trial of slander: deal in your righteousness with all those who spitefully assail the characters of holy men, and cause all who are smarting under calumny and reproach to come forth unsullied from the affliction, even as did your only-begotten Son. Amen.

Meditation: *Men's curses are impotent, God's blessings are omnipotent* (Matthew Henry).

Psalm 110:1-3

Suggested further reading: Matthew 22:41-46

David in spirit heard the solemn voice of Jehovah speaking to the Messiah from of old. What wonderful fellowship there has been between the Father and the Son! From this secret and intimate communion spring the covenant of grace and all its marvellous arrangements. All the great acts of grace are brought into actual being by the Word of God: had he not spoken, there would have been no manifestation of Deity to us. But in the beginning was the Word, and from of old there was mysterious fellowship between the Father and his Son Jesus Christ concerning his people and the great contest on their behalf between himself and the powers of evil.

Though David was a firm believer in the unity of the Godhead, he yet spiritually discerns the two persons, distinguishes between them, and perceives that he has a peculiar interest in the second, for he calls him 'my Lord'. This was an anticipation of the exclamation of Thomas, 'My Lord and my God,' and it expresses the psalmist's reverence, his obedience, his believing appropriation and his joy in Christ. It is well to have clear views of the mutual relations of the persons of the blessed Trinity; indeed, the knowledge of these truths is essential for our comfort and growth in grace. There is a manifest distinction in the divine persons, since one speaks to another; yet the Godhead is one.

Jehovah calls Adonai, our Lord, to the repose and honours of his celestial seat. His work is done, and he may sit; it is well done, and he may sit at his right hand; it will have grand results, and he may therefore quietly wait to see the complete victory that is certain to follow. The glorious Jehovah thus addresses the Christ as our Saviour; for, says David, he said 'to my Lord'. Jesus is placed in the seat of power, dominion and dignity, and is to sit there by divine appointment while Jehovah fights for him, and lays every rebel beneath his feet. He sits there by the Father's ordinance and call, and will sit there despite all the raging of his adversaries, till they are all brought to utter shame by his putting his foot upon their necks. In this sitting he is our representative. The mediatorial kingdom will last until the last enemy shall be destroyed, and then, according to the inspired word, 'comes the end, when he shall have delivered up the kingdom to God the Father'. The work of subduing the nations is now in the hand of the great God, who by his providence will accomplish it to the glory of his Son. His word is pledged to it, and the session of his Son at his right hand is its guarantee; therefore let us never fear as to the future.

Meditation: *It was a higher honour to have Christ for his son, than to be a king; yet David does not say that Christ is his son, but rejoices that Christ is his Lord, and he Christ's servant* (John Albert Bengel).

Psalm 110:4-7

Suggested further reading: Hebrews 7:14-28

We have reached the heart of the psalm, which is also the very centre and soul of our faith. Our Lord Jesus is a priest-king by the ancient oath of Jehovah. It must be a solemn and a sure matter which leads the Eternal to swear, and with him an oath fixes and settles the decree for ever; but in this case, as if to make assurance a thousand times sure, it is added, 'and will not relent'. Jesus is sworn to be the priest of his people, and he must abide so even to the end, because his commission is sealed by the unchanging oath of the immutable Jehovah. If his priesthood could be revoked, and his authority removed, it would be the end of all hope and life for the people whom he loves; but this sure rock is the basis of our security — the oath of God establishes our glorious Lord both in his priesthood and in his throne. It is the Lord who has constituted him a priest for ever, he has done it by oath, that oath is without repentance, is taking effect now, and will stand throughout all ages: hence our security in him is placed beyond all question.

The order of Melchizedek's priesthood was the most ancient and primitive, the most free from ritual and ceremony, the most natural and simple, and at the same time the most honourable. That ancient patriarch was the father of his people, and at the same time ruled and taught them; he swayed both the sceptre and the censer, reigned in righteousness, and offered sacrifice before the Lord.

There has never arisen another like him since his days, for whenever the kings of Judah attempted to seize the sacerdotal office they were driven back to their confusion; God would have no king-priest save his Son. Melchizedek's office was exceptional; none preceded or succeeded him. He comes upon the page of history mysteriously: no pedigree is given, no date of birth, or mention of death; he blesses Abraham, receives tithe, and vanishes from the scene amid honours which show that he was greater than the founder of the chosen nation. He is seen but once, and that once suffices. Our Lord Jesus, like Melchizedek, stands forth before us as a priest of divine ordaining; not made a priest by fleshly birth, as the sons of Aaron. He mentions neither father, mother, nor descent, as his right to the sacred office; he stands upon his personal merits, by himself alone; as no man came before him in his work, so none can follow after; his order begins and ends in his own person, and in himself it is eternal. The king-priest has been here and left his blessing upon the believing seed, and now he sits in glory in his complete character, atoning for us by the merit of his blood, and exercising all power on our behalf.

Meditation: *The present psalm grows up from the former psalm, as the Hill of Olivet, the Hill of Ascension rises up from the Vale of Gethsemane below it* (Christopher Wordsworth).

Psalm 111

Suggested further reading: Ecclesiastes 12:9-14

In design, in size, in number, in excellence, all the works of the Lord are great. Even the little things of God are great. Those who love their Maker delight in his handiwork, they perceive that there is more in it than appears upon the surface, and therefore they bend their minds to study and understand it. The devout naturalist ransacks nature, the earnest student of history pries into hidden facts and dark stories, and the man of God digs into the mines of Scripture, and hoards up each grain of its golden truth. God's works are worthy of our researches, they yield us wonderfully blended instruction and pleasure, and appearing to be far greater after investigation, they grow more than before. Men's works are noble from a distance; God's works are great when sought out.

Grace is as conspicuous as righteousness in the great work of God, indeed, a fulness of tender love is seen in all that he has done. He treats his people with great consideration for their weakness and infirmity, having the same pity for them as a father has towards his children. Should we not praise him for this? A silver thread of loving-kindness runs through the entire fabric of God's work of salvation and providence, and never once is it left out in the whole piece. Let the memories of his saints bear witness to this fact with grateful joy. No promise of the Lord shall fall to the ground, nor will any part of the great compact of eternal love be revoked or allowed to sink into oblivion. The covenant of grace is the plan of the great work that the Lord works out for his people, and it will never be departed from. The Lord has set his hand and seal to it, his glory and honour are involved in it, indeed, his very name hangs upon it, and he will not, even in the least jot or tittle, cease to remember it. His divine decree has made the covenant of his grace a settled and eternal institution: redemption by blood proves that the covenant cannot be altered, for it ratifies and establishes it beyond all recall. This, too, is reason for the loudest praise.

'The fear of the LORD is the beginning of wisdom.' It is its first principle, but it is also its head and chief attainment. The word 'beginning' in Scripture sometimes means the chief; and true religion is at one and the same time the first element of wisdom, and its chief fruit. To know God so as to walk aright before him is the greatest of all the applied sciences. Holy reverence of God leads us to praise him, and this is the point that the psalm drives at, for it is a wise act on the part of a creature towards his Creator.

Meditation: *The fear of the Lord and the laws of God give men a good understanding, and are able to make them wise unto salvation* (Matthew Henry).

Psalm 112:1-5

Suggested further reading: Colossians 3:12-17

According to the last verse of Psalm 111, 'The fear of the
LORD is the beginning of wisdom'; this man, therefore, has
begun to be wise, and wisdom has brought him present
happiness, and secured him eternal felicity. Jehovah is so
great that he is to be feared and revered by all those that are
round about him, and he is at the same time so infinitely
good that the fear is sweetened into filial love, and becomes
a delightful emotion, by no means engendering bondage.

The true seed of the righteous are those who follow them
in their virtues, even as believers are the seed of Abraham,
because they imitate his faith. These are the real heroes of
their era, the truly great men among the sons of Adam; their
lives are sublime, and their power upon their age is far
greater than appears at first sight. The race of sincere,
devout, righteous men, is kept up from age to age, and ever
abides under the blessing of God. The godly may be persecuted, but they shall not be forsaken; the curses of men
cannot deprive them of the blessing of God, for the words
of Balaam are true, 'He has blessed, and I cannot reverse it.'
Their children also are under the special care of heaven,
and as a rule it shall be found that they inherit the divine
blessing. Honesty and integrity are better cornerstones for
an honourable house than mere cunning and avarice, or
even talent and push. To fear God and to walk uprightly is
a higher nobility than blood or birth can bestow.

We are at best but humble copies of the great original; still we are copies, and because we are so we praise the Lord, who has created us anew in Christ Jesus. The upright man is 'gracious', that is, full of kindness to all around him; he is not sour and churlish, but he is courteous to friends, kind to the needy, forgiving to the erring, and earnest for the good of all. He is also 'full of compassion'; that is to say, he tenderly feels for others, pities them, and as far as he can assists them in their time of trouble. He does not need to be driven to benevolence, he is brimful of humanity; it is his joy to sympathize with the sorrowing. He is also said to be 'righteous': in all his transactions with his fellow men he obeys the dictates of right, and none can say that he goes beyond or defrauds his neighbour. His justice is, however, tempered with compassion, and seasoned with graciousness. Such men are to be found in our churches, and they are by no means so rare as the censorious imagine; but at the same time they are far scarcer than the breadth of profession might lead us to hope. Lord, make us all to possess these admirable qualities.

Meditation: *This psalm is a praising of God for blessing the believer, and the whole psalm proves that the believer is blessed* (David Dickson).

Psalm 112:6-10

Suggested further reading: Romans 2:1-16

God has rooted and established the righteous man so that neither men nor devils shall sweep him from his place. His prosperity shall be permanent, and not like that of the gambler and the cheat, whose gains are evanescent. His reputation shall be bright and lustrous from year to year, for it is not a mere pretence; his home shall be permanent, and he shall not need to wander from place to place as a bird that wanders from her nest; and even his memory shall be abiding, for a good man is not soon forgotten.

He shall have no dread that evil tidings will come, and he shall not be alarmed when they do come. His heart being fixed in solid reliance upon God, a change in his circumstances but slightly affects him; faith has made him firm and steadfast, and therefore if the worst should come to the worst, he would remain quiet and patient, waiting for the salvation of God. His love to God is deep and true, his confidence in God is firm and unmoved; his courage has a firm foundation, and is supported by omnipotence. He has become settled by experience, and confirmed by years. He is not a rolling stone, but a pillar in the house of the Lord. He is ready to face any adversary — a holy heart gives a brave face. All through the conflict, even till he seizes the victory, he is devoid of fear. When the battle wavers, and the result seems doubtful, he nevertheless believes in God, and is a stranger to dismay. Grace makes him desire his enemies' good: though nature leads him to wish to see justice done to his cause, he does not desire for those who injure him anything by way of private revenge.

The tenth and last verse sets forth very forcibly the contrast between the righteous and the ungodly, thus making the blessedness of the godly appear all the more remarkable. The ungodly shall first see the example of the saints to their own condemnation, and shall at last behold the happiness of the godly and to the increase of their eternal misery. The child of wrath shall be obliged to witness the blessedness of the righteous, though the sight shall make him gnaw his own heart. While the righteous shall endure for ever, and their memory shall be always green, the ungodly man and his name shall rot from off the face of the earth. He desired to be the founder of a family, and to be remembered as some great one: he shall pass away and his name shall die with him. How wide is the gulf which separates the righteous from the wicked, and how different are the portions which the Lord deals out to them. Oh, for grace to be blessed of the Lord! This will make us praise him with our whole heart.

Meditation: *None of us likes the idea of being forgotten, and yet the only way to avoid it is to be righteous before God* (C. H. Spurgeon).

Psalm 113:1-5

Suggested further reading: Isaiah 40:18-31

Praise is an essential offering at all the solemn feasts of the people of God. Prayer is the myrrh, and praise is the frankincense, and both of these must be presented to the Lord. How can we pray for mercy for the future if we do not bless God for his love in the past? The Lord has wrought all good things for us, let us therefore adore him. If God's own servants do not praise him, who will? The name of Jehovah is used three times, and may be regarded as a thinly veiled allusion to that holy mystery by those of us who understand the doctrine of the Trinity in unity. Let Father, Son and Holy Spirit all be praised as the one, only, living and true God. While praising him aloud, the people were also to bless him in the silence of their hearts, wishing glory to his name, success to his cause, and triumph to his truth. By mentioning 'the name', the psalmist is teaching us to bless each of the attributes of the Most High, which are, as it were, the letters of his name: not quarrelling with his justice or his severity, nor slavishly dreading his power, but accepting him as we find him revealed in the inspired Word and by his own acts, and loving him and praising him as such. We must not give the Lord a new name nor invent a new nature, for that would be the setting up of a false god. Every time we think of the God of Scripture we should bless him, and his august name should never be pronounced without joyful reverence.

From early morn till eventide ceaseless hymn should rise unto Jehovah's throne, and from east to west over the whole round earth pure worship should be rendered unto his glory. So ought it to be; and blessed be God, we are not without faith that it shall be. We trust that before the world's dread evening comes, the glorious name of the Lord will be proclaimed among all nations, and all people shall call him blessed. At the first proclamation of the gospel the name of the Lord was glorious throughout the whole earth. Will it not be much more so, before the end comes? At any rate, this is the desire of our souls. Meanwhile, let us endeavour to sanctify every day with praise to God.

Though the Gentiles did not know him, Jehovah was their ruler: their false gods were no gods, and their kings were puppets in his hands. The Lord is high above all the learning, judgement and imagination of heathen sages, and far beyond the pomp and might of the monarchs of the nations. None can be compared with him for an instant; Israel's God is without parallel; our own God in covenant stands alone, and none can be likened unto him.

Meditation: *It is the nature of love, that the one whom we love we prefer to all others, and we ask, 'Who is like my beloved?'* (Wolfgang Musculus).

Psalm 113:6-9

Suggested further reading: Isaiah 57:15-21

The Lord dwells so far on high that even to observe heavenly things he must humble himself. He must stoop to view the skies, and bow to see what angels do. What, then, must be his condescension, seeing that he observes the humblest of his servants upon earth, and makes them sing for joy like Mary when she said, 'You have regarded the low estate of your handmaiden'? How wonderful are these words of Isaiah: 'For thus says the high and lofty One who inhabits eternity, whose name is Holy; I dwell in the high and holy place, with him who has a contrite and humble spirit, to revive the spirit of the humble, and to revive the heart of the contrite ones.' Heathen philosophers could not believe that the great God was observant of the small events of human history; they pictured him as abiding in serene indifference to all the wants and woes of his creatures. 'Our Rock is not as their rock'; we have a God who is high above all gods, and yet who is our Father, knowing what we need before we ask him; our Shepherd, who supplies our needs; our Guardian, who counts the hairs of our heads; our tender and considerate Friend, who sympathizes in all our griefs. Truly the name of our condescending God should be praised wherever it is known.

The Lord does nothing by halves: when he raises men from the dust he is not content till he places them among the peers of his kingdom. We are made kings and priests unto God, and we shall reign for ever and ever. Instead of poverty, he gives us the wealth of princes; and instead of dishonour, he gives us a more exalted rank than that of the great ones of the earth. All his people are princes, and so the text teaches us that God places needy souls whom he favours among the princes of princes. He often enables those who have been most despairing to rise to the greatest heights of spirituality and gracious attainment, for those who once were last shall be first. Though less than the least of all saints Paul was, nevertheless, in no way considered beneath the very chief of the apostles; and in our own times, Bunyan, the blaspheming tinker, was raised into another John, whose dream almost rivals the visions of the Apocalypse. Such verses as these should give great encouragement to those who are lowest in their own esteem. The Lord pours contempt upon princes; but as for those who are in the dust and on the ash heap, he looks upon them with compassion, acts towards them in grace, and in their case displays the riches of his glory by Christ Jesus. Those who have experienced such amazing favour should sing continual hallelujahs to the God of their salvation.

Meditation: *If it is such condescension for God to behold things in heaven and earth, what an amazing condescension was it for the Son of God to come from heaven to earth and take our nature upon him, that he might seek and save them that were lost* (Matthew Henry).

Psalm 114

Suggested further reading: 1 Corinthians 10:1-13

The song begins with a burst, as if the poetic fury could not be restrained, but overleaped all bounds. The soul elevated and filled with a sense of divine glory cannot wait to fashion a preface, but springs at once into the middle of its theme. Israel emphatically came out of Egypt, out of the population among whom they had been scattered, from under the yoke of bondage, and from under the personal grasp of the king who had made the people into national slaves. Israel came out with a high hand and a stretched-out arm, defying all the power of the empire, and making the whole of Egypt travail in severe anguish, as the chosen nation was, as it were, born out of its midst.

In their exodus of Egypt all the people were separated unto the Lord as a peculiar people, a nation of priests whose motto should be, 'Holiness unto the Lord.' Judah was the Lord's 'holy thing', set apart for his special use. The nation was peculiarly Jehovah's dominion, for it was governed by a theocracy in which God alone was King. It was his domain in a sense in which the rest of the world was outside his kingdom. The whole people were the shrine of Deity, and their camp was one great temple. What a change there must have been for the godly amongst them, from the idolatries and blasphemies of the Egyptians to the holy worship and righteous rule of the great King in Jeshurun. They lived in a world of wonders, where God was seen in the wondrous bread they ate and in the water they drank, as well as in the solemn worship of his holy place. When the Lord is manifestly present in a church, and his gracious rule obeyed, what a golden age has come, and what honourable privileges his people enjoy! May it be so among us!

Our deliverance from under the yoke of sin is strikingly typified in the going up of Israel from Egypt, and so also was the victory of our Lord over the powers of death and hell. The Exodus should therefore be earnestly remembered by Christian hearts. Did not Moses on the mount of transfiguration speak to our Lord of 'the exodus' that he should shortly accomplish at Jerusalem; and is it not written of the hosts above that they sing the song of Moses the servant of God, and of the Lamb? Do we not ourselves expect another coming of the Lord, when before his face heaven and earth shall flee away and there shall be no more sea? We join then with the singers around the Passover table and make their Hallel ours, for we too have been led out of bondage and guided like a flock through a desert land, wherein the Lord supplies our wants with heavenly manna and water from the Rock of ages. Praise the Lord.

Meditation: *Christ is a fountain of living waters to his Israel, from whom they receive grace for grace* (Matthew Henry).

Psalm 115:1-2

Suggested further reading: 2 Kings 19:8-19

It will be well to remember that this psalm was sung at the Passover, and therefore it bears relationship to the deliverance from Egypt. Its burden seems to be a prayer that the living God, who had been so glorious at the Red Sea and at the Jordan, should again for his name's sake display the wonders of his power.

When Israel marched into Canaan, all the people round about were terrified, because of Jehovah, the mighty God; but the nations had shaken off this dread since there had been of late no remarkable display of miraculous power. The saddest part of all their trouble was that their God was no longer feared and dreaded by their adversaries. Therefore Israel cried unto her God that he would again make bare his arm. The repetition of the words 'not unto us' would seem to indicate a very serious desire to renounce any glory that they might at any time have proudly applied to themselves, and it also sets forth the vehemence of their wish that God would magnify his own name at any cost to them. How could the heathen think Jehovah a merciful God if he gave his people over to the hands of their enemies? How could they believe him to be faithful and true if, after all his solemn covenant engagements, he utterly rejected his chosen nation? God is very jealous of the two glorious attributes of grace and truth, and the plea that these may not be dishonoured has great weight with him. In these times, when the first victories of the gospel are only remembered as histories of a dim and distant past, sceptics are apt to boast that the gospel has lost its youthful strength and they even presume to cast a slur upon the name of God himself. We may therefore rightly entreat the divine interposition that the apparent blot may be removed from his badge, and that his own word may shine forth gloriously as in the days of old. We may not desire the triumph of our opinions, for our own sakes, or for the honour of a sect, but we may confidently pray for the triumph of truth, that God himself may be honoured.

Why should the nations be allowed with a sneer of contempt to question the existence, and mercy, and faithfulness of Jehovah? They are always ready to blaspheme; we may well pray that they may not derive a reason for so doing from the course of providence, or the decline of the church. Our honour and the honour of the church are small matters, but the glory of God is the jewel of the universe, of which all else is but the setting. We may come to the Lord and plead his jealousy for his name, being well assured that he will not allow that name to be dishonoured.

Meditation: *So much as we sacrifice to our own credit, to the dexterity of our hands, or the sagacity of our wit, we detract from God* (Stephen Charnock).

Psalm 115:3-8

Suggested further reading: 2 Kings 19:20-28

Supreme above all opposing powers, the Lord reigns on a throne high and lifted up. Incomprehensible in essence, he rises above the loftiest thought of the wise; absolute in will and infinite in power, he is superior to the limitations which belong to earth and time. This God is our God, and we are not ashamed to own him, although he may not work miracles at the beck and call of every vain-glorious boaster who may choose to challenge him. Even if our God is neither seen nor heard, and is not to be worshipped under any outward symbol, he none the less real and true, for he is where his adversaries can never be — in the heavens, from where he stretches forth his sceptre, and rules with boundless power.

However distasteful to his enemies, the Lord has accomplished all his good pleasure without difficulty; even when his adversaries raved and raged against him they have been compelled to carry out his designs against their will. Even proud Pharaoh, when most defiant of the Lord, was but as clay upon the potter's wheel, and the Lord's end and design in him were fully answered. We may well endure the jeering question, 'Where now is their God?' while we are perfectly sure that his providence is undisturbed, his throne unshaken, and his purposes unchanged. What he has done he will yet do, his counsel shall stand, and he will carry out all his desires. At the end of the great drama of human history, the omnipotence of God and his immutability and faithfulness will be more than vindicated to the eternal confusion of his adversaries.

How strange that a man should think that he can make a god! Can madness go further? Our God is a spirit, and his hands made the heavens and the earth. We may well worship him, and we need not be disturbed at the sneering question of those who are so insane as to refuse to adore the living God, and yet bow their knees before images of their own carving. We may make an application of all this to the times in which we are now living. The god of modern thought is the creation of the thinker himself, evolved out of his own consciousness, or fashioned according to his own notion of what a god should be. Now, it is evident that such a being is no God. A god who can be fashioned by our own thoughts is no more a god than the image manufactured or produced by our own hands. The true God must of necessity reveal himself. It is clearly impossible that a being who can be contrived and comprehended by man's reasoning should be the infinite and incomprehensible God. Their idols are blinded reason and diseased thought, the product of men's muddled brains, and they will come to nothing.

Meditation: *It is impossible that there should be a God at all except the God of revelation* (C. H. Spurgeon).

Psalm 115:9-18

Suggested further reading: 2 Kings 19:29-37

Whatever others do, let the elect of heaven keep fast to the God who chose them. Jehovah is the God of Jacob; let his children prove their loyalty to their God by their confidence in him. Whatever our trouble may be, and however fierce the blasphemous language of our enemies, let us not fear nor falter, but confidently rest in him who is able to vindicate his own honour, and protect his own servants.

The Lord has many blessings, each one worthy of remembrance; he blesses and blesses and blesses again. Where he has once bestowed his favour he continues it; his blessing delights to visit the same house very often and to abide where it has once lodged. Blessing does not impoverish the Lord: he has multiplied his mercies in the past, and he will pour them forth in great abundance in the future. He will have a general blessing for all who fear him, a peculiar blessing for the whole house of Israel, and a double blessing for the sons of Aaron. It is his nature to bless, it is his prerogative to bless, it is his glory to bless, it is his delight to bless; he has promised to bless, and therefore be sure of this: he will bless and bless and bless without ceasing.

Our afflictions and depressions of spirit shall not cause us to suspend our praises; neither shall old age and increasing infirmities damp the celestial fires, no, nor shall even death itself cause us to cease from the delightful occupation. The spiritually dead cannot praise God, but the life within us constrains us to do so. The ungodly may abide in silence, but we will lift up our voices to the praise of Jehovah. Even though for a time he may work no miracle, and we may see no peculiar interposition of his power, yet on the strength of what he has done in ages past we will continue to praise his name 'until the day break, and the shadows flee away', when he shall once more shine forth as the sun to gladden the faces of his children. The present time is auspicious for commencing a life of praise, since today he bids us hear his voice of mercy. 'From this time forth' is the suggestion of wisdom, for this duty ought not to be delayed; and it is the dictate of gratitude, for there are pressing reasons for prompt thankfulness. Once begin praising God and we have entered upon an endless service. Even eternity cannot exhaust the reasons why God should be glorified.

Meditation: *Mercy, according to the covenant of grace, gives the same grounds of faith and hope to everyone within the church; so that whatever favour is shown to one of God's people, it is of a general use and profit to others* (Thomas Manton).

Psalm 116:1-8

Suggested further reading: 1 Thessalonians 5:15-28

Every believer ought to be able to declare without the slightest hesitation, 'I love the Lord.' It was required under the law, but was never produced in the heart of man except by the grace of God, and upon gospel principles. It is a great thing to say 'I love the Lord': for the sweetest of all graces and the surest of all evidences of salvation is love. It is great goodness on the part of God that he condescends to be loved by such poor creatures as we are, and it is a sure proof that he has been at work in our heart when we can say, 'You know all things, you know that I love you.' The psalmist not only knows that he loves God, but he also knows why he does so. When love can justify itself with a reason, it is deep, strong and abiding. We have reason, superabundant reason, for loving the Lord; and so because in this case principle and passion, reason and emotion go together, they make up an admirable state of mind. David's reason for his love was the love of God in hearing his prayers.

David was enclosed in a ring of deadly grief. The psalmist was sought for by trouble and it found him out, and when he himself became a seeker he found no relief, but double distress. When the good man could not run to God, he called to him. In his extremity his faith came to the fore: it was useless to call on man, and it may have seemed almost as useless to appeal to the Lord; but yet with his whole soul he invoked all the attributes which make up the sacred name of Jehovah, and thus he proved the truth of his confidence.

In hearing prayer the grace and righteousness of Jehovah are both conspicuous. It is a great favour to hear a sinner's prayer, and yet since the Lord has promised to do so, he is not unrighteous to forget his promise and disregard the cries of his people. The combination of grace and righteousness in the dealings of God with his servants can only be explained by remembering the atoning sacrifice of our Lord Jesus Christ. At the cross we see how gracious is the Lord and righteous. The psalmist explained the reasons for his determination to call upon God as long as he lived, and none can question but that he had come to a most justifiable resolve. When from so great a depth he had been uplifted by so special an interposition of God, he was undoubtedly bound to be for ever the hearty worshipper of Jehovah, to whom he owed so much. May God the Holy Spirit help us so to pray without ceasing and in everything to give thanks, for this is the will of God in Christ Jesus concerning us.

Meditation: *Do we not all feel the force of the reasoning, and will we not carry out the conclusion?* (C. H. Spurgeon).

Psalm 116:9-13

Suggested further reading: 1 Corinthians 11:23-34

The psalmist's second resolution is to live as in the sight of God in the midst of the sons of men. By a man's walk is understood his way of life: some men live only as in the sight of their fellow men, having regard to human judgement and opinion; but the truly gracious man considers the presence of God, and acts under the influence of his all-observing eye. 'You, God, see me' is a far better influence than 'My master sees me.' The life of faith, hope, holy fear and true holiness is produced by a sense of living and walking before the Lord, and he who has been favoured with divine deliverances in answer to prayer finds his own experience the best reason for a holy life, and the best assistance to his endeavours. We know that God is near to his people in a special manner: what manner of persons ought we to be in all holy conversation and godliness?

No man should speak about the things of God unless he believes. The speech of the waverer is mischievous, but the tongue of the believer is profitable; the most powerful speech that has ever been uttered by the lips of man has emanated from a heart fully persuaded of the truth of God. Not only the psalmist, but also such men as Luther and Calvin, and other great witnesses for the faith, could each one most heartily say, 'I believed, therefore have I spoken.' It is of little use to be harping on the string of man's imperfection and deceitfulness; it is infinitely better to praise the perfection and faithfulness of God. The question is a very proper one: the Lord has rendered so much mercy to us that we ought to look about us, and look within us, and see what can be done by us to manifest our gratitude. We ought not only to do what is plainly before us, but also with holy ingenuity to search out various ways by which we may render fresh praises to our God. Each person should have his own peculiar mode of expressing gratitude. The Lord sends each one a special benefit. Let each one enquire, 'What shall I render? What form of service would be most becoming in me?' The psalmist will utter blessings and thanksgivings and prayers, and then drink of the cup that the Lord had filled with his saving grace. What a cup this is! Upon the table of infinite love stands the cup full of blessing. It is ours by faith to take it in our hand, make it our own, and partake of it, and then with joyful hearts to laud and magnify the gracious one who has filled it for our sakes that we may drink and be refreshed.

Meditation: *Beloved reader, let us pause here and take a long and deep draught from the cup which Jesus filled, and then with devout hearts let us worship God* (C. H. Spurgeon).

Psalm 116:14-19

Suggested further reading: 1 Peter 3:13-22

The psalmist has already stated his third resolution, to devote himself to the worship of God evermore, and here he commences the performance of that resolve. The vows that he had made in anguish, he now determines to fulfil. He does so at once, now, and in public, 'in the presence of all his people'. Good resolutions cannot be carried out too speedily; vows become debts, and debts should be paid. It is well to have witnesses to the payment of just debts, and we need not be ashamed to have witnesses to the fulfilling of holy vows, for this will show that we are not ashamed of our Lord, and it may be a great benefit to those who look on and hear us publicly sounding forth the praises of our prayer-hearing God. How can those who have never openly confessed their Saviour do this? O secret disciples, what do you say to this verse? Be encouraged to come into the light and own your Redeemer. If, indeed, you have been saved, come forward and declare it in his own appointed way.

Those who are redeemed with precious blood are so dear to God that even their deaths are precious to him. The death-beds of saints are very precious to the church, she often learns much from them; they are very precious to all believers, who delight to treasure up the last words of the departed; but they are most of all precious to the Lord Jehovah himself, who view the triumphant deaths of his gracious ones with sacred delight. If we have walked before him in the land of the living, we need not fear to die before him when the hour of our departure is at hand. In paying his vows the man of God re-dedicates himself unto God; the offering that he brings is himself. He is fond of this occupation, and several times in this psalm declares that 'he will call upon the name of the Lord', while at the same time he rejoices that he had done so many a time before. Good feelings and actions bear repeating: the more of hearty callings upon God the better.

The very thought of the beloved Zion touched his heart, and he writes as if he were actually addressing Jerusalem, whose name was dear to him. There would he pay his vows, in the abode of fellowship, in the very heart of Judea, in the place to which the tribes went up, the tribes of the Lord. God's praise is not to be confined to a closet, nor his name to be whispered in holes and corners, as if we were afraid that men should hear us; but in the thick of the throng, and in the very centre of assemblies, we should lift up heart and voice unto the Lord, and invite others to join with us in adoring him, saying, 'Praise the LORD.'

Meditation: *Be bold, be bold, you servants of the Lord, in sounding forth the praises of your God. Wicked men are over-bold in pouring forth their blasphemies to the dishonour of God; they care not who hear them. Shall they be more auda-cious to dishonour God, than you are zealous to honour him?* (William Gouge).

Psalm 117

Suggested further reading: Romans 4:13-25

This is an exhortation to the Gentiles to glorify Jehovah, and a clear proof that the Old Testament spirit differed widely from that narrow and contracted national bigotry with which the Jews of our Lord's day became so inveterately diseased. The nations could not be expected to join in the praise of Jehovah unless they were also to partake of the benefits that Israel enjoyed. Hence the psalm was an intimation to Israel that the grace and mercy of their God were not to be confined to one nation, but would in happier days be extended to all the race of man. This was how Moses had prophesied when he said, 'Rejoice, O Gentiles, with his people' (Deut. 32:43), according to the Hebrew. The nations were to be his people. He would call them a people that were not a people, and her beloved that was not beloved. We know and believe that no one tribe of men shall be unrepresented in the universal song which shall ascend unto the Lord of all. Individuals have already been gathered out of every kindred and people and tongue by the preaching of the gospel, and these have most heart-ily joined in magnifying the grace that sought them out, and brought them to know the Saviour. These are but the advance-guard of a number which no man can number, who will come before long to worship the all-glorious one. Having praised him once, do it again, and do it still more fervently, daily increasing in the reverence and zeal with which you extol the Most High. Not only praise him nationally by your rulers, but popularly in your masses. The multitude of the common folk shall bless the Lord. Inasmuch as the matter is spoken of twice, its certainty is confirmed, and the Gentiles must and shall extol Jehovah — all of them, without exception. Under the gospel age we worship no new god, but the God of Abraham is our God for ever and ever; the God of the whole earth shall he be called.

The Lord is kind to us as his creatures, and merciful to us as sinners, hence his merciful kindness to us as sinful creatures. This mercy has been very great, or powerful. The mighty grace of God has prevailed even as the waters of the flood prevailed over the earth: breaking over all bounds, it has flowed towards all portions of the multiplied race of man. In Christ Jesus, God has shown mercy mixed with kindness, and that to the very highest degree. We can all join in this grateful acknowledgement, and in the praise that is therefore due. He has kept his covenant promise that in the seed of Abraham should all nations of the earth be blessed, and he will eternally keep every single promise of that covenant to all those who put their trust in him. This should be a cause of constant and grateful praise, wherefore the psalm concludes as it began, with Hallelujah.

Meditation: *In God's worship it is not always necessary to be long; few words sometimes say what is sufficient, as this short psalm gives us to understand* (David Dickson).

Psalm 118:1-4

Suggested further reading: Ezra 3:8-13

Those who only praise God because he does them good should rise to a higher note and give thanks to him because he is good. In the truest sense he alone is good, therefore in all gratitude the Lord should have the royal portion. If others seem to be good, he is good. If others are good in a measure, he is good beyond measure. When others behave badly towards us, it should only stir us up to give thanks more heartily unto the Lord, because he is good; and when we ourselves are conscious that we are far from being good, we should bless him all the more reverently that 'he is good'. We must never tolerate an instant's unbelief as to the goodness of the Lord; whatever else may be questionable, this is absolutely certain, that Jehovah is good; his nature is always the same, and always good. It is not only that he was good, and will be good, but he is good, let his providence be what it may. Therefore let us even at this present moment, though the skies be dark with clouds, yet give thanks unto his name.

Mercy is a great part of his goodness, and one which more concerns us than any other, for we are sinners and have need of his mercy. Angels may say that he is good, but they do not need his mercy and cannot therefore take an equal delight in it; inanimate creation declares that 'he is good', but it cannot feel his mercy, for it has never transgressed; but man, deeply guilty and graciously forgiven, beholds mercy as the very focus and centre of the goodness of the Lord. The endurance of the divine mercy is a special subject for song: notwithstanding our sins, our trials, our fears, his mercy 'endures for ever'. The best of earthly joys pass away, and even the world itself grows old and hastens to decay, but there is no change in the mercy of God; he was faithful to our forefathers, he is merciful to us, and will be gracious to our children and our children's children.

The fourfold testimonies to the everlasting mercy of God which are now before us speak like four evangelists, each one declaring the very pith and marrow of the gospel; and they stand like four angels at the four corners of the earth holding the winds in their hands, restraining the plagues of the latter days that the mercy and long-suffering of God may endure towards the sons of men. Here are four cords to bind the sacrifice to the four horns of the altar, and four trumpets with which to proclaim the year of jubilee to every quarter of the world. Let not the reader pass on to the consideration of the rest of the psalm until he has with all his might lifted up both heart and voice to praise the Lord, 'for his mercy endures for ever'.

Meditation: *The Son of God himself when addressed by someone as 'Good Master', by one, namely, who beholding his flesh, and comprehending not the fulness of his divine nature, considered him as man only, replied, 'Why do you call me good? No one is good — except God alone.' And what is this but to say, If you wish to call me good, recognize me as God?* (Augustine).

Psalm 118:5-14

Suggested further reading: Isaiah 31:1-9

Prayers that come out of distress generally come out of the heart, and therefore they go to the heart of God. It is sweet to recollect our prayers, and often profitable to tell others of them after they are heard. Prayer may be bitter in the offering, but it will be sweet in the answering. The man of God had called upon the Lord when he was not in distress, and therefore he found it natural and easy to call upon him when he was in distress. He worshipped, he praised, he prayed: for all this is included in calling upon God, even when he was in a straitened condition.

The psalmist naturally rejoiced in the divine help; all men turned against him, but God was his defender and advocate, accomplishing the divine purposes of his grace. He does not say that he should not suffer, but that he would not fear: the favour of God infinitely outweighed the hatred of men, therefore setting the one against the other he felt that he had no reason to be afraid. He was calm and confident, though surrounded with enemies, and so let all believers be, for in this they honour the Lord. God is infinitely more able to help, and more likely to help, than man, and therefore prudence suggests that we put our confidence in him above all others. It is also morally better to do so, for it is the duty of the creature to trust in the Creator. God has a claim upon his creatures' faith, he deserves to be trusted; and to place our reliance upon another rather than upon himself is a direct insult to his faithfulness. It is better in the sense of safer, since we can never be sure of our ground if we rely upon mortal man, but we are always secure in the hands of our God. It is better in its effect upon ourselves: to trust in man tends to make us mean, crouching, dependent; but confidence in God elevates, produces a sacred quiet of spirit, and sanctifies the soul. It is, moreover, much better to trust in God, as far as the result is concerned; for in many cases the human object of our trust fails from want of ability, from want of generosity, from want of affection, or from want of memory; but the Lord, so far from failing, does for us exceeding abundantly above all that we ask or even think.

The poet warrior knew that he was saved, and he not only ascribed that salvation to God, but he declared God himself to *be* his salvation. Thus can all the Lord's redeemed say, 'Salvation is of the Lord.' We cannot endure any doctrine that puts the crown upon the wrong head and defrauds the glorious King of his revenue of praise. Jehovah has done it all; in Christ Jesus he is all, and therefore in our praises let him alone be extolled.

Meditation: *A servant of the Lord is better provided for than the greatest favourites and minions of princes* (Thomas Manton).

Psalm 118:15-21

Suggested further reading: Hebrews 10:19-25

The families of believers are happy, and they should take pains to give their happiness a voice by their family devotion. The dwelling-place of saved men should be the temple of praise; it is but righteous that the righteous should praise the righteous God, who is their righteousness. The struggling hero knew that the voice of woe and lamentation was heard in the tents of his adversaries, for they had suffered severe defeat at his hands. He was, however, delighted to be reminded that the nation for whom he had struggled would rejoice from one end of the land to the other at the deliverance which God had brought about by his means. That hero of heroes, the conquering Saviour, gives to all the families of his people abundant reasons for incessant song now that he has led captivity captive and ascended up on high. Let none of us be silent in our households: if we have salvation let us have joy, and if we have joy let us give it a tongue with which it may magnify the Lord.

Having reached the entrance of the temple, the grateful champion asks for admission, as if he felt that he could only approach the hallowed shrine by divine permission, and wished only to enter in the appointed manner. The temple of God was meant for the righteous to enter and offer the sacrifices of righteousness, hence the gates are called the gates of righteousness. Righteous deeds were done within its walls, and righteous teachings sounded forth from its courts. Only let the gate be opened, and the willing worshipper will enter; and he will enter in the right spirit, and for the best of purposes, that he may render homage to the Most High. Alas, there are multitudes who do not care whether the gates of God's house are opened or not; and although they know that they are opened wide they never care to enter, neither does the thought of praising God so much as cross their minds. The time will come for them when they shall find the gates of heaven shut against them, for those gates are peculiarly the gates of righteousness through which there shall by no means enter anything that defiles. Our champion might have praised the Lord in secret, and doubtless he did so; but he was not content without going up to the assembly, there to register his thanksgivings. Those who neglect public worship generally neglect all worship; those who praise God within their own gates are among those most ready to praise him within his temple gates. Public praise for public mercies is every way most appropriate, most acceptable to God, and most profitable to others.

Meditation: *Answered prayers bring God very near to us; realized salvation enables us to realize the immediate presence of God* (C. H. Spurgeon).

Psalm 118:22-29

Suggested further reading: Matthew 21:33-46

David had been rejected by those in authority, but God had placed him in a position of the highest honour and the greatest usefulness, making him the chief cornerstone of the state. In the case of many others whose early life has been spent in conflict, the Lord has been pleased to accomplish his divine purposes in a similar way; but to none is this text more applicable than to the Lord Jesus himself. He is the living stone, the tried stone, elect, precious, which God himself appointed from of old. The Jewish builders, scribe, priest, Pharisee and Herodian rejected him with disdain. They could see no excellence in him upon which they should build. He could not be made to fit in with their ideal of a national church, he was a stone of another quarry from themselves: not of like mind nor according to their taste. Therefore they cast him away and poured contempt upon him. They reckoned him to be as nothing, though he is Lord of all. In raising him from the dead the Lord God exalted him to be the head of his church, the very pinnacle of her glory and beauty. Since then he has become the confidence of the Gentiles, even of those that are afar off upon the sea, and so he has joined the two walls of Jew and Gentile into one stately temple, and is seen to be the binding cornerstone, making both one. This is a delightful subject for contemplation.

Jesus in all things has the pre-eminence, he is the principal stone of the whole house of God. We are accustomed to lay one particular stone of a public building with solemn ceremony, and to deposit in it any precious things which may have been selected as a memorial of the occasion: henceforth that cornerstone is looked upon as peculiarly honourable, and joyful memories are associated with it. All this is in a very emphatic sense true of our blessed Lord. God himself laid him where he is, and hid within him all the precious things of the eternal covenant; and there he shall for ever remain, the foundation of all our hopes, the glory of all our joys, the uniting bond of all our fellowship. He is 'the head over all things to the church', and by him the church is joined together, and grows into a holy temple in the Lord. Still the builders refuse him: even to this day the professional teachers of the gospel are far too apt to fly to any and every new philosophy sooner than maintain the simple gospel, which is the essence of Christ. Neverthe-less, he holds his true position amongst his people, and the foolish builders shall see to their utter confusion that his truth shall be exalted over all. Those who reject the chosen stone will stumble against him to their own hurt, and be-fore long will come his second advent, when he will fall upon them from the heights of heaven, and grind them to powder.

Meditation: *We observe the Lord's Day as our true Sabbath, a day made and ordained of God, for the perpetual remembrance of the achievements of our Redeemer* (C. H. Spurgeon).

Psalm 119:1-8

Suggested further reading: Psalm 1

These first eight verses are taken up with a contemplation of the blessedness that comes through keeping the statutes of the Lord. The subject is treated in a devout manner rather than in a didactic style. Heart-fellowship with God is enjoyed through a love of that word, which is God's way of communing with the soul by his Holy Spirit. Prayer and praise and all sorts of devotional acts and feelings gleam through the verses like beams of sunlight through an olive grove. You are not only instructed, but also influenced to holy emotion, and helped to express the same.

Lovers of God's holy words are blessed, because they are preserved from defilement (v. 1), because they are made practically holy (vv. 2-3), and are led to follow after God sincerely and intensely (v. 2). It is seen that this holy walking must be desirable because God commands it (v. 4); therefore the pious soul prays for it (v. 5), and feels that its comfort and courage must depend upon obtaining it (v. 6). In the prospect of answered prayer, indeed, while the prayer is being answered, the heart is full of thankfulness (v. 7), and is fixed in solemn resolve not to miss the blessing if the Lord will give enabling grace (v. 8). The changes are rung upon the words 'way' — 'undefiled in the way', 'walk in his ways', 'O that my ways were directed'; 'keep' — 'keep his testimonies', 'keep your precepts diligently', 'directed to keep', 'I will keep'; and 'walk' — 'walk in the law', 'walk in his ways'. Yet there is no tautology, nor is the same thought repeated, though to the careless reader it may seem so.

True religion is not cold and dry; it has its exclamations and raptures. It is always practical, for it does not permit us to delight ourselves in a perfect rule without exciting in us a longing to be conformed to it in our daily lives. A blessing belongs to those who hear and read and understand the word of the Lord; yet it is a far greater blessing to be actually obedient to it, and to carry out in our walk and conversation what we learn in our searching of the Scriptures. Purity in our way and walk is the truest blessedness. Rough may be the way, stern the rule, hard the discipline — all these we know and more — but a thousand heaped-up blessednesses are still found in godly living, for which we bless the Lord. It is not enough to believers to be blameless, they wish also to be actively righteous. A hermit may escape into solitude that he may do no iniquity, but a saint lives in society that he may serve his God by walking in his ways. The surest way to abstain from evil is to be fully occupied in doing good.

Meditation: *The best of God's servants are but students in the knowledge and obedience of his word* (Thomas Manton).

Psalm 119:9-16

Suggested further reading: 2 Timothy 3:10-17

Never was there a more important question for any man; never was there a more appropriate time for asking it than at the commencement of life. It is by no means an easy task that the prudent man sets before him. Here is the difficulty: first of beginning aright, next of being always able to know and choose right, and then of continuing in the right till perfection is ultimately reached; this is hard for any man, how will a youth accomplish it? The way, or life, of the man has to be cleansed from the sins of his youth behind him, and kept clear of the sins which temptation will place before him: this is the work, this is the difficulty.

No nobler ambition can lie before a youth, none to which he is called by so sure a calling; but none in which greater difficulties can be found. Let him not, however, shrink from the glorious enterprise of living a pure and gracious life; rather let him enquire the way by which all obstacles may be overcome. Let him not think that he knows the road to easy victory, nor dream that he can keep himself by his own wisdom; he will do well to follow the psalmist, and become an earnest enquirer asking how he may cleanse his way. Let him become a practical disciple of the holy God, who alone can teach him how to overcome the world, the flesh and the devil, that trinity of defilers by whom many a hopeful life has been spoiled. He is young and unaccustomed to the road, let him not be ashamed often to enquire his way of one who is so ready and so able to instruct him in it.

Young man, the Bible must be your chart, and you must exercise great watchfulness that your way may be according to its directions. You must take heed to your daily life, as well as study your Bible, and you must study your Bible that you may take heed to your daily life. With the greatest care a man will go astray if his map misleads him; but with the most accurate map he will still lose his road if he does not take heed to it. The narrow way was never hit upon by chance, neither did any heedless man ever lead a holy life. We can sin without thought, we have only to neglect the great salvation and ruin our souls; but to obey the Lord and walk uprightly will need all our heart and soul and mind. Let the careless remember this. God's Word is the best preventive against offending God, for it tells us his mind and will, and tends to bring our spirit into conformity with the divine Spirit. No cure for sin in the life is equal to the word in the seat of life, which is the heart.

Meditation: *There is no hiding from sin unless we hide the truth in our souls* (C. H. Spurgeon).

Psalm 119:17-24

Suggested further reading: Philippians 4:8-20

In this section the trials of the way appear to be manifest to the psalmist's mind, and he prays accordingly for the help which will meet his case. As in the last eight verses he prayed as a youth newly come into the world, so here he pleads as a servant and a pilgrim, who increasingly finds himself to be a stranger in an enemy's country. His appeal is to God alone, and his prayer is specially direct and personal. He speaks with the Lord as a man speaks with his friend.

The prayer of verse 17 shows that it is only through divine bounty or grace that we can live as faithful servants of God, and manifest obedience to his commands. If we give God service it must be because he gives us grace. We work for him because he works in us. Thus we may make a chain out of the opening verses of the three first octaves of this psalm: verse 1 blesses the holy man, verse 9 asks how we can attain to such holiness, and verse 17 traces such holiness to its secret source, and shows us how to seek the blessing. The more a man prizes holiness and the more earnestly he strives after it, the more will he be driven towards God for help with it, for he will plainly perceive that his own strength is insufficient, and that he cannot even so much as live without the bounteous assistance of the Lord his God. No bounty is greater than that which benefits our person, our soul, our mind, and benefits it in so important an organ as the eye. It is far better to have the eyes opened than to be placed in the midst of the noblest prospects and remain blind to their beauty. Some men can perceive no wonders in the gospel, but David felt sure that there were glorious things in the law: he did not have half the Bible, but he prized it more than some men prize the whole. He felt that God had laid up great bounties in his Word, and he begs for power to perceive, appreciate and enjoy the same. We need not so much that God should give us more benefits, as the ability to see what he *has* given.

The words of the Lord serve us for many purposes; in our sorrows they are our delight, and in our difficulties they are our guides; we derive joy from them and discover wisdom in them. If we desire to find comfort in the Scriptures we must submit ourselves to their counsel, and when we follow their counsel it must not be with reluctance but with delight. This is the safest way of dealing with those who plot for our ruin; let us give more heed to the true testimonies of the Lord than to the false witness of our foes.

Meditation: *David wanted divine teaching — the eye-salve of the Spirit; and therefore he would not open the Bible without this prayer, 'Open my eyes'* (Robert Murray M'Cheyne).

Psalm 119:25-32

Suggested further reading: Philippians 2:12-18

Here, it seems to me, we have the psalmist in trouble, bewailing the bondage to earthly things in which he finds his mind to be held. In these verses we see the influence of the divine word upon a heart which laments its downward tendencies, and is filled with mourning because of its deadening surroundings. The word of the Lord evidently arouses prayer (vv. 25-29), confirms choice (v. 30), and inspires renewed resolve (v. 32): it is the surest source of help in all tribulation, whether of body or mind. This portion has 'D' for its alphabetical letter: it sings of Depression, in the spirit of Devotion, Determination and Dependence.

When a person is depressed in spirit, weak and bent towards the ground, the main thing is to increase his stamina and put more life into him: then his spirit revives, and his body becomes erect. In reviving the life, the whole man is renewed. Shaking off the dust is a little thing by itself, but when it follows upon quickening, it is a blessing of the greatest value, just as good spirits that flow from established health are among our choicest mercies. The phrase 'according to your word' means, according to your revealed way of reviving your saints. The Word of God shows us that he who first made us must keep us alive, and it tells us of the Spirit of God who through the ordinances pours fresh life into our souls. We beg the Lord to act towards us in this, his own, regular method of grace.

Being truly sorry for his fault, and having obtained full forgiveness, he is anxious to avoid offending again, and hence he begs to be taught obedience. He was not willing to sin through ignorance, he wished to know all the mind of God by being taught it by the best of teachers. He pined after holiness. Justified men always long to be sanctified. When God forgives our sins we are all the more fearful of sinning again. Mercy, which pardons transgression, sets us longing for grace that prevents transgression. We may boldly ask for more when God has given us much; he who has washed out the past stain will not refuse that which will preserve us from present and future defilement. With energy, readiness and zeal he would perform the will of God, but he needed more life and liberty from the hand of God. The heart is the master; the feet soon run when the heart is free and energetic. God must work in us first, and then we shall will and do according to his good pleasure. He must change the heart, unite the heart, encourage the heart, strengthen the heart, and enlarge the heart, and then the course of the life will be gracious, sincere, happy and earnest; so that from our lowest up to our highest state in grace we must attribute all to the free favour of our God.

Meditation: *The strong action of the heart in all holy things comes from the blessed operation of the Spirit upon it; then only can we 'run' the way of God's commandments, when he has enlarged our heart* (Philip Bennet Power).

Psalm 119:33-40

Suggested further reading: John 17:6-19

A sense of dependence and a consciousness of extreme need pervade this section, which is all made up of prayer and plea. The psalmist will have the Lord for his teacher; for he feels that his heart will not learn from any less effectual instructor. A sense of great slowness to learn drives us to seek a great teacher. What condescension it is on our great Jehovah's part that he deigns to teach those who seek him. The lesson which is desired is thoroughly practical; the holy man would not only learn the 'statutes', but the 'way' of them, the daily use of them, their tenor, spirit, direction, habit, tendency. He would know that path of holiness that is hedged in by divine law, along which the commands of the Lord stand as signposts of direction and milestones of information, guiding and marking our progress. The very desire to learn this way is in itself an assurance that we shall be taught from them, for he who made us long to learn will be sure to gratify the desire.

When divine grace sets a man in the true way he will be true to it. Mere human wit and will have no such enduring influence: there is an end to all perfection of the flesh, but there is no end to heavenly grace except its own end, which is the perfecting of holiness in the fear of the Lord. Perseverance to the end is most certainly to be predicted of those whose beginning is in God, and with God, and by God; but those who commence without the Lord's teaching soon forget what they learn, and divert from the way upon which they professed to have entered. No one may boast that he will hold on his way in his own strength, for that must depend upon the continual teaching of the Lord: we shall fall like Peter, if we presume on our own firmness as he did. If God keeps us we shall keep his way; and it is a great comfort to know that it is God's way to keep the feet of his saints. Yet we are to watch that our keeping of the way does not depend wholly on ourselves; for our perseverance rests not on any force or compulsion, but certainly on the teaching of the Lord. Whoever is the teacher, there requires learning on the part of the taught one: no one can teach a man who refuses to learn. Let us, then, earnestly drink in divine instruction, so that we may hold fast our integrity, and follow on in the path of uprightness to life's latest hour! If we receive the living and incorruptible seed of the Word of God we must live; apart from this we have no eternal life, but only a name to live.

Meditation: *We need not only light to know our way, but a heart to walk in it* (Thomas Manton).

Psalm 119:41-48

Suggested further reading: 1 Peter 1:22 - 2:3

In these verses holy fear is apparent and prominent. The man of God trembles lest in any way or degree the Lord should remove his favour from him. The eight verses are one continued pleading for the abiding of grace in his soul, and it is supported by such holy arguments as would only suggest themselves to a spirit burning with love to God.

'Salvation' is the sum and crown of all mercies — deliverance from all evil, both now and for ever. Here is the first mention of salvation in the psalm, and it is joined with mercy: 'By grace you are saved.' Salvation is styled 'your salvation', thus ascribing it wholly to the Lord. What a mass of mercies are heaped together in the one salvation of our Lord Jesus! It includes the mercies that spare us before our conversion, and lead up to it. Then comes calling mercy, regenerating mercy, converting mercy, justifying mercy, pardoning mercy. Nor can we exclude from complete salvation any of those many mercies that are needed to conduct the believer safe to glory. Salvation is an aggregate of mercies incalculable in number, priceless in value, incessant in application, eternal in endurance. To the God of our mercies be glory, world without end!

Nothing more effectually binds a man to the way of the Lord than an experience of the truth of his word, embodied in the form of mercies and deliverances. Not only does the Lord's faithfulness open our mouths against his adversaries, but it also knits our hearts to his fear, and makes our union with him more and more intense. Great mercies lead us to feel an inexpressible gratitude which, failing to utter itself in time, promises to engross eternity with praises. God's grace alone can enable us to keep his commandments without break and without end; eternal love must grant us eternal life, and out of this will come everlasting obedience. There is no other way to ensure our perseverance in holiness but by the word of truth abiding in us, as David prayed it might abide with him. It was natural that he should reach out towards a law that he delighted in, even as a child holds out its hands to receive a gift which it longs for. When such a lovely object as holiness is set before us, we are bound to rise towards it with our whole nature, and till that is fully accomplished we should at least lift up our hands in prayer towards it. When mercy comes down, our hands will be lifted up; when God thinks favourably upon us, we are sure to think of him. Happy is he who stands with hands uplifted both to receive the blessing and to obey the precept; he shall not wait upon the Lord in vain.

Meditation: *Where holy hands and holy hearts go, the whole man will one day follow* (C. H. Spurgeon).

Psalm 119:49-56

Suggested further reading: Hebrews 6:13-20

This octet deals with the comfort of the word. It begins by seeking the main consolation, namely, the Lord's fulfilment of his promise. Then it shows how the word sustains us under affliction, and makes us so impervious to ridicule that we are moved by the harsh conduct of the wicked rather to feel horror at their sin than to any submission to their temptations. We are then shown how the Scripture furnishes songs for pilgrims, and memories for night-watchers; and the psalm concludes by the general statement that the whole of this happiness and comfort arises out of keeping the statutes of the Lord.

The psalmist does not fear a failure in the Lord's memory, but he makes use of the promise as a plea, and this is the form in which he speaks, after the manner of men when they plead with one another. When the Lord remembers the sins of his servant, and brings them before his conscience, the penitent cries, 'Lord, remember your word of pardon, and therefore remember my sins and iniquities no more.' There is a world of meaning in that word 'remember', as it is addressed to God; it is used in Scripture in the tenderest sense, and suits the sorrowing and the depressed. The psalmist cried, 'Lord, remember David, and all his afflictions'; Job also prayed that the Lord would appoint him a set time, and remember him. In the present instance the prayer is as personal as the 'Remember me' of the thief, for its essence lies in the words — 'to your servant'.

It would all be in vain for us if the promise were remembered to all others when it did not come true to ourselves; but there is no fear, for the Lord has never forgotten a single promise to a single believer.

The argument is that God, having given grace to hope in the promise, would surely never disappoint that hope. He cannot have caused us to hope without cause. If we hope upon his word we have a sure basis: our gracious Lord would never mock us by exciting false hopes. Our great Master will not forget his own servants, nor disappoint the expectation which he himself has raised. Because we are the Lord's, and endeavour to remember his word by obeying it, we may be sure that he will think upon his own servants, and remember his own promise by making it good. We are not rewarded for our works, but there is a reward in them. Many a comfort is obtainable only by careful living: we can surely say of such consolations, 'This has become mine, because I kept your precepts.'

Meditation: *Those that make God's promises their portion may with humble boldness make them their plea. God gave the promise in which the psalmist hoped, and the hope by which he embraced the promise* (Matthew Henry).

Psalm 119:57-64

Suggested further reading: 1 John 2:24 - 3:3

In this section the psalmist seems to take a firm hold upon God himself: appropriating him (v. 57), crying out for him (v. 58), returning to him (v. 59), solacing himself in him (vv. 61-62), associating with his people (v. 63), and sighing for personal experience of his goodness (v. 64).

The poet is lost in wonder while he sees that the great and glorious God is all his own! Well might he be so, for there is no possession like Jehovah himself. Like the Levites, he took God to be his portion, and left other matters to those who coveted them. This is a large and lasting heritage, for it includes all, and more than all, and it outlasts all; and yet no man chooses it for himself until God has chosen and renewed him. A fully assured possession of God does not set aside prayer, but rather urges us to it; he who knows God to be his God will seek his face, longing for his presence. The presence of God is the highest form of his favour, and therefore it is the most urgent desire of gracious souls: the light of his countenance gives us a foretaste of heaven. Oh, that we always enjoyed it! The good man entreated God's smile as one who begged for his life, and the entire strength of his desire went with the entreaty. Such eager pleadings are sure of success; that which comes from our heart will certainly go to God's heart. All God's favours are ready for those who seek them with their whole hearts.

Whatever may be the slips and wanderings of an honest heart, there remains enough of true life in it to produce ardent piety when once it is quickened by the visitations of God. The psalmist entreated for mercy, and when he received it he became eager and vehement in the Lord's ways. He had always loved them, and hence when he was enriched with grace he displayed great vivacity and delight in them. He made double speed: for positively, he 'made haste', and negatively, he refused to yield to any motive which suggested procrastination — he 'delayed not'. Thus he made rapid advances and accomplished much service, fulfilling in this the vow that is recorded in verse 57: 'I have said that I would keep your words.' The commands which he was so eager to obey were not ordinances of man, but precepts of the Most High. Many are zealous to obey custom and society, and yet they are slack in serving God. It is a crying shame that men should be served without delay, and that God's work should be bypassed, or be performed with dreamy negligence.

The first verse of this eight is fragrant with full assurance and strong resolve, and the last verse overflows with a sense of the divine fulness, and of the psalmist's personal dependence. Those who wish to keep a law are anxious to know all its clauses and provisions lest they should offend through inadvertence.

Meditation: *He who dares not care to be instructed of the Lord has never honestly resolved to be holy* (C. H. Spurgeon).

Psalm 119:65-72

Suggested further reading: Nahum 1:1-8

In this ninth section the verses all begin with the letter Teth. They are the witness of experience, testifying to the goodness of God, the graciousness of his dealings, and the preciousness of his word. The psalmist especially proclaims the excellent uses of adversity, and the goodness of God in afflicting him. The sixty-fifth verse is the text of the entire octave.

The psalmist tells the Lord the verdict of his heart; he cannot be silent, he must speak his gratitude in the presence of Jehovah, his God. It is something that God has 'dealt' at all with such insignificant and undeserving beings as we are, and it is far more that he has dealt 'well' with us, and so well, so wondrously well. He has done all things well: the rule has no exception. In providence and in grace, in giving prosperity and sending adversity, in everything Jehovah has dealt well with us. It is dealing well on our part to tell the Lord that we feel that he has dealt well with us; for praise of this kind is specially fitting and comely. This kindness of the Lord is, however, no chance matter: he promised to do so, and he has done it according to his word. It is very precious to see the word of the Lord fulfilled in our happy experience; it endears the Scripture to us, and makes us love the Lord of the Scripture. The book of providence tallies with the book of promise: what we read in the page of inspiration we meet with again in the leaves of our life-story. We may not have thought that it would be so, but our unbelief is repented of now that we see the mercy of the Lord to us, and his faithfulness to his word; henceforth we are bound to display a firmer faith both in God and in his promise.

Even in affliction God is good, and does good. This is the confession of experience. God is essential goodness in himself, and in every attribute of his nature he is good in the fullest sense of the term; indeed, he has a monopoly of goodness, for there is none good but one, that is God. His acts are according to his nature: from a pure source flow pure streams. God is not latent and inactive goodness; he displays himself by his doings, he is actively beneficent, he does good. How much good he does no tongue can tell! How good he is no heart can conceive! All the glory we can give to God is to reflect his own glory upon himself. We can say no more good of God than God is and does. We believe in his goodness, and so honour him by our faith; we admire that goodness, and so glorify him by our love; we declare that goodness, and so magnify him by our testimony.

Meditation: *See how this portion of the psalm is flavoured with goodness. God's dealings are good (v. 65), holy judgement is good (v. 66), affliction is good (v. 67), God is good (v. 68), and here the law is not only good but better than the best of treasure. Lord, make us good through your good word. Amen* (C. H. Spurgeon).

Psalm 119:73-80

Suggested further reading: Malachi 3:16-18

We have now come to the tenth portion, which in each stanza begins with Yod, but it certainly does not treat of jots and tittles and other trifles. Its subject would seem to be personal experience and its attractive influence upon others. The prophet is in deep sorrow, but looks to be delivered and made a blessing. Endeavouring to teach, the psalmist first seeks to be taught (v. 73), persuades himself that he will be well received (v. 74), and rehearses the testimony which he intends to bear (v. 75). He prays for more experience (vv. 76-77), for the baffling of the proud (v. 78), for the gathering together of the godly to him (v. 79), and for himself again that he may be fully equipped for his witness-bearing and may be sustained in it (v. 80). This is the anxious yet hopeful cry of one who is heavily afflicted by cruel adversaries, and therefore makes his appeal to God as his only friend.

God-fearing men are encouraged when they meet with experienced believers. A hopeful man is a God-send when things are declining or in danger. When the hopes of one believer are fulfilled his companions are cheered and established, and led to hope also. It is good for the eyes to see a man whose witness is that the Lord is true; it is one of the joys of saints to hold converse with their more advanced brethren.

David has two descriptions for the saints: they are God-fearing and God-knowing. They possess both devotion and instruction; they have both the spirit and the science of true religion. We know some believers who are gracious, but not intelligent; and, on the other hand, we also know certain professors who have all head and no heart; he is the man who combines devotion with intelligence. We neither care for devout dunces nor for intellectual icebergs. When fearing and knowing walk hand in hand they cause men to be thoroughly furnished unto every good work. If these are my choice companions I may hope that I am one of their order. Let such persons ever turn to me because they find me congenial company.

If the heart is sound in obedience to God, all is well, or will be well. If right at heart we are right in the main. This is even more important than to be held in esteem by good men. This is the root of the matter. If we are not sound before God, our name for piety is an empty sound. He who is right at heart has no reason for shame, and he never shall have any; hypocrites ought to be ashamed now, and they shall one day be put to shame without end; their hearts are rotten, and their names shall rot. Those who have learned their own frailty by sad experience are led to dive beneath the surface, and cry to the Lord for truth in their inner being.

Meditation: *The comforts of the word are the common portion of God's people* (Thomas Manton).

Psalm 119:81-88

Suggested further reading: 1 Peter 4:1-8

This octave is the midnight of the psalm, and very dark and black it is. Stars, however, shine out, and the last verse gives promise of the dawn. The strain will become more cheerful after this; but meanwhile it should minister comfort to us to see so eminent a servant of God so hardly used by the ungodly: evidently in our own persecutions, no strange thing has happened to us.

To read the word till the eyes can no longer see is but a small thing compared with watching for the fulfilment of the promise till the inner eyes of expectancy begin to grow dim with deferred hope. We may not set times to God, for this is to limit the Holy One of Israel; yet we may urge our suit with importunity, and make fervent enquiry as to why the promise is delayed. David sought no comfort except that which comes from God. He had placed his case in the Lord's hands, and he prayed that sentence might be given and put into execution. He desired nothing but justice, so that his character might be cleared and his persecutors silenced. He knew that God would certainly avenge his own elect, but the day of rescue tarried, the hours dragged heavily along, and the persecuted one cried day and night for deliverance. It was well for David that his enemies were God's enemies, and that their attacks upon him had no sanction from the Lord. It was also much to his gain that he was not ignorant of their devices, for he was thus put upon his guard, and led to watch his ways lest he should fall into their pits.

While he kept to the law of the Lord he was safe, though even then it was an uncomfortable thing to have his path made dangerous by the craft of wanton malice.

If we are revived in our own personal piety we shall be out of reach of our assailants. Our best protection from tempters and persecutors is more life. Loving-kindness itself cannot do us greater service than by making us to have life more abundantly. We look to the loving-kindness of God as the source of spiritual revival, and we entreat the Lord to quicken us, not according to our deserts, but after the boundless energy of his grace. If quickened by the Holy Ghost we shall be sure to exhibit a holy character. We shall be faithful to sound doctrine when the Spirit visits us and makes us faithful. None keep the word of the Lord's mouth unless the word of the Lord's mouth quickens them. We ought to greatly admire the spiritual prudence of the psalmist, who does not so much pray for freedom from trial as for renewed life that he may be supported under it. When the inner life is vigorous all is well. Lord, let it be heart-work with us, and let our hearts be right with you.

Meditation: *Hold fast Christ in the dark; surely you shall see the salvation of God* (Samuel Rutherford).

Psalm 119:89-96

Suggested further reading: Colossians 1:13-23

The strain is more joyful, for experience has given the sweet singer a comfortable knowledge of the word of the Lord, and this makes a glad theme. After tossing about on a sea of trouble the psalmist here leaps to shore and stands upon a rock. Jehovah's word is neither fickle nor uncertain; it is settled, determined, fixed, sure, immovable. Man's teachings change so often that there is never time for them to be settled; but the Lord's word is from of old the same, and will remain unchanged eternally. Some men are never happier than when they are unsettling everything and everybody; but God's mind is not with them. The power and glory of heaven have confirmed each sentence which the mouth of the Lord has spoken, and so confirmed it that to all eternity it must stand the same — settled in heaven, where nothing can reach it. In the former section David's soul fainted, but here the good man looks out of self and perceives that the Lord faints not, neither is weary, neither is there any failure in his word. The faithfulness and immutability of God are fit themes for holy song, and when we are tired with gazing upon the shifting scene of this life, the thought of the immutable promise fills our mouth with singing. God's purposes, promises and precepts are all settled in his own mind, and none of them shall be disturbed. Covenant settlements will not be removed, however unsettled the thoughts of men may become; let us therefore settle it in our minds that we abide in the faith of our Jehovah as long as we have any being.

Nature is governed by fixed laws; the globe keeps its course by the divine command, and displays no erratic movements: the seasons observe their predestined order, the sea obeys the rule of ebb and flow, and all other things are marshalled in their appointed order. There is an analogy between the Word of God and the works of God, particularly in that they are both constant, fixed and unchangeable. God's word, which established the world, is the same as that which he has embodied in the Scriptures; by the word of the Lord were the heavens made, and specially by him who is emphatically *the* Word.

When we see the world keeping its place and all its laws abiding the same, we have assurance here that the Lord will be faithful to his covenant, and will not allow the faith of his people to be put to shame. If the earth abides, the spiritual creation will abide; if God's word suffices to establish the world, surely it is enough for the establishment of the individual believer. If we are conscious that we are the Lord's, we may be confident that he will save us. We are the Lord's by creation, election, redemption, surrender and acceptance; and hence our firm hope and assured belief that he will save us.

Meditation: *If we have sought the Lord we may be sure that the Lord has sought us, and will certainly save us* (C. H. Spurgeon).

Psalm 119:97-104

Suggested further reading: 1 Corinthians 3:5-17

Wisdom is knowledge put to practical use. Wisdom comes to us through obedience. We learn not only from promise, and doctrine, and sacred history, but also from precept and command; in fact, from the commandments we gather the most practical wisdom, and that which enables us best to cope with our adversaries. A holy life is the highest wisdom and the surest defence. He who is taught of God has a practical wisdom such as malice cannot supply to the crafty; while harmless as a dove he also exhibits more than the serpent's wisdom.

That which the Lord had taught him had been useful in the camp, and he finds it equally valuable in the schools. Our teachers are not always to be trusted; in fact, we may not follow any of them implicitly, for God holds us to account for our personal judgements. It behoves us then to follow closely the chart of the Word of God, that we may be able to save the vessel when even the pilot errs. If our teachers should be sound and safe in all things, they will be really glad for us to excel them, and they will ever be ready to acknowledge that the teaching of the Lord is better than any teaching which they can give us. Disciples of Christ who sit at his feet are often better skilled in divine things than doctors of divinity. The instruction derived from Holy Scripture is useful in many directions, superior from many points of view, unrivalled everywhere and in every way. As our soul may make her boast in the Lord, so may we boast in his word.

God's words are many and varied, and as a whole they make up what we call 'the Word': David loved them each one, individually, and all of them as a whole; he tasted an indescribable sweetness in them. He expresses the fact of their sweetness, but as he cannot express the degree of their sweetness he cries, 'How sweet!' Being God's words they were divinely sweet to God's servant; he who put the sweetness into them had prepared the taste of his servant to discern and enjoy it. David makes no distinction between promises and precepts, doctrines and threatenings; they are all included in God's words, and all are precious in his esteem. Oh, for a deep love to all that the Lord has revealed, whatever form it may take. The final verse of the strophe marks a great advance in character, and shows that the man of God is growing stronger, bolder and happier than before. He has been taught of the Lord, so that he discerns between the precious and the vile, and while he loves the truth fervently he hates falsehood intensely. May all of us reach this state of discrimination and determination, so that we may greatly glorify God.

Meditation: *By meditation we preach to ourselves, and so we come to understand more than our teachers, for we come to understand our hearts, which they cannot* (Matthew Henry).

Psalm 119:105-112

Suggested further reading: John 12:42-50

We are walkers through the city of this world, and we are often called to go out into its darkness; let us never venture there without the light-giving word, lest we slip with our feet. Each man should use the Word of God personally, practically and habitually, that he may see his way and see what lies in it. When darkness settles down upon all around me, the Word of the Lord, like a flaming torch, reveals my way. One of the most practical benefits of Holy Writ is guidance in the acts of daily life; it is not sent to astound us with its brilliance, but to guide us by its instruction. It is true the head needs illumination, but, even more, the feet need direction, else head and feet may both fall into a ditch. Happy is the man who personally appropriates God's Word, and practically uses it as his comfort and counsellor — a lamp to his own feet.

He chose the 'testimonies' as his lot, his portion, his estate; and what is more, he laid hold upon them and made them so — taking them into possession and enjoyment. David's choice is our choice. If we might have our desire, we would desire to keep the commands of God perfectly. To know the doctrine, to enjoy the promise to practise the command — this is a kingdom large enough for me. Here we have an inheritance which cannot fade and cannot be alienated; it is for ever, and ours for ever, if we have so taken it. Sometimes, like Israel at the first coming into Canaan, we have to take our heritage by hard fighting, and, if so, it is worthy of all our labour and suffering; but always it has to be taken by a decided choice of the heart and grip of the will. What God gives we must take. The gladness, which had come to him through the Word of the Lord, had caused him to make an unalterable choice of it. All the parts of Scripture had been pleasing to David, and were so still, and therefore he stuck to them, and meant to stick to them for ever. That which rejoices the heart is sure to be chosen and treasured. It is not the head-knowledge but the heart-experience that brings the joy.

Many are inclined to preach, but the psalmist was inclined to practise; many are inclined to perform cere-monies, but he was inclined to perform statutes; many are inclined to obey occasionally, but David would obey always; and, alas, many are inclined towards temporary religion, but this godly man was bound for eternity. He would perform the statutes of his Lord and King even to the end.

Meditation: Lord, send us such a heavenly inclination of heart as this: then shall we show that you have quickened and taught us. To this end create in us a clean heart, and daily renew a right spirit within us, for only so shall we incline in the right direction (C. H. Spurgeon).

Psalm 119:113-120

Suggested further reading: Matthew 7:21-29

The last octave was practical, this is thoughtful; there the man of God attended to his feet, and here to his heart. The emotions of the soul are as important as the acts of the life, for they are the fountain and spring from which the actions proceed. When we love the law it becomes a law of love, and we cling to it with our whole heart. In this paragraph the psalmist deals with thoughts and things and persons which are the opposite of God's holy thoughts and ways. He is evidently in great fear of the powers of darkness, and of their allies, and his whole soul is stirred up to stand against them with a determined opposition. Just as he began the octave from verse 97 with, 'O how I love your law', so here he begins with a declaration of hatred against that which breaks the law. The opposite of the fixed and infallible law of God is the wavering, changing opinion of men. David had an utter contempt and abhorrence for this; all his reverence and regard went to the sure word of testimony. In proportion to his love to the law was his hate of men's inventions. The thoughts of men are vanity; but the thoughts of God are verity.

Those who make a conscience of their thoughts are not likely to tolerate evil company. If we fly to God from vain thoughts, how much more shall we avoid vain men. Kings are all too apt to be surrounded by a class of men who flatter them, and at the same time take liberty to break the laws of God. David purged his palace of such parasites; he would not harbour them beneath his roof. A house is all the better for being rid of liars, pilferers, lewd talkers and slanderers. We are bound at all hazards to keep ourselves clear of such companions as come to us by our own choice if we have any reason to believe that their character is vicious. Evildoers make evil counsellors. Those who say to God, 'Depart from us,' ought to hear the immediate echo of their words from the mouths of God's children, 'Depart from us. We cannot eat bread with traitors.'

Such was his awe in the presence of the Judge of all the earth, whose judgement he had just been considering, that he was exceedingly fearful and trembling. God's words of judgement are solemn, and his deeds of judgement are terrible; they may well make us afraid. At the thought of the Judge of all — his piercing eye, his books of record, his day of assize, and the operations of his justice — we may well cry for cleansed thoughts, and hearts, and ways, lest his judgements should fall on us. When we see the great Refiner separating the precious from the vile, we may well feel a godly fear, lest we should be put away by him, and left to be trodden under his feet.

Meditation: *Depart from them that depart from God* (Thomas Manton).

Psalm 119:121-128

Suggested further reading: Psalm 19:7-14

Our heart has more rest in the cry, 'God be merciful to me', than in appealing to justice. It is well to be able to say, 'I have done justice and righteousness', and then to add in all lowliness, yet 'deal with your servant according to mercy'. The Lord condescendingly deals, or has communications, with his servants, not spurning them, but communing with them; and this he does in a tender and merciful way, for in any other form of dealing we should be crushed into the dust. We may expect a master to teach his own servant the meaning of his own orders. Yet since our ignorance arises from our own sinful stupidity, it is great mercy on God's part that he condescends to instruct us in his commands. For our ruler to become our teacher is an act of great grace, for which we cannot be too grateful. Among our mercies this is one of the choicest.

He sought teaching; but he goes much further, and craves for understanding. Usually, if the instructor supplies the teaching, the pupil finds the understanding; but in our case we are far more dependent, and must beg for understanding as well as teaching: this the ordinary teacher cannot give, and we are thrice happy that our Divine Tutor can furnish us with it. We are to confess ourselves fools, and then our Lord will make us wise, as well as give us knowledge. The best understanding is that which enables us to render perfect obedience and to exhibit intelligent faith, and it is this which David desires — 'understanding, that I may know your testimonies'. Some would rather not know these things; they prefer to be at ease in the dark rather than possess the light that leads to repentance and diligence. The servant of God longs to know in an understanding manner all that the Lord reveals of man and to man; he wishes to be so instructed that he may apprehend and comprehend that which is taught him.

As it was God's time to work so it was David's time to love. So far from being swayed by the example of evil men, so as to join them in slighting the Scriptures, he was rather led into a more vehement love of them. As he saw the commandments slighted by the ungodly, his heart was in sympathy with God, and he felt a burning affection for his holy precepts. It is the mark of a true believer that he does not depend upon others for his religion, but drinks water out of his own well, which springs up even when the cisterns of earth are all dried. Our holy poet amid a general depreciation of the law felt his own esteem of it rising so high that gold and silver sank in comparison. He judged God's holy commands to be better than the best earthly thing, indeed, better than the best sort of the best earthly thing.

Meditation: *As the wicked are hurt by the best things, so the godly are bettered by the worst* (William Jenkyn).

Psalm 119:129-136

Suggested further reading: John 1:1-14

Jesus the eternal Word is called Wonderful, and all the uttered words of God are wonderful in their degree. Those who know them best wonder at them most. It is wonderful that God should have borne testimony at all to sinful men, and more wonderful still that his testimony should be of such a character, so clear, so full, so gracious, so mighty.

The mere hearing of the word with the external ear is of small value by itself, but when the words of God enter into the chambers of the heart then light is scattered on all sides. The word finds no entrance into some minds because they are blocked up with self-conceit, or prejudice, or indifference; but where due attention is given, divine illumination must surely follow upon knowledge of the mind of God. The sincere and candid are the true disciples of the word. To such it gives not only knowledge, but understanding. By his grace he enables us to put our feet step by step in the very place which his word ordains. This prayer seeks a very choice favour, namely, that every distinct act, every step, might be arranged and governed by the will of God. This does not stop short of perfect holiness, neither will the believer's desires be satisfied with anything beneath that blessed consummation. 'And let no iniquity have dominion over me.' This is the negative side of the blessing. We ask to do all that is right, and to fall under the power of nothing that is wrong. God is our sovereign, and we would have every thought in subjection to his sway. Believers have no choice, darling sins to which they would be willing to bow. They pant for perfect liberty from the power of evil, and being conscious that they cannot obtain it for themselves, they cry to God for it.

He wept in sympathy with God to see the holy law despised and broken. He wept in pity for men who were thus drawing down upon themselves the fiery wrath of God. His grief was such that he could scarcely express it; his tears were not mere drops of sorrow, but torrents of woe. In this he became like the Lord Jesus who beheld the city, and wept over it; and like Jehovah himself, who had no pleasure in the death of him that dies, but that he turn to him and live. None are so affected by heavenly things as those who are much in the study of the Word, and by which they are taught the truth and essence of things. Carnal men are afraid of brute force, and weep over losses and crosses; but spiritual men feel a holy fear of the Lord himself, and most of all lament when they see dishonour cast upon his holy name.

Meditation: *Godly men are affected with deep sorrow for the sins of the ungodly* (Robert Leighton).

Psalm 119:137-144

Suggested further reading: Daniel 9:3-15

This passage deals with the perfect righteousness of Jehovah and his word, and expresses the struggles of a holy soul in reference to that righteousness. The initial letter with which every verse commences sounds like the Hebrew word for righteousness: our keynote is righteousness.

The psalmist has not often used the name of the LORD in this vast composition. The whole psalm shows him to have been a deeply religious man, thoroughly familiar with the things of God; and such persons never use the holy name of God carelessly, nor do they even use it at all frequently in comparison with the thoughtless and the ungodly. Familiarity begets reverence in this case. Here he uses the sacred name in worship. He praises God by ascribing to him perfect righteousness. God is always right, and he is always actively right, that is, righteous. This quality is bound up in our very idea of God. We cannot imagine an unrighteous God. He extols God's word, or recorded judgements, as being right, even as their Author is righteous. That which comes from the righteous God is itself righteous. Jehovah both says and does that which is right, and that alone. This is a great stay to the soul in time of trouble. When we are most sorely afflicted, and cannot see the reason for the dispensation, we may fall back upon this most sure and certain fact, that God is righteous, and his dealings with us are righteous too. It should be our glory to sing this brave confession when all things around us appear to suggest the contrary. This is the richest adoration — this which rises from the lips of faith when carnal reason utters about undue severity, and the like.

First he had said that God's testimonies were righteous, then that they were everlasting, and now that their righteousness is everlasting. Thus he gives us a larger and more detailed account of the Word of God the longer he is engaged in writing upon it. The more we say in praise of Holy Writ, the more we may say and the more we can say. To live without understanding is not to live the life of a man, but to be dead while we live. Only as we know and apprehend the things of God can we be said to enter into life. The more the Lord teaches us to admire the eternal rightness of his word, and the more he quickens us to the love of such rightness, the happier and the better we shall be. As we love life, and seek many days that we may see good, it behoves us to seek immortality in the everlasting word which lives and abides for ever and to seek good in that renewal of our entire nature which begins with the enlightenment of the understanding and passes on to the regeneration of the entire man.

Meditation: *Here is our need of the Holy Spirit, the Lord and giver of life, and the guide of all the quickened ones, who shall lead us into all truth. O for the visitations of his grace at this good hour!* (C. H. Spurgeon).

Psalm 119:145-152

Suggested further reading: 2 Peter 1:16-21

This section is given up to memories of prayer. The psalm-ist describes the time and the manner of his devotions, and pleads with God for deliverance from his troubles. He who has been with God in the closet will find God with him in the furnace. If we have cried we shall be answered. Delayed answers may drive us to importunity; but we need not fear the ultimate result, since God's promises are not uncertain, but are 'founded for ever'. The whole passage shows us: how he prayed (v. 145); what he prayed for (v. 146); when he prayed (v. 147); how long he prayed (v. 148); what he pleaded (v. 149); what happened (v. 150); how he was res-cued (v. 151); what was his witness as to the whole matter (v. 152).

His whole soul pleaded with God, his entire affections, his united desires all went out towards the living God. It is well when a man can say as much as this of his prayers: it is to be feared that many never cried to God with their whole heart in all their lives. There may be no beauty of elocu-tion about such prayers, no length of expression, no depth of doctrine, nor accuracy of diction; but if the whole heart is in them they will find their way to the heart of God. He desires of Jehovah that his cries may not die in the air, but that God may have regard to them. True supplicants are not satisfied with the exercise itself, they have an end and object in praying, and they look out for it. If God does not hear prayer we pray in vain. The term 'hear' is often used in Scripture to express attention and consideration. In one sense God hears every sound that is made on earth, and every desire of every heart; but David meant much more; he desired a kindly, sympathetic hearing, such as a physician gives to his patient when he tells him his pitiful story. He asked that the Lord would draw near, and listen with friendly ear to the voice of his complaint, with the view of pitying him and helping him.

He knew at the very first that the doctrines of God's Word were settled before the world began, that they had never altered, and never could by any possibility be altered. He had begun by building on a rock, by seeing that God's testimonies were 'founded', that is, grounded, laid as foundations, settled and established; and that with a view to all the ages that should come, during all the changes that should intervene. It was because David knew this that he had such confidence in prayer, and was so importunate in it. It is sweet to plead immutable promises with an immutable God. It was because of this that David learned to hope: a man cannot have much expectation from a changing friend, but he may well have confidence in a God who cannot change.

Meditation: *God's testimonies are unalterable and everlasting as the attributes of their great Author and can never fail those who rely upon them, in time or eternity* (George Horne).

Psalm 119:153-160

Suggested further reading: Habakkuk 3:1-7

In this section the psalmist seems to draw still nearer to God in prayer, to state his case and to invoke divine help with more boldness and expectation. It is a pleading passage, and the keyword of it is 'consider'. With much boldness he pleads his intimate union with the Lord's cause as a reason why he should be aided. The special aid that he seeks is personal reviving, for which he cries to the Lord again and again.

The writer has a good case, though a grievous one, and he is ready, indeed anxious, to submit it to the divine arbitration. His matters are right, and he is ready to lay them before the Supreme Court. His manner is that of one who feels safe at the throne. Yet there is no impatience: he does not ask for hasty action, but for consideration. In effect he cries, 'Look into my grief, and see whether I do not need to be delivered. From my sorrowful condition judge as to the proper method and time for my rescue.' The psalmist desires two things, and these two things blended: first, a full consideration of his sorrow; secondly, deliverance; and, then, that this deliverance should come with a consideration of his affliction. It should be the desire of every gracious man who is in adversity that the Lord should look upon his need, and relieve it in such a way as shall be most for the divine glory, and for his own benefit.

'Revive me.' He prays this three times, using the same words. We may understand that David felt like one who was half stunned with the assaults of his foes, ready to faint under their incessant malice. What he wanted was revival, restoration, renewal; therefore he pleaded for more life, 'O you who revived me when I was dead, revive me again that I may not return to the dead! Revive me that I may outlive the blows of my enemies, the faintness of my faith, and the swooning of my sorrow.' The third time he does not say, 'Revive me according to your judgements,' but 'Revive me, O Lord, according to your loving-kindness.' This is the great gun that he brings up last to the conflict: it is his ultimate argument, if this does not succeed he must fail. He has long been knocking at mercy's gate, and with this plea he strikes his heaviest blow. When he had fallen into great sin this was his plea, 'Have mercy upon me, O God, according to your loving-kindness,' and now that he is in great trouble he flies to the same effectual reasoning. Because God is love he will give us life; because he is kind he will again kindle the heavenly flame within us.

Meditation: *We need not desire to be revived any further than God's loving-kindness will revive us* (Matthew Henry).

Psalm 119:161-168

Suggested further reading: 1 Samuel 30:16-31

David's awe of the word did not prevent his joy; his fear of God was not of the kind which perfect love casts out, but of the sort which it nourishes. He trembled at the word of the Lord, and yet rejoiced at it. He compares his joy to that of one who has been long in battle, and has at last won the victory and is dividing the spoil. The profits made in searching the Scriptures were greater than the trophies of war. We too have to fight for divine truth; every doctrine costs us a battle, but when we gain a full understanding of it by personal struggles it becomes doubly precious to us. In these days godly men have a full share of battling for the Word of God; may we have for our spoil a firmer hold upon the priceless word. Perhaps, however, the psalmist may have rejoiced as one who comes upon hidden treasure for which he had not fought, in which case we find the analogy in the man of God who, while reading the Bible, makes grand and blessed discoveries of the grace of God laid up for him — discoveries which surprise him, for he was not looking for such a prize. Whether we come by the truth as finders or as warriors fighting for it, the heavenly treasure should be equally dear to us. With what quiet joy does the ploughman steal home with his golden find! How victors shout as they share the plunder! How glad should that man be who has discovered his portion in the promises of holy writ, and is able to enjoy it for himself, knowing by the witness of the Holy Spirit that it is all his own.

All David's hope was fixed upon God, he looked to him alone for salvation; and then he endeavoured most earnestly to fulfil the commands of his law. Those who place least reliance upon good works are very frequently those who have the most of them; that same divine teaching which delivers us from confidence in our own doings leads us to abound in every good work to the glory of God. In times of trouble there are two things to be done: the first is to hope in God, and the second is to do that which is right. The first without the second would be mere presumption; the second without the first mere formalism. It is well if in looking back we can claim to have acted in the way that is commanded of the Lord. If we have acted rightly towards God we are sure that he will act kindly with us.

Meditation: *The more we store our minds with heavenly truth, the more deeply shall we be in love with it: the more we see the exceeding riches of the Bible the more will our love exceed measure, and exceed expression* (C. H. Spurgeon).

Psalm 119:169-176

Suggested further reading: Jude 20-25

The psalmist is approaching the end of the psalm, and his petitions gather force and fervency; he seems to break into the inner circle of divine fellowship, and to come even to the feet of the great God whose help he is imploring. This nearness creates the lowliest view of himself, and leads him to close the psalm upon his face in deepest self-humiliation, begging to be sought out like a lost sheep.

David wants the Lord's attention to his prayer to be very close and considerate. He uses a figure of speech and personifies his prayer. We may picture his prayer as Esther, venturing into the royal presence, entreating an audience, and begging to find favour in the sight of the blessed and only Potentate. It is a very sweet thing to a suppliant when he knows for sure that his prayer has obtained audience, when it has trodden the sea of glass before the throne, and has come even to the footstool of the glorious seat around which heaven and earth adore. It is to Jehovah that this prayer is expressed with trembling earnestness — our translators, filled with holy reverence, translate the word, 'O LORD'. We crave audience of none else, for we have confidence in none beside. A man may fitly ask help from God's hand when he has dedicated his own hand entirely to the obedience of the faith. God's law, contained in the Ten Commandments, gives joy to believers. God's law, that is, the entire Bible, is a well-spring of consolation and enjoyment to all who receive it. Though we have not yet reached the fulness of our salvation, yet we find in God's Word so much concerning a present salvation that we are delighted even now.

Many times in the psalm David has defended his own innocence against foul-mouthed accusers, but when he comes into the presence of the Lord his God he is ready to confess his transgressions. He sums up, not only his past, but also his present life, under the image of a sheep which has broken from its pasture, forsaken the flock, left the shepherd, and brought itself into the wild wilderness, where it has become as a lost thing. The sheep bleats, and David prays, 'Seek your servant.' Now, if the grace of God enables us to maintain in our hearts the loving memory of God's commandments it will surely yet restore us to practical holiness. Let the reader remember the first verse of the psalm while he reads the last, the major blessedness lies not in being restored from wandering, but in being upheld in a blameless way even to the end. May the Lord uphold us to the end! Yet even then we shall not be able to boast with the Pharisee, but shall still pray with the publican, 'God be merciful to me a sinner'; and with the psalmist, 'Seek your servant.'

Meditation: *The godly never so fall but there remains in them some grace, which reserves a hope of medicine to cure them: so David here. Albeit he transgressed some of God's commandments, yet he fell not into any full oblivion of them* (William Cowper).

Psalm 120

Suggested further reading: Mark 14:43-50

It is of little use to appeal to our fellows on the matter of slander, for the more we stir in it the more it spreads. It is of no avail to appeal to the honour of the slanderers, for they have none, and the most piteous demands for justice will only increase their malignity and encourage them to fresh insult. We may as well plead with panthers and wolves as with black-hearted traducers. However, when cries to man would be our weakness, cries to God will be our strength. To whom should children cry but to their father? Does not some good come even out of that vile thing, falsehood, when it drives us to our knees and to our God? Jehovah hears. He is the living God, and hence prayer to him is reasonable and profitable. The psalmist remembered and recorded this instance of prayer-hearing, for it had evidently much affected him; and now he rehearses it for the glory of God and the good of his brethren.

Those who fawn and flatter, and all the while have enmity in their hearts, are horrible beings; they are the seed of the devil, and he works in them after his own deceptive nature. It is better to meet wild beasts and serpents than deceivers: these are a kind of monster whose birth is from beneath, and whose end lies far below. It should be a warning to liars and deceivers when they see that all good men pray against them, and that even bad men are afraid of them. For the believer here is good cause for prayer. 'Deliver us from evil,' may be used with emphasis concerning this business. From gossips, talebearers, and all sorts of liars, good Lord deliver us!

Gracious men are vexed with the conversation of the wicked. Our poet felt himself to be as ill at ease among lying neighbours as if he had lived among savages and cannibals. The traitors around him were as bad as the unspeakable Turk. He cries, 'Woe is me'. Their sin appalled him; their enmity galled him. Those who defame the righteous are worse than cannibals; for savages only eat men after they are dead, but these wretches eat them up alive. Let those who dwell with such pugilistic company console themselves with the remembrance that both David and David's Lord endured the same trial. It is the lot of the saints to find foes even in their own households. Others besides David dwelt in the place of dragons. Others besides Daniel have been cast into a den of lions. Meanwhile, let those who are in quiet resting-places and peaceful habitations be greatly grateful for such ease. God has given us this tranquillity. May we never inflict upon others that from which we have been screened ourselves!

Meditation: *God's help is seasonable; it comes when we need it* (R. Mayhew).

Psalm 121:1-4

Suggested further reading: 2 Thessalonians 3:1-5

It is wise to look to the strong for strength. The holy man who here sings a choice sonnet looked away from the slanderers by whom he was tormented, to the Lord who saw all from his high places, and was ready to pour down succour for his injured servant. Help comes to saints only from above, they look elsewhere in vain; let us lift up our eyes with hope, expectancy, desire and confidence. Satan will endeavour to keep our eyes upon our sorrows that we may be disquieted and discouraged. Let us firmly resolve to look out and look up, for there is good cheer for the eyes, and they that lift up their eyes to the eternal hills shall soon have their hearts lifted up also. The purposes of God; the divine attributes; the immutable promises; the covenant, ordered in all things and sure; the providence, predestination, and proved faithfulness of the Lord — these are the hills to which we must lift our eyes, for from these our help must come. It is our resolve that we will not be bandaged and blindfolded, but will lift up our eyes.

What we need is help — help powerful, efficient, constant, we need a very present help in trouble. What a mercy that we have it in our God. Our hope is in Jehovah, for our help comes from him. Jehovah, who created all things, is equal to every emergency; heaven and earth are at the disposal of him who made them, therefore let us be very joyful in our infinite helper. He will sooner destroy heaven and earth than permit his people to be destroyed, and the perpetual hills themselves shall bow rather than he, whose ways are everlasting, shall fail. We are bound to look beyond heaven and earth to the one who made them both. It is vain to trust the creatures: it is wise to trust the Creator. Though the paths of life are dangerous and difficult, yet we shall stand fast, for Jehovah will not permit our feet to slide; and if he will not suffer it we shall not suffer it. If our foot will be thus kept, we may be sure that our head and heart will be preserved also.

When dangers are awake around us we are safe, for our Preserver is awake also, and will not permit us to be taken unawares. No fatigue or exhaustion can cast our God into sleep; his watchful eyes are never closed. It may also be worthy of mention that in verse 3 the Lord is spoken of as the personal keeper of one individual, and in verse 4 of all those who are in his chosen nation, described as Israel. Mercy to one saint is the pledge of blessing to them all. Happy are the pilgrims to whom this psalm is a safe conduct; they may journey all the way to the celestial city without fear.

Meditation: *God never closes his eyes on the condition of his people, on the needs of the world* (Albert Barnes).

Psalm 121:5-8

Suggested further reading: John 10:22-30

Here the Preserving One, who had been spoken of by pronouns in the two previous verses, is distinctly named —
Jehovah is your keeper. What a mint of meaning lies here:
the sentence is a mass of bullion, and when coined and
stamped with the king's name it will bear all our expenses
between our birthplace on earth and our rest in heaven.
Here is a glorious person — Jehovah, assuming a gracious
office and fulfilling it in person — Jehovah is your keeper,
on behalf of a favoured individual — 'your', and a firm
assurance of revelation that it is even so at this hour —
Jehovah is 'your keeper'. Can we appropriate the divine
declaration? If so, we may journey onward to Jerusalem
and know no fear; indeed, we may journey through the
valley of the shadow of death and fear no evil.

There is a most delightful double personality here.
Jehovah keeps the believer, not by agent, but by himself;
and the person protected is definitely pointed out by the
word 'you' — it is not our estate or name which is shielded,
but the proper personal man. To make this even more
intensely real and personal another sentence is added, 'The
Lord shall preserve you from all evil; he shall preserve your
soul', or Jehovah will keep your soul. Soul-keeping is the
very soul of keeping. If the soul is kept all is kept. The
preservation of the greater includes that of the less so far as
it is essential to the main design: the kernel shall be
preserved, and in order to accomplish this, the shell shall

be preserved also. God is the sole keeper of the soul. Our soul is kept from the dominion of sin, the infection of error, the crush of despondency, the puffing up of pride; kept from the world, the flesh and the devil; kept for holier and greater things; kept in the love of God; kept unto the eternal kingdom and glory. What can harm a soul that is kept of the Lord?

When we go out in the morning to labour, and come home at evening to rest, Jehovah shall preserve us. When we go out in youth to begin life, and come in at the end to die, we shall experience the same preserving. Three times we have the phrase 'the Lord shall preserve', as if the sacred Trinity thus sealed the word to make it sure. What anxiety can survive this triple promise? This preserving is eternal, continuing from this time forth, even for evermore. The whole church is thus assured of everlasting security: the final perseverance of the saints is thus ensured, and the glorious immortality of believers is guaranteed. None are so safe as those whom God preserves; none so much in danger as the self-secure. Glory to the Preserver of Israel, who is endeared to us under that title, since our growing sense of weakness makes us feel more deeply than ever our need of being kept.

Meditation: *He has not led me so tenderly thus far to forsake me at the very gate of heaven* (Adoniram Judson).

Psalm 122:1-5

Suggested further reading: Ephesians 4:1-6

David's heart was in the worship of God, and he was delighted when he found others inviting him to go where his desires had already gone: it helps the ardour of the most ardent to hear others inviting them to a holy duty. The word was not 'go', but 'let us go'; hence the ear of the psalmist found a double joy in it. He was glad for the sake of others: glad that they wished to go themselves, glad that they had the courage and liberality to invite others. He knew that it would do them good; nothing better can happen to men and their friends than to love the place where God's honour dwells. If we are glad to be called by others to our Father's house, how much more glad shall we be actually to go there. We love our Lord, and therefore we love his house, and pangs of strong desire are upon us that we may soon reach the eternal abode of his glory. Our gladness at the bare thought of being in God's house is detective as to our character, and prophetic of our being happy one day in the Father's house on high. What a sweet Sabbath psalm is this! At the prospect of the Lord's Day, and all its hallowed associations, our soul rejoices. How well, also, may it refer to the church! We are happy when we see numerous souls ready to unite themselves with the people of God. The pastor is specially glad when many come forward and ask him for assistance in entering into fellowship with the church. No language is more cheering to him than the humble request, 'Let us go into the house of the Lord.'

David saw in vision the city built; no more a waste, or a mere collection of tents, or a city upon paper, commenced but not completed. Thanks be to God, Jerusalem is built: the Lord by his glorious appearing has built up Zion. The church is a permanent and important institution, founded on a rock, and arranged with wisdom. In a church one of the most delightful conditions is the compactness of unity: 'one Lord, one faith, one baptism'. A church should be one in creed and one in heart, one in testimony and one in service, one in aspiration and one in sympathy. Those who would build dividing walls within our Jerusalem greatly injure her; she needs compacting, not dividing. There is no joy in going up to a church which is rent with internal dissension: the gladness of holy men is aroused by the adhesiveness of love, the unity of life; it would be their sadness if they saw the church to be a house divided against itself. Some bodies of Christians appear to be periodically blown to fragments, and no gracious man is glad to be in the way when the explosions take place. The tribes do not go up there, for strife and contention are not attractive forces.

Meditation: *To go into the house of the Lord signifies . . . to come together where we may have God present with us, hear his word, call upon his holy name, and receive help and succour in our necessity* (Martin Luther).

Psalm 122:6-9

Suggested further reading: Philippians 2:1-11

Peace was Jerusalem's name, pray that her condition may verify her title. Abode of Peace, peace be to you. Here was a most sufficient reason for rejoicing at the thought of going up to the house of the Lord, since that sacred shrine stood in the centre of an area of peace; well might Israel pray that such peace should be continued. In a church peace is to be desired, expected, promoted and enjoyed. If we may not say, 'Peace at any price,' yet we may certainly cry, 'Peace at the highest price.' Those who are daily fluttered by rude alarms are charmed to reach their nest in a holy fellowship, and abide in it. In a church one of the main ingredients of success is internal peace: strife, suspicion, party-spirit, division — these are deadly things. Those who break the peace of the church deserve to suffer, and those who sustain it win a great blessing. Peace in the church should be our daily prayer, and in so praying we shall bring down peace upon ourselves.

It is to the advantage of all Israel that there should be peace in Jerusalem. It is for the good of every Christian, indeed, of every man, that there should be peace and prosperity in the church. Here our humanity and our common philanthropy assist our religious prayer. By a flourishing church our children, our neighbours, our fellow-countrymen are likely to be blest. Moreover, we cannot but pray for a cause with which our dearest relatives and choicest friends are associated; if they labour for it,

we must and will pray for it. He prays for Jerusalem because of Zion. How the church salts and savours all around
it. The presence of Jehovah, our God, endears to us every
place in which he reveals his glory. Well may we seek good
for those within whose walls dwells God, who alone is good.
We are to live for God's cause, and to be ready to die for it.
First we love it (v. 6) and then we labour for it; we see its
good, and then seek its good. If we can do nothing else we
can intercede for it. Our covenant relation to Jehovah as
our God binds us to pray for his people — they are 'the
house of the Lord our God'. If we honour our God we desire
the prosperity of the church which he has chosen for his
indwelling. Thus is the poet glad of an invitation to join
with others in the Lord's service. He goes with them and
rejoices, and then he turns his delight into devotion, and
intercedes for the city of the great King. O church of the
living God, we hail your assemblies, and on bended knee
we pray that you may have peace and felicity. May our
Jehovah so send it. Amen.

Meditation: *'May they prosper that love you.' The reverse is
also true. 'None ever took a stone out of the Temple, but the
dust flew into his eyes' (Jewish Proverb).*

Psalm 123

Suggested further reading: Nehemiah 9:32-38

God is, God is in heaven, God resides in one place, and God is evermore the same, therefore will I look to him. When we cannot look to any helper on a level with us it is greatly wise to look above us; in fact, if we have a thousand helpers, our eyes should still be toward the Lord. The higher the Lord is, the better for our faith, since that height represents power, glory and excellence, and these will all be engaged on our behalf. We ought to be very thankful for spiritual eyes; the blind men of this world, however much human learning they may possess, cannot behold our God, for in heavenly matters they are devoid of sight. Yet we must use our eyes with resolution, for they will not go upward to the Lord of themselves, but they incline to look downward, or inward, or anywhere but to the Lord. Let it be our firm resolve that the heavenward glance shall not be lacking. If we cannot see God, at least we will look towards him. God is in heaven as a king in his palace; he is there revealed, adored and glorified. From there he looks down on the world and sends succours to his saints as their needs demand; hence we look up, even when our sorrow is so great that we can do no more. It is a blessed condescension on God's part that he permits us to lift up our eyes to his glorious high throne; indeed, more, that he invites and even commands us so to do. When we are looking to the Lord in hope, it is well to tell him so in prayer: the psalmist uses his voice as well as his eye.

Observe the covenant name, 'the Lord our God': it is
sweet to wait upon a covenant God. Because of that covenant he will show mercy to us; but we may have to wait
for it. God has his time and season, and we must wait until
it comes. For the trial of our faith our blessed Lord may
delay for a while, but in the end the vision will be fulfilled.
Mercy is that which we need, that which we look for, that
which our Lord will manifest to us. Even those who look to
the Lord, with that holy look which is described here, still
need mercy, and as they cannot claim it by right they wait
for it till sovereign grace chooses to vouchsafe it. Blessed
are those servants whom their Master shall find so doing.
Waiting upon the Lord is a posture suitable both for earth
and heaven; it is, indeed, in every place the right and fitting condition for a servant of the Lord. Nor may we leave
the posture so long as we are, by grace, dwellers in the
realm of mercy. It is a great mercy to be enabled to wait for
mercy.

Meditation: *He who previously lifted his eyes unto the hills,
now has raised his heart's eyes to the Lord himself* (The
Venerable Bede).

Psalm 124:1-5

Suggested further reading: Acts 12:1-11

The opening sentence is abrupt, and remains a fragment. By such a commencement attention was aroused as well as feeling expressed: and this is ever the way of poetic fire — to break forth in uncontrollable flame. The glorious Lord became our ally; he took our part, and entered into treaty with us. If Jehovah was not our protector, where should we be? Nothing but his power and wisdom could have guarded us from the cunning and malice of our adversaries; therefore, let all his people say so, and openly give him the honour of his preserving goodness. Here are two 'ifs', and yet there is no 'if' in the matter. The Lord was on our side, and is still our defender, and will be so from henceforth, even for ever. Let us with holy confidence exult in this joyful fact. We are far too slow in declaring our gratitude, hence the exclamation, 'Let Israel say'. We murmur without being stirred up to it, but our thanksgiving needs a spur, and it is well when some warm-hearted friend bids us say what we feel. Imagine what would have happened if the Lord had left us, and then see what has happened because he has been faithful to us. Are not all the materials of a song spread before us? Let us sing to the Lord.

When all men combined, and the whole race of men seemed set upon stamping out the house of Israel, what must have happened if the covenant Lord had not interposed? When they stirred themselves, and combined to make an assault upon our peace and safety, what should we have done in their rising if the Lord had not also risen? No one who could or would help was near, but the bare arm of the Lord sufficed to preserve his own against all the leagued hosts of adversaries. There is no doubt as to our deliverer, we cannot ascribe our salvation to any second cause, for it would not have been equal to the emergency; nothing less than omnipotence and omniscience could have wrought our rescue. We set every other claimant on one side, and rejoice because the Lord was on our side. Had not God been with us our disdainful enemies would have made nothing of us, and dashed over us as a mountain torrent sweeps down the side of a hill, driving everything before it. Not only would our goods and possessions have been carried off, but our soul, our courage, our hope would have been borne away by the impetuous assault, and buried beneath the insults of our antagonists. Let us pause here, and as we see what might have been, let us adore the guardian power which has kept us in the flood, and yet above the flood. In our hours of dire peril we must have perished had not our Preserver prevailed for our safe keeping.

Meditation: *We are taught how to think of our troubles and afflictions past, lest the sense and feeling of God's grace vanish out of our minds* (Martin Luther).

Psalm 124:6-8

Suggested further reading: Acts 12:12-24

The Lord is heartily praised for not permitting his servants to be devoured when they were between the jaws of the raging ones. It implies that none can harm us till the Lord permits: we cannot be their prey unless the Lord gives us up to them, and that our loving Lord will never do. Hitherto he has refused permission to any foe to destroy us, blessed be his name. The more imminent the danger the more eminent the mercy which would not permit the soul to perish in it. God be blessed for ever for keeping us from the curse. Jehovah be praised for checking the fury of the foe, and saving his own. The verse reads like a merely negative blessing, but no boon can be more positively precious. He has given us to his Son Jesus, and he will never give us to our enemies. Blessed be God, many of us can make joyous music with these notes, 'Our soul has escaped'. Escaped from our natural slavery; escaped from the guilt, the degradation, the habit, the dominion of sin; escaped from the vain deceits and fascinations of Satan; escaped from all that can destroy; we do indeed experience delight. What a wonder of grace it is! What a miraculous escape that we who are so easily misled should not have been permitted to die by the dread fowler's hand. The Lord has heard the prayer that he taught us to pray, and he has delivered us from evil.

'Our help', our hope for the future, our ground of confidence in all trials present and to come 'is in the name of the LORD'. Jehovah's revealed character is our foundation of confidence, his person is our sure fountain of strength. Our Creator is our preserver. He is immensely great in his creating work; he has not fashioned a few little things alone, but all heaven and the whole round earth are the works of his hands. When we worship the Creator let us increase our trust in our Comforter. Did he create all that we see, and can he not preserve us from evils that we cannot see? Blessed be his name, he that has fashioned us will watch over us; indeed, he has done so, and rendered us help in the moment of jeopardy. He is our help and our shield, even he alone. He will to the end break every snare. He made heaven for us, and he will keep us for heaven; he made the earth, and he will aid us upon it until the hour comes for our departure. Every work of his hand preaches to us the duty and the delight of reposing upon him only. All nature cries, 'Trust in the Lord for ever, for in the Lord Jehovah there is everlasting strength.' 'Comfort one another with these words.'

Meditation: *Now commit your souls to the same faithful creator* (Thomas Manton).

Psalm 125

Suggested further reading: Galatians 6:11-18

Zion cannot be removed, and does not remove; so the people of God can neither be moved passively nor actively, by force from without or fickleness from within. Faith in God is a settling and establishing virtue; he who by his strength sets fast the mountains, by that same power stays the hearts of them that trust in him. This steadfastness will endure 'for ever', and we may be assured therefore that no believer shall perish either in life or in death, in time or in eternity. We trust in an eternal God, and our safety shall be eternal.

Though they do not make a circular wall, the mountains around the holy city are, nevertheless, set like sentinels to guard her gates. God does not enclose his people within ramparts and bulwarks, making their city to be a prison; but yet he so orders the arrangements of his providence that his saints are as safe as if they dwelt behind the strongest fortifications. What a double security the verses set before us! First, we are established, and then entrenched; settled, and then guarded; made like a mount, and then protected as if by mountains. This is no matter of poetry, it is so in fact; and it is no matter of temporary privilege, but it shall be so for ever. Date when we please, 'from this time forth' Jehovah encircles his people: look on us as far as we please, the protection extends for ever. Note, it is not said that Jehovah's power or wisdom defends believers, but he himself is round about them: they have his personality for their protection, his Godhead for their guard. We are here taught that the Lord's people are those who trust him, for they are described in this way in the first verses: the line of faith is the line of grace, those who trust in the Lord are chosen of the Lord. The two verses together prove the eternal safety of the saints: they must abide where God has placed them, and God must forever protect them from all evil. It would be difficult to imagine greater safety than is set forth here.

The power and influence of wicked men when they have the upper hand are used to lead or drive the righteous astray; but the godly must not accept this as an excuse, and yield to the evil pressure. They must far rather resist with all their might till it shall please God to stay the violence of the persecutor, and give his children rest. Here the Lord promises to do this in due time. When God is smiting the unfaithful, not a blow shall fall upon the faithful. The chosen of the Lord shall not only be like Salem, but they shall have salem, or peace. He who has peace with God may enjoy peace concerning all things. Bind the first and last verses together: Israel trusts in the Lord (v. 1), and Israel has peace (v. 5).

Meditation: *Great is the stability of a believer's felicity* (John Trapp).

Psalm 126

Suggested further reading: 1 Corinthians 15:50-58

The heathen heard the songs of Israel, and the better sort among them soon guessed the cause of their joy. Jehovah was known to be their God, and to him the other nations ascribed the emancipation of his people, reckoning it to be no small thing that the Lord had thus done. For those who carried away the nations had never in any other instance restored a people to their ancient dwelling-place. These foreigners were no dreamers; though they were only lookers-on, and not partakers in the surprising mercy, they plainly saw what had been done, and rightly ascribed it to the great Giver of all good. It is a blessed thing when saints set sinners talking about the loving-kindness of the Lord, and it is equally blessed when the saints who are hidden away in the world hear of what the Lord has done for his church, and themselves resolve to come out from their captivity and unite with the Lord's people. Ah, dear reader, Jehovah has indeed done marvellous things for his chosen, and these 'great things' shall be themes for eternal praise among all intelligent creatures.

Even as the Lord sends floods down into the dry beds of southern torrents after long droughts, so can he fill our wasted and wearied spirits with floods of holy delight. The Lord can do this for any of us, and he can do it at once, for nothing is too hard for the Lord. It is well for us thus to pray, and to bring our suit before him who is able to bless us exceeding abundantly. Do not let us forget the past, but in the face of our present difficulty let us resort to the Lord, and beseech him to do that for us which we cannot possibly do for ourselves — that which no other power can perform on our behalf. Israel did return from the captivity in Babylon, and it was even as though a flood of people hastened to Zion. Suddenly and plenteously the people again filled the temple courts. In the latter days they shall also return to their own land in streams, and replenish it yet again. Like mighty torrents the nations shall flow unto the Lord in the day of his grace. May the Lord hasten it in his own time. Present distress must not be viewed as if it would last for ever: it is not the end, by any means, but only a means to the end. Sorrow is our sowing, rejoicing shall be our reaping. If there were no sowing in tears there would be no reaping in joy. Let us keep to the work of this present sowing time, and find strength in the promise that is here so positively given us. Here is one of the Lord's shalls and wills; it is freely given both to workers, waiters and weepers, and they may rest assured that it will not fail: 'in due season they shall reap'.

Meditation: *The Lord turns exile into ecstasy, and banishment into bliss* (C. H. Spurgeon).

Psalm 127

Suggested further reading: Colossians 3:18-25

The word 'vain' is the keynote here, and we hear it ring out clearly three times. Men desiring to build know that they must labour, and accordingly they put forth all their skill and strength; but let them remember that if Jehovah is not with them their designs will prove failures. Moses was faithful as a servant over all his house; and as long as the Lord was with that house it stood and prospered; but when he left it, its builders became foolish and their labour was lost. They sought to maintain the walls of Judaism, but sought in vain: they watched around every ceremony and tradition, but their care was idle. Of every church, and every system of religious thought, this is equally true: unless the Lord is in it, and is honoured by it, the whole structure must sooner or later fall in hopeless ruin. Much can be done by man; he can both labour and watch; but without the Lord he has accomplished nothing, and his wakefulness has not warded off evil.

Children are a heritage that Jehovah himself must give, or a man will die childless, and thus his house will be unbuilt. God gives children, not as a penalty nor as a burden, but as a favour. They are a token for good if men know how to receive them, and educate them. Where society is rightly ordered children are regarded, not as an encumbrance, but as an inheritance; and they are received, not with regret, but as a reward. Our best possessions are our own dear offspring, for whom we bless God every day. When sons and daughters are arrows, it is well to have a quiver full of them; but if they are only sticks, knotty and useless, the fewer of them the better. While those are blessed whose quiver is full, there is no reason to doubt that many are blessed who have no quiver at all; for a quiet life may not need such a warlike weapon. Moreover, a quiver may be small and yet full; and then the blessing is obtained. In any case we may be sure that a man's life does not consist in the abundance of children that he possesses.

He who is the father of a host of spiritual children is unquestionably happy. He can answer all opponents by pointing to souls who have been saved by his means. Converts are emphatically the heritage of the Lord, and the reward of the preacher's soul travail. By these, under the power of the Holy Ghost, the city of the church is both built up and watched, and the Lord has the glory of it.

Meditation: *It is true that unless the good hand of God is upon us we cannot prosperously build a place of worship for his name. Unless we have his blessing, a dwelling-house cannot be comfortably erected. And if his blessing is not on our children, the house (the family) may be built up; but instead of its being the house of God, it will be the synagogue of Satan. All marriages that are not under God's blessing will be a private and public curse* (Adam Clarke).

Psalm 128

Suggested further reading: 1 Timothy 6:6-10

The last psalm ended with a blessing — for the word there translated 'happy' is the same as that which is here rendered 'blessed', thus the two songs are joined by a catch-word. There is also in them a close community of subject. The fear of God is the cornerstone of all blessedness. We must reverence the ever-blessed God before we can be blessed ourselves. Some think that this life is an evil, an infliction, a thing upon which rests a curse; but it is not so, the God-fearing man has a present blessing resting upon him. He is happy now, for he is the child of the happy God, the ever-living Jehovah; and he is even here a joint-heir with Jesus Christ, whose heritage is not misery, but joy. This is true of every one of the God-fearing, of all conditions, in all ages: each and every one is blessed. Their blessedness may not always be seen by carnal reason, but it is always a fact, for God himself declares that it is so; and we know that those whom he blesses are blessed indeed. Let us cultivate that holy filial fear of Jehovah that is the essence of all true religion — the fear that consists of reverence, of dread to offend, of anxiety to please, and of entire submission and obedience. This fear of the Lord is the fit fountain of holy living, we look in vain for holiness apart from it: none but those who fear the Lord will ever walk in his ways. The religious life, which God declares to be blessed, must be practical as well as emotional. It is idle to talk of fearing the Lord if we act like those who have no care whether there be a God or no. God's ways will be our ways if we have a sincere reverence for him: if the heart is joined unto God, the feet will follow hard after him.

If we fear God we may dismiss all other fear. In walking in God's ways we shall be under his protection, provision, and approval; danger and destruction shall be far from us, for all things shall work for our good. In God's view it would not be a blessed thing for us to live without exertion, nor to eat the unearned bread of dependence. The happiest state on earth is one in which we have something to do, strength to do it with, and a fair return for what we have done. This, with the divine blessing, is all that we ought to desire, and it is sufficient for any man who fears the Lord and abhors covetousness.

Meditation: The fear of the Lord is the internal principle; but unless there is a corresponding expression in the outward life, what reason is there to suppose that it has any existence at all? Observe also that there is no walking in the ways of the Lord, until his fear is established in the heart. There can be no genuine morality apart from the fear of God. How can a man obey God while his affections are alienated from him? (N. M'Michael).

Psalm 129:1-4

Suggested further reading: Isaiah 10:5-14

The song begins abruptly. The trials of the church have been repeated again and again, countless times: the same afflictions are fulfilled in us as in our fathers. Jacob of old found his days full of trouble; each Israelite is often harassed; and Israel as a whole has proceeded from tribulation to tribulation. 'Many a time', Israel says, because she could not say how many times. She speaks of her assailants as 'they', because it would be impossible to write or even to know all their names.

The scourgers tore the flesh as ploughmen furrow a field. It is a grand piece of imagery condensed into few words. The afflicted nation was, as it were, lashed by her adversaries so cruelly that each blow left a long red mark, or perhaps a bleeding wound, upon her back and shoulders, comparable to a furrow which tears up the ground from one end of the field to the other. Many a heart has been in a similar situation; smitten and sorely wounded by those that use the scourge of the tongue; so smitten that their whole character has been cut up and scored by calumny. The true church has in every age had fellowship with her Lord under his cruel flagellations: his sufferings were a prophecy of what she would be called to endure from then on, and the foreshadowing has been fulfilled. Zion has in this sense been ploughed as a field. Well did Latimer say that there was no busier ploughman in all the world than the devil: whoever makes short furrows, he does not.

Whoever baulks and shirks, he is thorough in all that he does. Whoever stops work at sundown, he never does. He and his children plough like practised ploughmen; but they prefer to carry on their pernicious work upon the saints behind their backs, for they are as cowardly as they are cruel.

Whatever men may be, Jehovah remains just, and will therefore keep covenant with his people and deal out justice to their oppressors. Here is the hinge of the condition: this makes the turning-point of Israel's distress. The Lord bears with the long furrows of the wicked, but he will surely make them cease from their ploughing before he has done with them. Sooner or later a righteous God will interpose, and when he does so, his action will be most effectual; he does not unfasten, but cuts asunder the harness which the ungodly use in their labour of hate. Never has God used a nation to chastise his Israel without destroying that nation when the chastisement has come to a close: he hates those who hurt his people even though he permits their hate to triumph for a while for his own purpose. If any man would have his harness cut, let him begin to plough one of the Lord's fields with the plough of persecution. The shortest way to ruin is to meddle with a saint: the divine warning is, 'He that touches you touches the apple of his eye.'

Meditation: *God does not fail to sow blessings in the furrows, which the plowers plow upon the back of the church* (Jeremy Taylor).

Psalm 129:5-8

Suggested further reading: Isaiah 10:15-23

It is but justice that those who hate, harass and hurt the good should be brought to naught. Those who confound right and wrong ought to be confounded, and those who turn back from God ought to be turned back. Loyal subjects wish ill to those who plot against their king. How can we wish prosperity to those who would destroy what is dearest to our hearts? This present age is so flippant that if a man loves the Saviour he is styled a fanatic, and if he hates the powers of evil he is named a bigot. As for ourselves, despite all objectors, we join heartily in this denunciation; and would revive in our heart the old practice of Ebal and Gerizim, where those who bless God were blessed, and those who make themselves a curse to the righteous were cursed. The church of God is so useful, so beautiful, so innocent of harm, so fraught with good, that those who do her wrong are wronging all mankind and deserve to be treated as the enemies of the human race. Study a chapter from the *Book of Martyrs*, and see if you do not feel inclined to read an imprecatory psalm over Bishop Bonner and Bloody Mary. It may be that some wretched sentimentalist will blame you: if so, read another over him.

In harvest times men bless each other in the name of the Lord; but there is nothing in the course and conduct of the ungodly man to suggest the giving or receiving of a benediction. Upon a survey of the sinner's life from beginning to end, we feel more inclined to weep than to rejoice, and we feel bound rather to wish him failure than success. We dare not use pious expressions as mere compliments, and hence we dare not wish God-speed to evil men lest we be partakers of their evil deeds. When persecutors are worrying the saints, we cannot say, 'The blessing of the Lord be upon you.' When they slander the godly and oppose the doctrine of the cross, we dare not bless them in the name of the Lord. It would be infamous to compromise the name of the righteous Jehovah by pronouncing his blessing upon unrighteous deeds.

See how godly men are roughly ploughed by their adversaries, and yet a harvest comes of it which endures and produces blessing; while the ungodly, though they flourish for a while and enjoy complete immunity, dwelling, as they think, quite out of harm's reach, are soon found to have gone their way and to have left no trace behind. Lord, number me with your saints. Let me share their grief if I may also partake of their glory. Thus would I make this psalm my own, and magnify your name, because your afflicted ones are not destroyed, and your persecuted ones are not forsaken.

Meditation: *The faithful in suffering prevail and overcome; but the wicked in doing are overthrown, and miserably perish, as all the histories of all times and ages plainly witness* (Martin Luther).

Psalm 130:1-4

Suggested further reading: Jonah 1:17 - 2:10

The more distressed we are, the more excellent is the faith that trusts bravely in the Lord, and therefore appeals to him, and to him alone. Good men may be in the depths of temporal and spiritual trouble; but good men in such cases look only to their God, and they stir themselves up to be more instant and earnest in prayer than at other times. The depth of their distress moves the depths of their being; and from the bottom of their hearts an exceedingly great and bitter cry rises unto the one living and true God. If the Lord will but hear us we will leave it to his superior wisdom to decide whether he will answer us or not. It is better for our prayer to be heard than answered. If the Lord were to make an absolute promise to answer all our requests it might be rather a curse than a blessing, for it would be casting the responsibility of our lives upon ourselves, and we should be placed in a very anxious position. But now the Lord hears our desires, and that is enough; we only wish him to grant them if his infinite wisdom sees that it would be for our good and for his glory.

If Jah, the all-seeing, should in strict justice call every man to account for every want of conformity to righteousness, where would any one of us be? Truly, he does record all our transgressions; but as yet he does not act upon the record, but lays it aside till another day. If men were to be judged upon no system but that of works, who among us could answer for himself at the Lord's bar, and hope to stand clear and accepted? Jehovah, who sees all, and is our Lord, will assuredly bring us into judgement concerning those thoughts, and words, and works which are not in exact conformity to his law. Were it not for the Lord Jesus, could we hope to stand? Dare we meet him in the dread day of account on the footing of law and equity? Free, full, sovereign pardon is in the hand of the great King: it is his prerogative to forgive, and he delights to exercise it. Because his nature is mercy, and because he has provided a sacrifice for sin, therefore forgiveness is with him for all that come to him confessing their sins. The power of pardon is permanently resident with God: he has forgiveness ready to his hand at this instant. If the Lord were to execute justice upon all, there would be none left to fear him. If all were under apprehension of his deserved wrath, despair would harden them against fearing him: it is grace which leads the way to a holy regard of God, and a fear of grieving him.

Meditation: *There is a common error in the world, to think we may be the bolder to sin because God is merciful; but, O my soul, take heed of this error, for God's mercy is to no such purpose; it is not to make us bold, but to make us fear, the greater his mercy is, the greater ought our fear to be, for there is mercy with him that he may be feared* (Sir Richard Baker).

Psalm 130:5-8

Suggested further reading: Luke 2:25-35

Expecting the Lord to come to me in love, I quietly wait for
his appearing; I wait upon him in service, and for him in
faith. For God I wait and for him only, if he will manifest
himself I shall have nothing more to wait for; but until he
appears for my help I must wait on, hoping even in the
depths. This waiting of mine is no mere formal act, my
very soul is in it — 'My soul waits'. I wait and I wait —
mark the repetition! 'My soul waits', and then again, 'My
soul waits', to make sure work of the waiting. It is well to
deal with the Lord intensely. Such repetitions are the reverse of vain repetitions. If the Lord Jehovah makes us wait,
let us do so with our whole hearts; for blessed are all they
that wait for him. The waiting itself is beneficial to us; it
tries faith, exercises patience, trains submission and endears the blessing when it comes. The Lord's people have
always been a waiting people: they waited for the first advent, and now they wait for the second. They waited for a
sense of pardon, and now they wait for perfect sanctification. They waited in the depths, and they are not now
wearied with waiting in a happier condition. They have
cried and they do wait; probably their past prayer sustains
their present patience. Those who do not hope cannot wait;
but if we hope for what we do not see, then we wait for it
with patience. God's Word is a true word, but at times it
tarries; if ours is true faith it will wait the Lord's time. A
word from the Lord is as bread to the soul of the believer;

and, refreshed by it, it holds out through the night of sorrow expecting the dawn of deliverance and delight. Waiting, we study the word, believe the word, hope in the word, and live on the word; and all because it is 'his word' — the word of him who never speaks in vain. Jehovah's word is a firm ground for a waiting soul to rest upon.

God has great things in store for his people; they ought to have large expectations. Let us look out of self and its poverty to Jehovah and his riches of mercy. He can and will redeem all his people out of their many and great troubles; no, their redemption is already wrought out and laid up with him, so that he can at any time give his waiting ones its full benefit. The attribute of mercy and the fact of redemption are two most sufficient reasons for hoping in Jehovah; and the fact that there is no mercy or deliverance elsewhere should effectually wean the soul from all idolatry.

Meditation: *Are not these deep things of God a grand comfort, for those who are crying out of the depths? Is it not better to be in the deeps with David, hoping in God's mercy, than up on the mountaintops, boasting in our own fancied righteousness?* (C. H. Spurgeon).

Psalm 131

Suggested further reading: Proverbs 16:16-24

The psalm deals with the Lord, and is a solitary colloquy with him, not a discourse before men. We have a sufficient audience when we speak with the Lord, and we may say to him many things that were not proper for the ears of men. The holy man makes his appeal to Jehovah, who alone knows the heart: a man should be slow to do this upon any matter, for the Lord is not to be trifled with; and when anyone ventures on such an appeal he should be sure of his case. He begins with his heart, for that is the centre of our nature, and if pride is there it defiles everything, just as mire in the spring causes mud in all the streams. It is a grand thing for a man to know his own heart so as to be able to speak before the Lord about it. It is beyond all things deceitful and desperately wicked, who can know it? Who can know it unless taught by the Spirit of God? It is a still greater thing if, upon searching himself thoroughly, a man can solemnly protest unto the Omniscient One that his heart is not haughty; that is to say, neither proud in his opinion of himself, contemptuous to others, nor self-righteous before the Lord; neither boastful of the past, proud of the present, nor ambitious for the future. A man does well to know his own size. Ascertaining his own capacity, he will be foolish if he aims at that which is beyond his reach, straining himself, and thus injuring himself. Such is the vanity of many men that if a work is within their range they despise it, and think it beneath them: the only service which they are willing to undertake is that to which they have never been called, and for which they are by no means qualified. What a haughty heart must he have who will not serve God at all unless he may be trusted with five talents at the least! His looks are indeed lofty who disdains to be a light among his poor friends and neighbours here below, but demands to be created a star of the first magnitude to shine among the upper ranks, and to be admired by gazing crowds. It is just on God's part that those who wish to be everything should end in being nothing.

Blessed are those afflictions which subdue our affections, which wean us from self-sufficiency, which educate us into Christian manliness, which teach us to love God not merely when he comforts us, but even when he tries us. Well might the sacred poet repeat his figure of the weaned child; it is worthy of admiration and imitation; it is doubly desirable and difficult to attain. Such weaning from self springs from gentle humility, and partly accounts for its existence. If pride is gone, submission will be sure to follow; and, on the other hand, if pride is to be driven out, self must also be vanquished.

Meditation: *Your case can never be out of the reach of God's power and mercy* (Adam Clarke).

Psalm 132:1-10

Suggested further reading: 1 Chronicles 17:1-15

With David the covenant was made, and therefore his name is pleaded on behalf of his descendants, and the people who would be blessed by his dynasty. Jehovah, who changes not, will never forget one of his servants, or fail to keep his covenant; yet for this thing he is to be entreated. That which we are assured the Lord will do must, nevertheless, be made a matter of prayer. The request is that the Lord would 'remember', and this is a word full of meaning. We know that the Lord remembered Noah, and assuaged the flood; he remembered Abraham, and sent Lot out of Sodom; he remembered Rachel, and Hannah, and gave them children; he remembered his mercy to the house of Israel, and delivered his people. The plea is urged with God that he would bless the family of David for the sake of their progenitor; how much stronger is our master-argument in prayer that God would deal well with us for Jesus' sake! David had no personal merit; the plea is based upon the covenant graciously made with him: but Jesus has deserts that are his own, and of boundless merit — these we may urge without hesitation. When the Lord was angry with the reigning prince, the people cried, 'Lord, remember David'; and when they needed any special blessing, again they sang, 'Lord, remember David.' This was good pleading, but it was not as good as ours, which runs like this: 'Lord, remember Jesus, and all his afflictions.'

One cannot help remembering that the holy resolve of David gave to a place and a house much more importance than the Lord himself ever attached to such matters. It is a striking fact that true religion never flourished more in Israel than before the temple was built, and that from the day of the erection of that magnificent house the spirit of godliness declined. Good men may have on their hearts matters which seem to them of chief importance, and it may be acceptable with God that they should seek to carry them out; and yet in his infinite wisdom he may judge it best to prevent them executing their designs. God does not measure his people's actions by their wisdom or lack of wisdom, but by the sincere desire for his glory which has led up to them.

In verses 8-10, we have a prayer for the temple, the ark, the priests, the Levites, the people and the king: in each petition there is fulness of meaning well worthy of careful thought. We cannot plead too much in detail; the fault of most prayers is their indefiniteness. In God's house and worship everything needs a blessing, and every person connected with it needs it continually. As David vowed and prayed when he was minded to house the ark, so now the prayer is continued when the temple is consecrated, and the Lord deigns to fill it with his glory.

Meditation: *We shall never have done praying till we have done needing* (C. H. Spurgeon).

Psalm 132:11-18

Suggested further reading: Acts 13:22-37

Here we come to a grand covenant pleading of the kind that is always prevalent with the Lord. We cannot urge anything with God which is equal to his own word and oath. Jehovah swears that our faith may have strong confidence in it: he cannot forswear himself. He swears 'in truth', for he means every word that he utters; men may be perjured, but none will be so profane as to imagine this of the God of truth. Jehovah is not a changeable being. He never turns from his purpose, much less from his promise solemnly ratified by oath. He is not a man that he should lie, nor the son of man that he should repent. What a rock they stand upon who have an immutable oath of God for their foundation! We know that this covenant was really made with Christ, the spiritual seed of David, for Peter quotes it at Pentecost. Christ sits on a sure throne for ever and ever, seeing that he has kept the covenant, and through him the blessing comes upon Zion, whose poor are blessed in him. Jesus sprang from the race of David, as the evangelists are careful to record; he was 'of the house and lineage of David': at this day he is the King of the Jews, and the Lord has also given him the heathen for his inheritance. He must reign, and of his kingdom there shall be no end. God himself has set him on the throne and no rebellion of men or devils can shake his dominion. The honour of Jehovah is concerned in his reign, and therefore it is never in danger; for the Lord will not suffer his oath to be dishonoured.

God desires to abide with those whom he has loved with an everlasting love; and we do not wonder that it should be so, for we also desire the company of our beloved ones. It is a double marvel, that the Lord should choose and desire such poor creatures as we are. God in the church is the wonder of heaven, the miracle of eternity, the glory of infinite love. He calls Zion my 'rest'. Here his love remains and displays itself with delight, and this 'for ever'. He will not seek another place of repose, nor grow weary of his saints. In Christ the heart of Deity is filled with content, and for his sake he is satisfied with his people, and will be so world without end. These august words declare a distinctive choice — *this*, and no other; a certain choice — *this*, which is well known to me; a present choice — *this*, which is here at this moment. God has made his election of old, he has not changed it, and he never will repent of it, his church was his rest and is his rest still. As he will not turn from his oath, so he will never turn from his choice.

Meditation: *Oh, that we may enter into his rest, may be part and parcel of his church, and yield by our loving faith a delight to the mind of him who takes pleasure in them that fear him, in them that hope in his mercy* (C. H. Spurgeon).

Psalm 133

Suggested further reading: John 17:20-26

'Behold.' It is a wonder seldom seen, therefore behold it! It may be seen, for it is the characteristic of real saints — therefore, do not fail to inspect it! God looks on with approval, therefore consider it with attention. 'How good and how pleasant it is for brethren to dwell together in unity!' No one can tell the exceeding excellence of such a condition; and so the psalmist uses the word 'how' twice — 'Behold how good!' and 'How pleasant!' He does not attempt to measure either the good or the pleasure, but invites us to behold for ourselves.

As to brethren in spirit, they ought to dwell together in church fellowship, and in that fellowship one essential matter is unity. We can dispense with uniformity if we possess unity: oneness of life, truth and way; oneness in Christ Jesus; oneness of object and spirit — these we must have, or our assemblies will be synagogues of contention rather than churches of Christ. The closer the unity the better; for the more of the good and the pleasant there will be. Christian unity is good in itself, good for ourselves, good for the brethren, good for our converts, good for the out-side world; and for certain it is pleasant: for a loving heart must have pleasure and give pleasure in associating with others of like nature. A church united for years in earnest service of the Lord is a well of goodness and joy to all those who dwell round about it.

Christian affection knows no limits of parish, nation, sect or age. Is the man a believer in Christ? Then he is in the one body, and I must yield him an abiding love. Brotherly love comes from the head, but falls to the feet. Its way is downward. It 'ran down': love for the brethren condescends to men of low estate, it is not puffed up, but is lowly and meek. This is no small part of its excellence, oil would not anoint if it did not flow down, neither would brotherly love diffuse its blessing if it did not descend. Where love reigns God reigns. Where love wishes blessing, there God commands the blessing. Oh, for more of this rare virtue! Not the love which comes and goes, but that which dwells; not that spirit which separates and secludes, but that which dwells together; not that mind which is all for debate and difference, but that which dwells together in unity. Never shall we know the full power of the anointing till we are of one heart and of one spirit; never will the sacred dew of the spirit descend in all its fulness till we are perfectly joined together in the same mind; never will the covenanted and commanded blessing come forth from the Lord our God till once again we shall have 'one Lord, one faith, one baptism'. Lord, lead us into this most precious spiritual unity, for your Son's sake. Amen.

Meditation: *If God be one, let all that profess him be of one mind, and one heart, and thus fulfil Christ's prayer, 'that they all may be one'* (Thomas Watson).

Psalm 134

Suggested further reading: Luke 2:36-40

The word 'bless' is the characteristic word of the psalm.
The first two verses stir us up to bless Jehovah, and in the
last verse Jehovah's blessing is invoked upon the people.
Oh, to abound in blessing! May 'blessed' and 'blessing' be
the two words that describe our lives. Let others flatter their
fellows, or bless their stars, or praise themselves; as for us,
we will bless Jehovah, from whom all blessings flow. To be
a servant of Jehovah is an incalculable honour, a blessing
beyond all estimate. To be a servant in his temple, a domestic in his house, is even more a delight and a glory — if
those who are ever with the Lord, and dwell in his own
temple, do not bless the Lord, who will? We can well understand how the holy pilgrims half envied those consecrated
ones who guarded the temple, and attended to the necessary duties surrounding it through the hours of night. To
the silence and solemnity of night there was added the awful
glory of the place where Jehovah had ordained that his
worship should be celebrated; blessed were the priests and
Levites who were ordained to a service so sublime. That
these should bless the Lord throughout their nightly vigils
was most fitting: the people would have them mark this,
and never fail in the duty. They were not to move about
like so many machines, but put their hearts into all their
duties, and worship spiritually in the whole course of their
duty.

As the angels praise God day without night, so must the servants of the churches be instant in season and out of season. This is their main business. They are to bless men by their teaching, but they must bless Jehovah even more with their worship. Too often men look at public worship only from the side of its usefulness to the people; but the other matter is of even higher importance, we must see to it that the Lord God is adored, extolled, and held in reverence.

The benediction comes from the City of the Great King, from his appointed ministers, by virtue of his covenant, and so it is said to be 'out of Zion'. To this day the Lord blesses each one of his people through his church, his gospel and the ordinances of his house. It is in communion with the saints that we receive untold benedictions. May each one of us obtain yet more of the blessing which comes from the Lord alone. Zion cannot bless us; the holiest ministers can only wish us a blessing; but Jehovah can and will bless each one of his waiting people. So may it be at this good hour. Do we desire it? Let us then bless the Lord ourselves. Let us do it a second time. Then we may confidently hope that the third time we think of blessing, we shall find ourselves conscious receivers of it from the Ever-blessed One. Amen.

Meditation: *All men lie under the curse, till God brings them into the fellowship of his church, and pronounce them blessed by his word* (David Dickson).

Psalm 135:1-7

Suggested further reading: Romans 11:33-36

It is not enough for us to praise God ourselves, we are quite
unequal to such a work; let us call in all our friends and
neighbours, and if they have been slack in such service, let
us stir them up to it with loving exhortations. Let his character be extolled by you, and let all that he has revealed
concerning himself be the subject of your song; for this is
truly his 'name'.

The greatness of God is as much a reason for adoration
as his goodness, when we are once reconciled to him. God
is great positively, great comparatively, and great superlatively — 'above all gods'. Of this the psalmist had an assured personal persuasion. He says positively, 'I know'. It
is knowledge worth possessing. He knew by observation,
inspiration and realization; he was no agnostic, he was
certain and clear upon the matter. He not only knows the
greatness of Jehovah, but also that, as the Adonai, or Ruler,
'our Lord' is infinitely superior to all the imaginary deities
of the heathen, and to all great ones besides. His will is
carried out throughout all space. The king's warrant runs
in every portion of the universe. The heathen divided the
great domain; but Jupiter does not rule in heaven, nor Nep-
tune on the sea, nor Pluto in the lower regions; Jehovah
rules over all. His decree is not defeated, his purpose is not
frustrated: in no one point is his good pleasure set aside.
The word 'whatever' is of the widest range and includes all
things, and the four words of place which are mentioned

comprehend all space; therefore the declaration of the text knows neither limit nor exception. Jehovah works his will: he pleases to do, and he performs the deed. None can stay his hand. How different this from the gods whom the heathen fabled to be subject to all the disappointments, failures and passions of men! How contrary even to those so-called Christian conceptions of God which subordinate him to the will of man, and make his eternal purposes the football of human caprice. Our theology teaches us no such degrading notions of the Eternal as that he can be baffled by man. 'His purpose shall stand, and he will do all his pleasure.' No region is too high, no abyss too deep, no land too distant, no sea too wide for his omnipotence: his divine pleasure is dispatched over all the realm of nature, and his commands are obeyed.

Everything in the material world is under the immediate direction and control of the Lord of all. Observe how the psalmist brings before us the personal action of Jehovah: 'He causes ... he makes ... he brings.' Everywhere the Lord works all things, and there is no power that escapes his supremacy. It is well for us that it is so: one bandit force wandering through the Lord's domains defying his control would cast fear and trembling over all the provinces of providence.

Meditation: *God's distinguishing grace should make his elect lift up many a humble, joyful, and thankful heart to him* (John Trapp).

Psalm 135:8-14

Suggested further reading: Joshua 12:7-24

The nations of Canaan joined in the desperate resistance offered by their monarchs, and so they were smitten, while their kings, the ringleaders of the fight, were slain. He is prepared to mete out vengeance to those who oppose his designs: those who dream of him as too tender to come to blows have mistaken the God of Israel. He intended to bless the work through his chosen people, and he would not be turned from his purpose: cost what it might, he would preserve the candle of truth which he had lit, even though the blood of nations should be spilt in its defence. The wars against the Canaanite races were a price paid for the setting up of a nation that was to preserve for the whole world the lively oracles of God. Of old the Lord had given this land to Abraham and his seed by a covenant of salt, but he allowed the Amorites and other tribes to stay there till their iniquity was full, and then he bade his people come and take what was theirs out of the holders' hands. Canaan was their heritage because they were the Lord's heritage, and he gave it to them actually, because he had long before given it to them by promise.

The Lord's chosen still have a heritage from which none can keep them back. Covenant blessings of inestimable value are secured to them; and, as surely as God has a people, his people shall have a heritage. To them it comes by gift, though they have to fight for it. It often happens that when they slay a sin or conquer a difficulty they are enriched by the spoil: to them even evils work for good, and trials ensure triumphs.

God's name is eternal, and will never be changed. His character is immutable; his fame and honour also shall remain to all eternity. There shall always be life in the name of Jesus, and sweetness and consolation. Those upon whom the Lord's name is named in verity and truth shall be preserved by it, and kept from all evil, world without end. Men's memorials decay, but the memorial of the Lord abides evermore. What a comfort to despondent minds, trembling for the ark of the Lord! This must be construed in its connection, and it teaches us that the honour and glory gained by the Lord in the overthrow of the mighty kings would never die out. For a long time Israel reaped the benefit of the prestige which the divine victories had brought to the nation. Moreover, the Lord in thus keeping the covenant that he made with Abraham, when he promised to give the land to his seed, was making it clear that his memorial contained in promises and covenant would never be out of his sight. His name endures in all its truthfulness, for those who occupied Israel's land were driven out, that the true heirs might dwell there in peace.

Meditation: *God is, and will be always, the same to his church, a gracious, faithful, wonder-working God; and his church is, and will be the same to him, a thankful, praising people; and thus his name endures for ever* (Matthew Henry).

Psalm 135:15-21

Suggested further reading: Jeremiah 10:1-10

It is the height of insanity to worship metallic manufactures. Though silver and gold are useful to us when we rightly employ them, there is nothing about them that can entitle them to reverence and worship. If we did not know the sorrowful fact to be indisputable, it would seem to be impossible that intelligent beings could bow down before substances that they must themselves refine from the ore, and fashion into form. One would think it less absurd to worship one's own hands than to adore that which those hands have made. What great works can these mock deities perform for man when they are themselves the works of man? Idols are fitter to be played with, like dolls by babes, than to be adored by grown-up men. Hands are better used in breaking than in making objects that can be put to such an idiotic use.

The idol-worshippers are as bad as the idol-makers; for if there were none to worship, there would be no market for the degrading manufacture. Idolaters are spiritually dead, they are the mere images of men, their best being is gone, they are not what they seem. Their mouths do not really pray, their eyes see not the truth, their ears hear not the voice of the Lord, and the life of God is not in them. Those who believe in their own inventions in religion betray great folly, and an utter absence of the quickening Spirit. Gracious men can see the absurdity of forsaking the true God and setting up rivals in his place; but those who perpetrate this crime do not think so, on the contrary, they pride themselves upon their great wisdom, and boast of 'advanced thought' and 'modern culture'. May we be saved from such mimicry of divine work lest we also become like our idols.

The house of Israel comprehends all the chosen seed; then we come down to the smaller but more central ring of the house of Aaron, and we widen out to the whole tribe of Levi. Let reverence and adoration spread from man to man until the whole lump of humanity shall be leavened. The house of Levi had choice reasons for blessing God, read the Levite story and see. Remember that the whole of the Levites were set apart for holy service, and supported by the tribes allotted to them; therefore they were honour bound above all others to worship Jehovah with cheerfulness. Those who fear God need not wait for any other qualification for sacred service; godly fear proves us to be in the covenant with Israel, in the priesthood with Aaron, and in the service of the Lord with Levi. Filial fear, such as saints feel towards the Lord, does not hinder their praise; no, it is the main source and fountain of their adoration.

Meditation: *Idolatry is a benumbing sin, which bereaves the idolater of the right use of his senses* (David Dickson).

Psalm 136:1-9

Suggested further reading: 2 Chronicles 7:1-7

The exhortation is intensely earnest: the psalmist pleads
with the Lord's people with an 'Oh,' three times repeated.
Thanks are the least that we can offer, and these we ought
to give freely. The inspired writer calls us to praise Jehovah
for all his goodness to us, and all the greatness of his power
in blessing his chosen. We thank our parents, let us praise
our heavenly Father; we are grateful to our benefactors, let
us give thanks unto the Giver of all good. Let us thank him
that we have seen, proved and tasted that he is good. He is
good beyond all others; indeed, he alone is good in the
highest sense; he is the source of good, the good of all good,
the sustainer of good, the perfecter of good, and the
rewarder of good. For this he deserves the constant gratitude of his people.

Jehovah is the great unrivalled Wonderworker. None can
be likened unto him: he is alone in the seat of wonders, the
Creator and Worker of true marvels, compared with which
all other remarkable things are as child's play. His works
are all great in wonder even when they are not great in
size; in fact, in the minute objects of the microscope we
behold as great wonders as even the telescope can reveal.
All the works of his unrivalled skill are wrought by him
alone and unaided, and to him, therefore, must be undivided honour. None of the gods or the lords helped Jehovah
in creation, or in the redemption of his people: his own
right hand and his holy arm wrought for him these great

deeds. What have the gods of the heathen done? If the question be settled by doings, Jehovah is indeed 'alone'. It is exceedingly wonderful that men should worship gods who can do nothing, and forget the Lord who alone does great wonders. Even when the Lord uses men as his instruments, yet the wonder of the work is his alone; therefore let us not trust in men, or idolize them, or tremble before them.

Praise is to be rendered to Jehovah, 'for his mercy endures for ever'. The mercy of the wonder is the wonder of the mercy; and the enduring nature of that mercy is the central wonder of that wonder. The Lord causes us often to sit down in amazement as we see what his mercy has wrought out and prepared for us: 'wonders of grace to God belong', indeed, great wonders and unsearchable. What joy that there is mercy, mercy with Jehovah, enduring mercy, mercy enduring for ever. It is far-reaching, long enduring and all encompassing. Mercy gleams in every ray of light. We are ever needing it, trying it, praying for it, receiving it: therefore let us for ever sing of it. Oh, the depth! Glory to his name world without end!

Meditation: *Whatever instruments the Lord is pleased to use in any of his wonderful works, he alone is the worker, and will not share the glory of the work with any creature* (David Dickson).

Psalm 136:10-16

Suggested further reading: Exodus 15:1-10

We have heard of the glory of the world's creation, we are now to praise the Lord for the creation of his favoured nation by their exodus from Egypt. Because the monarch of Egypt stood in the way of the Lord's gracious purposes it became necessary for the Lord to deal with him in justice; but the great design was mercy to Israel, and through Israel mercy to succeeding ages, to the whole world. The last and greatest of the plagues struck all Egypt to the heart. The sorrow and the terror that it caused throughout the nation it is hardly possible to exaggerate. From king to slave, each one was wounded in the most tender point. The joy and hope of every household was struck down in one moment, and each family had its own wailing. The former blows had missed their aim compared with the last; but that 'struck Egypt'. The Lord's first-born had been oppressed by Egypt, and at last the Lord fulfilled his threat, 'I will slay your son, even your first-born.' Justice lingered, but it struck home at last.

Scattered as the tribes were up and down the country, and apparently held in a grasp that would never be relaxed, the Lord wrought their deliverance, and severed them from their idolatrous task-masters. None of them remained in bondage. The Lord brought them out; brought them out at the very hour when his promise was due; brought them out, brought them all out; despite their being mingled among the Egyptians; brought them out never to return. Not only the matter but also the manner of the Lord's mighty acts should be the cause of our praise. We ought to bless the Lord for adverbs as well as adjectives. In the Exodus the great power and glory of Jehovah were seen. He dashed the enemy in pieces with his right hand. He led forth his people in no mean or clandestine manner. He made a road across the sea-bottom, causing the divided waters to stand like walls on either side. Men deny miracles; but, granted that there is a God, they become easy to believe. The chariots were thrown over, the horses were overthrown. The King and his warriors alike were overwhelmed; they were hurled from their chariots as locusts are tossed to and fro in the wind. Broken was the power and conquered was the pride of Egypt. Jehovah had vanquished the enemy.

The Lord's mercy to his people endured, even to the extremity of vengeance upon a whole nation. He is slow to anger, and judgement is his strange work; but when mercy to men demands severe punishments he will not hold back his hand from the needful surgery. What were all the first-born of Egypt compared with those divine purposes of mercy to all generations of men, which were wrapped up in the deliverance of the elect people?

Meditation: *Let us even when the Lord's judgements are abroad in the earth continue to sing of his unfailing grace* (C. H. Spurgeon).

Psalm 136:17-26

Suggested further reading: Numbers 21:21-31

God's dealings are mysterious, but they must be right, simply because they are his. The people knew nothing of the way, but they were led; they were a vast host, yet they were all led; there were neither roads nor tracks, but being led by unerring wisdom they never lost their way. He who brought them out of Egypt also led them through the wilderness. Within sight of their inheritance Israel had to face powerful enemies. Kings judged to be great because of the armies at their back blocked up their road. This difficulty soon disappeared, for the Lord smote their adversaries, and a single stroke sufficed for their destruction. What good was their fame to them? As they opposed God they became infamous rather than famous. Their deaths made the Lord's fame increase among the nations while their fame ended in disgraceful defeat. Sihon smote Moab, but he could not smite Israel, for the Lord smote him. He was valiant and powerful, so as to be both great and famous; but as he wilfully refused to give a peaceful passage to the Israelites, and fought against them in malice, there was no choice but to let him run into the destruction that he courted. His fall was speedy and final, and the chosen people were so struck with it that they sang of his overthrow in their national songs. The fastnesses of Bashan were no defence against Jehovah. Og was soon ousted from his stronghold when the captain of the Lord's host led the war against him. The Lord's people were called upon to fight against him, but it was God who won the victory. As Lord of the whole earth he transferred his estate from one tenant to another. The land did not become the property of the Israelites by their own sword and bow, but by a grant from the throne. This was the great end that had been aimed at all along, from Egypt to Jordan. He who brought his people out also brought them in. He who had promised the land to the seed of Abraham also saw to it that the deed of gift did not remain a dead letter.

The Lord is God in the highest realms, and among celestial beings. His throne is set in glory, above all, out of reach of foes, in the place of universal oversight. He who feeds ravens and sparrows is yet the glorious God of the highest realms. Angels count it their glory to proclaim his glory in every heavenly street. See here the greatness of his nature, the depth of his condescension, and the range of his love. Mark the one sole cause of his bounty: 'For his mercy endures for ever.' He has done all things from this motive; and because his mercy never ceases, he will continue to multiply deeds of love world without end. Let us, with all our powers of heart and tongue, give thanks to the holy name of Jehovah for ever and ever.

Meditation: *If the end of one mercy were not the beginning of another, we were undone* (Philip Henry).

Psalm 137:1-6

Suggested further reading: 2 Chronicles 36:11-21

Glad to be away from the noisy streets, the captives sought the riverside, where the flow of the waters seemed to be in sympathy with their tears. It was some slight comfort to be out of the crowd, and to have a little breathing room, and therefore they sat down, as if to rest a while and comfort themselves in their sorrow. They sat down in little groups and made common lamentation, mingling their memories and their tears. Everything reminded Israel of her banishment from the holy city, her servitude beneath the shadow of the temple of Bel, her helplessness under a cruel enemy; and therefore her sons and daughters sat down in sorrow. Nothing else could have subdued their brave spirits; but the remembrance of the temple of their God, the palace of their king, and the centre of their national life, quite broke them down. Destruction had swept down all their delights, and therefore they wept — the strong men wept, the sweet singers wept! They did not weep when they remembered the cruelties of Babylon; the memory of fierce oppression dried their tears and made their hearts burn with wrath: but when the beloved city of their solemnities came into their minds they could not refrain from floods of tears. True believers mourn in just this way when they see the church despoiled, and find themselves unable to assist her: we could bear anything better than this. In these our times the Babylon of error ravages the city of God, and the hearts of the faithful are grievously wounded as they see truth fallen in the streets, and unbelief rampant among the professed servants of the Lord. We bear our protests, but they appear to be in vain; the multitude is mad upon their idols. May we weep in secret for the hurt of our Zion: it is the least thing we can do; perhaps in its result it may prove to be the best thing we can do. May we also sit down and deeply consider what is to be done. May we, in any case, keep upon our mind and heart the memory of the church of God that is so dear to us. The frivolous may forget, but Zion is graven on our hearts, and her prosperity is our chief desire.

The singers imprecate eternal silence upon their mouths if they forget Jerusalem to gratify Babylon. The players on instruments and the sweet songsters are of one mind, the enemies of the Lord will get no mirthful tune or song from them. The sacred city must ever be first in their thoughts, the queen of their souls; they would sooner be dumb than dishonour her sacred hymns, and give occasion to the oppressor to ridicule her worship. If such is the attachment of a banished Jew to his native land, how much more should we love the church of God of which we are children and citizens. How jealous should we be of her honour, how zealous for her prosperity!

Meditation: *A godly man lays to heart the miseries of the church* (Thomas Watson).

Psalm 137:7-9

Suggested further reading: Ezekiel 25:1-14

The case is left in Jehovah's hands. He is a God of recompenses, and will deal out justice with impartiality. We may rest assured that every unrighteous power is doomed to destruction, and that from the throne of God justice will be measured out to all whose law is force, whose rule is selfishness, and whose policy is oppression. Happy is the man who shall help in the overthrow of the spiritual Babylon, which, despite its riches and power, is 'to be destroyed'. Happier still shall he be who shall see it sink like a millstone in the flood, never to rise again. What that spiritual Babylon is, none need enquire. There is but one city upon earth that can answer to the name.

Fierce was the heart of the Jew who had seen his beloved city the scene of such terrific butchery. His heart pronounced a similar sentence upon Babylon. She should be scourged with her own whip of wire. The desire for righteous retribution is rather the spirit of the law than of the gospel; and yet in moments of righteous wrath the old fire will burn; and while justice survives in the human breast it will not lack for fuel among the various tyrannies which still survive. We shall be wise to view this passage as a prophecy. History informs us that it was literally fulfilled: in their terror the Babylonian people agreed to destroy their own offspring, and men thought they would be happy when they had put their own wives and children to the sword. Horrible as the whole transaction was, it is something to be glad of, if we take a broad view of the world's welfare; for Babylon, the gigantic robber, had for many a year slaughtered nations without mercy, and her fall was the rising of many people to a freer and safer state. The murder of innocent infants can never be sufficiently deplored, but it was an incident of ancient warfare that the Babylonians had not omitted in their massacres, and, therefore, they were not spared it themselves. The revenges of providence may be slow, but they are ever sure; neither can they be received with regret by those who see God's righteous hand in them. It is a wretched thing that a nation should need an executioner; yet if men commit murder, tears are more appropriately shed over their victims than over the assassins themselves.

The captives in Babylon did not make music, but they poured forth their righteous maledictions, and these were far more in harmony with their surroundings than songs and laughter could have been. Those who mock the Lord's people will receive more than they desire, to their own confusion: they shall have little enough to make mirth for them, and more than enough to fill them with misery. Shall despots crush virtue beneath their iron heel and never be punished? Time will show.

Meditation: *A feeling of universal love is admirable, but it must not be divorced from a keen sense of justice* (C. H. Spurgeon).

Psalm 138:1-3

Suggested further reading: Isaiah 42:21-25

His mind is so taken up with God that he does not mention his name; to him there is no other God, and Jehovah is so perfectly realized and so intimately known that the psalmist, in addressing him, thinks no more of mentioning his name than we should do if we were speaking to a father or a friend. He sees God with his mind's eye, and simply addresses him with the pronoun 'you'. He is resolved to praise the Lord, and to do it with the whole force of his life, even with his whole heart.

He would worship God in God's own way. The Lord had ordained a centre of unity, a place of sacrifice, a house of his indwelling; and David accepted the way of worship enjoined by revelation. Even so, the true-hearted believer of these days must not fall into the will-worship of superstition, or the wild worship of scepticism, but reverently worship as the Lord himself prescribes. The idol gods had their temples; but David averts his glance from them, and looks earnestly to the spot chosen by the Lord for his own sanctuary. We are not only to adore the true God, but to do so in his own appointed way: the Jew looked to the temple, we are to look to Jesus, the living temple of the Godhead. Praise would be the main part of David's worship; the name or character of God the great object of his song; and the special point of his praise, the grace and truth which shone so conspicuously in that name. The person of Jesus is the temple of the Godhead, and there we behold the glory of the Father, 'full of grace and truth'.

The word of promise made to David was, in his eyes, more glorious than everything else that he had seen of the Most High. Revelation excels creation in the clearness, definiteness and fulness of its teaching. The name of the Lord in nature is not so easily read as in the Scriptures, which are a revelation in human language, specially adapted to the human mind, treating of human need, and of a Saviour who appeared in human nature to redeem humanity. Heaven and earth shall pass away, but the divine word will not pass away, and in this respect especially it has a pre-eminence over every other form of manifestation. Moreover, the Lord lays all the rest of his name under tribute to his word: his wisdom, power, love and all his other attributes combine to carry out his word. It is his word that creates, sustains, quickens, enlightens and comforts. As a word of command it is supreme; and in the person of the incarnate Word it is set above all the works of God's hands. Let us adore the Lord who has spoken to us by his Word, and by his Son; and in the presence of unbelievers let us both praise his holy name and extol his holy Word.

Meditation: *God has a greater regard unto the words of his mouth, than to the works of his hand: heaven and earth shall pass away, but one jot or tittle of what he has spoken shall never fall to the ground* (Ebenezer Erskine).

Psalm 138:4-8

Suggested further reading: Philippians 1:3-11

'Great is the glory of the LORD.' This glory shall overshadow all the greatness and glory of all kings: they shall be stirred to obey and adore by a sight of it. Oh, that Jehovah's glory was revealed even now! Oh, that the blind eyes of men could once behold it, then their hearts would be subdued to joyful reverence! David, under a sense of Jehovah's glory, exclaimed, 'I will sing' (v. 1), and here he represents the kings as doing the same thing.

In greatness, dignity and power, Jehovah is higher than the highest. His nature is high above the comprehension of his creatures, and his glory even exceeds the loftiest soarings of imagination. He views 'the lowly' with pleasure, thinks of them with care, listens to their prayers and protects them from evil. Because they think little of themselves he thinks much of them. They are low in their own esteem, and he makes them high in his esteem. He does not need to come near 'the proud' in order to discover their utter vanity: a glance from afar reveals to him their emptiness and offensiveness. He has no fellowship with them, but views them from a distance; he is not deceived, but knows the truth about them, despite their blustering; he has no respect for them, but utterly abhors them. Our foes fall when the Lord comes to deal with them; he makes short work of the enemies of his people — with one hand he routs them. His wrath soon quenches their wrath; his hand stays their hand. Adversaries may be many, and malicious, and mighty; but our glorious Defender has only to stretch out his arm and their armies vanish. The sweet singer rehearses his assurance of salvation, and sings of it in the ears of the Lord, addressing him with this confident language. He will be saved — saved dexterously, decidedly, divinely; he has no doubt about it. God's right hand cannot forget its cunning; Jerusalem is his chief joy, and he will defend his own elect.

God is concerned in all that concerns his servants. He will see to it that nothing precious to them shall fail to come to completion; their life, their strength, their hopes, their graces, their pilgrimage, shall each and every one be perfected. Jehovah himself will see to this; and therefore it is most sure. Since we have it written upon our hearts that God will perfect his work in us, and we see it also written in Scripture that his mercy does not change, we entreat with holy earnestness that we may not be forsaken. If there is anything good in us, it is the work of God's own hands: will he leave it? Why has he wrought so much in us if he means to give us up? It will be a sheer waste of effort. He who has gone so far will surely persevere with us to the end. Our hope for the final perseverance of the believer lies in the final perseverance of the believer's God.

Meditation: *God does not leave off till he has finished* (Alexander Maclaren).

Psalm 139:1-6

Suggested further reading: Proverbs 8:22-36

Searching ordinarily implies a measure of ignorance which is removed by observation. Of course, this is not the case with the Lord; but the psalmist means that the Lord knows us as thoroughly as if he had examined us minutely, and had pried into the most secret corners of our being. This infallible knowledge has always existed: 'You have searched me'; and it continues to this day, since God cannot forget what he has once known. There never was a time in which we were unknown to God, and there never will be a moment in which we shall be beyond his observation. Note how the psalmist makes his doctrine personal. He does not say, 'O God, you know all things'; but, 'You have known me.' It is ever our wisdom to lay truth home to ourselves. How wonderful the contrast between the observer and the observed! Jehovah and me! Yet this most intimate connection exists, and therein lies our hope. Let the reader sit still a while and try to realize the two poles of this statement — the Lord and poor puny man — and he will see much to admire and wonder at.

I am observed when I quietly sit down, and marked when I resolutely rise up. My most common and casual acts, my most needful and necessary movements, are noted by you, and you know the inward thoughts which regulate them. Though my thought is invisible to the sight, though as yet I am not aware myself of the shape it is assuming, yet you have it under your consideration, and you perceive its nature, its source, its drift, its result. My path and my bed, my running and my resting, are also within the circle of your observation. You surround me even as the air continually surrounds all creatures that live. I am shut up within the wall of your being; I am encircled within the bounds of your knowledge. Waking or sleeping I am still observed by you. You are familiar with all I do; nothing is concealed from you, nor surprising to you, nor misunderstood by you. Our paths may be habitual or accidental, open or secret, but the Most Holy One is well acquainted with them all. This should fill us with awe, so that we do not sin; with courage, so that we do not fear; with delight, so that we do not mourn.

Can we attain to any idea of his power, his wisdom, his holiness? Our mind has no line with which to measure the Infinite. Do we therefore question? Say, rather, that we therefore believe and adore. We are not surprised that the Most Glorious God should in his knowledge be high above all the knowledge to which we can attain. It must of necessity be so, since we are such poor limited beings; and when we stand on tip-toe we cannot reach to the lowest step of the throne of the Eternal.

Meditation: *Compared with our stinted knowledge, how amazing is the knowledge of God!* (Henry Duncan).

Psalm 139:7-12

Suggested further reading: Amos 9:1-6

Here omnipresence is the theme — a truth to which omniscience naturally leads up. 'Where shall I go from your spirit?'
Not that the psalmist wished to go from God, or to avoid
the power of the divine life; but he asks this question to set
forth the fact that no one can escape from the all-pervading
being and observation of the Great Invisible Spirit. Observe
how the writer makes the matter personal to himself: 'Where
shall I go?' It would be well if we all applied truth to our
own cases in this way. It is wise for each one to say: 'The
spirit of the Lord is ever around *me*: Jehovah is omnipres-
ent to *me*. If, full of dread, I hastened to escape from that
nearness of God which had become my terror, which way
could I turn?' 'Where? … Where?' He repeats his cry. No
answer comes back to him. The reply to his first 'Where?'
is its echo — a second 'Where?' From the sight of God he
cannot be hidden, but that is not all; from the immediate,
actual, constant presence of God he cannot be withdrawn.
We must be, whether we will it or not, as near to God as our
soul is to our body. This makes it dreadful work to sin; for
we offend the Almighty to his face, and commit acts of treason at the very foot of his throne. Go from him, or 'flee'
from him we cannot: neither by patient travel nor by hasty
flight can we withdraw from the all-surrounding Deity. His
mind is in our mind; himself within ourselves. His spirit is
over our spirit; our presence is ever in his presence.

'The darkness and the light are both alike to you.' This sentence seems to sum up all that went before, and most emphatically puts the negative upon the faintest idea of hiding under the cover of night. Men cling to this notion, because it is easier and less expensive to hide under darkness than to journey to remote places; and therefore the foolish thought is here beaten to pieces by statements which in their varied forms effectually batter it. Yet the ungodly are still duped by their grovelling notions of God, and enquire, 'How does God know?' They must fancy that he is as limited in his powers of observation as they are, and yet if they would but consider for a moment they would conclude that he who could not see in the dark could not be God, and he who is not present everywhere could not be the almighty Creator.

Assuredly God is in all places, at all times, and nothing can by any possibility be kept away from his all-observing, all-comprehending mind. The Great Spirit comprehends within himself all time and space, and yet he is infinitely greater than these, or anything else that he has made.

Meditation: *A heathen philosopher once asked, 'Where is God?' The Christian answered, 'Let me first ask you, Where is he not?'* (John Arrowsmith).

Psalm 139:13-18

Suggested further reading: Job 10:1-12

Who can gaze even upon a model of our anatomy without wonder and awe? Who could dissect a portion of the human frame without marvelling at its delicacy, and trembling at its frailty? The psalmist had scarcely peered within the veil that hides the nerves, sinews and blood-vessels from common inspection; the science of anatomy was quite unknown to him; and yet he had seen enough to arouse his admiration of the work and his reverence for the Worker. These parts of my frame are all *your* works; and though they are personal works, close under my own eye, yet are they wonderful to the last degree. They are works within my own self, yet they are beyond my understanding, and appear to me as so many miracles of skill and power. We need not go to the ends of the earth for marvels, nor even across our own threshold; they abound in our own bodies. While the vessel was still upon the wheel, the Potter saw it all. The Lord knows not only our shape, but also our substance: this is substantial knowledge indeed. God saw us when we could not be seen, and he wrote about us when there was nothing of us to write about. When as yet there were none of our members in existence, all those members were before the eye of God in the sketchbook of his foreknowledge and predestination.

When we remember that God thought upon us from all eternity, continues to think upon us every moment, and will think of us when time shall be no more, we may well exclaim, 'How great is the sum' of your thoughts to me! Thoughts that are natural to the Creator, the Preserver, the Redeemer, the Father, the Friend, are evermore flowing from the heart of the Lord. Thoughts of our pardon, renewal, upholding, supplying, educating, perfecting, and a thousand more kinds perpetually well up in the mind of the Most High. It should fill us with adoring wonder and reverent surprise that the infinite mind of God should turn so many thoughts towards us who are so insignificant and so unworthy! The thoughts of God are altogether innumerable; for nothing can surpass in number the grains of sand which belt the main ocean and all the minor seas. The task of counting God's thoughts of love would be a never-ending one. Even if we could count the sands on the seashore, we should not then be able to number God's thoughts, for they are 'more in number than the sand'. This is not the hyperbole of poetry, but the solid fact of inspired statement. God thinks upon us infinitely, there is a limit to the act of creation, but not to the might of divine love.

Meditation: *A godly soul should fall asleep in God's arms, like a child in its mother's lap* (Thomas Horton).

Psalm 139:19-24

Suggested further reading: Jude 12-23

Crimes committed before the face of the Judge are not likely to go unpunished. If the eye of God is grieved with the presence of evil, it is only natural to expect that he will remove the offending object. God who sees all evil will slay all evil. With earthly sovereigns sin may go unpunished for lack of evidence, or the law may be left without execution from lack of vigour in the judge; but this cannot happen in the case of God, the living God. He does not bear the sword in vain. Such is his love of holiness and hatred of wrong that he will carry on war to the death with those whose hearts and lives are wicked. God will not always allow his lovely creation to be defaced and defiled by the presence of wickedness: if anything is sure, this is sure, that he will redress himself upon his adversaries.

To love all men with benevolence is our duty; but to love any wicked man with complacency would be a crime. To hate a man for his own sake, or for any evil done to us, would be wrong; but to hate a man because he is the foe of all goodness and the enemy of all righteousness, is nothing more nor less than an obligation. The more we love God the more indignant shall we grow with those who refuse him their affection. The loyal subject must not be friendly to the traitor. Since God is everywhere, he knows our feelings towards the profane and ungodly, and he knows that, so far from approving such characters, the very sight of them is grievous to our eyes.

David is no accomplice with traitors. He has disowned them categorically, and now he appeals to God that he does not harbour a trace of fellowship with them. He will have God himself search him, and search him thoroughly, till every point of his being is known, and read, and understood; for he is sure that even by such an investigation there will be found in him no complicity with wicked men. He challenges the fullest investigation, the innermost search: he would need to be a true man who can put himself deliberately into such a crucible. Yet we may, each one, desire such searching; for it would be a terrible calamity for sin to remain in our hearts, unknown and undiscovered. 'See whether there is in my heart, or in my life, any evil habit unknown to myself. If there is such an evil way, take me from it, take it from me. No matter how dear the wrong may have become, nor how deeply prejudiced I may have been in its favour, be pleased to deliver me from it altogether, effectually, and at once, that I may tolerate nothing which is contrary to your mind. As I hate the wicked in their way, so would I hate every wicked way in myself.'

Meditation: *I call upon you to be cautious in using this prayer. It is easy to mock God, by asking him to search you whilst you have made but little effort to search yourselves, and perhaps still less to act upon the result of the scrutiny* (Henry Melvill).

Psalm 140:1-5

Suggested further reading: Micah 2:1-5

David does not so much plead against an individual as against the species represented by him, namely, the being whose best description is — 'the evil man'. There are many such men abroad; indeed we shall not find an unregenerate man who is not in some sense an evil man, and yet all are not evil in the same way. It is well for us that our enemies are evil, it would be a horrible thing to have the good against us. When 'the evil man' exerts himself against the godly he is as terrible a being as a wolf, or a serpent, or even a devil. Fierce, implacable, unpitying, unrelenting, unscrupulous, he cares for nothing but the indulgence of his malice. The persecuted man turns to God in prayer; he could not do a wiser thing. Who can meet the evil man and defeat him save Jehovah himself, whose infinite goodness is more than a match for all the evil in the universe? We cannot of ourselves baffle the craft of the enemy, but the Lord knows how to deliver his saints. He can keep us out of the enemy's reach, he can sustain us when under his power, he can rescue us when our doom seems fixed, he can give us the victory when defeat seems certain; and in any and every case, if he does not save us from the man, he can keep us from the evil. Should we, at this moment, be oppressed in any measure by ungodly men, it will be better to leave our defence with God than to attempt it ourselves.

David's enemies were as violent as they were evil, as crafty as they were violent, and as persistent as they were crafty. It is hard dealing with persons who are only in their element when they are at daggers-drawn with you. Such a situation calls for prayer, and prayer calls on God. The Lord by providence and grace can keep us out of the power of the wicked. He alone can do this, for neither our own watchfulness nor the faithfulness of friends can secure us against the serpentine assaults of the foe. We need to be preserved from the smooth as well as the rough hands of the ungodly, for their flatteries may harm us as much as their slander. The hands of their example may pollute us, and so do us more harm than the hands of their oppression. Jehovah must be our keeper, or evil hands will do what evil hearts have imagined and evil lips have threatened. This is a forcible argument to use in prayer with God: he is the patron of holiness, and when the pure lives of his people are in danger of overthrow, he may be expected to interpose. Never let the pious forget to pray, for this is a weapon against which the most determined enemy cannot stand.

Meditation: *Good men live by prayer. He who gets to the throne of grace is covered by the cloud of glory, through which no sun can smite by day, nor moon by night* (William Swan Plumer).

Psalm 140:6-13

Suggested further reading: Hebrews 13:1-6

When hunted by man, the psalmist addressed himself to God. Often the less we say to our foes, and the more we say to our best Friend, the better it will fare with us; if we say anything, let it be said to the 'Lord'. David rejoiced in the fact that he had already said that Jehovah was his God: he was content to have committed himself, he had no wish to draw back. The Lord was David's own by deliberate choice, to which he again sets his seal with delight. The wicked reject God, but the righteous receive him as their own, their treasure, their pleasure, their light and delight. The prayers of saints have a voice in them; they are expressive pleadings even when they sound like inarticulate moanings. The Lord can discern a voice in our wailings, and he can and will listen to them. Because he is God he can hear us; because he is *our* God he *will* hear us. So long as the Lord hears us we are content — the answer may be according to his own will, but we entreat to be heard. A soul in distress is grateful to any one who will be kind and patient enough to hearken to its tale, but it is specially thankful for an audience with Jehovah. The more we consider his greatness and our insignificance, his wisdom and our folly, the more we shall be filled with praise when the Lord attends to our cry.

All through the psalm the writer is bravely confident, and speaks of things about which he had no doubt: in fact, no psalm can be more grandly positive than this protest against slander. The slandered saint knew Jehovah's care for the afflicted, for he had received actual proof of it himself. What confidence this should create within the bosoms of the persecuted and poverty-stricken! The prosperous and wealthy can maintain their own cause, but those who are otherwise shall find that God helps those who cannot help themselves. Many talk as if the poor had no rights worth noticing, but they will sooner or later find out their mistake when the judge of all the earth begins to plead with them. The former psalm had its 'surely', but this is a more pleasing one. As surely as God will slay the wicked he will save the oppressed, and fill their hearts and mouths with praises. Whoever else may be silent, the righteous will give thanks; and whatever they may suffer, the matter will end in their living through the trial, and magnifying the Lord for his delivering grace. How high have we climbed in this psalm — from being hunted by the evil man to dwelling in the divine presence; so faith raises up the saint from the lowest depths to heights of peaceful repose.

Meditation: *The one safety for simple and unlearned people when assailed by the crafty arguments of heretics and infidels is not controversy, but prayer, a weapon their adversaries seldom use, and cannot understand* (Bruno of Aste).

Psalm 141:1-6

Suggested further reading: Revelation 8:1-6

As incense is carefully prepared, kindled with holy fire, and devoutly presented unto God, so let my prayer be. We are not to look upon prayer as easy work requiring no thought, it needs to be 'set' forth; what is more, it must be set forth 'before the Lord', by a sense of his presence and a holy reverence for his name. Neither may we regard all supplication as certain of divine acceptance. It needs to be set forth before the Lord 'as incense', concerning the offering of which there were rules to be observed, otherwise it would be rejected by God. Whatever form his prayer might take, his one desire was that it might be accepted by God. Prayer is sometimes presented without words by the very motions of our bodies: bended knees and lifted hands are the tokens of earnest, expectant prayer. Certainly work, or the lifting up of the hands in labour, is prayer if it is done in dependence upon God and for his glory. There is a hand-prayer as well as a heart-prayer, and our desire is that this may be sweet unto the Lord as the sacrifice of eventide. Holy hope, the lifting up of hands that hang down, is also a kind of worship: may it ever be acceptable with God. The psalmist makes a bold request: he would have his humble cries and prayers to be as much regarded by the Lord as the appointed morning and evening sacrifices of the holy place.

The way the heart inclines the life soon tends: evil things desired bring forth wicked things practised. Unless the fountain of life is kept pure, the streams of life will soon be polluted. Alas, there is great power in company: even good men are apt to be swayed by association; hence the fear that we may practise wicked works when we are with wicked workers. We must endeavour not to be with them lest we sin with them. It is bad when the heart goes the wrong way alone, worse when the life runs in the evil road alone; but it is apt to increase to a high degree of ungodliness when the backslider runs the downward path with a whole horde of sinners around him. Our practice will be our perdition if it is evil; it is an aggravation of sin rather than an excuse for it to say that it is our custom and our habit. It is God's practice to punish all who make a practice of iniquity. Good men are horrified at the thought of sinning as others do; the fear of it drives them to their knees. Iniquity, which, being interpreted, is a want of equity, is a thing to be shunned as we would avoid an infectious disease.

Meditation: *Prayer is knowing work, believing work, thinking work, searching work, humbling work, and nothing worth if heart and hand do not join in it* (Thomas Adam).

Psalm 141:7-10

Suggested further reading: Esther 4:13 - 5:5

David's case seemed hopeless: the cause of God in Israel
was as a dead thing, even as a skeleton broken, and rotten,
and shovelled out of the grave, to return as dust to its dust.
There seemed to be no life, no cohesion, no form, order, or
headship among the godly party in Israel: Saul had demol-
ished it, and scattered all its parts, so that it did not exist as
an organized whole. David himself was like one of these
dried bones, and the rest of the godly were in much the
same condition. There seemed to be no vitality or union
among the holy seed; but their cause lay at death's door.
How often have good men thought like this about the cause
of God! Wherever they have looked, death, division and
destruction have stared them in the face. Cut and cloven,
hopelessly sundered! Scattered, indeed, scattered at the
grave's mouth! Split up and split for the fire! This is how
the cause of God and truth has seemed to be. Upon 'the
earth' the prospect was wretched; the field of the church
was ploughed, harrowed and scarified: it had become like
a wood-chopper's yard, where everything was doomed to
be broken up. We have seen churches in such a state, and
have been heartbroken. What a mercy that there is always
a place above the earth to which we can look! There lives
one who will give a resurrection to his cause, and a reunion
to his divided people. He will bring up the dead bones from
the grave's mouth, and make the dried kindling live again.
Let us imitate the psalmist, and look up to the living God.

He looked upward and kept eyes fixed there. He regarded duty more than circumstances; he considered his promise rather than the external providence; and he expected from God rather than from men. He did not shut his eyes in indifference or despair, neither did he turn them to the creature in vain confidence, but he gave his eyes to his God, and saw nothing to fear. Jehovah his Lord is also his hope. Thomas called Jesus Lord and God, and David here speaks of his God and Lord. These evil workers sought to catch David in his speech or acts. This was in itself a piece of inequity, and so in keeping with the rest of their conduct. They were bad themselves, and they wished either to make him like themselves, or to cause him to seem so. If they could not catch the good man in one way, they would try another; snares and traps should be multiplied, for they were determined to work his ruin anyhow. Nobody could preserve David but the Omniscient and Omnipotent One; he also will preserve us. It is hard to keep out of snares that you cannot see, and to escape traps that you cannot discover. Well might the much-hunted psalmist cry 'Keep me'.

Meditation: *If you would keep your mind fixed in prayer, keep your eye fixed. Much vanity comes in at the eye* (Thomas Watson).

Psalm 142

Suggested further reading: Daniel 6:10-23

Consider how the psalmist's prayer grew into shape as he
proceeded with it. He first poured out his natural longings,
'I cry'; and then he gathered up all his wits and arranged
his thoughts, 'I make my supplication'. True prayers may
differ in their diction, but not in their direction: an
impromptu cry and a preconceived supplication must in
the same way ascend towards the one prayer-hearing God,
and he will accept each of them with equal readiness. The
intense personality of the prayer is noteworthy: no doubt
the psalmist was glad of the prayers of others, but he was
not content to be silent himself. See how everything is in
the first person: 'I cry with my voice; with my voice ... I
make my supplication...'

As man would not regard him, David was driven to
Jehovah, his God. Was not this a gain made out of a loss?
Wealth gained by a failure? Anything which leads us to cry
unto God is a blessing to us. There is a sort of progressive
repetition all through this sacred song; he 'cried' first, but
he 'said' afterwards: his cry was bitter, but his saying was
sweet; his cry was sharp and short, but his saying was fresh
and full. It gives a believer great pleasure to remember his
own believing speeches: he may well desire to bury his
unbelieving murmurings in oblivion, but the triumphs of
grace in working in him a living faith, he will not dream of
forgetting. What a grand confession of faith was this! David
spoke to God, and of God: 'You are my refuge'; not, you

have *provided* me a refuge, but you, yourself, *are* my refuge. He fled to God alone; he hid himself beneath the wings of the Eternal. He not only believed this, but also said it, and practised it. Nor was this all; for David, when banished from his portion in the promised land, and cut off from the portion of goods which he inherited by right, found his portion in God, indeed, God *was* his portion. This was so, not only in reference to a future state, but also here among living men. It is sometimes easier to believe in a portion in heaven than in a portion upon earth: we could die more easily than live, at least we think so. But there is no living in the land of the living like living upon the living God. For the man of God to say these precious things in the hour of his dire distress was a grand attainment. It is easy to prate bravely when we dwell at ease, but to speak confidently in affliction is quite another matter.

Meditation: *Be very particular in secret prayer, both as to sins, wants and mercies... Be not ashamed to open out all your necessities* (Samuel Lee).

Psalm 143:1-6

Suggested further reading: Galatians 3:1-14

In the preceding psalm David began by declaring that he had cried unto the Lord; here he begs to be favourably regarded by Jehovah the living God, whose memorial is that he hears prayer. Saints desire to be answered as well as heard: they long to find the Lord faithful to his promise and righteous in defending the cause of justice. It is a happy thing when we dare appeal even to righteousness for our deliverance; and this we can do upon gospel principles, for 'if we confess our sins he is faithful and just to forgive us our sins'. Even the sterner attributes of God are upon the side of the man who humbly trusts, and turns his trust into prayer. With God's faithfulness and righteousness upon our side we are guarded on the right hand and on the left. These are active attributes, and fully equal to the answering of any prayer which it would be right to answer. Requests that do not appeal to either of these attributes it would not be for the glory of God to hear, for they must contain desires for things unpromised, and unrighteous.

None can stand before God upon the footing of the law. God's sight is piercing and discriminating; the slightest flaw is seen and judged; and therefore pretence and profession cannot avail where that glance reads all the secrets of the soul. David proclaimed the doctrine of universal condemnation by the law long before Paul had taken his pen to write the same truth. To this day it stands true even to the same extent as in David's day, no man living even at this moment may dare to present himself for trial before the throne of the Great King on the footing of the law. This foolish age has produced specimens of a pride so rank that men have dared to claim perfection in the flesh; but these vainglorious boasters are no exception to the rule laid down here: they are but men, and poor specimens of men. When their lives are examined they are frequently found to be more faulty than the humble penitents before whom they vaunt their superiority.

Saul's animosity drove David to haunt caverns and holes, like an unquiet ghost; he wandered out by night, and lay hid by day like an uneasy spirit which had long been denied the repose of the grave. Poor David! He was qualified to bless the house of the living, but he was driven to consort with the dead! Such may be our case, and yet we may be very dear to the Lord. One thing is certain, the Lord who permits us to dwell in darkness among the dead, will surely bring us into light, and cause us to dwell with those who enjoy life eternal.

Meditation: *So far from being able to answer for my sins, I cannot answer even for my righteousness* (Bernard of Clairvaux).

Psalm 143:7-12

Suggested further reading: James 1:1-8

The afflicted suppliant faints, and is ready to die. His life is ebbing out; each moment is important; it will soon be all over for him. No argument for speed can be more powerful than this. Who will not run to help a suppliant when his life is in jeopardy? God will not fail when our spirit fails, but, rather, he will hasten his course and come to us on the wings of the wind. Communion with God is so dear to a true heart that its withdrawal makes the man feel as though he were ready to die and utterly perish. God's withdrawals reduce the heart to despair, and take away all strength from the mind. Moreover, his absence enables adversaries to work their will without restraint; and thus, in a second way, the persecuted one is likely to perish. If we have God's countenance we live, but if he turns his back upon us we die. When the Lord looks with favour upon our efforts we prosper, but if he refuses to countenance them we labour in vain.

That which makes us flee to our God may be an ill wind, but it blows us good. There is no cowardice in such flight, but much holy courage. God can hide us out of reach of harm, and even out of sight of it. He is our hiding-place; Jesus has made himself the refuge of his people, the sooner, and the more entirely, we flee to him the better for us. Beneath the crimson canopy of our Lord's atonement believers are completely hidden; let us abide there and be at rest. David desired to be among the godly, in a land of

another sort from that which had cast him out. He sighed
for the upland meadows of grace, the table-lands of peace,
the fertile plains of communion. He could not reach them
by himself; he must be led there. God, who is good, can
best conduct us to the goodly land. There is no inheritance
like a portion in the land of promise, the land of precept,
the land of perfection. He who teaches us must guide and
conduct us to his own dwelling-place in the country of
holiness. The way is long, and steep, and he who goes
without a divine leader will faint on the journey; but with
Jehovah to lead, it is delightful to follow, and there is neither stumbling nor wandering. David was heavily afflicted.
Not only was there trouble in his soul, but his soul was in
trouble; plunged in it as in a sea, shut up in it as in a prison.
God could bring him out of it, and, especially, he could at
once lift up his soul or spirit out of the ditch. The prayer is
an eager one, and the appeal a bold one. We may be sure
that trouble was soon over when the Lord heard such
supplications.

Meditation: *We seek in vain temporal deliverances of God if
we neglect to seek spiritual graces, which are most necessary
for us* (Archibald Symson).

Psalm 144:1-8

Suggested further reading: Ephesians 6:10-20

When the heart is in a right state it must praise God, it cannot be restrained; its utterances leap forth as waters forcing their way from a living spring. With all his strength David blesses the God of his strength. We ought not to receive so great a boon as strength to resist evil, to defend truth, and to conquer error, without knowing who gave it to us, and rendering to him the glory for it. Not only does Jehovah give strength to his saints, but also he *is* their strength. God is full of power, and he becomes the power of those who trust him. David was called to be a man of war, and he was eminently successful in his battles; he does not trace this to his good generalship or valour, but to his being taught and strengthened for the war and the fight. If the Lord deigns to have a hand in such unspiritual work as fighting, surely he will help us to proclaim the gospel and win souls; and then we will bless his name with even greater intensity of heart. We will be pupils, and he shall be our Master, and if we ever accomplish anything we will give our instructor hearty blessing.

David trusts in God and finds him everything; he looks to man and sees him to be nothing; and then he wonders how it is that the great Lord can condescend to take notice of such a piece of folly and deceit as man. God is a consuming fire, and his touch kindles the peaks of the Alps, and makes them smoke. If Jehovah were to appear, nothing could stand before him; if the mighty mountains smoke at his touch, then all mortal power that is opposed to the Lord must end in smoke. How long-suffering he is to his adversaries, whom he could so readily consume. A touch would do it; God's finger of flame would set the hills on fire, and consume opposition of every kind. The artillery of heaven soon puts the enemy to flight, a single bolt sets the armies running hither and thither in utter rout. Jehovah never misses the mark; his arrows are fatal to his foes when he goes forth to war. It was no common faith which led the poet-king to expect the Lord to use his thunderbolts on behalf of a single member of that race which he had just now described as 'like a breath'. A believer in God may without presumption expect the almighty Lord to use on his behalf all the stores of his wisdom and power, even the terrible forces of tempest shall be marshalled to the fight, for the defence of the Lord's chosen. When we have once mastered the greater difficulty of the Lord's taking any interest in us, it is but a small thing that we should expect him to exert his great power on our behalf.

Meditation: *The Eternal can hurl his lightnings wherever he pleases, and effect his purpose instantaneously* (C. H. Spurgeon).

Psalm 144:9-15

Suggested further reading: Acts 9:20-31

David intended to tune his best instruments as well as to use his best vocal music: the best is all too poor for so great a God, and therefore we must not fall short of our utmost. In his many battles David would have perished had not almighty care preserved him. He had by his valour wrought salvation for Israel, but he lays his laurels at the feet of his Lord and Preserver. If any men need salvation kings do, and if they get it, the fact is so astonishing that it deserves a verse to itself in the psalm of praise. David traces his escape from death to the delivering hand of God. Note, he speaks in the present tense: 'delivers', for this was an act that covered his whole life. He puts his name to the confession of his indebtedness: it is David who without hesitation acknowledges the mercy granted to himself. He styles himself as the Lord's servant, accepting this as the highest title he had attained or desired.

With a special eye to the peace and prosperity that will follow, David seeks deliverance from the wicked, and the gracious presence of the Lord. The sparing of his life would mean the peace and happiness of a whole nation. We can scarcely judge how much happiness may hang upon the Lord's favour to one man. Under the Old Testament Israel had present earthly rewards for obedience; when Jehovah was their God they were a nation enriched and flourishing. All these temporal gifts are a part of happiness, but still the heart and soul of happiness lies in the people being right

with God, and having full possession of him. Those who
worship the happy God become a happy people. Then if
we do not have temporal mercies literally, we have something better; if we do not have the silver of earth we have
the gold of heaven, which is better still. With a little accommodation these verses may be applied to a prosperous
church, where the converts are growing and beautiful, the
gospel stores abundant, and the spiritual increase most
cheering. There, ministers and workers are in full vigour,
and the people are happy and united. May the Lord make it
so in all our churches evermore!

In this psalm David ascribes his own power over the
people, and the prosperity which attended his reign, to the
Lord himself. Happy was the nation that he ruled: happy
in its king, in its families, in its prosperity, and in possessing peace; but yet more in enjoying true religion and worshipping Jehovah, the only living and true God.

Meditation: *God is the author of all true happiness; he is
the donor of all true happiness; he is the maintainer of all
true happiness, and he is the centre of all true happiness;
and, therefore, he that has him for his God, and for his portion is the only happy man in the world* (Thomas Brooks).

Psalm 145:1-7

Suggested further reading: Isaiah 38:9-20

David determined that his praise should rise to blessing, should be intelligently spent upon the name or character of God, and should be continued world without end. He uses the word 'bless' not merely for variation of sound, but also to deepen and sweeten its sense. To bless God is to praise him with a personal affection for him, and to wish him well; this is an increasingly easy exercise as we advance in experience and grow in grace. David declares that he will offer every form of praise, through every form of existence.

Worship should be somewhat like its object — great praise for a great God. There is no part of Jehovah's greatness that is not worthy of great praise. Praise may be said to be great when the song contains great matter, when the hearts producing it are intensely fervent, and when large numbers unite in the grand acclaim. There shall be a tradition of praise: men shall hand on the service, they shall make it a point to instruct their descendants in this hallowed exercise. Let us see to it that we praise God before our children, and never make them think that his service is an unhappy one. The praise of the Lord enlarges the heart, and as it grows upon us our minds grow with it. God's works of goodness and acts of power make up a subject which all the eras of human history can never exhaust. A praiseful heart seems to live in all the centuries in delightful companionship with all the good. We are not afraid that the incense will ever cease to burn upon the altars of Jehovah: the priests die, but the adoration lives on. Having been filled with his great goodness, the Lord's redeemed people will retain a happy memory of it, and shall often be moved to utter those recollections. Not content with a scanty mention of such amazing love, they shall go on to an abundant utterance of such abundant favour. It shall be their delight to speak with one another of God's dealings with them, and to compare notes of their experiences. God has done nothing stintedly; all his goodness is great goodness, all worthy to be remembered, all suggestive of holy discourse. What do they sing of? They sing of that righteousness which is the sinner's terror, which even good men mention with deep solemnity. Righteousness received by gospel light is in reality the secret foundation of the believer's hope. God's covenant of grace is our strong consolation, because he who made it is righteous, and will not run back from it. Since Jesus died as our substitute, righteousness requires and secures the salvation of all the redeemed. This attribute is our best friend, and therefore we sing of it.

Meditation: *All glory be to him who remains the same Lord throughout all generations* (C. H. Spurgeon).

Psalm 145:8-16

Suggested further reading: Acts 14:8-18

This is how the Lord looks upon all living men: he is gracious, or full of goodness and generosity. He treats his creatures with kindness, his subjects with consideration, and his saints with favour. His words and ways, his promises and his gifts, his plans and his purposes all manifest his grace, or free favour. There is nothing suspicious, prejudiced, morose, tyrannical, or unapproachable in Jehovah — he is condescending and kind.

'The Lord is good to all.' No one, not even his fiercest enemy, can deny this; for the falsehood would be too barefaced, since the very existence of the lips that slander him is a proof that it is slander. He allows his enemies to live, he even supplies them with food, and smoothes their way with many comforts; for them the sun shines as brightly as if they were saints, and the rain waters their fields as plentifully as if they were perfect men. Is not this goodness to all? In our own land the gospel sounds in the ears of all who care to listen; and the Scriptures are within reach of the poorest child. It would be a wanton wresting of Scripture to limit this expression to the elect, as some have tried to do; we rejoice in electing love, but none the less we welcome the glorious truth, 'The Lord is good to all.' His meditation has brought him near to God, and God near to him, he speaks to him in adoration, changing the pronoun from 'his' to 'your'. He sees the great King, and prostrates himself before him. It is well when our devotion opens the gate of heaven, and enters within the portal to speak with God face to face, as a man speaks with his friend. The point upon which the psalmist's mind rests is the eternity of the divine throne. The Lord's kingdom is without beginning, without break, without bound, and without end. He never abdicates his throne, neither does he call in another to share his empire. None can overthrow his power, or break away from his rule. Neither this age, nor the age to come, nor ages of ages shall cause his sovereignty to fail. Here is rest for faith. Men come and go like shadows on the wall, but God reigns eternally. We distinguish kings as they succeed each other by calling them first and second; but this King is Jehovah, the First and the Last. In his generation Adam knew his Creator to be King, and the last of his race shall know the same.

Jehovah is adored for his gracious providence towards men and all other creatures; this aptly follows the proclamation of his royalty, for here we see how he rules his kingdom, and provides for his subjects. These verses refer to natural providence; but they may equally well apply to the stores of grace, since the same God is king in both spheres. The hand of grace is never closed while the sinner lives.

Meditation: *Even the worst taste of God's mercy; such as fight against God's mercy taste of it; the wicked have some crumbs from mercy's table* (Thomas Watson).

Psalm 145:17-21

Suggested further reading: Revelation 15:1 - 16:1

In these verses we behold our God in the realm of his free grace dealing well with his believing people. His ways and works are both worthy to be praised. Jehovah cannot be unjust or impure. Let his doings be what they may, they are in every case righteous and holy. This is the confession of the godly who follow his ways, and of the gracious who study his works. Whatever God is or does must be right. In the salvation of his people he is as righteous and holy as in any other of his ways and works: he has not manifested mercy at the expense of justice, but, rather, he has magnified his righteousness by the death of his Son. He does not leave praying men, and men who confess his name, to battle with the world alone, but he is ever at their side. This favour is not for a few of those who invoke him; but for each one of the pious company. All who place themselves beneath the shield of his glorious name by calling themselves by it, and by calling upon it in supplication, shall find him to be a very present help in trouble.

Wickedness is an offence to all holy beings, and therefore those who are determined to continue in it must be weeded out. As good sanitary laws remove all creators of pest and plague, so the moral government of God marks every evil thing for destruction; it cannot be tolerated in the presence of a perfectly holy God. What ruins wicked men frequently become in this life! What monuments of wrath will they be in the world to come! Like Nineveh and

Babylon, and other destroyed places, they shall only exist to declare how thoroughly God fulfils his threatenings.

All men of every race, condition, or generation should unite to glorify God. No man need think that he will be rejected when he comes with his personal note of praise; all are permitted, invited and exhorted to magnify the Lord. His holiness should be specially adored: this is the crown, and in a certain sense the sum, of all his attributes. Only holy hearts will praise the holy name, or character of the Lord. Oh, that all flesh were sanctified, then would the sanctity of God be the delight of all! Once let the song begin and there will be no end to it. If there were two for-evers, or twenty for-evers, they ought all to be spent in the praises of the ever-living, ever-blessing, ever-blessed Jehovah. Blessed be the Lord for ever for having revealed to us his name, and blessed be that name as he has revealed it; indeed, blessed be he above all that we can know, or think, or say. Our hearts revel in the delight of praising him. Our mouth, our mind, our lip, our life shall be our Lord's throughout this mortal existence, and when time shall be no more.

Meditation: *Notice this recurrent thought, that the guardianship of the good implies the destruction of the wicked* (A. S. Aglen).

Psalm 146:1-5

Suggested further reading: Proverbs 3:1-6

'Praise the LORD', or, Hallelujah. It is sad to remember how this majestic word has been trailed in the mire of late. Its irreverent use is an aggravated instance of taking the name of Jehovah our God in vain. Let us hope that it has been done in ignorance by the ruder sort; but great responsibility lies with leaders who countenance and even copy this blasphemy. Let us pronounce the word 'Hallelujah' with holy awe, and summon ourselves and all others by it to adore the God of the whole earth. Men need to be called to praise; it is important that they should praise; and there are many reasons why they should do it at once. Let all who hear the word 'Hallelujah' unite immediately in holy praise.

Men are always far too apt to depend upon the great ones of earth, and forget the Great One above; and this habit is the fruitful source of disappointment. Though you should select one son of man out of many, and should imagine that he differs from the rest and may be safely depended on, you will be mistaken. There is none to be trusted, no, not one. Adam fell; therefore lean not on his sons. Man is a helpless creature without God; therefore, do not look for help in that direction. All men are like the few men who are made into princes, they are more in appearance than in reality, more in promising than in performing, more apt to help themselves than to help others. How many have turned away heart-sick from men on whom they once relied! Never was this the case with a believer in the Lord. He is a very present help in time of trouble. The God of Jacob is the God of the covenant, the God of wrestling prayer, the God of the tried believer; he is the only living and true God. The God of Jacob is Jehovah, who appeared unto Moses, and led the tribes of Jacob out of Egypt, and through the wilderness. Those who trust him are happy, for they shall never be ashamed or confounded. The Lord never dies, neither do his thoughts perish: his purpose of mercy, like himself, endures throughout all generations. Hallelujah! He, who has placed all his confidence in Jehovah, his God by a covenant of salt, is content with help for the present and in hope for the future. Happy is he when others are despairing! Happiest shall he be in that very hour when others are discovering the depths of agony. Oh, how blessed a thing it is to know that God is our present help, and our eternal hope. Full assurance is more than heaven in the bud, the flower has begun to open. We would not exchange with Caesar; his sceptre is a bauble, but our bliss is true treasure.

Meditation: *This psalm gives in brief the Gospel of Confidence. It inculcates the elements of faith, hope and thanksgiving* (Martin Geier).

Psalm 146:6-10

Suggested further reading: John 9:6-7, 35-41

He who made heaven can make a heaven for us, and make us fit for heaven. He who made the earth can preserve us while we are on earth, and help us to make good use of it while we sojourn upon it. He who made the sea and all its mysteries can steer us across the pathless deeps of a troubled life, and make it a way for his redeemed to pass over. This God, who still makes the world by keeping it in existence, is assuredly able to keep us to his eternal kingdom and glory. The making of the worlds is the standing proof of the power and wisdom of that great God in whom we trust. It is our joy that he not only made heaven but the sea; not only things that are bright and blessed, but things that are deep and dark. Concerning all our circumstances, we may say the Lord is there.

He who made the eye can open it, and when he does so it is to his glory. How often is the mental eye closed in moral night! And who can remove this dreary effect of the Fall but the almighty God? This miracle of grace he has performed in a myriad of cases, and it is in each case a theme for loftiest praise. Jehovah consoles the bereaved, cheers the defeated, solaces the despondent, comforts the despairing. Let those who are bowed to the ground appeal to him, and he will speedily raise them up. This is greatly to his glory. Let those who enjoy the inestimable privilege of his love magnify his name with enthusiastic delight.

Jehovah is King, and his kingdom can never come to an end. Neither does he die, nor abdicate, nor lose his crown by force. Glory be to his name, his throne is never in jeopardy. As the Lord ever lives, so he ever reigns. Zion's God, the God of his worshipping people, he is the one who shall reign in every age. There will always be a Zion; Zion will always have Jehovah for her King; for her he will always prove that he is reigning in great power. What should we do in the presence of so great a King, but enter into his courts with praise, and pay to him our joyful homage? 'Praise the LORD.' Again they said Hallelujah. Again the sweet perfume arose from the golden vials full of sweet odours. Are we not prepared for an outburst of holy song? Do not we also say, 'Hallelujah'? Here ends this gladsome psalm. Here ends *not* the praise of the Lord, which shall ascend for ever and ever. Amen.

Meditation: *It ought not to pass without remark that the name Jehovah is repeated here five times in five lines, to intimate that it is an almighty power, that of Jehovah, that is engaged and exerted for the relief of the oppressed; and that it is as much to the glory of God to succour them that are in misery, as it is to ride on the heavens by his name JAH, Psalm 68:4* (Matthew Henry).

Psalm 147:1-6

Suggested further reading: Luke 1:68-79

The flow of the broad river of the Book of Psalms ends in a cataract of praise. The present psalm begins and ends with Hallelujah. Jehovah and happy praise should ever be associated in the mind of a believer. Jove was dreaded, but Jehovah is beloved. To one and all of the true seed of Israel the psalmist acts as choir-master, and cries, 'Praise the Lord.' Such an exhortation may fitly be addressed to all those who owe anything to the favour of God; and which of us does not? Pay him we cannot, but praise him we will, not only now, but for ever.

God appears both in the material and spiritual world as a builder and maker, and in that he is to be praised. His grace, wisdom and power are all seen in the formation and establishment of the chosen seat of his worship; once a city with material wall, but now a church composed of spiritual stones. The Lord is not only a builder, but a healer; he restores broken hearts as well as broken walls. His deep sympathy with mourners is a special mark of his goodness. Few will associate with the despondent, but Jehovah chooses their company, and abides with them till he has healed them by his comforts. He deigns to handle and heal broken hearts: he himself lays on the ointment of grace, and the soft bandages of love, and thus binds up the bleeding wounds of those convinced of sin. This is the compassion of a God. Those to whom he has acted so graciously may well praise him. The Lord is always healing and binding: this is no new work to him, he has done it of old; and it is not a thing of the past of which he is now weary, for he is still healing and still binding. Come, broken hearts, come to the Physician who never fails to heal: uncover your wounds to the one who so tenderly binds them up!

Our Lord and King is great — magnanimous, infinite, inconceivably glorious. None can describe his majesty, or assess the greatness of his excellence. His acts reveal something of his might, but the mass of his power is hidden, for all things are possible with God, even the things impossible with men. He is infinite in existence, in power, and in knowledge, as these phrases plainly teach us. And yet how condescending! For it is he who so tenderly nurses the sick souls, and waits to be gracious to sinful men. He brings his boundless power and infinite understanding to bear upon human distress for its assuagement and sanctification. For all these reasons let his praise be great: even if it were infinite, it would not exceed his due. In the building of his church and the salvation of souls, his greatness, power and wisdom are all displayed: let him be extolled because of each of these attributes.

Meditation: *God is so great that nothing is great to him, and he is so condescending that nothing is little to him: his infinite majesty thus naturally brings low the lofty and exalts the lowly* (C. H. Spurgeon).

Psalm 147:7-11

Suggested further reading: Isaiah 62:1-9

In this paragraph the contrast announced in the former section is enlarged upon from another point of view, namely, as it is seen in nature and in providence. All that he does is gracious, every movement of his hand is goodness; therefore let our hearts reply with gratitude, and our lips with song. Our lives should be responses to divine love. Jehovah is ever engaged in giving, let us respond with thanksgiving. He is 'our' God, and this fact is one choice joy of the song. We have chosen him because he has chosen us; and we see in him peculiarities that distinguish him from all the pretended deities of those among whom we dwell. He is 'our' God in covenant relationship for ever and ever, and to him be praise in every possible form.

He works in all things, above as well as below. Clouds are not caused by accident, but produced by God himself, and made to assume degrees of density by which the blue firmament is hidden. A skyscape might seem to be a mere fortuitous concourse of vapours, but it is not so: the Great Artist's hand thus covers the canvas of the heavens. By causing the grass to grow on the hills the Lord feeds the cattle. God cares for the brute creation. Men tread grass under foot as though it were nothing, but God causes it to grow; too often men treat their cattle with cruelty, but the Lord himself feeds them. The great God is too good, and, indeed, too great to overlook things that are despised. Greatness occupied with little things is one of the chief features

of this psalm. Ought we not all to feel special joy in praising one who is so specially remarkable for his care of the
needy and the forgotten? Ought we not also to trust in the
Lord? He who feeds the sons of the raven will surely nour-
ish the sons of God! Hallelujah to him who both feeds the
ravens and rules the stars! What a God you are, O Jehovah!

Oh, the matchless condescension of the Lord, that his
greatness should take pleasure in the insignificant creatures of his hand! As a father takes pleasure in his own
children, so the Lord solaces himself in his own beloved
ones, whose marks of new birth are fear and hope. They
fear, for they are sinners; they hope, for God is merciful.
God takes pleasure in them, both when they are afraid and
when they rejoice. Is there not rich cause for praise in this
special feature of the divine character? As men may be
known by the nature of the things which give them pleasure, so is the Lord known by the blessed fact that he takes
pleasure in the righteous, even though that righteousness
is as yet in its initial stage of fear and hope.

Meditation: *A sincere Christian is known by both these: a
fear of God, or a constant obedience to his commands, and
an affiance, trust, and dependence upon his mercies* (Thomas
Manton).

Psalm 147:12-20

Suggested further reading: Philippians 4:1-7

How the poet insists upon praise; he cries, 'Praise ... praise', as if it were the most important duty of all. A peculiar people should render peculiar praise. The city of peace should be the city of praise, and the temple of the covenant God should resound with his glories. If nowhere else, yet certainly in Zion, there should be joyful adoration of Zion's God. Note that we are to praise the Lord in our own houses in Jerusalem as well as in his own house in Zion. The holy city surrounds the holy hill, and both are dedicated to the holy God, therefore both should ring with hallelujahs.

Internal happiness is as truly the Lord's gift as external security. When the Lord blesses 'your children within you', you are, O Zion, filled with a happy, united, zealous, prosperous, holy people, who dwell in communion with God, and enter into the joy of their Lord. When God makes your walls salvation your gates must be praise. There would be little point in fortifying a wretched, starving city; but when the walls are strengthened, it is an even greater joy to see that the inhabitants are blessed with all good gifts. How much our churches need a present and abiding benediction! Quiet extends even to the boundaries; there are no enemies wrangling with those on the borders. If there is peace there, we may be sure that peace is everywhere. 'When a man's ways please the Lord he makes even his enemies to be at peace with him'. Peace comes from the God of peace. Considering the differing constitutions, conditions, tastes and opinions of men, it is a work of God when in large churches unbroken peace is found year after year; and it is an equal wonder if worldlings, instead of persecuting the godly, treat them with marked respect. He who builds Zion is also her Peacemaker, the Lord and Giver of peace.

The methods of Jehovah in the natural world are simple but effectual; equally so are those which he employs in the spiritual kingdom; for the breath of his Holy Spirit breathes upon frozen hearts, and streams of penitence and love gush forth at once. We are to praise the Lord above all things for the fact that he manifests himself to us in a way that he does not do to the world. Whatever part of his mind he discloses to us, whether it be a word of instruction, a statute of direction, or a judgement of government, we are bound to bless the Lord for it. He who causes summer to come in the place of winter has also removed the coldness and death from our hearts by the power of his word, and this is abundant cause for singing unto his name.

Meditation: *The godly man, when he dies, 'enters into peace' (Isa. 57:2); but while he lives, peace must enter into him* (Thomas Watson).

Psalm 148:1-6

Suggested further reading: Psalm 19:1-6

See how the psalmist trumpets out the word 'PRAISE'. It sounds forth some nine times in the first five verses of this song. Like repeating guns, exultant exhortations are sounded forth in tremendous force: 'Praise! Praise! Praise!' The drum of the great King beats round the world with this one note: 'Praise! Praise! Praise!' All this praise is distinctly and personally for Jehovah. Praise not his servants or his works; but praise HIM. Is he not worthy of all possible praise? Pour it forth before HIM in full volume; pour it only there!

Living intelligences, perfect in character and in bliss, lift up your loudest music to your Lord, each one of you. Not one bright spirit is exempted from this consecrated service. However many you are, O angels, you are all *his* angels, and therefore you are bound, all of you, to render service to your Lord. Whether you are named Gabriel, or Michael, or by whatever other titles you are known, praise the Lord. 'Praise him, all his hosts.' This includes angelic armies, but groups with them all the heavenly bodies. Though they are inanimate, the stars, the clouds, the lightning, have their ways of praising Jehovah. Let each one of the countless legions of the Lord of hosts show forth his glory; for the countless armies are all his: his by creation, and preservation, and consequent obligation. Both these sentences claim unanimity of praise from those in the upper regions who are called upon to commence the strain: 'all his angels ... all his hosts'. That same hearty oneness must pervade the whole orchestra of praising ones; hence, further on, we read of all stars of light, all deeps, all hills, all cedars, and all people. How well the concert begins when all angels, and all the heavenly host, strike the first joyful notes! In that concert our souls would at once take their part.

The Maker should have honour from his works, they should tell forth 'his' praise; and thus they should praise his 'name' — by which his character is intended. The name of Jehovah is written legibly upon his works, so that his power, wisdom, goodness and other attributes are there made manifest to thoughtful men, and thus his name is praised. The highest praise of God is to declare what he is. We can invent nothing which would magnify the Lord: we can never extol him better than by repeating his name, or describing his character. The Lord is to be extolled for creating all things that exist, and for doing so by the simple agency of his word. He created by a command; what a power is this! Well may he expect those who owe their being to him to praise him. Evolution may be atheistic; but the doctrine of creation logically demands worship; and hence, as the tree is known by its fruit, it proves itself to be true. Those who were created by command are under command to adore their Creator.

Meditation: *The voice which said 'Let them be', now says 'Let them praise'* (C. H. Spurgeon).

Psalm 148:7-14

Suggested further reading: Isaiah 43:14-21

The song descends to our abode, and so comes nearer home to us. Jehovah is to be praised not only 'in' the earth but 'from' the earth, as if the adoration ran over from this planet into the general accumulation of worship. In the first verse the song was 'from the heavens'; here it is going 'from the earth'; songs coming down from heaven are to blend with those going up from earth. The 'earth' meant here is our entire globe of land and water; it is to be made vocal everywhere with praise. There is room for every voice at this concert: fruitful trees and maidens, cedars and young men, angels and children, old men and judges — all may unite in this oratorio. None, indeed, can be dispensed with: for perfect psalmody we must have the whole universe aroused to worship, and all parts of creation must take their parts in devotion.

All that is contained in the name or character of Jehovah is worthy of praise, and all the objects of his creating care will be too few to set it forth in its completeness. His unique name should have a monopoly of praise. His royal splendour exceeds all that earth and heaven can express. He is himself the crown of all things, the excellency of the creation. He is the saints' glory: to him they render praise; and he by his mercy to them evermore gives them further reasons for praise, and higher motives for adoration. He is their God, and they are his saints; he makes them blessed, and they bless him in return. The Lord knows those who are his. He knows the name of him with whom he made a covenant, and how he came by that name, and who his children are, and where they are. In verse 11 all nations are called upon to praise the Lord; but here the call is specially addressed to his elect people, who know him more than all others: a 'people near to him', near by kin, and near by care; near as to manifestation and near as to affection. This is a highly honourable description of the beloved race; and it is even more emphatically true of the spiritual Israel, the believing seed. This nearness should prompt us to perpetual adoration. The Lord's elect are the children of his love, the courtiers of his palace, the priests of his temple, and therefore they are bound beyond all others to be filled with reverence for him, and delight in him. 'Praise the Lord' or, 'Hallelujah'. This should be the Alpha and Omega of a good man's life. Let us praise God to the end, world without end. The field of praise that lies before us in this psalm is bounded at beginning and end by landmarks in the form of hallelujahs, and all that lies between them, every word of it, is to the Lord's honour. Amen.

Meditation: *I could wish that all our lives might end like this book of psalms, in blessing and praising almighty God* (Thomas Cheshire).

Psalm 149

Suggested further reading: Revelation 7:9-17

Saints are precious, and a congregation of saints is a treasure house of jewels. God is in the midst of his saints, and because of this we may well long to be among them. They are so full of his praise that we feel at home among them when we are ourselves full of praise. The sanctuary is the house of praise as well as the house of prayer. All saints praise God: they would not be saints if they did not. Their praise is sincere, suitable, seasonable and acceptable. Personal praise is sweet unto God, but congregated praise has a multiplicity of sweetness in it. When holy ones meet, they adore the Holy One. Saints do not gather to amuse themselves with music, nor to extol one another, but to sing praise to the one whose saints they are. A congregation of saints is heaven upon earth: should not Jehovah, the Lord of saints, have all the praise that can come from such an assembly?

If our joy is pleasing to him, let us make it full. What condescension is this on Jehovah's part, to notice, to love, and to delight in his chosen! Surely there is nothing in our persons, or our actions, which could cause pleasure to the Ever-blessed One, were it not that he condescends to men of low estate. The thought of the Lord's taking pleasure in us is a mine of joy never to be exhausted. 'The meek' are humble, and feel their need of salvation; he is gracious, and bestows it upon them. They lament their deformity and he clothes them with a beauty of the choicest kind. He saves them by sanctifying them, and thus they wear the beauty of holiness, and the beauty of a joy that springs out of full salvation. He makes his people meek, and then makes the meek beautiful. Here is a grand argument for worshipping the Lord with the utmost exultation: he who takes such a pleasure in us must be approached with every token of exceeding joy. A meek and quiet spirit is called 'an ornament', and certainly it is 'the beauty of holiness'. When God himself beautifies a man, he becomes beautiful indeed and beautiful for ever.

All the godly shared in the triumphs of the Lord when he smote Israel's foes. We have similar honour, but it is shown in victories of another sort. All the holy ones are sent upon errands by their holy Lord. The honours described in this psalm are common to all the family of grace; and such service as the Lord appoints is to be undertaken by every one of them, without exception. The Lord honours all his chosen here, and he will glorify them all from now on: this rule is without exception. Surely in this we have the best argument for glorifying the Lord, and so we close our new song with another Hallelujah, 'Praise the Lord.'

Meditation: *The previous psalm was a hymn of praise to the Creator; this is a hymn to the Redeemer* (Matthew Henry).

Psalm 150

Suggested further reading: Revelation 5:8-13

Hallelujah! The exhortation is to all things in earth or in heaven. Should they not all declare the glory of him for whose glory they are, and were created? Jehovah, the one God, should be the one object of adoration. To give the least particle of his honour to another is shameful treason; to refuse to render it to him is heartless robbery. In his church below and in his courts above, hallelujahs should be continually presented. In the person of Jesus, God finds a holy dwelling or sanctuary, and there he is greatly to be praised. He may also be said to dwell in holiness, for all his ways are right and good; for this we ought to extol him with heart and with voice. Whenever we assemble for holy purposes our main work should be to present praises to the Lord our God. What an expanse we have in the boundless firmament of divine power! Let it all be filled with praise. Let the heavens, so great and strong, echo with the praise of the thrice holy Jehovah, while the sanctuaries of earth magnify the Almighty One.

With the loudest, clearest note, call the people together. Let all men know that we are not ashamed to worship. The sound of the trumpet is associated with the grandest and most solemn events, such as the giving of the law, the proclamation of jubilee, the coronation of Jewish kings, and the raging of war. It is to be thought of in reference to the coming of our Lord in his second advent and the raising of the dead. Let us never sound a trumpet before us to our own honour, but reserve all our trumpeting for God's glory. There is enough in our holy faith to create and to justify the utmost degree of rapturous delight. If men are dull in the worship of the Lord our God they are not acting consistently with the character of their religion.

'Let everything that has breath': that is to say, all living beings. He gave them breath, let them breathe his praise. In the Hebrew his name is composed rather of breathings than of letters, to show that all breath comes from him; therefore let it be used for him. Join all living things in the eternal song. Whether you are the least or greatest, do not withhold your praises. What a day it will be when all things in all places unite to glorify the one only living and true God! This will be the final triumph of the church of God. 'Praise the LORD.' Once more, Hallelujah! Thus is the psalm rounded with the note of praise; and thus is the Book of Psalms ended by a glowing word of adoration. Reader, will you not at this moment pause a while and worship the Lord your God? Hallelujah!

Meditation: *When we have said all we are able to say for God's praise, we are but to begin anew; for this are we taught by the renewing of the exhortation, in the close of sundry psalms, and here also at the end of all the psalms, 'Praise the LORD'* (David Dickson).

A wide range of excellent books on aromatherapy is available from Kavanagh Press. Please write to us for your free catalogue or contact us by email:

Kavanagh Press
Tynedale North Industrial Estate, Diddington LD13 0PJ, Tividale

Kavanagh Press, USA
P.O. Box 48, Auburn, MA 01501 USA

e-mail: sales@kavanaghal-press.com

http://www.kavanaghal-press.c